EXILE AND CREATIVITY

Edited by **SUSAN RUBIN SULEIMAN**

EXILE AND CREATIVITY

SIGNPOSTS, TRAVELERS, OUTSIDERS,

BACKWARD GLANCES

Duke University Press Durham and London 1998

091098 - 22

CONTENTS

SUSAN RUBIN SULEIMAN

INTRODUCTION

Of course, it's one hell of a way to get from Petersburg to Stockholm; but then for a man of my occupation the notion of a straight line being the shortest distance between two points has lost its attraction a long time ago.

JOSEPH BRODSKY, acceptance speech for the Nobel Prize in Literature

In order to rebuild one's life one has to be strong and an optimist. So we are very optimistic. Our optimism, indeed, is admirable, even if we say so ourselves.

HANNAH ARENDT, "We Refugees"

EMIGRÉS, EXILES, EXPATRIATES, refugees, nomads, cosmopolitans — the meanings of those words vary, as do their connotations. Expatriates can go home any time they like, while exiles cannot. *Cosmopolitan* can be a term of self-affirmation, straight or postmodernly ironic, or else an anti-Semitic slur. Over and above their fine distinctions, however, these words all designate a state of being "not home" (or of being "everywhere at home," the flip side of the same coin), which means, in most cases, at a distance from one's native tongue. Is this distance a falling away from some original wholeness and source of creativity, or is it on the contrary a spur to creativity? Is exile a cause for optimism (celebration, even) or its opposite?

Clearly, there is no simple answer to this question. The irony in Hannah Arendt's description of the "optimistic" refugees among whom she counted herself in 1943 is more bitter than Joseph Brodsky's wry self-characterization as one who can never take the shortest route between two points — and indeed, Brodsky had cause to celebrate when he made that remark in Stockholm in 1987. But wry or bitter, irony indicates a double edge. "Exile is strangely compelling to think about but terrible to experience," writes Edward Said in a well-known essay. And he goes on to ask: "If true exile is a condition of terminal loss, why has it been

All of the essays in this book, with one exception, first appeared in the special double issue of *Poetics Today*, "Creativity and Exile" (vol. 17, nos. 3–4, 1996), which I edited. Henry Louis Gates's essay first appeared in his book *Thirteen Ways of Looking at a Black Man* (New York: Random House, 1997) and is reprinted here (slightly modified) with the permission of the author.

transformed so easily into a potent, even enriching motif of modern culture? . . . Modern Western culture is in large part the work of exiles, émigrés, refugees" (Said 1994: 137). Besides, he concludes, exile has its pleasures, not the least of which is the "particular sense of achievement" one derives from "acting as if one were at home wherever one happens to be" (ibid.: 148).

On this side, on that side, on the one hand, on the other hand: few subjects elicit as much intellectual ambivalence—but also, especially of late, as much intellectual fascination—as the subject of exile. In its narrow sense a political banishment, exile in its broad sense designates every kind of estrangement or displacement, from the physical and geographical to the spiritual. Whence a good part of its fascination for contemporary analysts of culture. Seen in broad terms, exile appears not only as a (or even *the*) major historical phenomenon of our century, affecting millions of people, but as a focal point for theoretical reflections about individual and cultural identity (Bammer 1994), which in turn are intimately bound up with problems of nationalism, racism, and war. Victor Burgin, commenting on the violent racial confrontations in Spike Lee's film *Do the Right Thing*, notes ironically: "When the sons of émigré Italians confront the descendants of abducted Africans in Sal's Pizzeria they do so in a Black and Hispanic district with a Dutch name, which was stolen from Native Americans. Most of us know the melancholy tension of separation from our origins" (Burgin 1991: 29).

This book is devoted to exploring that "melancholy tension," in a variety of moods and modes. Given the diversity of experiences of exile, it would be a misguided attempt to reduce these wide-ranging essays to a single unifying perspective. As editor, I will, however, comment briefly on the shape (and shaping) of the book as a whole.

Signposts, travelers, outsiders, backward glances: the metaphor of the journey imposed itself as a way of organizing these critical forays, many of which venture into little-known territory. They are exploratory but not global, plying only the European-American route, and even so, incomplete. But who would claim completion in this domain? Perhaps a mad encyclopedist lost in the Andes, or a compiler of universal dictionaries in the rainforest? I will not apologize for the absences, the omissions of gender-geography-race-class. Take it as a given, many things are missing.

But many things are not. The variety of perspectives in these essays, in terms of discipline, temporal scope, geographical extension, and rhetori-

cal mode, is remarkable; especially if one considers how many themes recur, over and above (or under, as in a *basso continuo*) the divergent lines
of inquiry. As always, the editor's job of orchestrating differences has involved some arbitrary juxtapositions. If they produce a few surprises, or
even jarring notes, so much the better.

Signposts: indicators of possible itineraries. Christine Brooke-Rose, a
multilingual literary theorist and (to borrow a phrase from her) " 'poetic'
(exploring, rigorous)" novelist, points out some of the diverse meanings
and implications of exile and multilingualism in the work of writers from
the Romantics to the present. Thomas Pavel, a multilingual intellectual,
discusses the general phenomenon of intellectual exile, past and present,
before analyzing two specific versions in seventeenth-century French literature. Linda Nochlin introduces a reflection on visual art as one that
"loses less in translation," and also introduces a necessary reflection on
gender. Hélène Cixous, the whole of whose considerable oeuvre can be
placed under the sign of exile, returns here to her twin tutelaries and
"significant others," James Joyce and Clarice Lispector, themselves displaced persons writing far from the land of their birth. Denis Hollier,
who considers himself neither an exile nor an emigrant (and who is even
less a refugee—maybe a part-time expatriate?), reflects wittily, in epistolary form, on the paradoxes of crossing "as many borders as possible"
between France and the United States.

Travelers, Outsiders: All travelers are outsiders somewhere (some may
be so everywhere), but not all outsiders are travelers. Travelers can go
home, by definition, though they may choose not to; but one can be an
outsider in one's own home town, as members of minority groups know.
I have chosen these rather large, vague terms because they accommodate
a wide range of possibilities, and because I'm less interested in classifica-
tions than in suggestive cases. All of the essays in these sections deal, in
varying degrees of detail, with individuals in specific circumstances.

In the first group, Doris Sommer follows the travels, both literal and
textual, of a Renaissance man whose "very name is an oxymoron," the
Inca Garcilaso de la Vega. Alicia Borinsky follows those of a twentieth-
century Polish writer caught by war in Buenos Aires, who decides to
stay for a while (more than two decades) before crossing the Atlantic
again. Jacqueline Chénieux-Gendron traces some Surrealist journeys to

the New World at a time of historical collapse. Janet Bergstrom follows Jean Renoir's career from Paris to Hollywood and back, to conclude startlingly that only after his return to Paris did Renoir make his most Hollywood-like film. Ernst van Alphen looks at the work of his older fellow Dutchman Armando, whose obsession with the "past of the Second World War" (which is also the time of Armando's childhood) leads him to Germany and the condition of self-imposed exile.

In the second group, Svetlana Boym studies two types of homesickness in the autobiographies of Victor Shklovsky—who in my terms was a traveler, returning home—and Joseph Brodsky, who moved from the condition of notorious outlaw in Leningrad (as it was called then) to that of eminent outsider in New York. (Boym herself moved from Leningrad to New York and Boston, and from the status of Soviet refugee to that of American professor). John Neubauer, a Hungarian living and teaching in Amsterdam, studies two very different versions of "home" and of the novel in the works of Lukács and Bakhtin. Nancy Huston, an Anglophone Canadian writing in French in Paris, reflects on the life and work of the ever elusive Polish-Russian-French insider/outsider Romain Gary, whose split personalities included two best-selling novelists, a diplomat, a war hero, and a suicide.

Henry Louis Gates Jr., a famous African-American intellectual, reflects on his first meeting with the famous African-American intellectual James Baldwin in the south of France, and on the costs as well as the benefits of Baldwin's exile from the American scene during a crucial period of race relations in this country. Zygmunt Bauman, a Polish-Jewish sociologist and cultural critic living in Leeds, discusses the whole history of Jewish assimilation in the West before moving to his true subject, the place of eminent Jewish writers in a postwar Poland from which Jews have all but disappeared. Finally, we encounter in this group Tibor Dessewffy's reflections on strangerhood, as exemplified by (among others) the sociologist Alfred Schütz, who emigrated from Vienna to New York, and the Portuguese poet Fernando Pessoa, who remained at home but discovered several strangers, other poets, living in his own body. (Dessewffy is a Hungarian sociologist with a doctorate from Amsterdam.)

It is doubtless not an accident (though it was not planned from the start) that so many of these essays confront, more or less directly, the figure of the Jew. Even where one would least expect to find him—for example, in the work of the Inca Garcilaso, the 16th-century Spanish-Peruvian *mestizo*—the figure of the Jew turns up: as Doris Sommer shows, the inspiration for Garcilaso's first book was none other than a work by the expelled Spanish Jewish writer, León Hebreo, which Garcilaso translated from Italian. It would appear that in the European-American perspective, at least, the Jew as an emblematic figure of displacement is unavoidable, and not only in the twentieth century. In our century, of course, we are used to this: the Jew has been a long-standing figure embodying modern restlessness and uprootedness. Joyce intimated this idea in his choice of the urban walker Leopold Bloom as his everyman; Maurice Blanchot reiterated it in his notion of "être-Juif," "being-Jewish," a synonym for nomadic movement (Blanchot 1969: 183). Zygmunt Bauman—who may appear more entitled to speak about this, being himself a Jewish exile—has called the Jew in Kafka's works the "universal stranger," at whose experience "strangers of all walks of life could look . . . as a mirror and see the blurred and vaguely conveyed details of their own likeness" (Bauman 1988–89: 27).

Backward glances: Those who leave home with no thought of return and succeed, well or badly, in settling elsewhere, occasionally cast backward glances at what they left behind. Interestingly, so do their children, who may never have seen the left-behind place at all, except through the words—or the silences—of their parents. The last three essays take varying looks at such backward glances. Leo Spitzer, a historian whose parents, Jewish refugees, sailed from Europe in 1939 to settle (temporarily, it would turn out) in Bolivia, studies the Austrian refugee community in La Paz, where he grew up. Marianne Hirsch, the daughter of Rumanian refugees from the Bukovina, discusses work by artists and writers who, like herself, know their parents' native region only by hearsay or fantasy. My own essay, written by a transplanted Hungarian Jew, studies the war memoirs of . . . transplanted Hungarian Jews.

As I have tried, perhaps all too insistently, to suggest in the preceding pages, one of the most striking aspects of this scholarly examination of creativity and exile is that it is in large part the work of individuals who qualify, in a broad or narrow sense, as exiles. The element of autobiography in many of these learned essays bears out once more the power of the personal voice in criticism. Nor, one might say, should it be otherwise, especially when it comes to the subject of exile. Do those who have known it from inside out write with added urgency about the "melancholy tension of separation from our origins"? Perhaps; but I would not want to overstate the case. To the degree that exile is a matter not only

of physical displacement but of interior experience, we may all, independently of our actual religion, nationality, or place of birth, be (as the
walls of the Sorbonne proclaimed in 1968) "German Jews."

REFERENCES

Arendt, Hannah
    1978 "We Refugees" (1943), in *The Jew as Pariah: Jewish Identity and Politics in
       the Modern Age,* ed. Ron H. Feldman, 55–66 (New York: Grove Press).
Bammer, Angelica, ed.
    1994 *Displacements: Cultural Identities in Question* (Bloomington: Indiana
       University Press).
Bauman, Zygmunt
    1988–89 "Strangers: The Social Construction of Universality and Particu-
       larity," *Telos* (Winter): 7–42.
Blanchot, Maurice
    1969 *L'Entretien infini* (Paris: Gallimard).
Brodsky, Joseph
    1988 "Acceptance Speech" [for the Nobel Prize for Literature], *New York Re-
       view of Books* 34(21–22): 20.
Burgin, Victor
    1991 "Paranoiac Space," *Visual Anthropology Review* 7(2): 22–30.
Said, Edward
    1994 "Reflections on Exile" (1984), in *Altogether Elsewhere: Writers on Exile,*
      ed. Marc Robinson, 137–49 (Boston and London: Faber and Faber).

SIGNPOSTS

CHRISTINE BROOKE-ROSE

EXSUL

1

WHEN I WAS A CHILD in Brussels, brought up bilingually in French and English, I used to think that the word *exile* meant "ex-île," out of the island; not, I feel pretty certain, because of the British Isles, to and from which I was constantly taken and to which I nominally and paternally belonged, but because islands are magical to a child: Treasure Island, Crusoe's island, Peter Pan's never-never land, *Paul et Virginie* on their island, Coral Island, or whatever, a no-man's-land all the way to the island of solitudinous reading I loved to be in and hated to be suddenly thrust out of. And are not many utopias, even dystopias, islands, from Pindar's and Plato's to More's and Swift's and Golding's? Even science fiction's planets and galaxies and alternative worlds are felt as islands, isolated from our round earth's imagined corners of reality.

But no: exile (L. *exilium,* earlier *exsilium; exul,* earlier *exsul,* a banished man) was long thought to be linked to *solum,* soil, but is now (by Andrews 1987 [1879]) related to the root *sal,* Sanskrit *sar* (to go), L. *saline/saltare;* and L. *exsilio* meant "spring forth." But then later, in Old French, *exilier* or *essilier* meant "to ravage," "to devastate," a shift in meaning still traceable in *exterminate,* literally "to drive beyond boundaries."

Thus the clanging connotations are of suffering in banishment, but also of springing forth into a new life, beyond the boundaries of the familiar (beyond the boundaries of the island-self, I obstinately add, since no man is an island, even in no-man's-land). "Thou paradise of exiles, Italy!" Shelley wrote in 1818 (*Julian and Maddalo:* 1.57). That's for the springing forth connotation. But Pope Gregory VII's last words are said to have been: "I have loved righteousness and hated iniquity; wherefore I die in exile" (quoted in Bowden 1840, 2: bk. 3, chap. 20). This is a bitter adaptation of Psalm 45.7 Revised Standard Version:

Thou has loved righteousness and hated iniquity,
wherefore God, even thy God, hath anointed thee
with the oil of gladness above thy fellows.

That's for the suffering connotation, a suffering felt as unjust, a punishment for righteousness instead of the promised reward. To be sure, Gregory VII (Hildebrand) was not a poet or other writer of fiction (except perhaps in those last words), and in many ways deserved his fate in the deadly struggle for supremacy, between the papacy and the Holy Roman Empire, that bedeviled the whole of the Middle Ages. The emperor Henry VII had captured the "Leonine" city (after Leo IX) in 1083, Rome itself surrendered in 1084, but Gregory held out in the castle of Sant' Angelo. Then the pope's ally Robert Guiscard at last came to the "rescue," brutally sacking Rome and taking Gregory, almost as a captive, to the safety of Salerno, where he died on May 31, 1085.

It may seem absurd today that mere writers should ever have been considered powerful or influential enough to deserve exile, as opposed to political figures or, for that matter, to bakers and carpenters. But they have, and, being writers, offer a good deal more variety than political figures.

2

There are so many different kinds of literary exile. At random from memory, in roughly chronological, nonevaluative order: "Isaiah" (and in a very wide sense, all Jewish writers of the Diaspora), Ovid, Virgil, Cavalcanti, Dante (from Florence under Charles de Valois), Petrarch (to Provence), Thibault de Champagne (to his new kingdom of Navarre), Charles d'Orléans (imprisoned by the English), Voltaire, Mme de Staël, Adam Mickiewicz, Shelley, Keats, Byron, Cyprian Norwid, Charles Baudelaire (debts), Victor Hugo, Heinrich Heine, Oscar Wilde, Henry James, Joseph Conrad, Gabriele D'Annunzio (debts), W. B. Yeats, Edith Wharton, Tristan Tzara, Kurt Schwitters, T. S. Eliot, Ezra Pound, James Joyce, Gertrude Stein, Scott Fitzgerald, Ernest Hemingway, H. D., Djuna Barnes, Henry Miller, Radclyffe Hall, D. H. Lawrence, Max Beerbohm, Somerset Maugham, Stefan Zweig, Bertolt Brecht, André Breton, Christopher Isherwood, Aldous Huxley, W. H. Auden, Thomas Mann, Malcolm Lowry, Witold Gombrowicz, Vladimir Nabokov, Paul Bowles, Jane Bowles, Samuel Beckett, Eugene Ionesco, Jorge Semprún, Luis Cernuda, Milan Kundera, Aleksandr Solzhenitsyn, Harry Matthews, Italo Calvino, Anthony Burgess, Muriel Spark, and no doubt many others, all the way to the modern "foreigners" or "postcolonials" who write in English or

French today, from Kazuo Ishiguro to Salman Rushdie, an exile within an exile.

Clearly, this list alone covers a great variety of exiles, from temporary (e.g., Hugo) to permanent, though the exile can't always know this; early (e.g., Ishiguro, who came to England at six from Nagasaki) or *en fin de carrière* (Wilde). But the most obvious and commonly made distinction is between the following:

1. *Involuntary exile*, usually political or punitive ("Isaiah," Ovid, Dante, Thibault, Charles d'Orléans, Byron, Mickiewicz, and all the moderns such as Ionesco, Semprún, Cernuda, Kundera, Solzhenitsyn, etc., alas). And these can be further divided into those exiled for their books or their behavior (Ovid, Byron, Mme de Staël, Victor Hugo, Wilde, Solzhenitsyn) and those who as private persons fled from political conditions or war.

2. *Voluntary exile*, usually called expatriation, itself for many more personal reasons: social, economic, sexual (e.g., Radclyffe Hall and the lesbian group in Paris in the twenties), or simple preference (Beerbohm retired in Rapallo, Ezra Pound choosing Italy).

Involuntary exiles may tend to be unhappy, poor, bitter (like Gregory VII), nostalgic about the society left behind, self-righteous; voluntary exiles may tend to be happy, comfortable, satiric about the society left behind, self-righteous. But that is obviously a useless generalization, with too many exceptions on any one feature, and some, like Byron (a sexual scandal but rich and noble) or Wilde (a sexual scandal but broken by prison and poverty) hover between the two, while Cyprian Norwid, though a voluntary exile, lived and died in Paris in abject poverty and was buried in a pauper's grave.

It seems to me that there are more pertinent distinctions, which cut across the differences in causes and conditions. The first is formal and thematic, the second linguistic.

Formal/thematic

In older times, before the rise of the nation-state, when literary forms and themes were more restricted as well as more universal within a common temporal culture (medieval, classical, etc.), many writers in exile simply continued to write what they would have written at home. Petrarch, Charles d'Orléans, Thibault de Champagne (courtly lyrics); Shelley, Keats, Byron, Hugo (lyrics, romantic epics, classical elegies, etc.), Voltaire (satires, tragedies, *romans philosophiques,* essays), Mme de Staël (novels, essays). In other words, despite the inescapable language differences, the formal and thematic idiom was closer to the universal language of music: Handel could live in England but compose in the classical idiom, whereas it is impossible to consider Schubert or Dvořák apart from their use of folk song motifs. The analogy is of course inexact, but broadly helpful.

With the development of romantic realism in the nineteenth century, many exiled writers wrote about the society they had left behind. Although forms remained universally recognizable, however developing, there was a shift in subject matter, so that a new distinction can be made between those whose themes look back in either traditional or more experimental forms, and those whose themes, often with more formal experimentation, transcend the condition of exile. This distinction can be illustrated with, in the nineteenth century, Mickiewicz versus Norwid, or, in the twentieth, Joyce versus Beckett.

Mickiewicz, leaving Wilno in "Russian" Poland after the 1830 insurrection, first for Russia, then Dresden, and finally Paris, was immensely prolific for five years. The whole of *Pan Tadeusz,* a romantic patriotic epic poem with a Polish hero, full of passionate detail of landscape and customs down to every different kind of mushroom, was written in Paris. Then, perhaps exhausted after that immense effort of total recall, he dried up, at least on poetry, although as national bard he became deeply involved with Polish messianism. A modern counterpart is Solzhenitsyn. Norwid's poetry on the other hand, however essentially Polish, is not only more experimental but explores far less specifically Polish themes.

In a parallel if dissimilar way Joyce, though boldly experimental in form, continued to write about the Ireland of his youth, first realistically then mythologically in a wholly transformed, interlinguistic new idiom that transcends the earlier realism; whereas Beckett, also pushing the boundaries of novel or play beyond familiar forms, writes much simpler English (and later French), yet leaves Ireland far behind, and his postmodern successors, such as Calvino, also abandon regional or national locales and themes.

In a general sense this abandonment of the local is true of many modern writers. Thomas Mann's *The Magic Mountain* is not merely about a sanatorium, Djuna Barnes's characters are placeless, and so on. In *What Are Masterpieces?* Gertrude Stein said about herself: "I am an American and I have lived half my life in Paris, not the half that made me but the half that made what I made" (1970 [1940]: 62). Later, she elaborates: "What is adventure and what romance. Adventure is making the distant approach nearer but romance is having what is where it is which is not where you are stay where it is" (ibid.).

Those who make things "inside themselves," she goes on, do not need adventure but they do need romance:

It has always been true of all who make what they make come out of what is in them and have nothing to do with what is necessarily existing outside of them it is inevitable that they have always wanted two civilizations. . . . There is no possibility of mixing up the other civilization with yourself you are you and if you are you in your own civilization you are apt to mix yourself up too much with your civilization but when it is another civilization a complete other a romantic other another that stays there where it is you in it have freedom inside yourself which if you are to do what is inside yourself and nothing else is a very useful thing to have happen to you and so America is my country and Paris is my home town. (Ibid.: 62–63)

Whether we agree or not with this elaboration, it is true that the American expatriate in Paris is strangely immune to French influence, in much the same way that Joyce wrote about Dublin independently of Paris or Trieste. As Shari Benstock (1986: 78) has said about the English or American women who settled in France during the twenties (and it applies to most of the men, including Scott Fitzgerald), they wrote about the English and the Americans, and "were not affected by French mores and customs," since it was "the need for separateness that brought them to Paris," as well as, no doubt, economic and other advantages— the favorable rate of exchange, the sexual freedom, the liquor unavailable in Prohibition America, and "being geniuses together." (*Being Geniuses Together* is the title of Robert McAlmon's 1968 book, quoted in Gilbert and Gubar 1989, 2: 221. On the advantages of expatriation, see Gilbert and Gubar 1989, 2: 219.)

Hemingway, with his Parisian, Italian, Spanish, and African locales, is a notable exception, but then he hardly remained in one spot, and might be classed by Stein under "adventure." Perhaps the most exemplary exception, going back a generation or more, is Henry James, who shifted his subtle analyses from Boston to Europe, and more especially to the gulf between the two, skillfully inverting the cliché of Americans as vulgar and Europeans as civilized. His disciple Edith Wharton, on the other hand, though living in France, remained with American drawing-room society.

The Jamesian shift is more common today. Kundera is a good example, with *The Unbearable Lightness of Being* (1984) already mixing Geneva into a basically Czech story, and Salman Rushdie is another. *The Satanic Verses* (1988) is a real clash of Indian/London cultures. Kazuo Ishiguro moved from Japanese locales and themes to a tour de force in *The Remains of the Day* (1989), in which the thoughts and emotions of a typically British butler pierce through his pompously distancing, alienatingly "correct" idiom.

Apart from the last two, all these exiles—whatever their home/abroad themes or their familiar/innovative forms, whatever lands they left or went to, in whatever condition, Babylonish exile or prison, poor or relatively moneyed—nevertheless wrote in their native tongues.

Linguistic

The question of language is more complex, and examples of writers who adopt a language not their own are much rarer. Joseph Conrad is the modern archetype, writing *all* of his work in English. Apart from two poignant short stories, Conrad never wrote of Poland, but wrote instead of the sea, of Southeast Asia, South America, Marseilles, London. The other apparent exception, *Under Western Eyes* (1911), with an East European revolutionary theme, has a Russian hero, and a Moscow locale, and takes place partly in Geneva. As in all of Conrad's novels, the essential solitude of exile is transmuted away from Polish specificity.

Conrad was already born in exile (near Berdyczów), in the sense that this "Polish" part of Ukraine had been incorporated into Russia with the Partitions, although the idea of Poland and the Polish language remained very strong there. But Apollo Korzeniowski, Conrad's father and a literary man, was politically active and the family was further exiled when Conrad was seven, first to Vologda north of Moscow, then back south to Chernikov, not too far from Kiev; eventually, after his mother's death, Conrad returned at least to Lwów, then part of Austria, ending up as an orphan in Cracow (also part of Austria) under the guardianship of his maternal uncle. Conrad's dream was to go to sea, and at seventeen he left for Marseilles. In other words, he was born an involuntary exile in the East who became a voluntary exile in the West. But he was deeply read in Polish literature. A complex background.

Even today, Ionesco, Nabokov, and Beckett are rare examples of complete linguistic assimilation, possibly giving the distance needed for the transcending of regional/national themes into those of the human condition anywhere.

The phenomenon of language change, however, also cuts across geographical exile, since many writers from our ex-empires write in the ex-imperial languages of French and English. The Spanish/Portuguese situation is different, since those languages stamped out the native ones, at least for literary purposes, and became the first and native languages in much older ex-empires. But the Nigerians Chinua Achebe and Wole Soyinka, the Somali Nuruddin Farah, the Algerian Rachid Mimouni (and other African writers), Salman Rushdie (and other Indian writers), learning English/French young and perhaps even being bilingual, chose those second languages over their native idioms.

This modern phenomenon, though still rare, is an exact inversion of the medieval one, when the ex-imperial language, Latin, though much debased, was the only literary language, and was eventually stamped out by the new vernaculars. The effort to create a new literary language (Languedoc, Languedoil, Tuscan, Spanish, Middle English, Middle High German) or, earlier, simply to continue in the old vernacular (Saxon, Anglo-Saxon, Old High German) must have been an equivalent challenge, with this political and social difference: the medieval effort, though in each case individual, was also a generalized (if sometimes condemned) struggle in favor of the native, popular language as against the dying official one, whereas the modern effort of writers who use a language other than their native one is a purely individual struggle to merge into and contribute to the (as yet) not quite dying official language in order to reach a wider public rather than be restricted to a language this wider public can't be bothered to learn.

And yet, despite this inversion, the modern individual who decides to create in an idiom not his own, or only secondly his own, is surely making the same qualitative effort as that of Dante trying to create a new literary language out of his own spoken and popular idiom. That is, the effort is as great, the result at its best is as fresh, as cliché-escaping, as enriching, as that of Dante; unless the postcolonial, on the contrary, tries to follow the clichés (of language, of structure) of the ex-imperial culture, as happens, in my humble opinion, with Chinua Achebe (e.g., *Things Fall Apart* [1958]).

How then are these various clashing features of exile (involuntary/voluntary, home society/new society, own language/alien language) experienced today? Such a vast subject would deserve a whole book, examining each writer in detail. But since, more modestly, I have experienced both aspects of all those distinctions, as expatriate English writer and as ex-wife of Jerzy Peterkiewicz, a Polish exile writing in English, I propose to move on to a brief but more personal treatment, in the sense that I knew him well.

3

In 1958, the *Times Literary Supplement* (May 18, 1–2) published a long front-page article entitled "England Is Abroad," reviewing three English novels by foreigners: *An End to Dying,* by Sam Astrachan (Yiddish culture), *Black Midas,* by Jan Carew (Guiana), and *Future to Let,* by Jerzy Peterkiewicz. After over thirty-five years there is no point in summarizing the reviews, since reviews (like, sometimes, the books reviewed) are ephemeral. But it was the first time, to my knowledge, that the question of foreign writers in English was raised in the *TLS* and the article, like all *Times Literary Supplement* "fronts," dealt first, and at length, with the situation of the English novel. It starts:

Provincialism, like rheumatism, is the name of a disease which has as many cures as it has causes. . . . Provincialism is a kind of cultural rheumatism, a stiffness of the joints, a pained paralysis of the executory organs, an insidious and obscure malady that will in time deform the very structure of a language, altering its every statement into the posture of parody.   (Ibid.: 1)

I would qualify the metaphor by adding that rheumatism is a very conscious pain ("pained paralysis") while provincialism is unconscious and self-satisfied. The author goes on to suggest that the English idiom

was already in decay before the First World War. Already, by 1910, we find that many of the most accomplished writers in our language originate on the fringe of the English-speaking world and, more importantly, that they made no attempt to cover up their origins by conforming to the standards of the metropolis. On the contrary, they demand that London should accept them as they are and even suggest that it would benefit by following in their outlandish footsteps. What is more, London did. The centre of gravity of English literature shifted.   (Ibid.)

To be sure, the author is here thinking chiefly of "the American influx," in terms of which, he complains, this remarkable revolution is too often considered, and more particularly, of Yeats, rather than of writers who (like Peterkiewicz, alone of the three reviewed) learn English late. In other words, I have momentarily slid back to the "formal/thematic," non-"linguistic" part of the previous section. But not entirely. On Yeats, the author comments:

Had he been born a century earlier than he was, had he been a contemporary of Tom Moore, Yeats would either have written within the English conventions, or he would have been a much more modest poet than the one we know. He could not have been both an Irish poet and a great poet because there was no cultural context in which a great Irish poet could exist, unless perhaps, he wrote in Erse. The power of the English language was such that he would have been transformed by it into an English poet who happened to have been born in Ireland, just as Swift and Burke are English writers though they remain Irish men. (Ibid.)

In other words, Yeats would have been like Latin writers of the Late Empire or the Middle Ages (Macrobius, Pelagius, and such), whose land of residence is seldom relevant even if known (as in Gregory of Tours, Matthew of Vendôme, etc.).

Of the three writers considered by the *TLS*, Peterkiewicz was unique in having learned English late, in his twenties. Conrad was thus a frequent comparison in reviews of his English novels and, like Conrad, he was attacked by his compatriots for "betrayal," as are certain African writers today. But his situation, like his novels, was completely different from Conrad's. For one thing he had a Polish literary career behind him. In that sense at least, he is more like Beckett.

Born in 1916, Peterkiewicz left his Polish village in Dobrzyn (northeastern Poland) at fourteen, to study and later to conquer Warsaw, where he was quickly recognized as a highly original poet, and soon was editing a literary supplement. He was twenty-three when Hitler, and then Stalin, attacked Poland in 1939. He escaped to Romania, where he fell very ill, eventually arriving in France, and escaping again in 1940 to England, still too ill to fight. The Polish government in exile helped him to attend the University of St Andrews in Scotland, where he recovered and learned

English. In his autobiography (1993) he describes how he couldn't understand why a lecturer talked quite so often about Ovid, only to learn later that the lecturer merely pronounced "of it" in an emphatic way. That's how little English he knew at first.

I met him in the British Museum library when I was twenty-three and about to go to Oxford as an ex-service and grant-supported student after the war. By then he was finishing his Ph.D. thesis and continuing to publish articles and poems in the exile press.

Then, slowly, came the mutation: he not only stopped writing poetry, he turned to novels, and in English. Strange novels, both sad and funny, and deeply original. By then of course his English was fluent. And there occurred, equally slowly, a Jamesian shift in subject matter, from wholly Polish to partly Polish, to totally free and experimental. In slightly more detail (for I cannot of course give a proper critical evaluation here, nor is it my role): His first novel, *The Knotted Cord* (1953), was partly autobiographical, about a boy in a Polish village who, after an illness, is dedicated to Saint Anthony by his mother and dressed for three years in a Franciscan habit. In the second novel, *Loot and Loyalty* (1955), the scene shifts to Scottish mercenaries in seventeenth-century Poland (then powerful), including one Tobias Hume, a historical figure who composed songs and who, in the novel, gets involved with a newly imagined version of the False Dmitri in other words, the exile situation reversed. The scene shifts again in *Future to Let* (1958), to an Englishman caught up, via the exotic Celina, with Polish exiles in London.

And then the Polish scene is more or less over, if the essential solitude of exile is not, and the subsequent novels are among the most unusual of the time, or even, I would add, of the period since. *Isolation* (1959) also features an exotic foreign woman in London, but she is South American and a diplomat's wife, and meets her English lover in dramatically secretive ways and places, with a funny/sad eroticism that is part of the charm. *The Quick and the Dead* (1961) is literally about the dead and the dead living, in a weird, unplaceable limbo-locale, not in the least like a ghost story but both violent and gently poetic. We are completely out of the Polish/foreign versus London isolation.

That Angel Burning at My Left Side (1963) returns East, to the borderland between Poland and (now ex) East Prussia, with a hero searching for an unknown father, but it soon shifts to other regions, in sections named after the points of the compass (East, West, North, South, in that order), ending in Italy. Then comes my favorite, *Inner Circle* (1966), written in a spiral structure of recurring layers called "Surface," "Underground," and "Sky," apparently, but only apparently, unlinked. "Surface" describes a future people who emerge out of boxes to a much reduced living space on the surface, having barely a square meter each to stand on; "Underground" is the perpetual journey of a schizophrenic boy, Patrick, on the London tube train; and "Sky" is the story of Eve, already separated from Adam, living in a world of animals which is invaded by monkeys, with whom her daughter goes off to live. The link is in the title, the inner circle of solitude, echoed in the spiral structure. The treatment is like skating on thin ice, a light and graceful dance above cold, unseen depths.

The last novel, *Green Flows the Bile* (1969), about a dying British fellow traveler on a last visit to Eastern Europe, returns to a more realistic, satirical, even oddly prophetic vein, and was the first to be less well received. I myself like it less, but this may be subjective.

Why then was this highly original writer forgotten? Partly, I think, because he came too soon to be truly comprehended (in both senses); partly because England (and other places) woke up out of provincialism so that many other innovative novels (notably postmodern) began to attract all the attention; but mostly, I would venture, because Peterkiewicz stopped writing novels, though he continued writing in English (essays, radio plays, an autobiography). Sheer persistency can also be part of survival. Conrad, after all, did not really pierce through until *Chance* (1913), his twelfth novel (not counting various tales but including *Romance*, written with Ford Madox Hueffer, later Ford Madox Ford).

And why did he stop? He stopped when I left, but I have to insist here that there is no connection: literary gossips might say that he couldn't have written his novels without my support in English, or even, who knows, that I wrote them, but the second hypothesis is impossible (we are too different), and the first ridiculous. His English was perfect, nor did I ever correct more than actual (and rare) mistakes, as any publishing editor might, and I took great care not to touch the poetic oddity of his essential *ostranenie*. I contributed only encouragement and enthusiasm, and he had plenty of that elsewhere. The writer's block is always mysterious. Perhaps he got discouraged by the bad reception of the last novel, unusually sensitive (for we all get bad receptions here and there). Perhaps the sheer distance from his origins was too great. Conrad after all could and did revisit Poland; Peterkiewicz was blacklisted by the Communist regime and did not return to Poland until 1963 (for research), well after he became a British subject and teacher of Polish literature at the School of Slavonic Studies in London University, in other words a persona officially grata, and therefore protected, and even then he was followed. Now that Poland is free, he is welcome there again, his poetry is republished, his English works translated. Perhaps he is resourcing himself, or, more simply, returning to source.

This brings me back to the question of exile. I too am astride two languages and cultures, but since this fact is usually dealt with by the few who write about me as an expatriate in France, I shall say nothing of myself, except the following: exile is an immense force for liberation, for extra distance, for automatically developing contrasting structures in one's head, not just syntactic and lexical but social and psychological; it is, in other words, undoubtedly a leaping forth. But there is a price to pay. The distance can become too great, the loss of identity *as writer* in the alien society at least for one who shies away from other expatriates or "being geniuses together" (if any there be) can be burdensome; the new live language can feel more and more remote. So one has to fight all that as an extra effort, although that effort can also result in escaping the familiar phrase, the expected word, simply because it no longer comes into one's head, so even here there is advantage. But it is easy to drift into not making the effort at all.

4

Finally, I should like to widen the whole concept of exile beyond (or rather, back within) the notion of territorial or linguistic boundaries. For it is also possible to feel an exile in one's own country.

In *Born in Exile* (1982 [1892]) George Gissing follows the career of Godwin Peake, who as a poor boy gives up an opening to brilliant studies because his Cockney uncle decides to open an eating house, under the name of Peake, opposite the entrance to Midland College, which is giving Peake his chance. But he never gets over it, and longs to enter the society from which he has so snobbishly excluded himself (the parallel in Gissing's own life, marriage to a prostitute, was much more "shameful"). Since the only way a lower-class young man could do this was to marry an upper-class girl, and since the only way to do that was to become a parson, Godwin Peake as rationalist and nonbeliever goes through an elaborate pretense of studying to enter the church, partly to retain the financial help of his Midland benefactress, but mostly to gain entry into the magic circle of the girl's rich family and friends. Eventually he is not only found out but thoroughly ashamed, and, with his whole scheme and his genuine love collapsed, he leaves the country, catches a convenient fever, and dies in Vienna. But this seems purely fortuitous, for the sake of the last sentence, uttered by his friend Earaker: " 'Dead, too, in exile!' was his thought, 'Poor old fellow!' " (ibid.).

Peake is like Jude Fawley in *Jude the Obscure,* the archetype of the clever Victorian young man without means, stifled by conventions he hates yet acknowledges, akin to Wells's little man with social handicaps, and to many similar characters in Dostoevski, Turgenev, Gogol, or Lawrence, all the way to the English picaresque of the fifties, usually about misfits who make it.

Gissing made social exile his permanent theme, with infinite variations: all the characters living well below the poverty line in *The Nether World* (1974 [1889]) are social exiles, notably Clara Hewett, who tries to get out, with tragic consequences, and inversely Sidney Kirkwood, happy in a cut-above job, helpful to all, who sacrifices a possibly rich marriage to a girl he loves to marry Clara, now disfigured and discontented, out of pure generosity. Others are Bernard Kincote in *Isabel Clarendon* (1982 [1886]), and Jasper Milvain in *New Grub Street* (1976 [1891]).

Then, as Gissing moved upmarket (at least thematically), the social exile is often richly transmuted: Miriam Baske, a strictly puritan young widow among rich and cultivated English friends in Naples, fiercely resisting the lure of culture (*The Emancipated* [1977 {1890}]); Harvey Rolfe, a gentleman on the edge of frivolous society by choice, and his wife Alma, daughter of a dishonest and suddenly ruined millionaire, who thinks she can nevertheless make it in society as a professional singer (*The Whirlpool* [1977 {1897}]. And then there is the recurring feckless charlatan who comes to grief, faintly echoing Peake but with greater initial advantages and charm: Reuben Mallard in *The Emancipated,* Dyce Lashmar in *Our Friend the Charlatan* (1901) and, more subtly, Denzil in *Denzil Quarrier* (1979 [1892]), a brilliant young man fighting for a Parliamentary seat, but with a secret to hide. The best twist to this outsider theme, perhaps at last resolving Gissing's problem, at any rate treating it with humor, comes in *Will Warburton* (1981 [1905]), in which Will, a successful businessman, is ruined through generosity and trust in Godfrey Sherwood (another kind of charlatan) and decides to become a grocer.

He vanishes from his own society, but is unfortunately discovered, with, however, a happy ending: he marries for love and remains a grocer.

Rooted in all types of literary exile is the desire to integrate/not to integrate: the desire to remain integral to the society left behind rather than to merge with the society lived in (Mickiewicz, Joyce); the desire not to belong to the society left behind but to a more desirable society (Gissing, Conrad, James); the desire not to integrate either with the society left behind, except thematically (the need for separateness) or with the society lived in (the American expatriates); and many more ambiguous postmodern variations (Kundera, Calvino, Beckett, Ionesco, Nabokov, and, more tangentially perhaps, Peterkiewicz).

Ultimately, is not every poet or "poetic" (exploring, rigorous) novelist an exile of sorts, looking in from outside onto a bright, desirable image in the mind's eye, of the little world created, for the space of the writing effort and the shorter space of the reading? This kind of writing, often at odds with publisher and public, is the last solitary, nonsocialized creative art. Music needs performers, painting often needed teams in the past, and now often needs experts in modern inventions such as electronics or plastics, as sculpture and architecture always have. The dramatist needs production, the best-selling author needs media hype, the columnist needs editorial deadlines, the scriptwriter is the most minor contributor to a film. Reading, too, which used to be shared aloud, is the last solitary activity, compared with struggling against the crowd at an exhibition, going to the theater or the cinema. The circle of light on the page, excluding the world, the escapes from it in stray thoughts and imaginative leaps, for writer or reader: an imagined world, an "inner circle," within the island of exile, is that not also an island, the reader or writer exile, exsul?

REFERENCES

Achebe, Chinua
  1958 *Things Fall Apart* (London: Heinemann).
Andrews, E. A.
  1987 [1879] Harper's *Latin Dictionary,* revised, enlarged, and in great part rewritten by Charlton T. Lewis and Charles Short (Oxford: Clarendon).
Astrachan, Sam
  1958 *An End to Dying* (London: Barrie).

Benstock, Shari

    1986 *Women of the Left Bank: Paris, 1900–1940* (Austin: University of Texas Press).

Bowden, J. W.

    1845 *The Life and Pontificate of Gregory the Seventh.* Vol. 2 (New York: Dunham).

Carew, Jan

    1958 *Black Midas* (London: Secker and Warburg).

Conrad, Joseph

    1911 *Under Western Eyes* (London: Dent).

    1913 *Chance: A Tale in Two Parts* (London: Dent).

Gilbert, Sandra M., and Susan Gubar

    1989 *No Man's Land: The Place of the Woman Writer in the Twentieth Century.* Vol. 2, *Sexchanges* (New Haven, CT: Yale University Press).

Gissing, George

    1901 *Our Friend the Charlatan* (New York: AMS).

    1974 [1889] *The Nether World* (Brighton, UK: Harvester).

    1976 [1891] *New Grub Street* (Harmondsworth, UK: Penguin).

    1977 [1890] *The Emancipated* (Brighton, UK: Harvester).

    1977 [1897] *The Whirlpool* (Hassocks, UK: Harvester).

    1979 [1892] *Denzil Quarrier* (Brighton, UK: Harvester).

    1981 [1905] *Will Warburton* (Brighton, UK: Harvester).

    1982 [1886] *Isabel Clarendon* (Brighton, UK: Harvester).

    1982 [1892] *Born in Exile* (Hassocks, UK: Harvester).

Hall, Radclyffe

    1981 [1928] *The Well of Loneliness* (New York: Avon).

Ishiguro, Kazuo

    1989 *The Remains of the Day* (London: Faber and Faber).

Kundera, Milan

    1984 *The Unbearable Lightness of Being* (New York: Harper and Row).

McAlmon, Robert

    1968 *Being Geniuses Together, 1920–1930,* revised and with supplementary chapters by Kay Boyle (Garden City, NY: Doubleday).

Peterkiewicz, Jerzy

    1953 *The Knotted Cord* (London: Heinemann).

    1955 *Loot and Loyalty* (London: Heinemann).

    1958 *Future to Let* (London: Heinemann).

    1959 *Isolation* (London: Heinemann).

    1961 *The Quick and the Dead* (London: Macmillan).

    1963 *That Angel Burning at My Left Side* (London: Macmillan).

    1966 *Inner Circle* (London: Macmillan).

    1969 *Green Flows the Bile* (London: Michael Joseph).

    1993 *In the Scales of Fate: An Autobiography* (London: Marion Boyars).

Rushdie, Salman
   1988 *The Satanic Verses* (London: Viking).
Stein, Gertrude
   1970 [1940] *What Are Masterpieces?* (New York: Pitman).

THOMAS PAVEL

EXILE AS ROMANCE AND AS TRAGEDY

IS INTELLECTUAL EXILE a perennial phenomenon or a specifically modern one? Few centuries have experienced displacements of writers, artists, professors, and professionals as dramatic as those which accompanied the political upheavals of the twentieth century. Yet artists and thinkers like Ovid, Dante, Descartes, Poussin, Hobbes, and Pierre Bayle also spent their active lives in a foreign country, at least some of them forced to do so for political reasons. Invoking a quantitative criterion, one could of course reply that these were isolated cases. The flight of intellectuals from Germany after 1933, in contrast, reached mass proportions. Between 1933 and 1938, a staggering total of 3,120 academics left Germany, including 41 percent of full professors in the social sciences and 36 percent of those in law (Noakes 1993: 379). But the Huguenots flying from France to avoid persecution after the revocation of the Edict of Nantes (1685) also were quite numerous. Quantity, then, is probably not the only relevant factor.

A more striking difference between twentieth-century and premodern Europe is the permeability of the borders surrounding the ill-defined states of the latter. This feature encouraged mobility among professionals, making it easy for warriors, priests, artists, and professors to change patrons. Famous captains were for hire and switched sides when the fortunes of their masters declined. In a world in which education was dispensed in Latin and every cultivated person understood it, teachers, who usually belonged to religious orders, were dispatched wherever the order needed them, their native language being no obstacle. The most influential order involved in education, that of the Jesuits, was also the most international. This situation stands in marked contrast with the strong territoriality of nineteenth- and twentieth-century nation-states, which jealously yoked the army, the educational system, and the arts to the nation and its interests.

And in any case few premodern intellectuals chose to leave their homelands for political reasons per se. Ovid was sent away by Augustus as punishment for sexual misconduct involving the emperor's daughter. True, Dante's and Hobbes's troubles were political, and Bayle left France to avoid religious persecution, but Descartes retired from Paris for a number of reasons, one of which was the need for solitude, and Poussin chose Rome because in the middle of the seventeenth century it was the uncontested center of European artistic life. While Dante's wanderings might, in a sense, be compared to those of Thomas Mann and Czeslaw Milosz, Descartes's move to Holland seems closer to René Girard's move to America, whereas Poussin's decision to live in Rome resembles Brancusi's and Picasso's preference for Paris.

The notion of exile being a cloudy one, a few distinctions are in order. Taken metaphorically, exile may stand for many things, in particular the pervasive feeling human beings often experience that they do not entirely belong in the sublunar world. More on this meaning of the term later. Properly understood, exile is a subspecies of the more general notion of human mobility across geographic and political space. It implies the idea of forced displacement (as opposed to voluntary expatriation) that occurs for political or religious reasons rather than economic ones (as opposed both to slave trading and to voluntary immigration). In recent centuries it most often takes the form of individual mobility (as opposed to collective migration and diaspora), although in a more primitive historical environment it can involve an entire nation, for example, the Jewish exile to Babylon or the exile of the Crimean Tartars under Stalin. In these latter cases the element of forced displacement is present, as is another pervasive connotation of exile, the hope for return to the land of one's ancestors. Immigrants begin a new life and find a new home; exiles never break the psychological link with their point of origin. Among the features of exile must thus be included the coercive nature of the displacement, its religious or political motivation, and the exiled's faith in the possibility of homecoming.

In its strict definition, exile is a penalty imposed by society. Whereas in the form of ostracism and banishment it simply forbids the defendants to set foot in their homelands, deportation forcibly removes them to a place of exile assigned by the legal authority. Banished from Athens, Themistocles went to Persia, his country's archenemy; with greater foresight, French authorities imprisoned Colonel Dreyfus on Devil's Island in Guyana. In modern times, the term is also applied to those who leave their native land of their own accord, as a precautionary measure against the threat of religious or political persecution ("political" here includes totalitarian persecution in the name of ideology, race, and social class). In this extended sense, the German professors fleeing the Third Reich qualified as exiles, at least for as long as they kept alive the hope of returning to their homeland.

As a punishment, exile is reserved for those who count. Most commonly, it afflicts hereditary kings (from Tarquin to France's Charles X), powerful leaders (Alcibiades, Coriolanus, Napoleon, Trotsky), and influential members of the elite (Dante and his White Guelph friends, or the French nobility after 1790). At a slightly lower level, banishment may accompany the loss of favor with the ruler. The classic example is Ovid, who suffered *relegatio* (which did not entail loss of property and civic rights in Rome), rather than *exsilium* proper. Similarly, the many courtiers who incurred Louis XIV's displeasure were sent to their country houses. Lesser people need not be exiled: under Louis XIV, writers who failed to please were simply denied a pension. Precautionary flight is chosen by larger categories of individuals, but since it is a response to political or religious persecution, it also indicates that the category in question enjoys a certain prominence and visibility. The rulers who unleash their political or religious wrath against large groups of innocent people believe that these groups are powerful and pernicious. French Protestants, a prosperous community who, since the Edict of Nantes, enjoyed a special legal and administrative status, were more likely to attract the attention of Catholic fanatics in high places than, say, pagan villagers on the shores of Brittany. Success and prominence, at the individual level or at the level of the group, increase the chance of being exiled or of being forced to avoid persecution by choosing exile.

This last feature, the public importance of those who are likely to be exiled, helps to explain the increasing frequency of intellectual exile in Europe since the eighteenth century. If Racine and Corneille were never likely to flee their country in fear of their safety, as Victor Hugo had to after the rise of Louis Bonaparte, it is not that they weren't critical of absolute monarchy. They were. Beginning with *Rodogune* (1644), Corneille's tragedies depicted absolutism in an increasingly murky light; in Racine's plays, most monarchs are monsters. But at that time, writers in France did not yet carry enough weight to deserve exile. Voltaire, a century later, belonged to a different category. As one of the most influential critics of the ancien régime, he was listened to, feared, and respected. For his own safety, he also had to live at Fernay, on the Swiss border.

With the advent of the modern nation-states in the aftermath of the French Revolution, writers and intellectuals gained considerable importance. By emphasizing universal education, these states gave intellectuals a key role; at the same time, the nation-building process promoted them to a central symbolic role in the legitimation of national unity. The power and prestige they henceforth carried by virtue of what Paul Béni-chou (1973) called "the coronation of the writer" also made them more vulnerable to the fears and whims of the potentates, especially those who ruled with an iron hand at the apex of an illiberal system. The dissi-dent Germaine de Staël was banished by Napoleon I, Hugo left France in order to avoid living under Napoleon III; later, scores of intellectuals, writers, and artists fled Russia after 1917, Germany after 1933, and Spain after 1936. Today, many liberal Algerian intellectuals reside in France, and Iraqis in England and the United States. But even in a more lib-eral system, the prestige enjoyed by intellectuals in the modern world makes them oversensitive to political change. It is certainly not only for material reasons that so many English academics moved to the United States during Margaret Thatcher's term. Many must have felt that the explicit anti-intellectual stance of the new regime robbed them of their legitimate influence, as intellectuals, over the government of the country. As a group they reenacted, mutatis mutandis, the destiny of Alcibiades, Coriolanus, or Trotsky.

These remarks serve to explain why intellectual exile was not such a per-vasive theme in seventeenth-century French literature. Writers did not speak about it simply because it was not yet the conspicuous phenome-non it was to become a couple of centuries later. The retreat of Guez de Balzac or, more dramatically, of Rancé, the founder of the Trappe, were perceived as the withdrawal of wise men from a world ruled by vanity. Yet if classicist literature does not yet have intellectuals as its heroes, a loss of homeland sometimes affects the characters of the most popular of its serious genres romance and tragedy the former specializing in meta-phorical exile, the latter occasionally focusing on exile proper.

Heroic romance, an early modern offshoot of the Greek novel, in-herits from the latter the quest structure involving strong characters at odds with the world of contingency and relentlessly pursuing a noble good (usually faithful love) under the guidance of the gods. The heroes of Greek novels float above the sublunar world, despising the artifices of Fortune; their souls, in accordance with the Neoplatonic doctrine, are made from the same astral substance as are the incorruptible stars. The best example of the genre is Heliodorus's *The Aethiopian Story,* trans-lated into French by Jacques Amyot and widely read until the end of the eighteenth century. Its main character Chariclea, the daughter of the king of Aethiopia, was taken away from her parents as a child and brought up in Greece; she must return home, guided by the priest Kalasiris and followed by her lover Theagenes, a young Greek descended from Achilles. The two star-crossed lovers leave the Greek cities in which they grew up and undergo a long series of ordeals; their quest leads them through Egypt toward the earthly paradise of Aethiopia, where they are allowed to marry after being ordained priest and priestess of the Sun God. Their wandering in exile is a figure for the meandering path followed by Neoplatonic souls who, after having fallen from their Creator into the material world, strive to return to him. The true homeland of the young couple is no worldly city or kingdom, but the eternal divine order, symbolized by Aethiopia.[1]

The theme of the exiled child who, after a series of ordeals, returns home as a hero is a recurrent one in the seventeenth-century French heroic romance. Its initiatory connotations are weaker than those of the Greek novel (also weaker, by the way, than the mystical overtones of Céladon's exile from the sight of Astrea in Honoré d'Urfé's L'Astrée), yet such connotations linger to a certain extent, since the great deeds performed by the main character during his exile function as qualifying tests (Propp 1983; Eliade 1955). A lively instantiation of this topos is the subplot of Zelmatide, heir to the Inca empire, as narrated in Gomberville's Polexandre (1978 [1641]).[2]

Son of the glorious Inca Guina Capa and an Amazonian princess, Zelmatide is born in Quito during a war waged by his father against its inhabitants. Both parents having died in the conflict, the newborn Zelmatide is found by the envoys of the great Quasmez, emperor of the lands between Mexico and Quito. Because a prophecy has instructed Quasmez that the foundling will help him discover a lost treasure, Zelmatide

1. The notion of the ordeal novel comes from Bakhtin (1981), who describes the tension between the heroes of Greek novels and the forces of contingency.

2. A skillful and witty summary of Polexandre may be found in Bibliothèque universelle des romans, August 1776, 106–260. Zelmatide's story begins in Gomberville 1641 (1978 [1641], 1: 238) and is recounted beginning at p. 189 of the summary. Notice that the heroic romance is classified by the Bibliothèque universelle under "roman d'amour," the fourth in a Borgesian list of eight classes of novels, including (1) novels translated from Greek and Latin; (2) Chivalric novels; (3) novels about Italian history; (4) novels of love; (5) spiritual and moral novels; (6) comic novels; (7) novellas; and (8) supernatural novels.

is raised at the emperor's court. Although Quasmez knows Zelmatide's true identity, the young man believes that he is Quasmez's son. After Zelmatide accomplishes part of the prophecy by defeating all of Quasmez's enemies, he is sent alone to Mexico in order to recover Xaire, Quasmez's daughter, who had been abducted in her infancy by the Mexicans. A second prophecy assures his success on condition that he is stronger than himself. On his way to Mexico, Zelmatide releases a captive princess, liberates a province from bandits, and slays a malevolent giant — traditional methods of reaching the status of a hero.

At Montezuma's court he falls in love with Izatide, believed to be the daughter of Montezuma and Queen Hismélite. Despite the extraordinary services Zelmatide renders to the Mexican king, the young lovers are persecuted by Hismélite, and for good reason: she believes that Zelmatide is the foreigner who, according to Mexican astrologers, will one day bring down Montezuma's empire. The same astrologers predict that the salvation of Mexico depends on Izatide's being detained within. In spite of his love, then, Zelmatide has to leave Mexico.

More adventures lead him to discover his own identity, and to free his father Guina Capa who unexpectedly turns out to be alive. Together with his cosmopolitan confidant Garucca, an adventurous Peruvian who has traveled to Japan, China, and Portugal and has made an immense fortune, Zelmatide returns to Mexico in disguise, only to find that Izatide has died. In despair, he and Garucca set to sea, where they are taken prisoner by Bajazet, a most gallant and courteous pirate. Through Bajazet, Zelmatide meets Polexandre, a prince of French ancestry and ruler of the Canary Islands. Later, Zelmatide is reunited with Izatide, who also turns out to be alive. One of Polexandre's Spanish companions cures her of the blindness with which she had been afflicted in the interval. After discovering that Izatide is none other than Xaire, the lost daughter of Quasmez, the two lovers return to Peru as king and queen of the Incas.

Such a dry abstract inevitably fails to evoke the sumptuous setting of the story, the magic of the adventures, and the vigorous elegance of the style. Gomberville is undoubtedly one of the best storytellers of his century; his work is a precursor not only of Madeleine de Scudéry's immensely successful romances but also of Bernadin de Saint-Pierre's *Paul et Virginie*, Chateaubriand's *Les Natchez*, and Paul Claudel's *Le Soulier de satin*. In the Zelmatide episode, the theme of exile is intertwined with those of identity, self-knowledge, and self-worth the common stock of fairy tales and of the Greek novel. The hero wanders the world because he does not yet know who he is, and his identity is not revealed to him until he proves that he is worthy of it. As in the Greek novel, the Neoplatonic vision of earthly life as exile informs the plot as a whole. What at first appears to be the hero's family and home are in fact mere substitutes: the father who raised him, Quasmez, is not his genuine parent but only a caretaker, just as the land in which he grew up is merely a preparation for his true homecoming. In such a world, characters don't know much about who they are, or where they come from; moreover, they mistake the identities even of those they love most: Izatide is not Izatide but Xaire. Reality is shrouded in a veil of ignorance through which, guided by ambiguous prophecies, they attempt to peep. The sole maxim a hero can follow is to keep on behaving heroically, as if the ambiguities of reality did not exist, and to hope for the best. Zelmatide's heroism (like Polexandre's in the main plot) is vindicated in the end, for the evil characters' machinations are thwarted, those who are thought dead return to life, and the hero's identity and homeland are regained. Exile as initiatory ordeal ends in recovery, both worldly and spiritual. After having redeemed himself *in via,* the hero is welcomed *in patria.*

As we know, before returning to Peru the Inca prince makes friends with Bajazet and Polexandre, spontaneously sharing their sense of courage, nobility, and solidarity. Though separated by their geographic origins, Zelmatide, Bajazet, and Polexandre speak the same moral language and obey the same maxims, as if, before their birth, they had learned them in a true, heavenly homeland. To remind them of their astral origin, Providence regularly sends them signs of election and recognition. To these heroes, the caprices of Fortune are but superficial tremors on the surface of the glorious and reliable ocean of Life. In the company of the strong and generous, the world becomes at once adventurous and magically familiar. Ultimately, with all of its improbabilities, *Polexandre*'s fictional universe evokes a vast, hospitable canopy under which every character feels at home, greeted by friendly faces and reassured by Providence. In this serene environment, exile has no traumatic connotation: it is simply an exalting opportunity to discover the unity of the world.

Tragedy, in contrast, looks with a cold eye on the reality of political exile. Since tragedy presents the rise and fall of the mighty, exile is germane to its interests; a large population of exiled monarchs do in fact haunt Greek, French, and English tragedies. Usually, however, their plight is seen as part of the predicament of power and treated on a par with other calamities that afflict the rulers of the world: loss of life and limb, demotion from power, captivity, incest, and, in the French tragedies, unrequited love. In French classicist tragedy, demotion from power is usually treated in the context of monarchic legitimacy. Rotrou's *Cosroès,* Corneille's *Héraclius,* and Racine's *Athalie* all insist on the evil nature of tyrants and define tyranny as illegitimate rule (Prigent 1986). Struggles involving not just a change of ruler, but a change in the political system as a whole, are represented far less frequently. Yet, as avid readers of Plutarch and Livy, seventeenth-century dramatists were perfectly familiar with the political convulsions of the Roman republic.

Corneille, who knew Plutarch's lives of Pompey and of Sertorius, used the former in *La Mort de Pompée* (1643). Defeated by Julius Caesar at Pharsalus, Pompey seeks refuge in Egypt, whose king, young Ptolemy, indirectly owes him his throne. Advised by evil ministers who put the reason of state above morality, Ptolemy orders the assassination of Pompey as the illustrious refugee is about to land in Egypt. In this tragedy, the curse of exile is so effective that the fugitive general dies before reaching the stage. But the main emphasis of the play is less on Pompey's exile than on his defeat. To be defeated is a crime for which Pompey only has his destiny to blame, as Photin, the cynical minister who recommends the murder, argues:

> Puisqu'il est vaincu qu'il s'en prenne aux Destins.
> J'en veux à sa disgrâce et non à sa personne.
> (Since he has been defeated, he should blame Destiny.
> I resent his fall, not his person.)
> (1.1.96–97)

Almost twenty years later, in the only other Cornelian tragedy inspired by the Roman civil war, exile becomes the central focus. The Fronde (1648–52) was still a recent event, and literary historians find several allusions to it in *Sertorius* (1662) (see Couton 1949, 1951).[3] French classicists believed that setting a contemporary event against the background of a Greek or Roman story enhanced the depth, if not indeed the

3. Couton (1987) argues that Corneille's play transposes the conflict among Mazarin (Sulla), Turenne (Pompey), and Condé (Sertorius). Couton judiciously notices that in 1660, just a year before Corneille began working on *Sertorius,* Condé finally asked to be pardoned and returned from exile, thus healing one of the last wounds left by the Fronde, the disunion of the House of Bourbon.

universality, of the lessons drawn from both. In the case of *Sertorius,* this belief is probably vindicated, since few literary presentations of political exile highlight more vividly its appeal and its dangers.

Sertorius, a republican general of humble origins, has for a long time resisted the dictatorship of Sulla. Having withdrawn to Spain, he is followed by a group of Romans who declare themselves a Senate in exile. Since under Sulla Rome has been reduced to servitude, Roman freedom, they claim, survives only in exile. Pompey, who serves the victorious Sulla, comes to Spain in order to appease Sertorius and lure him back to Rome. In act 3, scene 1, the protagonists weigh two equally problematic solutions to the predicament created by civil war: in Sertorius's solution, the price of freedom is exile, while in Pompey's, national reconciliation can be achieved only through acquiescence to despotism.

To Pompey's plea for civil unity, Sertorius answers that Sulla, with Pompey's help, has reduced the Romans to slavery:

> C'est vous qui sous le joug traînez des coeurs si braves,
> Ils étaient plus que Rois, ils sont moindres qu'esclaves.
> (You yourself put such brave souls under the yoke,
> They were more than Kings, now they are less than slaves.)
>   (3.1.837–38)

In a civil war, answers Pompey, both sides have rights and wrongs. Moreover, since it is difficult to gauge the justice of the cause ("Le plus juste parti [est] difficile à connaître" [3.1.853] [It is difficult to know which party is right]), what counts is loyalty to one's party. Finally, Sulla may not always rule as a despot: the future may bring a form of liberalization. Sertorius, who prefers to make decisions based on present information ("jugeons tout sur la foi de nos yeux" [3.1.871] [in judging everything we should trust our eyes]), can only conclude that Pompey supports Sulla because he hopes to replace him as the master of Rome:

> Vous aidez aux Romains à faire essai d'un maître
> Sous cet espoir flatteur qu'un jour vous pourrez l'être
> (You help the Romans try to live under a master
> Hoping that someday you'll play that role)
>   (3.1.881–82)

Hurt by this accusation, Pompey points out that power is equally abusive everywhere:

Ne vit-on pas ici sous les ordres d'un homme?
N'y commandez-vous pas, comme Sylla dans Rome?
(Doesn't everyone obey the orders of one man here?
Don't you command here, as Sulla does in Rome?)

(3.1.893–94)

Legitimacy and consent are Sertorius's defense: he obeys his own Senate ("Si je commande ici, le Sénat me l'ordonne" [3.1.903] [If I command here, the Senate orders me to do it]) and those who obey him, love him ("Et si l'on m'obéit, ce n'est qu'autant qu'on m'aime" [3.1.910] [And if people obey me, it is only because they love me]). But Pompey understands repressive tolerance and crowd seduction:

votre empire en est d'autant plus dangereux

.   .   .   .

Qu'on croit n'être en vos fers qu'esclave volontaire
(Your power is all the more dangerous

.   .   .   .

Since those in chains believe that their slavery is voluntary)

(3.1.911, 914)

And how does Sertorius dare speak of legitimacy? His so-called Senate is nothing more than a band of outlaws ("un amas de bannis" [3.1.919]). Moving from disparagement to flattery, Pompey asks whether it wouldn't be better to give Rome back one of her greatest men. Rome herself, urges Pompey, invites Sertorius to return.

But for Sertorius Rome, deprived of her freedom, has been reduced to a spatial notion ("un enclos de murailles" [3.1.929] [an enclosure surrounded by walls]), or worse yet, a prison, populated by false Romans. The real Rome is in exile, gathered around Sertorius:

Rome n'est plus dans Rome, elle est toute où je suis.
(Rome is no more in Rome, she is only where I am.)

(3.1.934)

From the heights of his hubris, Sertorius asks Pompey to join the rebels and offers him the command of the army of exiles. In a rush of enthusiasm, Pompey promises that if Sertorius returns to Rome, Sulla will abdicate. Wisely, neither takes up the other's offer, and the dialogue ends. The two positions are utterly incompatible.

Since, in classicist tragedies, the norms of stoic morality are always valued above their rivals, Sertorius appears to have won the argument and securely occupied the moral high ground. Pompey's collaboration with tyranny is repulsive, as are his sophistry and his mendacious promises. Against Pompey, Sertorius is clearly right: present tyranny is a fact, future liberalization a mirage. Once accepted by a political community, despotism only softens after its subjects have lost their drive for freedom. Sertorius's concluding syllogism seems irrefutable: Rome is defined by its freedom, not by its geographical location; but Rome has lost its freedom, and the free Romans live elsewhere; therefore, true Rome is where the free Romans are.

Yet in a tragic twist, events belie Sertorius. His own lieutenant, Perpenna, jealous of the old commander's superiority, organizes a conspiracy against him and kills him at a banquet. True Rome was not after all where Sertorius decided it was. Rather, Pompey's diagnosis grasped the depressing truth: Sertorius's followers were little more than a bunch of outlaws. Political exile, with its deadly mixture of intoxicating high ideals and a missing reality principle, fosters its own variety of moral degradation. Sertorius's self-righteousness weakened his prudence; his idealism prevented him from recognizing his own isolation.

In Corneille's tragedy, political exile is no metaphor. In contrast to the heroes of romance, political figures live in a strictly human world, without a Providence to offer them warning signs, chivalrous friends to share their ideals, or a magic cohesion to keep the world together. Theirs is a cold, treacherous life, in which homeland is synonymous neither with freedom nor with virtue but denotes instead a shared past, shared suffering, and, yes, shared enslavement. Early modern writers were able to distinguish between fiction and politics; they also knew that rootedness and dignity often fail to coincide.

REFERENCES

Bakhtin, Mikhail
   1981 *The Dialogic Imagination: Four Essays,* translated by Caryl Emerson and Michael Holquist (Austin: University of Texas Press).
Bénichou, Paul
   1973 *Le Sacre de l'écrivain, 1750–1830; Essai sur l'avènement d'un pouvoir spirituel laïque dans la France moderne* (Paris: J. Cōrti).

Couton, Georges
  1949 *La Vieillesse de Corneille* (Paris: Maloine).
  1951 *Corneille et la Fronde* (Clermont-Ferrand, France: Bussac).
  1987 "Notice" to *Sertorius,* in Corneille, *Oeuvres complètes,* 3: 1444–50 (Paris: Gallimard).
Eliade, Mircea
  1955 *Littérature orale,* in *Histoire des littératures,* edited by Raymond Queneau, 1: 3–26 (Paris: Gallimard).
Gomberville, Marin Le Roy
  1978 [1641] *Polexandre,* 5 vols. (Geneva: Slatkine Reprints).
Noakes, Jeremy
  1993 "The Ivory Tower under Siege," *Journal of European Studies* 23: 371–407.
Prigent, Michel
  1986 *Le Héros et l'état dans la tragédie de Pierre Corneille* (Paris: Presses Universitaires de France).
Propp, Vladimir
  1983 *Les Racines historiques du conte merveilleux,* translated by Lise Gruel-Apert (Paris: Gallimard).

LINDA NOCHLIN

ART AND THE CONDITIONS OF EXILE:

MEN/WOMEN, EMIGRATION/EXPATRIATION

WHEN IT COMES TO EXILE, artists would seem to be in a better position than writers. Somehow, the visual world loses less in translation. For the writer, exile and the loss of native language may be devastating, depriving the subject of access to the living world. "This radical disjoining between word and thing is a desiccating alchemy, draining the world not only of significance but of its colors, striations, nuances its very existence. It is the loss of a living connection," declares writer Eva Hoffman (1989: 107). "What has happened to me in this new world?" she asks in her moving exploration of the meaning of exile, *Lost in Translation* (1989). "I don't know. I don't see what I've seen, don't comprehend what's in front of me. I'm not filled with language anymore, and I have only a memory of fullness to anguish me with the knowledge that, in this dark and empty state, I don't really exist" (ibid: 108).

For artists, on the whole, exile, at least insofar as the work is concerned, seems to be less traumatic. While some art is, indeed, site specific, visual language, on the whole, is far more transportable than the verbal kind. Artists traditionally have been obliged to travel, to leave their native land, in order to learn their trade. At one time, the trip to Rome was required, or a study-voyage in Italy; at other times and under special circumstances, it might be Munich or Spain or Holland or even North Africa; more recently, Paris was where one went to learn how to be an artist in the company of one's peers; and after New York stole the heart of the art world from Paris, it was here that ambitious young practitioners came to immerse themselves in the action. For every Constable enamored of the very slime on the logs of his native landscape, the few miles of the river Stour near his father's mill, for every Courbet finding his subjects in the people and landscapes of his native Franche-Comté or Cézanne repeatedly embracing the Montagne Ste. Victoire, we can point to a Sargent triumphantly catering to an international clientele; a Picasso finding himself and his modernism in Paris rather than in Barcelona; a displaced Mondrian inventing *Broadway Boogie Woogie* in New York rather than in his native Holland.

For some artists, getting away from home and its restrictions has been the sine qua non of a successful art career. "After all, give me France," said the great American artist Mary Cassatt, writing to Sarah Hallowell. "Women do not have to fight for recognition here, if they do serious work" (quoted in Mathews 1994: 217). For women, whether they be artists or writers, as Janet Wolff has pointed out in *Resident Alien* (1995), the conditions of exile have especially ambiguous or even ambivalent implications. On the one hand, "for the woman writer who is either geographically displaced . . . or culturally marginalized . . . it may be her very identity as woman which enables a radical re-vision of home and exile" (Wolff 1995: 7). "Displacement . . . can be quite strikingly productive. First, the marginalization entailed in forms of migration can generate new perceptions of place and, in some cases, of the relationship between places. Second, the same dislocation can also facilitate personal transformation, which may take the form of 'rewriting' the self, discarding the lifelong habits and practices of a constraining social education and discovering new forms of self-expression" (ibid.). Shari Benstock has pointed out that for some American women early in the century living and working in Paris, emigration was considered an escape from the constraints on women in their home cultures (quoted in Wolff 1995: 11). But, as Wolff also points out, there is little evidence that even adventurous women writers or artists had the same access to the city as their male contemporaries. Indeed, women artists themselves were often seen as a kind of threat to properly organized gender relations (ibid.: 107).

EXILE IN THE FEMININE: FINDING ONESELF TOGETHER

Yet in other situations, somewhat later in the early twentieth century, the condition of exile enabled at least a few women artists to join together in productive mutual support that would never have been possible in their original homelands. Such was the case with the English artist Leonora Carrington and her friend, Remedios Varo, both of whom fled to Mexico (from France and Spain, respectively) to escape revolution and war.

Mexico seemed extraordinary to Carrington—vivid, exotic, and additionally enlivened by an active group of exiled painters and writers. But most important for this second-generation surrealist was the presence of another woman artist whom she had already met in France: Remedios

Varo. The two now became "fellow travelers on a long and intense journey that led them to explore the deepest resources of their creative lives," to borrow the words of Whitney Chadwick in her study of women and surrealism. "For the first time in the history of the collective movement called Surrealism," Chadwick continues, "two women would collaborate in attempting to develop a new pictorial language that spoke more directly to their own needs" (1985: 194). Leonora Carrington declared in no uncertain terms: "Remedios's presence in Mexico changed my life" (Chadwick, private conversation with Carrington, 1983. Quoted in ibid.). For Remedios Varo, who came to Mexico with her husband, the surrealist poet Benjamin Péret, in 1942, searching for peace in a war-torn world, exile meant, quite literally, the end of all travel. Once settled in Mexico City, she developed a terrible fear of moving and rarely strayed outside her neighborhood. As her last husband, Walter Gruen, recalled: "She said she didn't have to go to the trouble of traveling because the best and the most beautiful travel was within her imagination" (Engel 1986: 2).

Paradoxically, it was as an exile that Varo, like her friend Leonora Carrington, found herself and her way as an artist. "As an emigrée, uprooted and exiled from her homeland, she embarked on a search for self-knowledge, a pilgrimage, both psychological and spiritual, to find deeper, more reliable roots," declares Varo's major biographer, Janet Kaplan. "Having been subject to the outside forces of world events shaping her life, she now sought metaphoric control through her art work by creating an alternative world of her own design peopled with characters bearing her own features. Like an actress taking on roles, she consistently used the self portrait device as a way to experiment with alternative identities. Finally able to settle in, and now distanced from the intimidations of the Surrealist circle, she developed a distinctive mature style that was to become her signature" (Kaplan 1984: 5–6). Exile, then, in the case of these two women artists, provided a fertile site for independent development and growth.

The case of Leonora Carrington and Remedios Varo is a relatively unusual one, and part of its unusualness has to do with the gender of the artists concerned. Nevertheless, despite the terrible destruction wrought by the Second World War on the vanguard artistic communities of Europe; and although the resulting displacement was inevitably hard on artists as well as writers, disrupting many careers irrevocably; many of the former landed on their feet and exerted considerable influence on their places of refuge: Albers disseminated his ideas at both Black Mountain and Yale; Breton and the surrealists in exile made a considerable splash in their new surroundings; Beckmann did some of his most serious and memorable work outside of Germany. Emigrants like de Kooning and Arshile Gorky found themselves at the center of the most innovative artistic movement of their times.[1]

R. B. KITAJ: EXILE IS MY BUSINESS

Although many artists have been exiled or have chosen expatriation or emigration, no other artist has so deeply engaged with exile as a subject, explored so obsessively the role of dispersion and fragmentation in the foundation of a pictorial language as R. B. Kitaj. Indeed, one might say that in his unceasing concentration on the signifiers of diaspora, Kitaj has become what one might call a specialist in exile. As such, his work, and his life, deserve further exploration in the context of this essay.

Although self-exiled from his native United States, Kitaj feels himself equally marginalized in his adoptive Britain. Indeed, it is significant that, as a young artist, Kitaj chose England, rather than the more obvious and "central" Paris, as his site of expatriation. Central to his casting himself in the role of universal exile is, of course, his sense of himself as a Jew, an identity which provided a growing inspiration for his art since about 1970. As art historian Richard Morphet observes in his highly intelligent catalog introduction to the recent Kitaj retrospective: "Kitaj's concern with the Jewish theme is powerfully coloured, and in many ways driven, by his horror of the Holocaust; in its originality and its insistence, his is one of the most powerful bodies of work on this topic. But for all the exceptional reinforcement given to it by the Holocaust, the notion of not belonging to any settled society is, for Kitaj, inherent in the very nature

1. For an excellent exploration of the effects of emigration on American art, see the exhibition catalog *The Golden Door: Artist-Immigrants of America, 1876–1976* (McCabe 1976). The list of artists includes such notables as Hans Hoffmann, George Grosz, Agnes Martin, Joseph Albers, Fritz Glarner, Andre Kertész, Walter Gropius, Lazlo Moholy-Nagy, Marcel Breuer, Mies van der Rohe, Josep Lluis Sert, Kurt Seligmann, Friedel Dzubas, Yves Tanguy, Piet Mondrian, Richard Lindner, Hans Richter, Jacques Lipchitz, Saul Steinberg, Naum Gabo, Marisol, and Max Beckmann. For further information on this issue see "The Great Flight of Culture," *Fortune*, December 24, 1941; Fleming and Bailyn 1969; and Sweeney 1946.

of existence as a Jew (1994: 9–10).[2] For this artist, whose work most obviously inscribes the conditions of exile in its very structure, fragmentation, both formal and iconographic, lies at the heart of his pictorial project. One might say that diaspora is enacted as much in the centrifugal energies and fragmented condition of his compositions as it is in his often ambiguous subjects with their equally provocative titles, made even more complex by the often lengthy narratives with which he supplements his paintings.

Fragmentation is Kitaj's strategy of choice, more obvious in the early works, like *Kennst du das Land?* (1962), a meditation on the Spanish Civil War among other events, where fragmentation signifies an inability, or perhaps a refusal to create a totalizing picture of such outrage.[3] Here, the fragment and compositional dispersal operate in a more conscious and readable way, but fragmentation is a generating impulse in many of the later works, too. In the ambitious *If Not, Not* of 1975–76 the perspective is centripetal. The prototypical "Jew" figure, the ubiquitous Joe Singer, identifiable by his hearing aid, sprawls in the left corner, braced by a nude woman. A fragmentary fallen figure, reminiscent of Goya's, Manet's, and Daumier's imagery of the victim, marks the front center stage, moving into the space of the viewer. A man in a bed—a self-portrait detail, according to the lengthy text provided by Kitaj to accompany the catalog illustration—cuddles a child, while a disembodied child's head, much larger in scale, floats at the end of the bed; in a glade of palm trees at the upper right is the headless figure of a female nude as well as some other figures. On the lower right, a guerilla crawls into the painting, supplying the missing upper torso of the figure in the center, and to his left, the fragmentation theme is reinforced by a fallen and dismembered image of Matisse's *Jeannette* portrait bust. Although the artist refers to a variegated and richly contradictory cluster of sources, ranging from Eliot's *Wasteland* to Auschwitz, from a Bassano battle scene to Giorgione's *Tempest,* the work makes me think of Gauguin gone mad, exploded and disembodied, with its sly exoticism and wonderfully dissonant pink, pale, chalky colors. *Cecil Court (The Refugees)* (1983–84) may be said to enact both diaspora and the Shoah in its composition, with

2. For studies of Kitaj's Jewish identity and his relation to the Holocaust, see Barsky 1990 and Amishai-Maisels 1993. Also see Kitaj 1989.

3. Reproductions of all works mentioned in the text are available in the 1994 exhibition catalog *R. B. Kitaj: A Retrospective,* edited by Richard Morphet.

Figure 1   R. B. Kitaj, *The Autumn of Central Paris (After Walter Benjamin)*,
1972–73. Courtesy of Marlborough Fine Art, London.

its dispersed figures, so oddly articulated that they almost seem to have
been stitched together, strewn about a corridor-like urban street, unrelated either to this alien space or to one another.

In one of his finest, most moving, and, for me, most nostalgia-produc-
ing works, *The Autumn of Central Paris (after Walter Benjamin)* of 1972–
73 (Figure 1), Kitaj again emphasizes the signifiers òf exile, alienation,
and breakup in the visual structure of the canvas. Although he avoids the
economic basis of Benjamin's analysis of alienation—capitalism and the
cult of the commodity simply do not play a role in Kitaj's sense of modernity—the political is much in evidence in this homage to Benjamin's
"addiction to fragment-life, the allusive and incomplete nature of his
work" as Kitaj terms it in his textual accompaniment to the painting
(1994: 94). A spectral red worker with a pickax marches across the border of Manet-inspired red café chairs in the foreground; a brutal thug

looms in the rear. Disjunction rules everywhere, alienation is borrowed from specifically French sources: the figure marking the back plane to the right wanders off into ominous blankness like the figure in the rear of Cézanne's eerie *Picnic*. The whole work is redolent of Manet's *Concert at the Tuileries*, which was, after all, an homage to the creative Paris of the Second Empire, but it projects a vision of the intellectual life of the city now abjected, ominous, torn apart.

Kitaj, who talks a lot about his work and himself, clearly relates his cult of the fragment to his Jewishness, and his Jewishness in turn to what he characterizes in broader, more embracing terms as "Diasporism" in his *First Diasporist Manifesto* (1989). Itself a collection of random thoughts, musings, and citations, illustrated by evocative fragments of his own paintings, the *Diasporist Manifesto* puts together whatever Kitaj finds inspiring, no matter how historically and culturally unlikely—and Benjamin would seem to lie at the heart of it all.

Almost thirty years ago, under the spell of Diasporists like Aby Warburg, Fritz Saxl, Edgar Wind and the Surrealists, I made a little painting called *His Cult of the Fragment*. I was a fragmented cultist ten years before I discovered Walter Benjamin (1892–1940), the exemplary and perhaps ultimate Diasporist and *his* cult of the fragment. It would be fifteen years before I ever heard the term Midrash and became transfixed by the artful and highly Diasporist history of that very real exegetical tradition within Jewish history. Thirty years later, I've learned of the Diasporists of the Ecole de Yale and their crazed and fascinating Cult of the Fragment. (Kitaj 1989: 59)

It is the philosopher Richard Wollheim who best summarizes the crucial position of the fragment in Kitaj's work. Says Wollheim: "The fragment serves three purposes. It attaches the work of art to its past by embedding some of the past in the present: it reproduces the condition of modern life, and, in particular, of modern urban life, to which modernist art is wedded; and it allows the artist to capture intimations of the uncanny, and the daemonic and the dreamlike, which are integral to any art of a confessional kind, which modern art is committed to being" (1994: 38).

Wollheim then goes on to look "at how Kitaj in his own work, uses the fragment to tap these three wellsprings of modern art," examining first his borrowings from earlier art and its various dimensions; then the fragment in its relation to modern life; and, finally, exploring the fragment and its use to convey the "darkness of the mind." It is to the

second of these uses of the fragment in Kitaj's art, as "the better por-
trayal of modern life" (ibid.: 39), that I would like to turn, for Wollheim
has, I believe, caught something specific about both Kitaj's sense of the
fragment *and* his concept of history and, although he may not be fully
aware of it, about the position of gender within history. He differentiates
Kitaj's take on modernity from that of his colleague, David Hockney.
For Hockney, the modern is equated with the contemporary. "Not so
for Kitaj," declares Wollheim. "For him, modern life is the life of that
legendary metropolis, of that mechanized Babylon, where all the great
writers and painters, and all the great idlers and noctambulists, and all
the great madams and their clients, real and fictional, of the last hundred
years and more, would have been equally at home; where Baudelaire
might have strolled with Svevo, and Walter Benjamin had a drink with
Polly Adler, and John Ashbery written poetry at a café table, and where
Cavafy and Proust and Pavese could have negotiated with Jupien for the
sexual favours they craved" (ibid.: 39). This is not merely evocative word
painting on Wollheim's part, it is an amazingly accurate condensation of
Kitaj's fragmentary, and basically nonhistorical, view of modernity, what
Kitaj himself might denominate as his diasporist vision. As Wollheim
says: "In K's world picture, the term *modernity* has a denotation that has
been distended over time; it is used to refer to everything that it has ever
been used to refer to since it first gained circulation as a tool of criticism,
now more than a hundred years ago" (ibid.).

What is dramatically absent from Kitaj's nostalgic and seductive vision
of modernity, and Wollheim's incisive summary of it, is any place for
women other than the brothel. Surely, there are women who might
populate the utopian vistas of the city of modernity, who have names —
Sarah Bernhardt, Gertrude Stein, Simone Weil, Virginia Woolf — who are
not whores? Evidently not when all is said and done. This would seem
to be, despite its numerous aesthetic and intellectual seductions, an Old
Boys' diaspora, created and shared by all of the guys mentioned above,
where women exist to swell the crowd in a sexy way, to pose as anonymous victims perhaps, but rarely to have a subject position offered them,
either inside or outside the picture.

Although the artist associates his painting *Women and Men* (1991–93)
with "beauty and good cheer and erotic pleasure" and talks about the
pleasures of depicting men and women together in his textual accompaniment to the work, associating it with Degas's *Young Spartans* (Kitaj
1994: 180), the latter is hardly a painting of happy relations between

Figure 2   R. B. Kitaj, *The Rise of Fascism*, 1979–80. Courtesy of Marlborough Fine Art, London.

the sexes. Its full title is, in fact, *Young Spartans Exercising*, and while I agree that it is indeed a wonderful painting, it is one in which Degas makes clear, through its very structure, the almost unbridgeable gap separating male from female; a gap that is enlarged in Kitaj's painting into a veritable abyss in the form of the blood red table separating male clients from female commodities. It is difficult to associate this desolate vision of the relations between men and women—the world as a giant brothel—with erotic pleasure between the sexes, despite Kitaj's good intentions. There is little sense of pleasurable interaction here, where the vast, blood-colored gap of the table, a giant cunt, belies the artist's positive words. In visual terms, sex is figured as something women sell to men and men buy from women, and it is dirty.

Why is the woman's body figured so repeatedly as the whore, the very allegory of debased fascism, as it was in the work of Grosz and Dix? One feels so often, in all those men's work, that a profound misogyny, a lust for and hatred of female flesh, provided an excuse for their reiterated allegorization of grotesquely whorish women as signs of a corrupt social order. Yet it is precisely this strain in Kitaj's work—with its insistence on women's bodies as both voluptuous and threatening, and its corollary, both stated and unstated, that the Jew is by definition male; that the diasporist sensibility is for men only—that puts me off, sets up a barrier. "The bather on the left is the beautiful victim, the figure of Fascism is in the middle and the seated bather is everyone else," Kitaj explains in his catalog statement on *The Rise of Fascism* of 1979–80 (Figure 2) (1994: 218). The artist is being either disingenuous or facetious in his explanation of the work: there is nothing in the painting itself—a dark-haired nude displaying her cunt to the viewer; an older, less attractive blond woman in a black bathing suit center stage; and a younger nude with red stockings to the right—that signifies fascism. It would do just as well entitled "Bathers with a Black Cat." Even the most arcane allegories, the most personal ones, should offer the spectator some clues to meaning within the work itself, especially when the subject is announced as something as portentous as the rise of fascism.

Arthur Danto, exploring the baffling quality of many of Kitaj's works in a fair-minded review of the artist's retrospective in *The Nation,* considers at length a painting that I found particularly offensive in the exhibition, the 1984 *Self-Portrait as a Woman.* This provocative title was surely meant to arouse expectations of something interesting, but, as Danto points out, "No one would know, I think, that it was a self-portrait unless one were told. The painting shows us a woman, naked rather than nude, since she is wearing high heels and red socks." And he continues:

"Self-portrait as . . ." implies that the artist has chosen to take on the bodily attributes of a woman for some metaphorical purpose the painting itself does not clarify. Indeed, nothing visually shows the difference between a painting of a naked woman standing outdoors and a portrait of the artist as a woman. Were it not for the title we would see it as no doubt symbolically charged in some way, but have no clear sense of what specifically it might mean. . . . Kitaj's title complicates our attitude, but it does not complicate the picture enough to help us understand why it is a self-portrait as a woman.   (Danto 1995: 467–68)[4]

Despite the long and sympathetic narrative provided by the artist in the catalog, the painting *qua* painting remains a large, meaty, sexy nude with some mysterious accoutrements. I feel taken in: any artist can paint a voluptuous nude deployed for masculine delectation and call it anything he wants—"The Free Woman," "The Spirit of Women's Liberation," "The Diasporist Manifesto," or, alternatively, "The Rise of Fascism"—

4. Danto goes on to explain that since "there is no way to tell what has to be told visually, without benefit of an explanatory narrative. . . . Kitaj tells us about the genesis of the picture, who the woman was, and her humiliating fate as a woman in Vienna who had slept with a Jew" (1995: 468).

take your pick. Since women have no identity in themselves, they can signify anything the artist wants them to, as allegories, or, more obliquely, as the bearers of secret meanings, known only to the artist himself.

Despite the occasional verbal or visual bone Kitaj throws to the occasional woman, and despite his no doubt sincere attempt to link women and homosexuals with diasporism and exile — "A Diasporist picture is marked by Exile and its discontents as subtly and unclearly as pictures painted by women or homosexuals are marked by their inner exilic discontents" (Kitaj 1989: 96–97) — his work exiles me from the diasporist tradition, to which I feel, so profoundly, that I belong, and which Kitaj has so movingly, if at times annoyingly and self-servingly, articulated. Turning away from his female nudes to his series of portraits of literary and art historical friends, I want to know why Anita Brookner (the novelist) can't turn around (charming and revealing though the back view image is), face us, and assert her dominion over the picture space as do Philip Roth, Sir Ernst Gombrich, or Michael Podro as *The Jewish Rider?* Obviously, there is an exile within the exile so poignantly enacted by Kitaj's images: the exile of women. What angers and disappoints me most about his work and writing, which aroused such high expectations, is that I, as a Jewish woman, have been exiled from Jewish exile by the mere fact of my sex; it is men who lay claim to the diasporist tradition of modernity.

If, as Richard Morphet claims, Kitaj's vision is indeed "one through which we are able . . . to recognize significant aspects of the condition of our age" (1994: 10), then we must also recognize the fact that one of the conditions of that vision, and of our age, is that woman exists in the masculine creative imagination as pure difference and in a state of almost inevitable abjection. Or, to put it another way: if Kitaj's work indeed engages with the conditions of exile as those most deeply imbricated in the historical fabric of our times, then women exist within it in a second exile, as prisoners of exile in the second degree, as objects of the desires and repugnances, each equally strong, or at times, of the ironic allegorizing, of a dominant male subjectivity, for the pleasure and instruction of a male audience.

OTHER ALTERNATIVES: THE WOMAN ARTIST AS EXPATRIATE

There are, of course, alternative positions for women within the discourses of exile, and I would like to explore one of them in some detail: the position of the woman artist who chooses, or is obliged, to live abroad. I have chosen two American women artists living in Paris, Shirley Jaffe and Zuka, women of approximately the same generation as Kitaj, whom I have known over the course of many years, and whose work I have followed with deep sympathy and interest. Both, incidentally, are first generation Americans themselves: Zuka was the child of Russian émigrés — her father was an officer in the White Russian Army — who settled in the colorful Russian colony of Los Angeles; Shirley, the offspring of Jewish immigrants who settled first in New Jersey, then in New York. Both came to Paris shortly after World War II: Zuka, as a young artist who felt she needed to see the great art in museums and galleries there, eventually met her husband there, had children, and stayed on; Shirley, as a painter married to a scholar studying in Paris under the GI Bill, found a circle of like-minded young American artists there, eventually divorced her husband, and stayed on. Neither as artists nor as individuals are they alike, although they are very good friends. It is rather the *difference* in their work and in their stories that is interesting, calling into question any easy explanation of either "woman" or "exile" in relation to the production of art. Yet both feel that being an American in Paris has been important to the evolution of their art and the ways in which it deviates from what one might call "mainstream" modernism or postmodernism.

Shirley Jaffe: The Search for Independence

For Shirley Jaffe, an abstract artist, being in Paris in the fifties meant a kind of independence from the dominant strains of American abstract expressionism, and, at the same time, it meant the support of a group of expatriate American artists — Sam Francis, Joan Mitchell, Norman Bluhm, Ellsworth Kelly, Jack Youngerman, Sidney Geist, and the Canadian Riopelle, to name some. In addition, other artists like Biala, Charlie Semser, Kimber Smith, Hugh Weiss, and of course, Zuka, provided moral support and friendship. "The fact that I lived here allowed me to concentrate on my painting," replied Jaffe to a question by Yves Michaud in a 1989 article. "In New York, you are totally absorbed into a modern and materialist civilization. With all the difficulties of living and all the possibilities of things to do, the time for painting can be very circumscribed" (quoted in Boudou 1994: 56).

Coming to Paris after studying at Cooper Union in New York and the Phillips Art School in Washington was both a shock and a revelation. In Paris, she wanted to see everything but felt totally uprooted at the same time. Her memory of this crucial moment in her "condition of exile," her life as an expatriate artist, is revealing both in its ambivalence and its concreteness.

I was very upset at having left America; I had the intense feeling of having made a break with something I was very familiar with. You can't imagine how dramatic it was. I felt as though I had made a real break, once I was here. I don't know why. A great wave, a great strength filled me. It was as if I had changed something of the utmost importance. It wasn't like going to Chicago from New York; it was something altogether different. I remember the first night in the hotel, near the gare St. Lazare. I burst into tears. I was in a very upset, conflicted state. A neighbor had brought us a bottle of champagne. I was very unhappy to have made this separation. Unconsciously I had prepared for this rupture. I only understood what had happened once I was here. It was a break like the one I made in my painting later. It was the idea of calling everything into question, of going after something totally different. I think I don't like getting into something already established. I emerged from a cocoon: school, family. . . . There was nothing here like what I had known before.   (quoted in Girard 1994; my translation)

The critic Xavier Girard relates the word *exhilaration,* used by Jaffe in the context of talking about the art that stimulated her at this time, to the word *exile,* "exil vivifiant, en français." [5] One might well refer to this crucial liminal experience in Jaffe's life as "an experience of exhilarating exile." It was an experience that was to be repeated, that she felt the need to repeat, in Berlin, in 1963–64. Here, she renewed the condition of exile, with all its exhilarating sense of estrangement and alienation, when she accepted a Ford fellowship to work in that city, away from the circle of American artists to which she (marginally) belonged in Paris. [6]

5. Girard explains his title "Exhilaration" in a footnote: "Shirley Jaffe utilise le mot exhilaration (de exhilarate: vivifier, ragaillardir, émoustiller): gaité de coeur, joie de vivre. Je luis fais remarquer que le mot fait aussi penser a exil, exil vivifiant, en français" (ibid.) (Shirley Jaffe uses the word *exhilaration* [from *exhilarate:* to enliven, cheer up, put into good spirits]: gaiety of heart, *joie de vivre.* I remarked to her that, in French, the word also evokes exile, a revivifying exile).

6. "I was considered a sub-product of 'Abstract Expressionism' in Paris. Sam Francis, Riopelle, Joan Mitchell had strong personalities. I was not integrated into

Figure 3 Shirley Jaffe, *Big Blue,* 1973. Courtesy of the artist.

In Berlin, she was in a totally strange world, where she was more a foreigner than ever. It was partly a question of language. "The language was completely foreign to me. I didn't want to find a place in that world. I did, however, try to learn German, in a much more conscious way than French, without great success. I visited the city intensely. I had a friend who took me everywhere, I began to read German novels" (quoted in ibid.). But something more important happened in Berlin, in this exile from expatriation. "In Berlin I was able to think with more precision. Composition seemed to me much more readable to the detriment of gesture" (quoted in ibid.). It was not until 1968 four years later that the full impact of that second exile became evident in her work, for it was in that year that she began to give her work a clearer coloristic, geometric definition, in a process of clarification but also of increasing complexity, of refusal of harmony or intuitive brio in favor of something more unexpected, even irritating, in terms of conventional rules

their circle; I was somewhat on the edges. My direction was personal. The painters saw me as someone who had interesting ideas about painting but who was difficult to identify" (quoted in Girard 1994; all translations mine).

Figure 4   Shirley Jaffe, *West Point,* 1988. Courtesy of the artist.

of formal composition. In short, she began to find her own style, a style in opposition to all the current "givens" of abstraction, both French and American (Figure 3). "I searched," she explained, "for the moment in a painting which was unexpected," the structural element which put into question, even threatened, the whole equilibrium of the composition (quoted in ibid.). *Discord, dislocation, disjunction, coloristic dissonance* all these terms have been used to define the precise quality of Jaffe's abstract deviations from the norm, her serious play on the borderline of chaos, her search for formal autonomy (Figure 4). This autonomy, it would seem, could only have developed in exile, away from the known, the familiar, the acceptable: everything that stands for home, and that home stands for.

Zuka and the Issue of American Identity

Zuka, born Zenaida Gurievna Booyakovitch in Los Angeles's lively Russian expatriate colony, where her father worked in the margins of the film industry (literally: his uniform-clad leg appears at the edge of a poster for a Garbo movie!) went to Paris in the early 1950s in search of art in both its historical and contemporary manifestations. She married Louis Mitelberg, renowned as a political cartoonist under the nom de plume "Tim," had two sons, and pursued her career in that city. Working as a figurative artist in Paris, her being American has had a good deal to do with her work. In a sense, one might say that Paris brought out the American in her; had she gone on living in the United States, her sense of herself as an American and her choice of uniquely American-inflected subjects might not have come into being. Going against the grain of the fashionable, she has dedicated herself to several narrative series, in which subject matter and formal invention have both played an important role. Being in Paris, away from the heartland of American avant-garde production, enabled her to rebel against the strictures of the trendy abstraction then in vogue in New York. "The subject," as she put it, "seems to be my object" (Zuka 1995). And the subject seemed to be, even more unfashionably, historical, taken from either American or French history. She started with portraits of Washington, Adams, and Jefferson and scenes from traditional American history, a kind of pictorial nostalgia for a distant homeland, made even more distant by the passage of time. Then she came even closer to home, with California history as her subject. In an important series dedicated to Father Junípero Serra, founder of a series of missions for the California Indians, an important historical figure of her native California, she worked in collage, a medium she loves because one can be so inventive with it and at the same time tell a story. Collage, with its emphasis on the material and its transformation, almost naturally prevents narrative from lapsing into banal realism, focusing the observer's eye on the formal side of the image. In a picture from the series, representing a group of witch doctors dancing around a bonfire, working in cut wallpaper constituted an exciting challenge: in a sense, the artist felt that she was creating, in the decorativeness of cut paper, an equivalent to the way the Indians decorated their own bodies with paint and beads.

In the 1980s, caught up in the excitement of the preparations for the celebration of the bicentenary of the French Revolution, and its concomitant political disputes, Zuka began work on an ambitious series dedicated to the French Revolution that was shown in both France and the United States. It was a most unusual version of history painting: "The French Revolution through American Eyes" of 1988. Indeed, only an American could have painted it. What was uniquely American about it was not only Zuka's insistence on seeing the past through the eyes of the present, but her insistence on the important role played by women in the French Revolution (Figure 5). Indeed, I titled the essay I wrote for the catalog of the exhibition devoted to the series' collages and paintings "Zuka's French Revolution: A Woman's Place Is Public Space" (Nochlin 1988). In the series, the artist stands conventional history painting on its ear:

> The representation of major political events in the visual arts is generally thought of as pompous, solemn and frozen: conservative in the worst sense of the word. . . . Nothing could be further from Zuka's spirited take on the French Revolution. Like all good historians—and all original artists—she knows that the past can only come to life in terms of the present. Although she has looked long and hard at the documents of the French Revolution and has appropriated a wide cross-section of its visual imagery, she has brought the revolution to life in terms of her own experience of it in the 20th Century, and through a language in which wit, playfulness, modernist irreverence, and awareness of the deflationary possibilities inherent to the formal means of art itself are fused by pictorial energy to create a vision of history that is at once idiosyncratically contemporary yet historically accurate. (Nochlin 1988: 3–4)

Zuka, in this ambitious series of works, deliberately emphasized the importance of women in revolutionary activity as had no other artist before her. "In so doing," I declared, "she has acted not merely as a feminist, but as a responsible historian, bringing to light and visually rearticulating a lost reality" (ibid.: 4).[7]

Yet Zuka's interest in women participants doesn't make her give up other sources of pictorial pleasure, even those least associated with women artists: she loves battle painting, both seeing it and doing it herself. Her rendition of the *Battle of Valmy* is one of the most spirited and

---

7. It might be interesting to contrast Zuka's approach to the relation of woman and history to that of Kitaj, who relegates women to the role of the allegorical and the abject.

Figure 5   Zuka, *Olympe de Gouges,* ca. 1989. Courtesy of the artist.

original of the bunch (Figure 6). Zuka states: "My father's family was in
the artillery; my grandfather was a general in the Russian army." There
are several paintings dedicated to Valmy among the eighty-five works in
the series, of which thirty are dedicated to women. Zuka definitely has
not exiled herself from traditionally "masculine" subjects. On the contrary, she loves everything to do with military history, frequently visiting
the Musée de l'Armée at Invalides and its exhibitions: out-of-the-way

Figure 6   Zuka, *Battle of Valmy, First Victory of Republican Troops against the Prussians,* 1989. Courtesy of the artist.

subjects like "Napoleon's doctor" get to her.[8] It is hard to imagine too many contemporary French artists of whom one could say the same; but it is interesting to remember that England's leading military painter in the late nineteenth century was a woman: Lady Elizabeth Butler.

Zuka's next series was at once more personal and more nostalgically imprinted with the world she had left behind: Hollywood and the loves of her youth. Entitled *The Men in My Life,* it included images of Johnny Weissmuller as Tarzan; Errol Flynn as Captain Blood; Michelangelo's *David* in Forest Lawn Cemetery (where the sculpture "sang" "Ah Sweet Mystery of Life," courtesy of Nelson Eddy); and most notably, Paul

8. This information comes from the rough cut of a film by Judith Wechsler about three women artists in Paris entitled "Biala, Zuka, and Shirley Jaffe."

Robeson singing in Moscow with Pushkin in the background. (Robeson had studied Russian with Zuka's mother, and the artist was, as she put it, "madly in love with him.") These paintings of her heroes were accompanied by three angels who were at once guardians and signs of love. As a series, despite some notable successes, she felt they didn't work and instead turned to the less overtly narrative subject of cows — a subject she became familiar with at her country house in Burgundy. The cows are extraordinary: specifically French cows, but, one might say, universal in their appeal: colorful, formally adroit, original in their odd shapes and unique relation to the demands of the surface of the canvas. Zuka's cows now exist in a variety of formats, ranging from brilliantly colored, non-naturalistic large-scale oil paintings to altered postcards of Paris scenes and jazzy bookmarks.[9]

For both Zuka and Shirley Jaffe, the fact of being Americans in exile, expatriates in Paris, has played a significant role, but not one that can easily be defined in terms of specific causes and effects. Paradoxically, one might say that the rhythms and "deep structures" of modern Paris have perhaps affected the abstract painter more than the figurative one. In 1967, for a brief period, Jaffe wandered around Paris taking pictures of street scenes, especially the old Gare Montparnasse, which was then being torn down to make way for the Tour Montparnasse (Rubinstein 1995: 87). Although Paris is never literally present in her abstract canvases, the sense of the disjunctive energy of the modern city has been seen by more than one critic to play an important role in her work. In the words of Raphael Rubinstein, in an article entitled "An Eye in the City" (1995): "Resisting the notion that forms worthy of contemplation require calm and isolation, her canvases make one contend with interference and confusion, just as in the real world, and just as in those photographs of the half-demolished Gare Montparnasse that so fascinated her 30 years ago" (ibid.). For Zuka, living in Paris has put her more deeply in touch not merely with French history, as seen through American eyes, to be sure, but with her own self-constructed and nostalgic identity as an American. The cows, of course, are French; but she remembers seeing her first cow in Michigan when she was seventeen. In any case, her vividly stylized, orange, pink, and purple bovines are as far from com-

9. This information is derived from interviews with the artist by the author over the past three years.

prising a record of specific sites as are Shirley Jaffe's abstractions. Nor can they be categorized as signifiers of that timeless natural order, French or otherwise, with which women are so often identified. For each of these expatriate artists, the work of art is a work of transformation, and the role of expatriation an overdetermined one, positive on the whole. The radical "disjoining between word and thing," to borrow Eva Hoffman's locution once more, far from being a "desiccating alchemy" (Hoffman 1989: 107), has provided them with the means to reinvent the world. And this world is not only replete with significance, but heightened, yes exhilarated, to use a word Shirley Jaffe is fond of, by the conditions of exile.

REFERENCES

Amishai-Maisels, Ziva
  1993 *Depiction and Interpretation: The Influence of the Holocaust on the Visual Arts* (Oxford: Pergamon).
Barsky, Vivian
  1990 " 'Home Is Where the Heart Is': Jewish Themes in the Art of R. B. Kitaj," in *Art and Its Uses: The Visual Image and Modern Jewish Society,* edited by Ezra Mendelsohn, 149–85 (Jerusalem: Institute of Contemporary Jewry, Hebrew University of Jerusalem).
Boudou, Dominique
  1994 "Shirley Jaffe, a la lisière du signe," *Beaux Arts Magazine* (November): 54–58.
Chadwick, Whitney
  1985 *Women Artists and the Surrealist Movement* (London: Thames and Hudson).
Danto, Arthur
  1995 "Art: R. B. Kitaj," *The Nation* (April 3): 465–69.
Engel, Peter
  1986 "Remedios Varo: Science into Art," in *Science in Surrealism: The Art of Remedios Varo,* exhibition catalog (New York: New York Academy of Sciences).
Fleming, Donald, and Bernard Bailyn, eds.
  1969 *The Intellectual Migration: Europe and America, 1930–1960* (Cambridge, MA: Belknap Press of Harvard University Press).
Girard, Xavier
  1994 "Exhilaration," *Le Journal du Musée Matisse* 1.
Hoffman, Eva
  1989 *Lost in Translation: A Life in a New Language* (New York: E. P. Dutton).

Kaplan, Janet
    1984 "Remedios Varo: Voyages and Visions." Paper presented at the Berkshire
    Conference on the History of Women, Smith College, Northhampton, MA.
Kitaj, R. B.
    1989 *First Diasporist Manifesto* (New York: Thames and Hudson).
    1994 *R. B. Kitaj: A Retrospective,* edited by Richard Morphet, exhibition cata-
    log (London: Tate Gallery).
Mathews, Nancy Mowll
    1994 *Mary Cassatt: A Life* (New York: Villard).
McCabe, Cynthia Jaffee
    1976 *The Golden Door: Artist-Immigrants of America, 1876–1976,* exhibition
    catalog (Washington, DC: Hirshhorn Museum and Sculpture Garden and
    Smithsonian Institute).
Morphet, Richard
    1994 "The Art of R. B. Kitaj: 'To thine own self be true,' " in Kitaj 1994: 9–34.
Nochlin, Linda
    1988 "Zuka's French Revolution: A Woman's Place Is Public Space," *The French
    Revolution through American Eyes,* exhibition catalog, 3–7 (Washington,
    DC: National Museum of Women in the Arts).
Rubinstein, Raphael
    1995 "An Eye in the City," *Art in America* 93(4): 87–91.
Sweeney, James Johnson
    1946 "Eleven Europeans in America," *Museum of Modern Art Bulletin* 13(4–5):
    1–39.
Wolff, Janet
    1995 *Resident Alien: Feminist Cultural Criticism* (Cambridge, UK: Polity).
Wollheim, Richard
    1994 "Kitaj: Recollections and Reflections," in Kitaj 1994: 35–42.
Zuka
    1995 "Five American Women Artists in Paris." Paper presented at the meeting
    of Mount Holyoke Alumnae, Paris.

HÉLÈNE CIXOUS

"MAMÃE, DISSE ELE," OR, JOYCE'S SECOND HAND

I WILL BEGIN WITH A PAIR OF ENDINGS:

A:

16 *April:* Away! Away!

The spell of arms and voices: the white arms of roads, their promise of close embraces and the black arms of tall ships that stand against the moon, their tale of distant nations. They are held out to say: We are alone. Come. And the voices say with them: We are your kinsmen. And the air is thick with their company as they call to me, their kinsman, making ready to go, shaking the wings of their exultant and terrible youth.

26 *April:* Mother is putting my new secondhand clothes in order. She prays now, she says, that I may learn in my own life and away from home and friends what the heart is and what it feels. Amen. So be it. Welcome, O life! I go to encounter for the millionth time the reality of experience and to forge in the smithy of my soul the uncreated conscience of my race.

27 *April:* Old father, old artificer, stand me now and ever in good stead. (Joyce 1964 [1916]: 252–53)

A':

Ele tinha acabado de nascer um homem. Mas, mal assumira o seu nascimento, e estava também assumindo aquele peso no peito: mal assumira a sua glória, e uma experiência insondável dava-lhe a primeira futura ruga. Ignorante, inquieto, mal assumira a masculinidade, e uma nova fome ávida nascia, uma coisa dolorosa como um homem que nunca chora. Estaria ele tendo o primeiro medo de que alguma coisa fosse impossível? A moça era um zero naquele ônibus parado, e no entanto, homem que agora ele era, o rapaz de súbito precisava se inclinar para aquele nada, para aquela moça. E nem ao menos inclinar-se de igual para igual, nem ao menos inclinar-se para conceder . . . Mas, atolado no seu reino de homem, ele precisava dele. Para quê? para lembrar-se de uma cláusula? para que ela ou outra qualquer não o deixasse ir longe demais e se perder? para que ele sentisse em sobressalto, como estava sentindo, que havia a possibilidade de erro? Ele precisava dela com fome para não esquecer que eram feitos de mesma carne, essa carne pobre de qual, ao subir no ônibus como um macaco, ela parecia ter feito um caminho fatal. Que é! mas afinal que é que está me acontecendo?, assustou-se ele.

Nada. Nada, e que não se exagere, fora apenas um instante de fraqueza e vacilação, nada mais que isso, não havia perigo.

Apenas um instante de fraqueza e vacilação. Mas dentro desse sistema de duro juízo final, que não permite nem um segundo de incredulidade senão o ideal desaba, ele olhou estonteado a longa rua — e tudo agora estava estragado e seco como se ele tivesse a boca cheia de poeira. Agora e enfim sozinho, estava sem defesa à mercê da mentira pressurosa com que *os outros* tentavam ensiná-lo a ser um homem. Mas e a mensagem?! a mensagem esfarelada na poeira que o vento arrastava para as grades do esgoto. Mamãe, disse ele.

(He had finished being born a man. But scarcely had he assumed his birth when he assumed also this weight in the breast: scarcely had he assumed his glory when an unfathomable experience gave him his first future wrinkle. Ignorant, worried, scarcely had he assumed masculinity when a new avid hunger was born, a painful thing like a man who never cries. Was he feeling the first fear that something was impossible? The girl was a zero in that bus at the stop, and yet, as the man which henceforth he was, the boy all of a sudden needed to lean on this nothing, on this girl. And not even to lean at least from equal to equal, not even to lean at least so as to concede . . . But sunk into his man's kingdom, he needed her. Why? to remind himself of a clause? so that she or another would not let him go too far and get lost? so that he should sense with a start, as he sensed, that there was a possibility of error? He needed her with hunger so as not to forget that they were made of the same flesh, this poor flesh with which, on climbing into the bus like a monkey, she seemed to have made a fatal path. Hey! but in the end what is happening to me?, he alarmed himself.

Nothing. Nothing, one mustn't exaggerate, it was just an instant of weakness and hesitation, nothing more than that, there was no danger.

Just an instant of weakness and hesitation. But within this system of inflexible last judgment, which does not permit even a second of incredulity or else the ideal collapses, he looked dumbfounded at the long road — and everything henceforth was ruined and dry as if he had his mouth full of dust. Henceforth and at last alone, he was without defense at the mercy of the eager lie with which *the others* tried to teach him to be a man. But and the message?! the message shredded in the dust which the wind carried toward the grill of the sewer. Mama, he said.)   (Lispector 1981 [1971]: 140–41)[1]

Mamãe, disse ele. *Mater ait.* This is the final utterance of the last sentence of Clarice Lispector's text *The Message* ("A mensagem") (1981 [1971]). It is also the first of the sentences whose trace I will be following, a trace which is familiar and yet foreign. We all have the impression of having already heard it, but otherwise, and in another language. Mater, ait. Mater? Lapsus? No. Lapwing. Or else we have already said it. Mamãe, disse ele. A little sentence like this, at the end of a text, such a sentence to end with, is rare. What is more, it is the sentence of a "beginner."

Who says "mama"? It is the infant who says this. (The Brazilian emphasizes that it is the *masculine* infant.) But how old is the infant? Ours, I mean the son that the texts we are reading give us, or else the son that we are, is a "young man" of sixteen (Clarice Lispector) or of eighteen (James Joyce). Here we have a wee little eighteen year old who says: mama. Later the child could be seventy — or eighty years old. Mama, he says; the sentence does not have an exclamation point. But the fact that there is no exclamation point does not mean that there is no exclamation. What living being can say mama without making the *call* resonate more or less clearly? Whoever says "mama" calls for help.

But one can utter a mute cry, or call without noise, or without the call tearing the air. Moreover, Clarice Lispector's text tells us that the infant man calls the mother who is not there, has never been there, has never been named in the text titled *The Message.* But who, at the last second, literally *comes out* of the son, summoned by the call, so as to return at least to his ears.

I note that the utterance is Mamãe, *disse* ele (he *said*). And not Mama, he *cried.* In the noncry of the saying, in this calm torment, there is a greater force, more disturbing than the panic of a cry.

But I recall that the utterance we believe we know by heart is not exactly that one. According to the tradition, the call is addressed to the father. Which tradition? The grecolatinojudeochristian tradition. Joyce's tradition. Our own. Yet here the expression *the call of the father* has called forth its other. If I say the call of the father or the call of the mother, being familiar with the use of the genitive case and its secrets, I will receive

1. All translations from the Portuguese are by Eric Prenowitz.

the call and its double or the call divided and reversed, the call which is addressed to the father or to the mother (they are not the same calls), and the call that the mother, the father, addresses to the son. It suffices that I say *call* or *mama* for the *address,* the destination to be forcefully inscribed: in the call (whether paternal or maternal) the addressee is understood to be *the son.* I will keep *the son* as the term common to my texts, as does Clarice Lispector in *The Message* where the word *filho, son,* very often applies to both sexes, boy and girl (even though other distinct nouns exist to say boy and girl, *rapaz, moça . . .*). Does the call always speak of the son, or is it the son who makes the call? In the texts we are going to touch on it so happens that it is always the son. Perhaps this is also our human tradition. Everywhere in all cultures, it is the son who is the hero of the call, because it's he who departs, who is parted from, detached, separated, who carries out or undergoes the separation. And it is the son who *complains about it.* Who appeals it.

I will add now another scene, another citation. It has to do with *Pater ait.*

> Stephen looked on his hat, his stick, his boots.
>
> *Stephanos,* my crown. My sword. His boots are spoiling the shape of my feet. Buy a pair. Holes in my socks. Handkerchief too.
>
> —You make good use of the name, John Eglinton allowed. Your own name is strange enough. I suppose it explains your fantastical humour.
>
> Me, Magee and Mulligan.
>
> Fabulous artificer, the hawklike man. You flew. Whereto? Newhaven-Dieppe, steerage passenger. Paris and back. Lapwing. Icarus. *Pater, ait.* Seabedabbled, fallen, weltering. Lapwing you are. Lapwing be.   (Joyce 1960 [1934]: 270)

Which is the son who calls the father *in Latin?* Who enters, into the text, between Newhaven and Paris, through the door of quotation? This text, indeed all of *Ulysses,* is thick with a company of quotations. Citation is the voice of the other, and it highlights the double playing of the narrative authority. We constantly hear the footsteps of the other, the footsteps of others in language, others speaking in Stephen's language or in Ulysses', I mean the book's, language.

I said *citation:* the last sentence of *The Message,* in paternal (or maternal) form, is without doubt one of the most cited sentences and perhaps the most cited sentence in the world. It reminds us that we have been caught up in citation ever since we said the first words mama or papa.

Joyce took care in *Ulysses* to call papa in Latin, that is, to thus make us hear a good many messages. Among them, the following: (1) that when I call the Father, I am Latin, I am Greek, I am Icarus (and quite a few others who will be evoked), and above all I am of the *past;* (2) that through Latin I am taken back to the ecclesiastical domains; (3) that it is too late, I am dying or I am already dead. Dead, drowned, my mouth underwater, I call the father in vain, and no one hears me.

In a certain sense, and the author of the *Tristia* and the *Metamorphoses* knew this well, the call for help is always grief stricken. There is a picture I would have liked to show you, the Portrait of the Stillborn Artist: it is a painting you know, Brueghel's *Fall of Icarus.* To the right of the picture or in the picture, one sees Icarus's two little pink legs emerging; perhaps he is saying papa, but if so it is underwater. This picture is one of the most magnificent stories there are. In a single glance it permits us to see all the fatalities, all the destinies, human destinations, and life and death in a single instant. In the relationships between measures, between the big and the small, as seen by me, what is most important, what is the biggest, what is the smallest? As seen by me, the shepherd or the plowman, nothing is more important and bigger than my furrows, my ox. And what is tragedy for me as I plow my life? Moreover, what I am saying is a tautology, to live and to plow are the same, I am in the process of living, and to my right someone is in the process of dying, I am in the process of plowing toward my east, and someone is in the process of dying to my west, and how could I integrate, in my own dimensions, tragedy (and even if one speaks to me every day of Sarajevo, or Rwanda . . .). It's not that it isn't there; it is there, but those are its dimensions: we pass each other, some go toward the left, others go toward the right, we don't meet and yet we are in the same landscape.

Let us speak of Icarus, that is to say of Daedalus, that is to say of death and of the name. The name of the father and the name of the son. Let us speak of the survival of the name.

In speaking of this father, of this son, of their names, I will only be returning to the point of departure. To the point of departure which begins *A Portrait of the Artist as a Young Man,* the epigraph taken from Ovid: *Et ignotas animum dimittit in artes,* and to the final point of departure; but a departure engenders a departure, in these texts which are related to each other, recognize each other, and cite each other by the complex motif, or concept, of departure. What does it mean to depart? What does one want, what does one wish to accomplish with a departure? Does one want to depart or does one want to arrive?

In going to Berlin, Kafka would say, does one want to go to Berlin or does one want to leave Prague? Where does the departure lead Stephen Dedalus? (We know a bit about this: leaving a Dublin is perhaps a way of arriving in a Dublin.)

Let us return to our characters on the front lines of departure. And to their names. Because all of this mythical and mystical adventure is closely linked to the question of the name one carries, of the importance carried by the proper name, of the force hidden in the name. Force of the name of D(a)edalus, beneficial and malefic force. And do not forget that the name has the power to *survive,* to *outlive* the person who carries it, and thus—above all in the case of the artist—to be given over to "the space of the epitaph." There is nothing more and less proper to a person than the name, and nothing which carries life and death more mysteriously. The cunning Daedalus, Daidalos, has succeeded in spreading his name to every city. And above all in French where we speak commonly of daedaluses (*dédales*), without knowing that Daedalus existed. And fallen into the ranks of the common name, he connotes no more than losing one's way. Poor Daedalus. Daedalus has become the synonym of his work: the labyrinth and vice versa.

Father and son make one or two, or heads and tails, as soon as they appear in Ovid, as Joyce saw and repeated. Indeed, ever since there has been the question of a boy being "born a man" we repeat the path and tragedy. Daedalus does not come without Icarus. Neither does he go without him. Each one is the uncontained part of the other.

On the one hand, the father is Leonardo da Vinci; he invents flight, he is both mathematician and physicist, and he does not miss the mark. On the other hand, there is the son, who is the unmastered part of what must be called curiosity. There is a curiosity which brings progress or technical success; and then there is excessive curiosity, which goes hand in glove with *hubris,* with pride, with the in-addition, nonreflection, with disobedience. But one could also spend dizzying hours analyzing the scene of the sacrifice of the son to the father's desire by reading the Latin song carefully; and detecting with anxiety the strangely murderous and non-oedipal projection of the old man onto the child. The first Daedalus is the anti–Stephen Dedalus by definition:

Dædalus interea Creten longumque perosus
Exilium tactusque loci natalis amore,
Clausis erat pelago.

(Meanwhile Daedalus, tired of Crete and of his long exile, was filled with longing for his own country, but he was shut in by the sea.)   (Ovid 1985 [1955]: bk. 8, 11. 183–85)[2]

Daedalus is also *a learned artist*. He produces works which, like all works of art, contain in fact a seed of death. Ultimately, the only people able to move about in art without risk are those who are in effect strong citizens having some authority within the art. Daedalus is the master of dead ends *and* of evasions. He is at the turning point, at the passageway. Author of works which lead to going astray, inventor of the labyrinth; and also inventor of the antidote, maker of wings which on the one hand give man a superhuman power; and which on the other attribute to him a supplementary *genos,* a supplementary genus. Is the man who flies still and only a man? When he is a bit bird? Thus *hybrid.*

Through Daedalus, who steers from one extreme to the other, we thus have access to the passage, to the *trans,* to the crossing of borders, to the de-limitation of genuses-genders-genres and species, to construction and to deconstruction, to metamorphosis. Through Daedalus I mean a Joyce.

With the call of his name, Daedalus leads monsters, mutants, chimeras. His story is an entanglement of prison and freedom. He had constructed the labyrinth under the orders of Minos, to lock up the Minotaur; this implies also that the monster, half-bull half-man, was to be preserved. The Minotaur is very much a monster, but after all Icarus and Daedalus are other monsters, other human anomalies. Daedalus revealed the secret of the labyrinth's exit to Ariadne to help her save Theseus, who had been sent to confront the Minotaur in the labyrinth no one can leave. All it takes is not letting go of the thread.

This is also a lesson in reading, when you are in the labyrinth of a text, and a text *is* a labyrinth, a text which was not a labyrinth would not be a text, a labyrinth has its coherence, the rooms communicate with one another, and as a rule one cannot escape, which is a good thing, one must enter the labyrinth of a text with a thread.

But, friend of the lovers, Daedalus was punished and locked up *without thread.* His line was cut; it's the same old story of the telephone. He was thus locked up without a thread but with his son Icarus, and as always

2. All English versions of Ovid are from Mary M. Innes's translation of the *Metamorphoses,* which has been slightly modified throughout.

he finds the easiest way to escape what's inescapable. When one has no thread and cannot go by land, one goes by air. This is what poets do. Thus he invents human wings, he assembles feathers with wax. He needs time, because to make a sufficient collection he has to wait for birds to drop their feathers. The technical moment plunges the poet into voluptuous pleasure. This is how Ovid watches Daedalus adjust the wings:

> et ignotas animum dimittit in artes,
> Naturamque novat. Nam ponit in ordine pennas,
> A minima coeptas, longam breviore sequenti,
> Ut clivo crevisse putes: sic rustica quondam
> Fistula disparibus paulatim surgit avenis.
> Tum lino medias et ceris alligat imas,
> Atque ita compositas parvo curvamine flectit,
> Ut veras imitetur aves.
>
> . . . .
>
> Postquam manus ultima coeptis
> Inposita est, geminas opifex libravit in alas
> Ipse suum corpus, motaque pependit in aura.

(he set his mind to arts never explored before, and altered the laws of nature. He laid down a row of feathers, beginning with tiny ones, and gradually increasing their length, so that the edge seemed to slope upwards. In the same way, the pipe which shepherds used to play is built up from reeds, each slightly longer than the last. Then he fastened the feathers together in the middle with thread, and at the bottom with wax; when he had arranged them in this way, he bent them round into a gentle curve, to look like real birds' wings. . . . When Daedalus had put the finishing touches to his invention, he raised himself into the air, balancing his body on his two wings, and there he hovered, moving his feathers up and down.) (Ibid.: 8.188–202)

Secondhand feathers. "Mother is putting my new secondhand clothes in order."

Yes, it's true, it is the mother—Daedalus the mother—who prepares the clothes of departure. Which are structurally secondhand. Yes, it is mother who prepares the second hand. The hand of the artist which is always second. But what is a mother? And a father? That is the enigma. Enigma through which Joyce is going to set the thinking on genealogy reeling. After all, one can also imagine a new secondhand mother or father; and one knows that the stability of the reference to the mother, in opposition to the instability or to the improbability of paternity of which Freud spoke, has foundered over this last decade since a mother has become potentially replaceable and fictitious, surrogate. I will add that from Freud to Joyce there is also a bit of second hand concerning the theme of improbable paternity.

But before Joycefreud, Ovid had already begun to challenge the stability of the names which "govern" us.

I will cite and comment on the wombtext of *A Portrait of the Artist* as I need it for James Joyce and because it is so beautiful:

Rapidi vicinia solis
Mollit odoratas, pennarum vincula, ceras;
Tabuerant cerae; nudos quatit ille lacertos
Remigioque carens non ullas percipit auras,
Oraque caerulea patrium clamantia nomen
Excipiuntur aqua; quae nomen traxit ab illo.
At pater infelix, nec jam pater: "Icare," dixit,
"Icare," dixit "ubi es? Qua te regione requiram?"
"Icare," dicebat, pennas aspexit in undis,
Devovitque suas artes, corpusque sepulchro
Condidit, et tellus a nomine dicta sepulti.

(he came too close to the blazing sun, and it softened the sweet-smelling wax that bound his wings together. The wax melted. Icarus moved his bare arms up and down, but without their feathers they had no purchase on the air. Even as his lips were crying his father's name, they were swallowed up in the deep blue waters which are called after him. The unhappy father, a father no longer, cried out: "Icarus!" "Icarus," he called. "Where are you? Where am I to look for you?" As he was still calling "Icarus" he saw the feathers on the water, and cursed his art. He laid his son to rest in a tomb, and the land took its name from that of the boy who was buried there.)   (Ibid.: 8.225–35)

This is a story of name giving, and how one passes from the name of the father to the name of the son. It is the son who gives the name (and not the father). Because he is dead. Thus the dead son can be a kind of name of the father. The name of (the) father *which is not pronounced here, oraque caerulea patrium clamantia nomen. Excipiuntur aqua,* on the one hand the name of the father is engulfed in the waters to which *he* gave his name, *quae nomen traxit ab illo,* which gets its name from him, but from which one? We know there is an Icarian Sea, but after all *ab illo* could be Daedalus or Icarus. Here in the bursting forth of the name, in the circulation of the name between water and air, the names of the father and the son, and the call of the names, in the amphibology and the precipitated dislocation of times and spaces, the attribution of paternity of the name of the sea is undecidable *in* the text.

"The unhappy father, a father no longer." *At pater infelix, nec jam pater: Icare, dixit.* In Ovid, we have here a magnificent foreshortening of the question *what is a father?* which runs through all of Joyce's texts: what is a father, what makes the father, what is a father who is no longer father, one would need to imagine, a father father, a prefather, a father still father, a father more or no more father, a father already no longer father, or an already no longer father, a never again father. If we were not so lazy in language, we would weave more precise and more just family ties, following Ovid's example here (the unhappy father who was already no longer father) and we would not simply say father, or mother. We could also say father-son, or son-father, or mother-son or mother-daughter. We would be sensitive to the presence of several kinds of mothers in a mother. We would come to say to ourselves, like Artaud: "I, Antonin Artaud, am my son, my father, my mother, and myself."

But we say: my parents, my children. But what are parents and what are children? Are there not children who are parents? Is there a parental essence? Does one become parent for eternity? Once parent, will one never again be child, etc.? Our thoughts are unfortunately finite, that is to say finishing, that is to say murderous.

It is an unsoned father, already half-dead and a bit deconstructed, the father-who-is-no-longer-father who says: Icarus, Icarus where are you? where must I search for you? *Icare, dixit, ubi es?* thus *he said,* not he cried. *Icare, dicebat, pennas aspexit in undis;* Icarus, he said, he perceived feathers in the waters, so he damned his art. The stripped-down quality of Ovid's text and of Icarus, *of whom only feathers remain,* is extraordinary. Ovid's writing is also the writing of tragedy. Tragedy is all the more tragic in that it is sober and elliptical. The peak of tragedy is the posthumous inscription, the impossible dialogue between the still living and the scarcely dead. Icarus, he said: he saw the feathers in the water. This is the answer. Performatively.

Icare, dixit, Icarus said he, son he said, is a phrase which I will connect with Joyce's *Pater ait,* father he says. Who knows, when Daedalus the father who is no longer father says "Icarus," who knows if he is not calling his father, who knows if when he says "Icarus" the situation as it is depicted in Ovid is not such, in the depths of the soul, that Daedalus is calling his father. Would the father who is no longer father, and who sees himself stripped of his child, not always be calling the father? Which one? The father that he was and that he is no longer, and the father that every child is for the father. The parent who first flies in front of the child and constantly turns around to see if the child is following: this is the parent of the early years, but then the parent's destiny is that the child should fly in front and that the child should turn around constantly to see if the parent-become-child is following.

From one fall to the other—from Icarus to Stephen—the call has changed its addressee, as we have known since *Ulysses*.

> Fabulous artificer, the hawklike man. You flew. Whereto? Newhaven-Dieppe, steerage passenger. Paris and back. Lapwing. Icarus. *Pater, ait.* Seabedabbled, fallen, weltering. Lapwing you are. Lapwing be.   (Joyce 1960 [1934]: 270)

A rare example in literature, here Ovid's song comes back broken in two, departure in *A Portrait of the Artist* and let us say *consequence* of the departure in *Ulysses*. Thus it is resurrection or ghostly reapparition. The drowned Icarus-Stephen reappears, a bit damp perhaps, in the library. He takes a place among the numerous ghosts that he himself calls to in this chapter. All are phantoms. Among those who are recalled and agitated we recognize father, son, brothers, uncles, the whole masculine species. But the mother?

The mother is the first-phantom, and perhaps the only real returning ghost. It is she who enters scene one:

> Stephen, an elbow rested on the jagged granite, leaned his palm against his brow and gazed at the fraying edge of his shiny black coatsleeve. Pain, that was not yet the pain of love, fretted his heart. Silently, in a dream she had come to him after her death, her wasted body within its loose brown graveclothes giving off an odour of wax and rosewood, her breath, that had bent upon him, mute, reproachful, a faint odour of wetted ashes. Across the threadbare cuffedge he saw the sea hailed as a great sweet mother by the wellfed voice beside him. The ring of bay and skyline held a dull green mass of liquid. A bowl of white china had stood beside her deathbed holding the green sluggish bile which she had torn up from her rotting liver by fits of loud groaning vomiting.
> Buck Mulligan wiped again his razorblade.

—Ah, poor dogsbody, he said in a kind voice. I must give you a shirt and a few noserags. How are the secondhand breeks?   (Ibid.: 4–5)

In a dream, silently, she had come to him, her wasted body within its loose graveclothes giving off an odour of wax and rosewood, her breath, bent over him with mute secret words, a faint odour of wetted ashes.

Her glazing eyes, staring out of death, to shake and bend my soul. On me alone. The ghostcandle to light her agony. Ghostly light on the tortured face. Her hoarse loud breath rattling in horror, while all prayed on their knees. Her eyes on me to strike me down.   (Ibid.: 10–11)

Let us return to April 16, the date on which the departure is *declared*. As one declares war. Or as one launches an attack. (I note in passing that the use of dates gives the last pages of *A Portrait of the Artist* this air of urgency and of the concrete which makes the move to action felt.)

16 *April:* Away! Away!

It is the end and it is the beginning.

What could be stronger for a text than such an "ending"?

It is the *Adieu.*

As is well known, Stephen's "notes" of April 26 are from Joyce's "first(?)-hand," they are a self-citation of epiphany 30, which he uses in *Stephen Hero* before citing it a second time here, slightly altered.

As is perhaps less well known, they are the reapparition of another adieu, that of a young man of eighteen who writes in French (he is *leaving* the Latin Quarter)—and who is named *Rimbaud*. I will recall it here:

Adieu

L'automne déjà!—Mais pourquoi regretter un éternel soleil, si nous sommes en-gagés à la découverte de la clarté divine,—loin des gens qui meurent sur les saisons.

L'automne. Notre barque élevée dans les brumes immobiles tourne vers le port de la misère, la cité énorme au ciel taché de feu et de boue. Ah! les haillons pour-ris, le pain trempé de pluie, l'ivresse, les mille amours qui m'ont crucifié! Elle ne finira donc point cette goule reine de millions d'âmes et de corps morts *et qui seront jugés!* Je me revois la peau rongée par la boue et la peste, des vers plein les cheveux et les aisselles et encore de plus gros vers dans le coeur, étendu parmi les inconnus sans âge, sans sentiment... J'aurais pu y mourir... L'affreuse évocation! J'exècre la misère.

Et je redoute l'hiver parce que c'est la saison du confort!

— Quelquefois je vois au ciel des plages sans fin couvertes de blanches nations en joie. Un grand vaisseau d'or, au-dessus de moi, agite ses pavillons multi-colores sous les brises du matin. J'ai créé toutes les fêtes, tous les triomphes, tous les drames. J'ai essayé d'inventer de nouvelles fleurs, de nouveaux astres, de nouvelles chairs, de nouvelles langues. J'ai cru acquérir des pouvoirs surnaturels. Eh bien! je dois enterrer mon imagination et mes souvenirs! Une belle gloire d'artiste et de conteur emportée!

Moi! moi qui me suis dit mage ou ange, dispensé de toute morale, je suis rendu au sol, avec un devoir à chercher, et la réalité rugueuse à étreindre! Paysan!

Suis-je trompé? la charité serait-elle soeur de la mort, pour moi?

Enfin, je demanderai pardon pour m'être nourri de mensonge. Et allons.

[Autumn already! — But why yearn for an eternal sun, if we are committed to the discovery of divine light, — far from the people who die by the seasons.

Autumn. Our boat lifted up through the motionless mists turns toward the port of poverty, the enormous city with its sky stained by fire and mud. Ah! the putrid rags, the rain-drenched bread, the drunkenness, the thousand loves that have crucified me! Will she not stop at all, then, this ghoul queen of millions of souls and of dead bodies *which will be judged!* I see myself again, my skin pitted by mud and pestilence, my hair and my armpits full of worms, and even bigger worms in my heart, lying among strangers without age, without feeling. . . . I could have died there. . . . Frightful recollection! I abhor poverty.

And I dread winter because it is the season of comfort!

— Sometimes I see in the sky endless beaches covered with joyful white nations. A great golden ship, above me, waves its multicolored pennants in the morning breezes. I have created all festivals, all triumphs, all dramas. I have tried to invent new flowers, new stars, new flesh, new tongues. I believed I acquired supernatural powers. Well! I must bury my imagination and my memories! A great glory as an artist and storyteller swept away!

I! I who called myself a seer or an angel, exempt from all morality, I am re-stored to the earth, with a duty to seek, and rugged reality to embrace! Peasant!

Am I deceived? would charity be the sister of death, for me?

Finally, I shall beg pardon for having nourished myself on falsehood. Then let's go.]   (Rimbaud 1973 [1873]: 102–5)

I will not take the time to comment on it because the other Icarus, the Irishman, is calling me. But I will quickly underline several similar themes here: whiteness, the call of the open sea, invention, the fall (here *in* the earth), the call for help, etc.

Everything in the last pages of *A Portrait* is inscribed under the sign of passage if not rupture—beginning with the first takeover by force, the narrative anacoluthon inaugurated on March 20, where suddenly the journal form irrupts into the book, the *I* irrupts into the story, and "the artist" goes from the status of character to the status of narrator.

Away! Away! is in the same movement of detachment and of interruption.

Away! is the bursting out of voice. The narrator's own voice operates an interrupting irruption, interruption-irruption which will be reedited explicitly in what follows by the apparition of the *Voices*.

But Away! Away! twice also expresses the duplicity of the exclamation: Convocation! Revocation!

Let us listen now to what the new I who has come out of this story writes to himself *in the present*.

The spell of arms and voices: the white arms of roads, their promise of close embraces and the black arms of tall ships that stand against the moon, their tale of distant nations. They are held out to say: We are alone. Come. And the voices say with them: We are your kinsmen. And the air is thick with their company as they call to me, their kinsman, making ready to go, shaking the wings of their exultant and terrible youth.   (Joyce 1964 [1916]: 252)

Strange epiphany, whose strangeness will be redoubled by the *entry* which follows. In a minute we will be able to see, though just barely, that these two apparently dissimilar moments are nonetheless linked: over there and right here, afar and anear, it is a question of family. But at first it is from the angle of a defamilialization that the theme is played out. Neither father nor mother. And with roads and voices for *Kin*. Such perfect defamilialization, omission, or effacement of the parents which is not even declared, but only indicated by the substitution of *kin*. As if the family were surpassed or replaced by an archaic *genos* and which insists on fraternal consanguinity. At least for that day.

Because a few days later, and one line lower, the family comes back, premonitorily, to *Ulysses*. "On ne part pas," Rimbaud would say.

Into the space of the domestic household, the landscape of the paragraph gathers poetic regions, crosses between land and sea, and between unknown "divinities" and exultant youths.

What or he who speaks here is already the stranger, who comes from the other world. And he is not the only one to speak. It's a concert. "The spell of arms and voices"—syllepsis of a metaphor—takes *arms* and *voices* at once figuratively and literally. In the second segment ("the white arms of roads, their promise of close embraces and the black arms of tall ships") the body becomes lexicalized metaphor. The tropic passion grows. Thus the arms begin to speak, in a prosopopoeia with a pressing and, it seems, paradoxical message:

"We are alone — come."

But how can one say *we* are alone when the *we* already expresses the more-than-one? Unless — on the occasion of the paradox — it is to make heard the fact that those who speak are a "company" of *Loners*. "I am alone"; these are the poet's words, we recognize them. *Aber ich bin allein,* Holderlin's words. Every poet's words. (1) I am alone, you who are alone come with us, this will not break the solitude. (2) Whoever says "I am alone" breaks the solitude and affirms it by this act of speech.

The arms speak. Discourse of the arms. Discourse of the voices. As if the voices were kinds of arms. The arms have voices. But the voices also have voices. And all these prosopopoeias remind us that for whoever has poeticizing ears, there is the call.

But all of this resonates in the labyrinth of the inner ear.

Voice. Whose voice? (You would think we were already with Circe.) Voices of the *kinsmen*. Kin, *genos* — tells of the common origin of consanguinity.[3] In sum, we hear the voice of the Blood. The blood brothers of the kinsman are . . . roads with white incestuous arms. It's that all things touch one another and interchange themselves, away in the distance. And this common blood which circulates in the masts and the arms is — *the voice*.

Of *kinsmen*. Voices of "brothers" in race, of unknown species. You are of the race of voices and of ships, say these prophets without form. We are voice brothers.

"And the air is thick with their company as they call to me, their kinsman, making ready to go, shaking the wings of their exultant and terrible youth." Here is a superbly oneiric, coalescent construction where the syntactic amphibology prevents us from identifying who with what; a little labyrinth, with *their kinsman making ready to go* packed into the main proposition. To such an extent that the one who has not yet taken flight is already beating wings, the others' wings or the other wings.

This whole paragraph (or this verse, or this stanza) is worked on by the transferential force: the departure is already here, it propagates itself by hypallage, transferring the qualities from one subject to another, hy-

---

3. Etymology of *kin:* Old English: *cyn.* Old Teutonic: *Kunjo* to engender, to beget.

pallage from the exultant youth to the ships. And this is how the arms become wings.

Who? There is youth and distance. And, subtly, sexual difference. White arms, black arms, love, virile friendship. And what is the sex of the voices? The winged sex.

Indeed we do not forget that we have already experienced a first heralding version of this scene, at the end of chapter four. In the course of this long apocalyptic episode which took place on the beach in view of Howth Castle, we had been witness to the symbolic death of Stephen the schoolboy, to the ecstasy at the hallucinatory vision of a "hawklike man flying sunward above the sea" (Joyce 1964 [1916]: 169), and to the resurrection of the soul destined through art for immortality.

It is there that the newborn, alone ("He was alone. He was unheeded, happy and near to the wild heart of life" [ibid.: 171]) had glimpsed his other: "A girl stood before him in midstream, alone and still, gazing out to sea" (ibid.). This is an encounter which is at once real and chaste and sublimated in Dantesque concord.

During this scene which ended in *rose* and apotheosis as he "rose," Stephen had gathered and superimposed the triumphant and threatening promises of all his imaginary relatives, because "all ages were as one to him" (ibid.: 168). All ages. The medieval age, the classical age, the Danish age, the Dantesque age. And all that flies and flutters was also a single great magic wing for him: the ghost of Hamlet, the ghost of Daedalus, and "the likeness of a strange and beautiful seabird" (ibid.: 171) of the "crane-like girl."

This immense mythical material finds an airy synthesis here and where the girl element has evaporated. This artist will depart *alone,* masculine, leaving Mother behind. Our Joyce, who always fed his work with his life, having swallowed Nora as Zeus did his Metis.

(A word about the signifier *kinsman* which stands out here: in epiphany 30 the word which appeared was *people*. With *kinsman,* a word of Teutonic origin, Joyce relates his hero to races that are much more ancient, more barbarian, and more legendary. The *Kin* rings in the gathering of the Siegfrieds, working back from Norway's Ibsen all the way to Iceland, blood brothers, brothers by adoption and sworn brothers of the Icelandic sagas.)

The sixteenth of April thus goes about its preparations for the voyage in the form of a literary exercise. An old-young style, in part biblical by the anaphora of *and;* in part Rimbaudian or Verlainian.

But on April 26, the same preparations for the same voyage take place in a familiar, familial version, with the return of the motif *away* in the domesticated maternal mode. As above, so below.

"Mother is putting my new secondhand clothes in order." We have returned to the house. *Oikos*. Family economy, realism, poverty. Yes. But at the same time there is the *play* of the writing, and the infinite richness of the themes. Mother does the work of Daedalus here. And from all sides the theme of transmission resonates. With the very beautiful English expression *secondhand*, the idea of the heritage is introduced in all its complexity; in this case what is to be inherited is not a paternal possession, but rather what has been *cast off*. We can recognize the figure of borrowing which gives emphasis to the bitter relationship with Stephen's false brothers, in particular Mulligan in *Ulysses*.

So here is our artist who will be clothed in these garments which have been abandoned, rejected, but not given, making of him a doubled lining and the reticent inhabitant of a costume, such that he is destined to be the kinsman of phantoms, himself a ghost who haunts a borrowed form and who is haunted by his predecessor. A single costume for two: this engenders the violent opposite of that admirable friendship which Montaigne celebrated, a friendship in which the sharing and the indivision was shared out thus: a single soul for two bodies. But to inhabit someone else's costume is to enter into the nightmarish labyrinth of alienations and of the schema of expropriation. In the first place the *new secondhand clothes* concretely introduce an element of interpretation for the powerful exile drive that animates James Joyce and Stephen Dedalus. *I do not want to belong,* they repeat. I do not want my soul to be clothed in a borrowed appearance which will phantomize me.

The entire ambition of the young man is to deconstruct the ties of kinship and of appearance and to remake for himself a sublime kinship. (This Joyce who signed his very first texts with the name Stephen Dedalus a name which had not been lent him, but which he had seized upon and adorned himself with.)

But if borrowing hurts and humiliates, it is also the figure of an entirely different relationship. *Secondhand* expresses also the art of borrowing, of collecting (feathers) and of *the graft* which brings forth that "loveliness which has *not yet* come into the world" dreamed of by Stephen.

Let us follow along the wily text. *Et ignotas animum dimittit in artes.*
"She prays now, she says, that I may learn in my own life and away

from home and friends what the heart is and what it feels. Amen. So be it. Welcome, O life!" But who writes this *in the present??* Who is taking notes while she prays? All of this in free indirect style, with this confusion of the narrative authority with the character, thus of the son with the mother. Who says "Amen"? Who says "so be it"? The one translates itself into the other. The mother's prayer "that I may learn in my own life and away from home and friends what the heart is and what it feels" returns inverted in the son's grandiloquent declaration: "I go to encounter for the millionth time the reality of experience and to forge in the smithy of my soul the uncreated conscience of my race."

Go learn, I will be master.

The sentences are spiced with irony, because this Stephen is slightly undermined by Icarus's megalomania.

Dedalus the son bloated with the father uses the romantic cliché: "Welcome, O life! I go to encounter for the millionth time the reality of experience and to forge in the smithy of my soul the uncreated conscience of my race."

Thus the discourse of the mother in him is covered over by the discourse of the smith father *that he is. In this sentence.* Father in this sentence. And in the next calling the father: "Old father, old artificer, stand me now and ever in good stead." So is he a father or not a father? Both, alternately, in slippage, by the metonymies of the unconscious.

Who is calling whom in these lines of adieu? Because calls abound. Calling on notes, calling for the gods, calling to life. The call of the mother . . . However, some of them are called to help, invoked, and not even named, if not by antonomasia. Who are these clandestine companions who flank the young man with their phantomatic presence? In the last sentence we hasten to think that the "old artificer" is Daedalus. But my colleague at the Sorbonne thinks it is the word *stead* which prevails, being the last word of the book, and perhaps the proper name — of a sort of symbolic father.

But in the *smithy* we can hear the semantic ambivalence of the *forge* resonating. Our artist will, in effect, forge truth and conscience, but simultaneously he will *forge forgeries.* These will perhaps be noble, as were the forgeries of Thoth who haunted him a bit earlier, Thoth the inventor of the fake which is writing.

Thus one can also *forge* oneself as a fake father or a fake son, that is a fabricated father . . .

Is he the smith, this boy of eighteen, who will forge the conscience of his race? But the smith is Daedalus, not Icarus; it is the father, not the son. As for genealogies, as for filiations, it is difficult to say in this text that Stephen sees himself or presents himself as a son. His mother says to him: go learn what the heart is, and *I* respond: I am the creator, I the son am the father of the progenitors. So in the labyrinth (in the dédale) the son is the father. I am the son of my mother whose father I am, I am the son-father. And this does not prevent me, the son-father, from calling for the help of the ancient father.

There is not only the Daedalus-Icarus couple, which in addition mirrors itself, reverses itself, exchanges itself in this text, but someone else who slips in here and who is imperceptible, a heroic character who forges something very particular, someone named Siegfried. This Siegfried went about as a bird a few pages earlier, in the University of Dublin. "They crossed the quadrangle together without speaking. The birdcall from *Siegfried* whistled softly followed them from the steps of the porch" (Joyce 1964 [1916]: 237). Siegfried takes an underground path in the text like the old Shakespearean mole. In the Wagnerian legend, Siegfried is the fixer of the broken sword of his father, Sigmund, and after millions of attempts and difficulties he manages to resolder, to reforge, his father's sword.

Certain texts are on the one hand labyrinths, and on the other forges where one performs operations like Siegfried's: one melts, like wax, one makes alloys, one resolders and rewelds.[4] Siegfried's sword is also *secondhand*? It is new because it is refounded, and at the same time it is secondhand. A text is necessarily secondhand and second *ad infinitum*. It is made of numerous swords which have been broken, then founded, then reforged to remake a new sword, and this is the case for Joyce's texts, into which all the world's great texts are thrown founded alloyed and remade. There is no body proper (of our culture) without the graft right from birth.

A body, a sword, a wax tablet so old and so new, *new secondhand,* this is our culture and its writing; indeed, we no longer know what old means. If Daedalus and Siegfried are in the same smithy as Stephen and ourselves, how old are we? Our culture has a strange, composed, chi-

---

4. One melts what? Swords? Instruments of the mastery of phallic signs, perhaps. Signatures.

merical body, encrusted and grafted with philosophies, with testaments, with laws, with geneses one hundred times regenerated; it is Neualt like a Prague synagogue and it is too jungfraud to forget and not to forget that "there is no body proper without this graft" (Derrida 1994: 213). There is no artist without cast-off feathers. Everything begins with this prosthesis.

There is no simple or proper portrait of the artist as a young man.

But rather a portrait of the Old as Young man, of the Father as Son, that is to say of the son as father of the Jung as Fraud and of the Son as Mother.

It is a prosthesis and a borrowing that bring us back to Dublin, which we have never left, to the library.

We hear in the following passage, with more or less innocent or alert ears, the footsteps of hidden names, the footsteps of survivors, depending on what we have already read:

> Stephen looked on his hat, his stick, his boots.
> *Stephanos*, my crown. My sword. His boots are spoiling the shape of my feet. Buy a pair. Holes in my socks. Handkerchief too.   (Joyce 1960 [1934]: 270)

The theme of the *new secondhand clothes* returns enriched by amphibologies: "Stephen looked at his hat, his stick, his boots." Hearing this sentence, I do not know who possesses the hat that is possessing Stephen. This hat, this cane refer to a third person; I do not know any more than Stephen himself who owns the hat itself. Indeed, this is why Stephen tries to take over borrowed attributes in a stroke of poetic magnification reminiscent of Genet. Let this bowler be my kingdom. Now he is king. Now he is knight. Who? Hamlet? Siegfried? Ephemeral illumination: it is impossible to sublimate the boots which are blistering his feet. And it is quite beautiful: with a kick this inscribes the conflict, the hostility, the complex problematic of the hated friend, the bad brother. At the same time, this telegraphic interlude again plays out the elevation and the fall, crowning and misery. Ineluctable modality of the double carriage of the name toward the heights and toward the depths always in the same movement. "You make good use of the name. . . . Your own name is strange enough" says the librarian who in the first case is correct, though in the second (your own name) he gives to Caesar what is not Caesar's. "Own," that is the problem. "Ourselves we do not owe," said brother Shakespeare already. The name in question is not in fact pronounced: so it rises and makes a ghostly apparition in the text like King Hamlet.

Fabulous artificer, the hawklike man. You flew. Whereto? Newhaven-Dieppe, steerage passenger. Paris and back. Lapwing. Icarus. *Pater, ait*. Seabedabbled, fallen, weltering. Lapwing you are. Lapwing be.   (Ibid.)

This is how one departs Daedalus and one returns Icarus, one departs hawk and en route one "turns" lapwing. One departs third person and one falls into second person, that is to say first person. According to the technique of the steerage passenger. Between *A Portrait of the Artist* and *Ulysses* a voyage took place outside of books, fallen between two books. This makes of Joyce's works a play in several acts reminiscent of Shakespeare, with an unfulfilled voyage, just like that of Hamlet who leaves Denmark only to return. But could this be the other lapwing??

At this point my grafted text speaks Latin and says: *Pater, ait*. I believe that Icarus is speaking. And that this is Ovid's voice. Yes, but in the *Metamorphoses,* I find: *Icare, dixit*. It is the father and not the son who calls softly. Indeed the son has called the father, no, *the name of the father,* but under-water. They call themselves, each other. The two of them. And they do not hear each other, themselves.

But this call alerts us; we recall a younger and older mouth which says the name of the father and complains. It is Christ. *Eli Eli lema sabaqthani* he says, and there is no response. Father, why have you let me down? We are the forsaken. Who are we when this is what we call out? And we are always sounding Christ's cry.

I am darning like Stephen's mother, and I would say that this is the cry of the nursling, it is the nursling who is forsaken by the mother, who is dropped in birth; it is as if there were a sort of ancient and impossible cry of the trauma of birth. What is splendid here is that this is said to the father: why have you let me fall, while in general we say this to the mother. The sensation we have when we are abandoned, and against which we protest, affects us more as the abandonment by the mother than as the abandonment by the father. When one is abandoned, one feels one's orphanage in relation to coming into the world, in relation to the substrate, to the uterine matrix, even if it is a man who abandons.

Returning to Clarice Lispector, you will understand why I have compared *Pater, ait* to the last sentence of *The Message*: Mother, he said, *Mama, said he*. Clarice Lispector knows that it is the mother one calls, or that there is calling of the mother; she knows it with a poetic knowledge, and she knows it also because she knows Joyce very well. After all, her first text is the portrait of the artist as a young woman, *Near to the Wild Heart* (Perto do coração selvagem) (1980 [1944]), which is also a bildungsroman. According to what she said, she named it thus because a friend told her that it was reminiscent of *A Portrait of the Artist as a Young Man*. Clarice Lispector says that she had not read Joyce at the time, but that the title of her book is indeed a citation from *A Portrait of the Artist*. Her first book thus calls on a *kinsman*. After the fact, she owed it to Joyce all the same to read *A Portrait of the Artist*. And for whoever has a bit of memory, the good wax, the kind which does not melt, which does not approach the sun, in this wax there is inscription, or engraving, of the artistic structures of kinship, which Joyce labored over, worked on, reinscribed so much.

Should we therefore attribute to Joyce the paternity of certain themes we find activated in Clarice Lispector? For example, the theme of initiation? of passage? of apprenticeship? No. These themes which are familiar to Joyce scholars belong—and this is what is exciting—originally, equally, but with a startling difference to the world of Clarice Lispector. We have much to learn from these differences between resemblances.

It is in this way that the story called *The Message* relates in a dense and dazzling form the experience of initiation-detachment-departure toward the age *called* man-woman, of these two inseparable entities the boy with the girl. Inseparable in what we can call the prehistoric age, so as to make themselves, to rub themselves the one against the other, leading to a separation by differentiation. Inseparable at first, and above all the two of them "artists," both destined for poetry, like Stephen. How each one is a bit the other, how each one takes the other a bit for him and herself, how each one is confused, is torn, in a rich sequence of alliances, of conjunctions, of disjunctions, of dislocations.

But here the metamorphosis is possible only by a dual movement.

usavam-se para se exercitarem na iniciação; usavam-se impacientes, ensaiando um com o outro o modo de bater asas para que enfim—cada um sozinho e liberto—pudesse dar o grande vôo solitário que também significaria o adeus um do outro.

(they used each other to practice for initiation; they used each other impatiently, the one with the other trying out the way to beat wings so as to be able at last— each one alone and free—to give the great solitary flight which would also signify the adieu of the one from the other.) (Lispector 1981 [1971]: 128–29)

This *Message* is very much Clarice's message. The experience Stephen speaks of: "I go to encounter for the millionth time the reality of experience"; yes it is true, every day we encounter for the millionth time the experience which is the first one, because it's the millionth, but it's the first on this particular day. Thus what Clarice's text does is to work at the message for the millionth time, it is the millionth message, but received for the first time, always just as enigmatic, and such that it will bring our characters to a moment of revelation which tears from them this unbursting cry which will not be *Pater, ait,* but rather *Mater, ait, Mama, he said.*

Clarice reminds us, after Kafka, that we cannot hope to receive the message; the person who will receive the message must not expect it; if it is waited for, it does not arrive. One cannot have a voluntarist attitude. The message arrives on condition that one not wait for it; it arrives *unhoped-for, the goal attained unexpectedly.*

So the message arrives unexpectedly, on condition that it be unhoped-for, and on condition that the receiver be receptive, that he be ready (*pronto* in Brazilian). But this is not to be ready like the schoolboy in the morning or like the soldier; it is to be the *place* capable of receiving, prepared, without being voluntarily prepared, but having been prepared in a good passivity, by dint of looking and of not knowing what one is looking for, by dint of stamping the ground, of getting edgy, of trampling, of knocking against things without knowing, in a sort of anguished openness, because one does not know what for, without anticipation, without forecast, without prediction, and then the message can arrive:

E nunca, nunca acontecia alguma coisa que enfim arrematasse a cegueira com que estendiam as mãos e que os tornasse prontos para o destino que impaciente os esperava, e os fizesse enfim dizer para sempre adeus.

(And never, never did anything arrive which would have at last put an end to the blindness with which they held out their hands and which would have made them ready for the destiny which waited impatiently for them, and would have at last made them say adieu forever.)   (Ibid.: 131)

When I am sixteen years old, I do not know that destiny is waiting impatiently for me. But, and this is sublime, as in Brueghel's painting, while I am there with my wings, perhaps the plowman or the shepherd or I the painter see something Icarus with his wings does not see: destiny. It is destiny which waits for me; I do not wait for it. And destiny (we are speaking Greek, but how can we do otherwise), destiny will arrive, but it will arrive when I am ready. It will arrive. He will arrive. We recognize the gaping forewarning of messianism.

Talvez estivessem tão prontos para se soltarem um do outro como uma gota de água quase a cair

(Perhaps they were so ready to detach themselves the one from the other like a drop of water about to fall)   (Ibid.: 132)

One must manage to detach one's selves the one from the other like *a single* drop of water. Which means that it is not easy. It is in falling that the drop of water will detach itself the one from the other. Carried by its own weight. Like a tear.

e apenas esperassem algo que simbolizasse a plenitude da *angústia* para paderem se separar. Talvez, maduros como uma gota de água, tivessem provocado o acontecimento de que falarei.

(and they only awaited something which symbolized the plenitude of *anguish* to be able to separate themselves. Perhaps, ripe like a drop of water, they had provoked the event of which I will speak.)   (Ibid.)

The detachment and the fall (of the tear, of the drop, of the child) happens when the subject has arrived at maturity. Maturity and anguish go together and change places.

The message? But what message? That is the enigma.

The first condition is the dispatch of the dispatch. The message is not necessarily a letter, or at least the letter is not necessarily composed of letters. There are substitutes for letters. The message arrives. It travels. It is a traveler. Let us say that the cannonade, the arrow, all that is sent without voice and by air or by sea mail, all that travels with a direction and which is at once mute and extremely eloquent, is a message. One sends messages to oneself hidden in the form of symptoms. Stephen is constantly sending himself these. For the moment I am working here rather on the message coming from a foreign elsewhere, it could be my own elsewhere, and which comes bringing what is called so beautifully in French *une nouvelle*, news, something unknown, which at the same time ought to be decipherable in one way or another. The second condition is thus that the addressee be capable of receiving the message.

This text warns us: I am sending you a message. To start with I am called *The Message,* which is already a message, and then I send you a message.

In the end I also constitute the message through my own reading. If I receive, if I read, if I perceive something given to me to read in French or English and taking this form — the message — perhaps I will not react. If, however, I line up the following in a translating game — *Le Message /* *A Mensagem / (The Message)* — I will perhaps be sensitized to the grammatical gender: in French the message is masculine, in English neutral, while in Brazilian it is feminine.

E vira-a, toda cheia de impotente amor pela humanidade, subir como um macaco no ônibus — e viu-a depois sentar-se quieta e comportada, recompondo a blusa enquanto esperava que o ônibus andasse.

(And he had seen her, all full of an impotent love for humanity, climbing like a monkey into the bus — and then he saw her sitting tranquil and proper, readjusting her blouse while waiting for the bus to start.)   (Ibid.: 140)

Here we are with this text *The Message,* a bit in the same situation, hesitating or feeling uncertainty and the origin of uncertainty, which is the mystery of sexual differences, ever since the beginning of the text. And what's more the text is unabashed; this is not hidden, it is incessantly reinscribed, reedited. It is constantly a question of sex, and at the same time in a slightly unexpected way, not entirely classical. When the word *sex* appears, neat and clean, it is not always in a form or a place that is obvious and familiar to us. There are words which make sex, brutally. Not only is sexual opposition or sexual difference or sexual indifferentiation in the text on every page, but what's more there are slightly unusual sexes, for example new sexes; sometimes the new sex is a word, sometimes the sex begins to speak. In the stroke of a wing we find our young man in the process of being born in Brazil. In the process of being born what? Bird? Artist? Man? No. *A* man. A singular, indeed masculine individual, and a poet.

Enquanto ela saiu costeando a parede como uma intrusa, já quase mãe dos filhos que um dia teira, o corpo pressentindo a submissão, corpo sagrado e impuro a carregar. O rapaz olhou-a, espantado de ter sido ludibriado pela moça tanto tempo, e quase sorriu, quase sacudia as asas que acabavam de crescer. Sou homem, disse-lhe o sexo em obscura vitória.

(While she went off skimming the wall like an intruder, already almost the mother of the children she would have one day, her body anticipating the submission, a body sacred and impure to assume. The boy watched her, stupefied at having been tricked for so long by the girl, and almost smiled, almost shook the wings which were finishing to grow. I am a man, the sex said to him in obscure victory.)   (Ibid.: 139)

One would think here that a boy is not born unto his destiny without wings. But of course, detachable wings. I will only follow here, for lack of space, the boy's voyage, because he is our Icarus. And because it is he who calls mama, he who could not be born a man without going, like Stephen, through Mother.

Here he is beating his wings like the bird at the edge of the nest. But no. It is not he. It is his sex which has wings. And what's more, the sex speaks. It speaks Brazilian; it says I and it says I in the place of and addressing itself to the I. "I am a man" are the words of the sex, not of the boy. There is a group of subjective authorities which constitute the "boy." Joyce distinguishes soul, body, clothing. For Clarice Lispector these are *all the parts of bodies,* the sensitive interior body which expresses itself in sweat, in heartbeats, and the other one, which on its feet has size forty-four shoes. And among all these emanations of the ego, there is one which is the sex, and which says "I am a man." All of the boy does not say "I am a man." Clarice Lispector works on the exact location of places of enunciation. This text permits us to recall that messages are sent from, they originate in the different mouths of the different regions of the body. The penis says "I am a man" with pride. The sex addresses itself to its chief. It is a very limited message. I do not know what the heart says.

But the message? Where is it? The last paragraph is going to arrive and still no message? The sublime last paragraph comes after a moment of anguish for the boy:

but in the end what is happening to me? he alarmed himself.

Nothing. Nothing, one mustn't exaggerate, it was just an instant of weakness and hesitation, nothing more than that, there was no danger.

Just an instant of weakness and hesitation.   (Ibid.: 141)

The repetition almost inverts the meaning of the remark. It has passed, and it returns. It was nothing; well no, quite precisely it was *nothing. Nada. Nada,* the other name of the girl. What happens to him is this *nothing* which is everything.

But within this system of inflexible last judgment, which does not permit even a second of incredulity or else the ideal collapses, he looked dumbfounded at the long road—and everything henceforth was ruined and dry as if he had his mouth full of dust. Henceforth and at last alone, he was without defense at the mercy of the eager lie with which *the others* tried to teach him to be a man. But and the message?! the message shredded in the dust which the wind carried toward the grill of the sewer. Mama, he said.   (Ibid.)

End of story.

But and the message?! Whose cry is this?

Mine, yours, the narrator's, and the boy's. After all, this story was called *The Message*. It promised. And here it ends, with its mouth full of dust, and it has not given me the message?? We're not really going to finish, to die perhaps, without having received the message?

And the message?

Alarum! we have slept five thousand years and all of a sudden the text cries: *And the message?!* The question is an answer. The form is elliptical. The *and* presupposes interlocution, presupposes dialogue, presupposes that something has preceded. But what has preceded? We have dealt with many mysteries in the story, and all of a sudden there arrives this *And the message?!* which indicates to us that the message arrives *in supplementary position*. Maybe it has always been in supplementary position in the text. I give a start because I had forgotten. Recollection is a start.

What makes me wake with a jump: "Just an instant of weakness and hesitation." There is a crack; it is this moment of anguish and agitation for the boy, who realizes, once he is born separate from the girl, that *he needs her,* the woman, "sunk," as he is, "into his kingdom." But we are "within this system of inflexible last judgment." It is a fortified system, which permits not an instant of weakness, "which does not permit even a second of incredulity." We have seen this before; it is the "phallocratic system." This is how Clarice Lispector, who did not think in terms of phallogocentrism, who does not belong to what is already the heritage of thought and language of our half-century, this is how she conceives of it: a "system of inflexible last judgment, which does not permit even a second of incredulity." The phallogocentric system is a fragile one, which does not stand for hesitation, for incredulity, not even for a second: a second would suffice for the entire edifice to crack. This is what is called resistance to castration, a gigantic bastion, but it can fall in a second;

therefore this second must not take place. What is described rapidly for us here is the condition of the subsistence and even of the survival of the inflexible masculine and phallocratic system. What is it that one must never approach? What is it that causes the fall of Icarus? On what does the solidity of phallicity depend?

"Just an instant of weakness and hesitation. But within this system of inflexible last judgment," which he is in, which he lives in like a fortified tower, "which does not permit even a second of incredulity or else the ideal collapses, he looked dumbfounded at the long road." There was a second. The road we have already seen, the road where there was the sphinx, etc., "and everything henceforth was ruined and dry as if he had his mouth full of dust." There is confusion by metonymy between the road and the mouth, the road and his body proper. And we may remember "this poor flesh with which, on climbing into the bus like a monkey, she seemed to have made a fatal path." The path of all flesh which is dust. Here he is with his mouth full of dust, as if that instant where he had seen the girl—who will one day be a mother—was sufficient to give him a taste of death, not of his own death, but of the destiny of every human being, which is dust. "He looked at the long road" and "his mouth full of dust." He looked at the mouth full of dust. With his mouth full of dust. What he takes into his eye he takes into his mouth.

And then we have the tragic moment of this text: "Henceforth and at last alone," without her, but without her he is "without defense." Such are the paradoxes of resistance; he defends himself from being with her, but alone he is without defense against everything, "at the mercy of the eager lie with which *the others* tried to teach him to be a man." In the ambivalence of solitude, he wants to be without her, but without her he is with "the others," whom he does not want. So what can be done?

At this very moment the text remembers in an explosion, *But and the message?!* It is now that we must latch on and try to hear if there is a message, what message. "The message shredded in the dust which the wind carried toward the grill of the sewer. Mama, he said." The last two sentences of the text are nonverbal. "And the message?" Response: "The message shredded . . ." The message is that the message has no verb, the message does not have a word, the message is not, the message is without being; I cannot even say the message *is* shredded. The carried off message, the wind, the dust message, toward the grill of the sewer. Shades of Ecclesiastes. In linguistics, the message is the signified; now the signified is just that: shredded in the dust carried off by the wind. In the logocentric tradition, the message is pure speech, revelation. The message is treated in the poetic mode as a letter in its materiality; but in fact, in its concrete materiality a message has two meanings: it is on the one hand the content, and on the other hand the container, or else, the message, that is the content, is the shredded container. The message: the container shredded in the dust which the wind carries toward the grill of the sewer. You want a message: here it is, says Ecclesiastes: and there is no message. In other words, it's a message. And here is what it gives as a response — it gives: Mama.

Mama, said he. This last sentence is without exclamation point. It is the first time in the story that we find the interpolated clause *he said;* it is also the first word of the nursling. The last word of the text is this *he* (Mama, said he) of the narrative authority. It is the he of a dying person. The he of Icarus who wants to survive. And then *Mama,* to end with. A small boy's word. But where is mama? At the end of this text we do not know what it is the boy names *mama. Mama* calls what or whom? Perhaps the message, perhaps the girl, perhaps the dust, perhaps the road. We do not know. Who is mama? We are in dust. It is as if this last word were saying to us the word which is uttered both by the person being born and by the person dying. Clarice changed the message. As if finally what one could hear is that even in a civilization that wants to conform to the inflexible system which allows not a second of incredulity, and where the woman seen from behind by the man is moved to cower along the wall, even here, being alone is no solution, and what makes itself felt stronger than everything at the very last minute, is the need at least to name mama. To avow. To recognize that the *one* needs the *zero.*

This is because the zero is not the nonvalue we think it is. The originary zero (*zero* comes from the Arabic *sifron,* the cipher, the number) is the key cipher, the one which permits the writing of numbers with the notation of position. To write *10, 100, 1000* we use the same numbers, but the ciphers have different values according to their position in the writing. If I want to say *100* I put the *1* in third position from right to left. Thus I need a first and a second position, I need a position *marker.* The *o* was introduced at first as an empty and necessary position. It is a *space.* Originally zero is not a number, but a marker of space. I transpose my zero in the omnibus and in life. And this is what the boy called *nada,* which is the key to the world for the one. The girl is a nothing which changes the value of the *1* according to its position.

Everything began with zero. Zero is how much there is when there isn't any. When there isn't any, there is, nonetheless. This is what permits us to conceive of the father already no longer father, and the mother not yet mother.

Now I could tell you of the birth of Zero in Babylon, but that would be another story . . .

TRANSLATED BY ERIC PRENOWITZ

REFERENCES

Derrida, Jacques
   1994 *Politiques de l'amitié* (Paris: Galilée).
Joyce, James
   1960 [1934] *Ulysses* (London: Bodley Head).
   1964 [1916] *A Portrait of the Artist as a Young Man* (New York: Viking).
Lispector, Clarice
   1980 [1944] *Perto do coração selvagem* (Rio de Janeiro: Nova Fronteira).
   1981 [1971] "A mensagem," in *Felicidade clandestina,* 125–41 (Rio de Janeiro: Nova Fronteira).
Ovid
   1985 [1955] *Metamorphoses,* translated by Mary M. Innes (London: Penguin).
Rimbaud, Arthur
   1973 [1873] *Une Saison en enfer/A Season in Hell,* translated by Enid Rhodes Peschel (New York: Oxford University Press).

DENIS HOLLIER

LETTER FROM PARIS (FOREIGN MAIL)

PARIS, JUNE 9, 1995

Dear Susan,

After hanging up the telephone, I was seized with a fit of bad conscience. I will continue my defense in writing. Yes, I am late. I should have sent you my contribution several months ago; I had committed myself. I even remember that, in accepting your invitation to participate in the volume on exile, I had a precise idea, if not of what I would say, at least of the text I counted on prompting me to say something, an essay by Hugo von Hofmannsthal, "Gallicisms" (1980a [1897]), written on the occasion of the publication of a textbook titled *Gentilities of the French Language: A Choice of Pretty Words and Expressive Phrases Proper to Giving a Very French Appearance to the Language and Style of Foreigners* (1896).[1]

What happened? Why, when you invited me, did I let myself be tempted? And why, since then, have I obviously done everything to forget this promise? Everything rather than remember it? I made it to you, last year, in New York. I was leaving for Paris for one year. Could I have let myself be overwhelmed by this return to my native country?

That is the excuse I improvised over the telephone, by pleading an unforeseen and selective unavailability. There was doubtless an element of bad faith in that justification made to order. It would have been astonishing if you who are organizing this volume on exile had refused to be swayed by an argument thus framed. One does not write anything anywhere. There is a minimum of "site specificity" in writing; what one writes is never absolutely indifferent to the place (ethnologists would say, the "terrain") in which the writing is being performed.

The argument could moreover be refined and take the form of a performative demonstration: when one is not oneself in the position of the exiled, the most eloquent way of demonstrating the fecundities of exile

---

1. The title in French is *Gentillesses de la langue française, choix de jolis mots et de locutions expressives propres à donner au langage et au style des étrangers un air bien français.*

is to put down one's pen. One does not return to one's home to contribute to the literature of exile: the place would mitigate the message. Proof *a contrario* of the fecundity of exile, I could have sent for your volume a blank page with my signature and the date: Paris, June 9, 1995. The author, having returned home, sent in a nonsubmission.

The argument would have been too beautiful to be true: too formal to be convincing.

It is nonetheless true that my presence in Paris and its limited duration gave priority to other subjects of meditation and objects of research (to keep myself to a studious register). The manuscripts of Michel Leiris, for example, or the archives of French radio, although granted that one day it will no longer be necessary to go to Paris to consult them, have still not been digitalized, have still not entered cyberspace, do not fall under the jurisdiction of "anywhere." They have not yet entered a space with neither places nor frontiers. Have not yet left the closed world for the infinite universe.

JUNE 10, 1995

So blame Paris. Am I going to start believing all these stories? They smack of pretext, of the rationalization of a more profound resistance. Yesterday, on the telephone, your insistence forced me to realize that my desertion was not merely circumstantial. Too bad for Hofmannsthal. This resistance you made me discover interests me. *Voilà.* Here I go.

It interests me because the same conversation made me understand, finally understand (you will excuse my slowness), the reasons for your insistence. Whereas I was hesitating to take my first steps on a terrain for which I was not feeling prepared, a mined terrain conducive to misunderstandings, on which each word is easily overinterpreted, the terrain less of exile itself than of the discourse of exile, you reminded me that I had been there for a long time. "Why new?" you said. "Everything is already in what you say in the introduction to *A New History of French Literature.* You can just return to that." There I was, trapped. Caught in my own snare.

I got out the book.

" 'What French person,' asked Chateaubriand, 'would not smile at the idea of a history of French literature composed outside France's own frontiers?' This *New History of French Literature* has been written from both sides of as many borders as possible" (Hollier 1989: xxv). These are the last lines of the introduction. Let's try to take a closer look. (Adieu to the gentilities of the French language.)

Why not profit from my presence on this side of the border (of one, and not just any one, of the borders generously evoked by those lines) in order to test the sound they make here: take advantage of my passage to the other side (*this* side, *diesseits*) of the border, the side I would call cis-atlantic, the side which was neither that of their sender nor that of their addressee but that of their referent, to see how they cross the border, in order to test the sound they make in the space of their referent.

Moreover, this is not the first time I am rereading these words of mine outside their original context. Two years ago, for the translation of the volume, I had to put them back into French (and, on that occasion, I had changed the title of the introductory text: "On Writing Literary History" had become "Literature without Borders?"). This book, published in English, on American soil, but dedicated to the literature or literatures of the French language, could truly be said to have been "written," at least in the larger sense of the word, from both sides of the border. A border crossed it from the beginning, one that passed between the language in which it was published and that of the literature it treated. How, then, was one to qualify the translation, that passage: import or export? Was it a voyage out or a voyage back for this volume, which returned to the country of its object at the same time that it left that of its language? At once a voyage to and from the native country? For fans of the figure of chiasmus, the translation which distanced it from one of its origins in order to bring it closer to the other was a godsend. But who are those fans? How had this book—which prided itself on being above borders, which claimed its authority from the reversibility of literary space, which claimed equal authority on both sides of the border—crossed the border around which it was itself constituted?

"This *New History of French Literature* has been written from both sides of as many borders as possible." In this sentence, the word which strikes me today is *possible* (as many as *possible*). If I may make an autoexplication of the text, it was supposed to suggest the idea that by multiplying borders, one will end up writing from both sides. As long as there was only a single border, one had to choose one's side. But their multiplication could induce a vertigo that would make one lose one's bearings. The optimism of this sentence results from what I will call (following the analysis proposed by Freud of the multiplication of snakes about the Medusa's head) denial by multiplication. It was a matter, in other words, of drowning the fish. For this optative has been revealed to possess no performative value: the translation of this sentence did not make it across the border. The exchange of smiles did not take place: the wink at Chauteaubriand did not suffice to ward off the condescending smile it was anticipating. This last word, contrary to what it said, butted up against the border, found itself back in the place from whence it came.

Lanson, Valéry, Borges, Genette have developed, each in his own way, the utopia of a history of literature which would finesse proper names. But the names of countries are proper names, too. And although the idea of delivering literary space from national constraints is not without nobility, it would be absurd to want to keep for that same deterritorialized literature its national frame. Literature without frontiers, so be it. But a French literature without frontiers? Why not a France without frontiers?

This fantasy—of a history of French literature that would have cut off all access to what Jean-Claude Milner calls "the signifier France" (1984: 128)—evokes a sequel to *Blade Runner,* "The Return of the Memory Snatchers." Extraterrestrials, natives (or rather, nonnatives) of a space without frontiers, of a space without geography (a psychasthenic space), have decided to invade a literature which continues to call itself French. They have learned by heart the sites of memory. But that's only a figure of speech: their hearts are not in it. One feels that they force themselves to remember in order to speak in the first person. Their tone rings false, like those foreigners we admire, who astonish us, who make us feel nervous because they speak our language without an accent. In the end, we always notice that frontiers leave them indifferent, that they do not even perceive them, that they see no difference between a voyage out and a voyage back, between a departure and an arrival. One sees that they come from another space, that they come from elsewhere, from anywhere, "anywhere out of this world," outside of the closed world, from a world without frontiers, without proper names, without names for countries, without places. The space of neon. Of neo-. New world, the world of the new. New England. New York. New Orleans. New History of French Literature. It's neo-French.

JUNE 12, 1995

I don't see very clearly to which of your categories I belong: to exile, certainly not, nor to emigration.

I remember that, after I had left France (for Italy), the first review copy I received was Derrida's *La Dissémination* (1972). Without a dedication but that's another story, to which Derrida referred in a separate note (it forms part of the history of *Tel Quel*). *La Dissémination* reprints "Plato's Pharmacy," which I had heard (in 1968) in Paris, and had read in *Tel Quel*. I read it again in my new cisalpine space.

A number of us were seduced by the simultaneously topological and topographical reading of Plato's *Phaedrus* with which this essay opens. Phaedrus lures Socrates outside of Athens by promising to read him a speech by the sophist Lysias which he has just procured. With extraordinary deftness, Derrida interlaces these two reroutings: that of discourse put on reserve by writing and that of Socrates, whom this same writing makes deviate from his right path. He associates Socrates' resistance to writing with his refusal to leave Athens, up to and including fire or hemlock. Socrates: he who does not write, but also he who never left Athens. Foreign to the foreign, he prefers death to exile. He will refuse to live if that means he must cross the city's border. He always thought, and philosophized, within earshot. Hence the importance Derrida attaches to this extramural excursion, which he goes so far as to call an *exodus*. "The thin pages of writing act as a *pharmakon* which pushes or lures outside of the city the one who never wanted to leave it" (Derrida 1972: 79). Writing is already in and of itself proof of the foreigner.

What relation does this have to *A New History of French Literature*? Shall we say that, like Socrates lured by Lysias's writing, a literature, seduced by writing, allowed itself to be carried outside the walls, abroad? A literature infatuated with writing to the point where it would have forgotten not only, as did Plato's cicadas, to drink and to eat, but moreover and especially, to speak. I arrived in the United States during an epoch when the most anodyne reference to writing, never mind the language in which it was made, sufficed in order for an angel to pass — in French. From the celebration of intransitive writing by Barthes to Derrida's grammatology, a religious silence, whether approving or not, accompanied the evocation of "what the French call *écriture*." Protected by distance against the illusions of phonocentrism, the French reference prospered by virtue of writing, acceding, far from the places where one might actually hear it, to the status of the astonishing, the unheard-of. No longer having to answer to its spoken version, like a shadow emancipated from its object. A language which prospered through writing, far from the paternalism or patriarchy of speech.

Should we regret that a language loses its voice upon exportation, that it leaves its linguistic frontiers only by renouncing speech, by becoming a silent and unheard *traviata*? A language: any language? According to a view profoundly anchored in the national linguistic consciousness, French is constantly threatened by a graphic schism, threatened with scission into two languages, the written and the spoken (one thinks of Malherbe, Céline, Queneau). As if writing were actually exposing the French language to an alienation at the end of which it risked becoming a language foreign to itself. What would be a French language which, in being written, would be distanced from itself to the point of detaching, of separating from itself?

Have we not ourselves, year after year, experienced this widening separation between an oral and a written French, that is, a foreigner's French, often qualified in France as a French for exportation? A French for places where French is not spoken. A French without gentility, as Hofmannsthal's professor would have styled it. And I will not trace here the etymology of the word *genteel*.

JUNE 13, 1995

I don't know if I told you that, since my return to (or my arrival in) Paris, I have been struck by the recentering of the French cultural consciousness around oral or phonetic motifs (a Francophonocentrism). And I'm not thinking only of the motif of a Francophony which would oppose (inside as well as outside France's borders) the French language to other, competing languages, nor even of a Francophony which it would not be absurd to oppose to a Francography (in which knowledge of French deals essentially with written material: reading knowledge). Nor am I thinking of the multiplication of sound libraries, the growing importance of sound archives, oral history, the memory of voices, radiophonic culture. Mind you, it is quite possible that this recentering is less recent than I think. For lack of living in France, for lack of being within earshot, it could very well have escaped me. Nevertheless, one almost has the impression that the French (those on the inside) are not having too much difficulty abandoning writing to those "outside." They celebrate speech without worrying too much about the accusations of phonocentrism to which they thus expose themselves.

Graphic decentering, oral recentering. Writing outside, speech inside. They abandon to the foreigner a writing which is emancipated from speech. But is this only about space, about a division of spheres of influence between speech and writing? If a series which, thirty years ago, began by publishing Michel Foucault celebrates today the sites of memory (*Les Lieux de mémoire,* published by Gallimard in the "Bibliothèque des Sciences Humaines" series), does this mutation arise only from a geopolitics of language? The so-called 1968 generation privileged centrifugal spaces: writing and deterritorialization. Today, in reaction, one returns to gathering shared memories and to oral history. One is busy, to quote Derrida, keeping the outside outside.

Marc Fumaroli's contributions to the last volumes of *Les Lieux de mémoire,* "Conversation" (La Conversation [1992]) and "The Genius of the French Language" (Le Génie de la langue française [1993]) are a striking example of this recentering. This return of speech does not present itself as a criticism of deconstruction. The two discourses do not seem to cross paths (do not respond to each other). Deconstruction speaks of phonocentrism, of the historico-metaphysical epoch of the sign. It avoids proper names, uses them only with prudence and under erasure or between quotation marks. An important part of Derrida's strategy suspends nominal references. In fact, he even associates writing with what he calls the original effacement of the proper name (Derrida 1967: 159). Fumaroli, for his part, begins by reintroducing the proper name. He is not dealing with the problems of deconstruction (metaphysics or the reversal of metaphysics), nor even with those of linguistics. For one can talk about phonocentrism, and the abasement of writing with which Derrida associates it (the demotion of writing to the rank of servant, of supplement, etc.), without referring to any natural language in particular. Fumaroli's object is a philology that, because it always bears upon a singular object, Milner (1978) has called love of the language. Everything follows from the choice of this singular love object and the utterance of its proper name.

Fumaroli's object is not phonocentrism but the French language, a language bound to the "oral secret of correct speech" (Fumaroli 1992: 699). "In order to last," he writes, "the French literary text must borrow the apparent oral facility, the sonorous happiness of live speech addressed to someone" (ibid.: 689–90). Literature in France makes a vocation of "high fidelity": writing has no say in the matter except to submit itself to the master's voice. Thus French literature triumphs in the genres close to orality. The great genre is that of the *Mémoires,* which Fumaroli characterizes as "*written* oral improvisations" (ibid.). Malherbe: he was "all the more careful not to make of them a *written* language, in mourning for voice and hearing" (Fumaroli 1993: 938). Concerning Marivaux: "To listen to Marivaux is to hear once again 'voices which have fallen silent,' their harmonies, their melody, their ingenuity. . . . The high fidelity of written literature thus preserves, if not the letter, at least the spirit of those circles which aspired to being 'Islands of the Blessed' " (Fumaroli: 1992: 709). Proust reproached Sainte-Beuve for having placed literature on the same level as conversation. But for Fumaroli, books are everything but the children of silence. "For Sainte-Beuve, a French work is literary because it is the written, lasting echo chamber of a cultivated society and its voices" (ibid.: 722). It is no longer speech which asks the written word to endure, but the written word which lives and survives because it has known how to preserve speech. Strangely, Derrida had also wished for the end of the book, but he saw in this the beginning of writing, not the return to the reign of conversation and live speech.

This restoration of speech to its position of authority entails a system of political metaphors whose inspiration recalls Charles Péguy's. In "Plato's Pharmacy," Derrida commented on the myth of the origin of writing proposed by the *Phaedrus.* Thamous, King of Egypt, is suspicious when Teuth proposes his invention to him. What need does a king have for writing? "His word suffices" (Derrida 1972: 86). "Writing will have value only if and in the measure that God-the-King determines" (ibid.). These could be Fumaroli's words, with the slight difference that he wouldn't use quotation marks. The merging of the motifs of royalty and living speech is the axis of his celebration of a language he qualifies as "French and royal" (Fumaroli 1993: 914). "This kingdom, one can never insist upon this enough, subordinates the written word to speech" (ibid.: 944). Beyond revolutions, France will remain faithful to its monarchical vocation as long as French will continue to be spoken there. Literature, our kingdom of France.

This reverse parallel between the gestures of Derrida and Fumaroli could be extended. Socrates' excursion (or exodus) in the *Phaedrus* has its equivalent in Fumaroli's essay, in the figure of Dante. Dante's exile is the occasion for a comparison of the literary and political destinies of the Île-de-France and Tuscany: "for want of kings, [Tuscany] had poets" (ibid.: 924). Dante is a "poetic monarch in exile" (ibid.). We are at the antipodes of the "sacre de l'écrivain," the consecration of the writer.[2] The sacralization of literature compensates for political powerlessness. Exile is responsible for a poetic inflation on the part of a literature in mourning for its language. Commenting upon the theses developed by Dante in *De vulgari eloquentia,* Fumaroli writes: "These foundations remain in the realm of the written text, not speech. They authorize a literature, not a kingdom: a written literary language, and not a living social and political bond."

A final example. Fumaroli — and this is one of the reasons why he prefers the seventeenth to the eighteenth century — does not share the compulsory enthusiasm concerning the universality of the French language in the eighteenth century. The kingdom was undermined by those faraway triumphs. Language, extending beyond the frontiers of the kingdom, "was escaping its control" and "the nascent universality began, as early as the reign of Louis XIV, to turn against French royalty" (ibid.: 964). On this subject, he quotes a sentence of the Abbé Desfontaines that one could perhaps have written on the walls of French departments when its first half still had a semblance of pertinence: "What is the source of this attraction for the language, joined to an aversion for the nation?" (ibid.). It all hangs together. It is fashionable to speak of traveling thought, but languages do not travel. He who loves his language must abide by the fable of the two pigeons. Lovers, happy lovers. Stick to nearby shores, avoid faraway driftings. Derrida: "Keep the outside outside" (1972: 147).

Obviously, this evolution poses all sorts of practical difficulties for those of us who teach French abroad. For, as opposed to the tragedies of Racine, the *Mémoires* of Saint-Simon, or the *Lundis* of Sainte-Beuve, conversation, that literary essence of France, does not export. Sartre used to say that jazz, like bananas, must be consumed on the spot: the same holds true for conversation. It is a genre which only exists around Saint-Germain des Près or La Muette. The more oral these cultural objects are, the less they are transportable. Conversations cannot be bought at the FNAC, do not benefit from tax breaks upon exportation. Bad object for any dream of *translatio studii.*

2. I allude here to Paul Bénichou's classic study of the rise of the writer in the nineteenth century (1973).

It is all the more significant to see Fumaroli's "The Genius of the French Language" being selected to conclude the editorial undertaking of the seven volumes called *Sites of Memory*. Indeed, memory reunites relatives but keeps at a distance those who do not share our past. It maintains itself in the "sites" where one finds shelter from those whom those sites remind of nothing. Shelter from the *memory snatchers*. The sites of memory protect against the space of "anywhere" (which rhymes with "l'univers"). The ritual collectivization of memory reunites the ensemble of subjects who can pronounce the same sentences in the first person. Me too, I remember. I too remember this or that. Those memories are also mine. Me too, I remember that for a long time I went to bed early.

Must one impose on literature the first person plural? Should literature be reduced to a "site of memory"? After all, the first words of *A la recherche du temps perdu* are not "For a long time we all went to bed early."

JUNE 15, 1995

I have been wanting to talk for a long time about "Gallicismes," a short text that could be claimed by a dubious genre, the discourse of the presentation of a medal to a worthy servant. Hofmannsthal wrote it on the occasion of the publication by his former French tutor, Gabriel Dubray, of a French manual destined for Austrian travelers, *Gentilities of the French Language*. One may find in it the idealized portrait of the language professor abroad: as the language in this case is French, I could never read those lines without finding in them, *ready-made,* a sort of self-portrait (or a self-caricature) by proxy.

Gabriel Dubray was Swiss. Why did he leave his native country for Austria? Hofmannsthal says nothing about it. But from the manner in which he speaks of this prisoner who was his professor, it is probable that this exile (Hofmannsthal uses the word) nourished his pupil's adolescent imagination. He did so sufficiently, in any case, to inspire him to write this sentence: "I truly believe that no one, not even poets, loves his language so much as the exiled" (Hofmannsthal 1980a [1897]: 73).

The exiled who become foreign language teachers: an ungrateful country may have obliged them to renounce everything except their language, expelled them from every paradise except that of their mother tongue. No matter where, "anywhere out of the world," until their last breath, those irreducible irredentists will remain intractable linguistic foreign bodies (xenophones), faithful to their native language.

Did Gabriel Dubray's teaching also include literature? Perhaps it was Montaigne, encountered through Dubray as intermediary, who taught Hofmannsthal that love of the language should not be sought among philologists. It is only to be found among the last aristocrats, the exiled, those who scorn the vulgarity of modern nations, etc. To love one's language, he says, one must miss it. The philologists' tragedy is that it would not occur to anyone to exile them: they would have to be noticed first. Those who teach their language abroad were once "real men": "banished princes, discharged officers, unknown poets, disappointed actors, young girls who have too many brothers and sisters, students, inventors, outlaws"; they have "become by chance professors of language" (ibid.: 69).

If the exile stoops to teach, it is not because he must stay alive, but because he cannot live without speaking his language. But precisely, exile washes away the sin of teaching, *it cleanses from the sin of teaching* those princes, officers, poets, etc., those male or female Toscas, who, for love of their language, have agreed to prostitute themselves on teaching's streets. One can illustrate with a more noble scenario the separation between the nobility of those hearts and the baseness of their work: by evoking, for example, the storybook prince who disguised himself as a servant in order to be able to live near his beloved. "And nearly always it happens that they teach their own language in a foreign country" (ibid.). *Gentilities of the French Language* is a celebration of orality, complementary in many respects to that of *Babette's Feast*.

These noble thoughts were inspired in Hofmannsthal by the honorable Gabriel Dubray, a Swiss speaker of French. However, if one believes Fumaroli and the tradition he speaks for, nothing is less French, nothing is more contrary to the genius of the French language, than this image heroized through the loving projection of a foreign student. It is the most un-French view of French to imagine it as a language loved only from afar, from the outside, from which one would take pleasure through distance, remoteness, silence. Even if it is a French professor who supports it, such a projection attests to an essentially Germanic conception of love of the language: Hofmannsthal speaks elsewhere of the "German mania for what is foreign" (1980d [1926]: 381).

The same idealization of the foreigner's status inspires Hofmannsthal's "Letters from a Voyager upon His Return," but it no longer detours through an identification with the other. It is no longer necessary for the Austrian writer to dream of a Frenchman's exile. Independently of the different nationalities of their authors, the two texts point to inverse situations. Gabriel Dubray, by a typically French linguistic hospitality, wanted to initiate his Viennese readers into the *gentilities* that would allow them to pass for native Frenchmen on the terraces of Parisian cafés. The voyager of the "Letters" is animated by the inverse movement, centrifugal rather than centripetal. The native who has returned (revenu) feels spectral, nearly a ghost (revenant), and dreams of leaving again. The pattern is that of Gide's Prodigal Son, who comes back only in order to leave again, in order to win over his brother to the seductions of distance. It's not a question of convincing foreigners that they will feel at home among us, but rather of showing that an Austro-German is at home only when he is not at home. For such a person, there is no such thing as a one-way trip. The voyage out is always already shaped as a voyage back. One does not lose less in coming back than one gained in leaving.

The traveler has roamed over all the continents. In the most exotic lands, each time a spectacle moved him, he writes "I thought to myself: home!" (Hofmannsthal 1980c [1907]: 177). "In the same way I *was* in Germany each time that something in Uruguay, or Canton, or finally on the islands, touched my soul" (ibid.: 178). Far away, an epiphany sufficed: small naked children, the frugality of an old Chinese man, the gaze of a gaucho's daughter. Here, nothing calls out to him. He needed to be in others' homes in order to feel at home. He never felt so much in Germany as when he was outside her borders. He has a passion for Germany structured by what neo-Lacanians call "extimacy." And that is how this voyager represents the quintessence of Germany. The Germans? "I can find them nowhere," he writes, "because the totality of their being is no longer anywhere, because in truth they are nowhere" (ibid.: 183). This "cahier d'un retour au pays natal," as Aimé Césaire would call it, this notebook of a return to the native country glorifies the chiasmuses of *Unheimlichkeit*. Whence the troubadour linguistics which organizes the many versions of the heart in love with its language that one finds in Hofmannsthal: seductive because abandoned, a mother tongue is never more beautiful than when one has left it; never more alive in us than when we no longer live in it. Such, at least, is the case with German, even if the apprenticeship of this chiasmus was done by proxy, through the mother tongue of the other.

As for Hofmannsthal's opinion of the French language, it is not fundamentally different from the one echoed by Fumaroli. One has but to look at the pages titled, appropriately, "Conversation in Salé," a dialogue on the comparative virtues of the two languages which unfolds in an upliftingly austere colonial setting (the Moroccan desert). Chiasmus rules the scene: it's Hofmannsthal who pays tribute to French and his interlocutor, Pierre Viénot, a French officer, to German. Hofmannsthal (jealous of French): "Your conversation is purely and simply the intellectual omnipresence of the nation" (Hofmannsthal 1980b [1907]: 366). Viénot (on the glory of German): "Inconvenient, but grandiose. Unsociable . . . unaware of the world's rules . . . but carrying a world in itself" (ibid.: 370). German risks devouring those who choose it to express themselves. "What a possibility, however, for genius to reach, in this language, nearly beyond the frontiers of humanity!" (ibid.: 371).

JUNE 18, 1995

I need hardly say that this way of being at home only on the other side of the border, this way for a community to begin only where it ends (beginning at its border as the Phoenix rises from its ashes) complicates the geography of exile. For if the return to one's native country is the true test of exile, or rather if one is equally, indifferently exiled on both sides of the border, then there is no longer a difference between exile and its contrary, between exile and anything at all.

Perhaps one can have today a slightly easy exile? A slightly metaphysical (and poetic) exile? Today, Gabriel Dubray's manual would be entitled rather *Gentilities of Exile*. Or *Exile without Pain*. Or, why not, *Exile at Home*. Could exile have ceased to be a punishment? A condemnation? Is it not curious to see an epoch that, following Walter Benjamin, tracks the aestheticization of politics, that values so highly exilographers and exilophiles? For if the fundamental equation of fascist aesthetics identifies the production of beauty with the destruction of utility, this equation is not an exclusivity of war: exile also aims, in its own way, to render useless if not productive goods, at least individuals. To keep them from being useful, that is, to "neutralize their ability to harm" — not by destroying them, but by decontextualizing them. If the aestheticization of war is a fascist symptom, that of exile could very well be its leftist equivalent. Can one be sure that the result of what Brecht called *Verfremdungseffekt* is really of the political order, without an aesthetic plus value?

A historian of the Second World War has recently criticized the growing metaphorization of the word: everybody wants to be exiled. But, in order to speak of exile, a political or judicial decision must forbid the exile's return. Not only must the community deprive him of the means to live, it must refuse him the right to live there (Bédarida 1989).

Thus the portrait of the condition of the (German) writer that emerges from Albrecht Betz's (1991) study of German emigration to Paris during the Hitler period is very far from the nostalgic anxieties and the poetic gentilities that the theme inspired in Hofmannsthal. Certainly, it goes without saying, some of those refugees were reduced (like Gabriel Dubray, even if for less pure motives than love of the language) to teaching German (one thinks of the Von Stroheim character in the film by Claude Autant-Lara, *Les Disparus de Saint-Agil*). It is nonetheless true, and hardly surprising, that these years of exile were not a happy period on either the linguistic or the literary level. Exile obliged the majority of those writers to bracket their love of the language, to leave behind not only Germany, but also literature, or at least literature as they had conceived and practiced it in Germany. Exile and engagement: the chiasmus which Betz describes is nearly the inverse of Hofmannsthal's. "The majority of emigrants," Betz writes, "in the situation imposed on them, abandoned as a lost illusion the idea of a pure literature, free from the convulsions of politics. . . . 'To make "literature" today is pure escapism,' writes Döblin in 1935 to Thomas Mann" (ibid.: 131).

JUNE 20, 1995

For the publication of the French edition of *A New History of French Literature*, the editor asked me to write, in the guise of a *captatio benevolentiae* intended for the book's new public (not just *any* public), an ad hoc presentation that would stroke the horse's neck and encourage it to take the bit. In a word, that would, despite the distance, make this history of French literature recognizable to the French.

But this kind of gentle text must be precisely what I am incapable of writing. My addition was much less courteous. To wit: "1989. On the occasion of the bicentennial of the French Revolution, Harvard University Press publishes *A New History of French Literature*" (subtitle— borrowed from Montesquieu's *Lettres persanes—How Can Anyone Be French?*). In a general tone of lamentation or "deploration" concerning

French language-and-literature, I organized the article around an un-easiness shared by many French authors today: Why are the Americans no longer interested in us?

I was anticipating the resistances (the smiles) that its claim to having been written on both sides of the border would garner in France for this so patently American book. As if it were enough to evoke this ambition to see it immediately contradicted: the border in question closes and a space is created in which, like two china dogs, each on its side of the Atlantic, a literature and its history, a literary history and its referent, stare at each other, break off all contact, all dialogue, all negotiation, decide to maintain separate rooms. On the French side: the literature refuses to recognize itself in the discourses it elicits abroad. On the American side: the authorized discourse about French literature clamors more and more loudly that it is still hungry, that what its object serves up is very little and no longer suffices. That in order to survive it will move to more nourishing fields.

But my first idea for the additional article had been quite different. It would have closed the book on a note at once more optimistic (a "happy end," as we say in French) and less self-referential. The entry would have been called: "1990. The original edition of *Immortality*, by Milan Kundera, is published in French." With a subtitle: "A New Recruit." Instead of concluding on the disappointments of exportation, this history of French literature would have concluded on its latest conquest through importation.

I will not go into the complicated arithmetic of the reasons which made me abandon this idea. I will mention only two of them. There was first the fact that *L'Immortalité* was not written in French: although its French version is copyrighted as the original edition, it mentions a translator, Eva Bloch. (Kundera is credited with revising the translation, but it was not until *Les testaments trahis* [1994] that the mention of a translator disappears from his work.) But there was a more substantial reason: Kundera did not leave one national literature for another. By no longer having himself translated from the Czech, he did not enter *into* French literature, he came *out* of exile. The border crossed in 1970 gradually underwent a radical transformation, in the course of years spent in France. It separated first two national spaces, two linguistic spaces; now it passes between national literatures and a genre which, Kundera says, is essentially transnational, the novel. Exile and disengagement: the movement here is the inverse of what Betz had described. Hofmannsthal saw in exile a "beyond" of poetry. Kundera sees in the novel a "beyond" of exile. The novel, he repeats, is required for the denationalization of exile.

And this is one of its major differences from the French national literary genre, conversation. Strictly speaking, one could say that Kundera's conversion to French, failing to be a conversion to the genius of this language, does not open to him the gates of French literature, even less so if one accepts the hierarchy of genres which Fumaroli makes a part of his definition: it is not a conversion to conversation, nor to the literary forms which assign conversation pride of place. "There is an essential difference," Kundera insists, "for example, between the novel on the one hand and, on the other, *Mémoires,* biography, autobiography" (1994: 307).

JUNE 21, 1995

I must leave you, although there would remain an infinity of paths to follow.

I will sketch just this one to conclude: Several weeks ago, *Le Monde* published an article by Kundera which began with a denunciation of the nationalization of literature by the university. "University practice examines literature almost exclusively in its national frame. . . . I have always found this practice limited" (Kundera 1995: 1). This condemnation, it seems to me, aims at two different targets and involves two types of borders: national borders on the one hand, and the border between literature and the university on the other.

National borders are emphasized by the academic importation of a foreign literature, which is accompanied, in effect, by a contextualizing discourse. Pedagogical internationalization attempts, paradoxically, to make of literature a national, historico-cultural symptom. It is difficult not to agree with this view. It is also difficult for someone within the university to remedy it. At a time when departments of comparative literature are being absorbed by cultural studies programs, if one abandons the frame of national literatures, chances are it won't be to the benefit of anything like a transnational literature.

Which poses the question of the other border, the one that runs between literature and the university. This is the one that counts for Kundera; the nationalization of literature is only one of his numerous complaints against the university. To cite the title of his first real French book, the one he published exactly one year ago when I arrived in France, the university is the place where one is trained in betraying testaments (Kundera 1994). The university is the place where dead writers are read against their will. Where one learns (and demonstrates) that a testament never arrives at its destination.

One could ask here whether Kundera, exiled in Paris, did not choose the French language because literature in France owes relatively little to the university. But that will be for another time.

I must prepare for my return. The fall semester approaches, sabbatical is over. *Back to school.* Adieu, Paris.

Excuse me for having been so long, so late.

TRANSLATED BY MARTI HOHMANN AND SUSAN R. SULEIMAN

REFERENCES

Bédarida, François
  1989 *De l'exil à la résistance: Réfugiés et immigrés d'Europe Centrale en France, 1933–1945* (Paris: Arcanterie).
Bénichou, Paul
  1973 *Le Sacre de l'écrivain* (Paris: Gallimard).
Betz, Albrecht
  1991 *Exil et engagement: Les Intellectuels allemands et la France,* translated by Pierre Rausch (Paris: Gallimard).
Derrida, Jacques
  1967 *De la grammatologie* (Paris: Minuit).
  1972 *La Dissémination* (Paris: Minuit).
Fumaroli, Marc
  1992 "La conversation," in *Les Lieux de mémoire,* edited by Pierre Nora, 3: 678–743 (Paris: Gallimard).
  1993 "Le Génie de la langue française," in *Les Lieux de mémoire,* edited by Pierre Nora, 3: 910–73 (Paris: Gallimard).
Hofmannsthal, Hugo von
  1980a [1897] "Gallicismes," in *Lettre de Lord Chandos et autres essais,* translated by Albert Kohn and Jean-Claude Schneider, 68–74 (Paris: Gallimard).
  1980b [1907] "La Conversation de Salé," in *Lettre de Lord Chandos et autres essais,* translated by Albert Kohn and Jean-Claude Schneider, 363–71 (Paris: Gallimard).
  1980c [1907] "Lettres du voyageur à son retour," in *Lettre de Lord Chandos et autres essais,* translated by Albert Kohn and Jean-Claude Schneider, 174–212 (Paris: Gallimard).
  1980d [1926] "La Revue européene," in *Lettre de Lord Chandos et autres essais,*

translated by Albert Kohn and Jean-Claude Schneider, 377–88 (Paris: Galli-mard).

Hollier, Denis, ed.

  1989 *A New History of French Literature* (Cambridge, MA: Harvard University Press).

  1993 *De la littérature française,* with François Rigolot (Paris: Bordas).

Kundera, Milan

  1994 *Les Testaments trahis* (Paris: Gallimard).

  1995 "L'Art de la fidélité," *Le Monde des livres* (May 26): 1.

Milner, Jean-Claude

  1978 *L'Amour de la langue* (Paris: Seuil).

  1984 *De l'école* (Paris: Seuil).

TRAVELERS

DORIS SOMMER

AT HOME ABROAD:

EL INCA SHUTTLES WITH HEBREO

Di, pues, ya; y si vieres que se indigna contra ti, desdezirte has de lo que huvieres dicho y pedirle has perdon. . . . Ya puedes dezir lo que se te antojare, que segun veo, bien sabes el modo de rescatarte.

(Say it, then, already; and if you see that he becomes indignant against you, you must unsay what you have said and ask his pardon. . . . You can already say whatever you want, because as far as I can see, you're the master of rescuing yourself.)

SOPHÍA, in *Diálogos de amor*

THE "INCA GARCILASO."[1] His very name is an oxymoron that forces together two imperial codes without reconciling them. It also condenses a personal history of impossible translations between mother tongue and fatherland, a history of borrowed and inexact belongings. As part of the New World and as a participant in its Spanish renewal, Garcilaso is a guide back to a classic past and forward to a modern empire. The bilateral movement is practically in his blood. His name announces a story of passionate crossings, violent contact, reversals, and doubled identities. A royal Peruvian mother and her aristocratic Spanish conqueror managed to produce a remarkable child in 1539, just after Francisco Pizarro's easy triumph over an internally divided empire. But the Castilian-speaking captain didn't develop his desire into marital love for the Quechua-speaking Incan (by 1549 he had married a Spanish girl), perhaps because the passionate parents never learned each other's language. Their son's name commemorates the double nobility of his bifurcated heritage, and the incommensurable clash.

Christened in 1539 as Gómez Suárez de Figueroa, the future author of the *Royal Commentaries of the Incas* (1609), as well as of *La Florida* (1605) and *Garci Pérez* (1596), would sign his books with an assumed and more

I am grateful to Joseph Dan for his generous contributions to this essay.
1. English translations are mine.

illustrious name. It had belonged to his deceased father, whose name he had been signing anyway as his sire's scribe and confidant. The son hoped, no doubt, to take the place, and the pension, that the conqueror's name promised in Spain's legal order. When Captain Sebastián Garcilaso de la Vega died in 1559, leaving the beloved bastard enough money and unmistakable instructions to study in Spain, the young man left ancient Cuzco for a new world.

There he tried, like his father's generation of warriors in Peru, to win glory and privilege as a soldier, fighting bravely, for example, in the War of Alpujarras to put down rebels of Moorish descent. But the *mestizo* scourge of rebellious *moriscos* never advanced very far as military defender of the empire, either in rank or in the progressively more pressing issue of salary. Spaniards were evidently reading him wrong, as a half-breed, a misfit, an unauthorized outsider. In response, Garcilaso would spend his next career showing that each half was a whole in its own right, that he was an insider both here and there, and that with both Peruvian and peninsular parents of noble lineage, he was doubly authorized as privileged participant in both worlds. With unquestionable authority, then, he put down the ungrateful sword and began to wield a more promising pen that would endorse his self-authorized name: El Inca Garcilaso de la Vega. But prefixing the legitimating Spanish name with a royal title from his mother's Tahuantisuyu, proclaiming a bicultural pride, was also saying too much. The foreign title appended to Spanish nobility was a destabilizing supplement in the paranoid purity of Inquisitorial language. Garcilaso would later learn to deploy the loopholed logic of supplements; but first he was its victim. His cultural as well as legal claims to Spain foundered on the dangerously doubled identity of a youth who declared that he was at home abroad.

"As his name is, so is he," goes the Hebrew saying. The doubly dignifying signature did more than signal entitlements; it apparently also gave some unimpressed authorities signs of divided loyalty and inconstancy. The ambitious youth evidently chose to meet that danger through the problematic but promising name. That he took pride in the family name is obvious. Garcilaso de la Vega was not only the venerated captain in Cuzco, so generous and popular that he became the target of invidious reports by rivals, and the defendant of elegantly written responses by his son the scribe. The name also belonged to perhaps the best poet of the Spanish Renaissance, and to more relatives who were famous bards and ambassadors: the Marqués de Santillana, Fernán Pérez de Guzmán, Pero

López de Ayala, the Manriques. No wonder the overseas scion of such literary and legislative glory chose to activate that lineage, using the kind of sympathetic magic that changes reality with a merely nominal adjustment.

If I invoke a Hebrew expression to describe the Inca Garcilaso's belated, even nostalgic self-fashioning, the borrowed words are not entirely out of place. Because the place of frustrated homecomings is Spain, where the category of alienated national had become almost synonymous with Hebrews, and Hebreo was literally the name of an exiled Jew whose book Garcilaso would translate from Italian into Spanish as his apprenticeship in writing. León Hebreo's *Dialoghi d'amore* (1535) is a Neoplatonic treatise in two voices that shuttles between classical and Mosaic codes of belief, as the lover Philón reads them allegorically and explains their compatibility to his wise Sophía. She never gets enough of his talk and finds endless details for him to develop.[2]

Writing became Garcilaso's career in a kind of internal exile, after his attempt to win an inheritance fell flat, ostensibly because of his father's double-dealing with the Crown. Captain Sebastián had insisted he was loyal to the Spanish crown, but histories documented his "treacherous" loyalty to Gonzalo Pizarro. The brother of Peru's leading conqueror had been loath to cede his privileges to anyone, including the king of Spain, who had decided to curtail the conquerors' control by limiting their entitlements. During the civil war that followed, Pizarro saved his own

---

2. Publishing the exercise was another matter. For one thing, the performance might have seemed redundant, only six years after Carlos Montesa had published his Spanish translation in Zaragoza (1584). Garcilaso may have been unaware of the work, despite the meticulously documented and time-consuming process of Inquisitorial approval and public licensing that publishing involved. Could he have overlooked a book by a professor at an established Spanish university, a book that had recently gotten through the same publication procedure, and the same church and state apparatus, that Garcilaso would have appealed to? It makes a reader wonder if he was indeed performing a translator's service for other readers, or if he was simply performing as an actor does, taking on the role of intellectual weaver in Hebreo's script. Through the translation, Garcilaso may well have been laying public claim to Hebreo, openly impersonating a voice that might well have been originally Spanish, and bringing it home. Maybe he was maneuvering an engagement that would recognize Hebreo's (and the translator's) Spanish legitimacy. Probably so. Yet, the likely editorial redundance was only one reason for readers to ponder Garcilaso's choice. Another was the nature of the dialogues: they were difficult and apparently so foreign to Garcilaso's indigenist interests.

mutinous life by escaping on the horse that Sebastián offered him. Garcilaso was sure that the allegations of treason were exaggerated, that his father's service to the state far outshone the small stain that the courts first ignored but later stubbornly inspected. And the son persisted for years on behalf of, and in, his father's good name. He was also entitled to something, or should have been, as an Incan aristocrat. Guamán Poma de Ayala was making his own appeal on precisely those grounds, and Rolena Adorno underlines his objections to countrymen so undone by the Spanish conquest that they failed to engage its opportunities for legal petitioning (Adorno 1992: 391). Garcilaso's persistent engagement was neither desperate nor naive. In fact he proudly points out that his defense of Incan nobility had practical results (González-Echevarría 1990: 124). The label "mestizo" was therefore not simply a stamp of corrupted blood. "I call myself mestizo openly, and do myself honor thereby," writes the slightly self-defensive chronicler (Garcilaso 1609, pt. 1, bk. 9, chap. 31). But more often than not, extramarital mestizo "heirs" inherited more legal hot air than anything else. Whatever legitimate or hopeful appeals Garcilaso could voice as the beloved son of his heroic father were muted by louder concerns in Spain's courts.

The country was waging an internal crusade to establish *pureza de sangre:* "natural children," as illegitimate offspring were delicately known (are legitimate children unnatural in baroque Spanish?), were vulnerable to legal dispute, especially in the case of a visibly mixed-blood bastard. The authorities had their reasons, and Garcilaso mentions some by name. His ex-schoolmates Juan Arias Maldonado and Pedro del Barco are two such reasons. These Hispanized mestizos had led significant interregional rebellions during the rash of resistance between 1562 and 1567 (ibid., pt. 2, bk. 8, chap. 17). And the rebellions would recur for a long time, sometimes fueled by the past glories that Peruvians read out of the *Commentaries* themselves. The most notorious case is the war against Spain led by a direct descendant of the last Incas, Tupaq Amaru, who had been reading the indigenous history before his campaign of 1780–81. José Mazzotti's recent study reads backwards from the sometimes aggressively Andean appeal of the *Comentarios reales* to argue that they have a dual appeal: along with the evidently European bias that celebrates the improvements of Spanish civilization over the already formidable achievements of the Incas, there is a Peruvian perspective. It is pitched to insiders as an expert guide to political and cultural survival (Mazzotti 1993).

A memorable passage in Garcilaso's writing will try to legitimate the very expression *hijo natural* precisely as homeboy, he who has undeniable rights and privileges in his father's, and his mother's, houses. But significantly, the passage describes his own reception in Portugal, not in Spain. It describes the friendly fiction of belonging there, as if to underline rather than to erase his foreignness. In Portugal, "la primera tierra que vi cuando vine de la mía, que es el Perú" (the first land I saw when I came from my own, which is Peru), generous and God-fearing people of the islands and the capital received him "*como si yo fuera hijo natural de alguna de ellas*" (as if I were one of their homeboys) (Garcilaso 1605: "Dedicatoria"; my emphasis). In one gesture of appreciation of (and appeal for support to) the Portuguese, Garcilaso dedicated *La Florida* (1605) to Teodosio de Braganza, explaining that many of the duke's countrymen had accompanied Hernando de Soto on the famous, if inconclusive, expedition. How could the Incan immigrant have imagined that another natural child of Lisbon was León Hebreo, Garcilaso's literary and philosophical trainer? And, what is still more striking, Hebreo's father had ties with the very same Braganza family that Garcilaso was courting. Those ties turned out to be so damaging at court that they forced the family from Portugal back to its earlier Spanish homeland.

The name Hebreo was, of course, no more native to the man who became one of Italy's foremost philosophers of love than was Italy itself. A few years before March 31, 1492, the date of the infamous edict of expulsion, the same man was living at the court of the Catholic kings Ferdinand and Isabel. His famous father Isaac had become minister of finance and a political adviser to the monarchs, and the son himself was probably their royal physician. That was before ethnic and religious differences became absolutely intolerable in Spain, and while the court doctor could still take self-evident pride in his legitimate name. It was Yehuda Abravanel, of the long line of poetic and political Abravanels that allegedly reached back to King David and forward to the true messiah (Dorman 1983: 17). The family's Spanish roots were deep, probably going back to the beginnings of Jewish settlement there, after Rome dispersed the Jews from Judea. Documented credentials reached back at least to 1284, when Hebreo's namesake, Don Yehuda of Seville and Córdoba, began to serve Sancho IV (1284–95) as royal tax collector, a job he continued for Fernando IV (1295–1312). By the end of the fourteenth century, with the first Inquisitorial rumblings, the patriarch Don Samuel Abravanel decided that if he could no longer be both Spanish and Jewish, an apparently threatening and therefore threatened combination, he would solve the contradiction by choosing sides. Samuel converted, and was henceforth known as Juan Sánchez de Sevilla (Gebhardt 1934: 236; Dorman 1983: 19). The family members who remained Jewish didn't remain in Spain for very long; they moved to neighboring Portugal, which was then bent on winning independence from Castile. The Abravanels settled in Lisbon, where they entered into the service of King Alfonso V, and where Don Isaac was born in 1437, followed by his son Yehuda in about 1460. After three generations of Portuguese prosperity, King John II accused Isaac of conspiracy. The patriarch barely escaped to the precarious security of Spain in 1484, the same year Christopher Columbus arrived there. Everyone knows what happened to the Jews only eight years later.

Spain rid itself of a people who had come to identify so stubbornly with that unnatural mother of a country that for centuries thereafter they would distinguish themselves from their Balkan and North African neighbors as "ispanioles." After that unhealthy purging, the young Doctor Abravanel — already into his second exile — translated himself in every sense of the word. He moved from one country to another and traded his Hebrew name, Yehuda, for its Spanish counterpart, León. As for the particularly distinguished Sephardic surname, he gave it up altogether for a generic label, "the Jew." Hebreo's modern Hebrew translator says, in fact, that the author's name could have referred to almost any of the many Jewish men exiled in Italy. If our only information were the man's name as it appears in the first published edition of his work, it would be impossible to establish his identity. We know it thanks to some biographical details, mostly from Don Isaac's mention of the family in prologues to his prolific work (references that exclude Don Samuel the convert) (Dorman 1983: 20); from Claudio Tolomei's letters (1566) (Dorman 1983: 15, 86–88); and from the detailed title of the first Spanish translation of the *Dialogues*. It is a version (by Guedella Ibn Yahiya, a third-generation exile and friend of the Abravanels) that Garcilaso would almost surely not have known. The translation was published in Venice in 1568, and dedicated (strangely?) to Spain's Felipe II as defender of the Catholic faith: *Los Dialogos de Amor de Mestre Leon Abrabanel Médico y Filósofo excelente. De nuevo traduzidos en lengua castellana, y deregidos a la Maiestad del Rey Filippo*. For some reason, the Jewish translator insisted to his ideal imperial reader that the book's argument developed very "católicamente" (Dorman 1983: 125), even though the author had evidently refused to be limited to that kind of approval. He left instead.

The Catholic kings would have been happy to retain Yehudah and his father Isaac, the court's physician and the country's finance minister. They would gladly have overlooked the stain of ethnicity in the glow of professional services during this first wave of forced conversions or flight, before "limpieza de sangre" became a patriotic requirement. What good options would the royal clients have had, anyway, at a time when money matters and worldly medicine seemed to be monopolies of miscreants? Faculties of medicine, we might remember, were the first to admit Jewish professors (Gaon 1993: 3). Don Isaac counted on his usefulness, no doubt, in that famous scene (as Cecil Roth calls it [1937: ix–xv]) when he threw himself before his majestic masters and pleaded with them, in vain, to rescind the decree. Instead, Ferdinand and Isabel offered the family "a dispensation" from the expulsion edict; that is, they offered to sponsor the family's conversion. Other illustrious Jewish subjects were doing it. In the introduction to his *Commentary on the Book of Kings,* Don Isaac doesn't mention them. He is as silent on the many thousands of last minute conversions as on the particular case of his personal friend, Rabbi Abraham Shneiur, head of Spain's Jewish congregation, whose decision to change cult rather than country precipitated so many other capitulations (Dorman 1983: 46). Instead, Isaac describes a seamless scene of exodus, as "one man says to the next, 'Let us stay strong in our faith, and hold on to God's Law, however we are pursued by enemies. If we survive, so be it; and if we die, we will die without breaking our covenant'" (Dorman 1983: 40–41; my translation from Hebrew). This kind of determination withstood even Ferdinand's plots to keep them (Roth 1937: x; Gebhardt 1934: 243–44).[3]

3. Ferdinand was no less determined to keep the Abravanels, as hostages if need be, than they were to keep their religion. The king arranged to have Yehuda's baby son kidnapped in order to hold the family nearby; but they intercepted the abduction and sent the child and his nurse to Portugal, where he was apparently seized and baptized anyway. Twelve years later, on the eve of what would have been a bar mitzvah, Yehudah wrote a rending elegy about the depth of his loss. Gebhardt's more detailed version speculates that father and son must have been reunited in Italy, because there is a document of 1560 recording a meeting in Salonica between Yehuda's grandson (and namesake), who was trying to get his grandfather's *Harmonica Coeli* published, and the neo-Christian doctor Amatus Lusitanus (Juan Rodrigo de Castel-Branco). The manuscript was written at the request of Pico della Mirandola, and Amatus had read it frequently. The young Abravanel seems to have died soon afterward in an epidemic (Gebhardt 1934: 246–47).

Rather than live the ignominy of descending from David and dissolving into the camp of Israel's enemies, Isaac and his son chose loss and exile. Instead of the ethnic erasure that the Crown offered as a personal solution to his Jewish problem, the young doctor of his own dilemma developed a less lethal treatment. His prescription against death by purification was a life of conscious contamination. He would thrive as a Spanish Jew. Since he would not erase his Jewishness in order to stay at home, he used his home language to broadcast his "infidel's" identity, signing his name as "Jew" in bold Spanish strokes.

The point would not have been lost on Hebreo's mestizo translator. El Inca Garcilaso, of the ethnically mixed name and culturally conflicted heritage, may very well have recognized the self-exiled Spaniard as a figure for himself. Abravanel had been an intimate of the Iberian kings, their compatriot of countless generations. Hebreo was a homeboy, even if he was hounded by fanatics as a foreigner. He had a cultural claim on Spain, the kind of claim Garcilaso was making when he assigned himself the paternal name.

The overlapping circumstances make for an almost uncanny echo system between the "Italian" writer and his "Castilian" interpreter, as if one life simply evoked a surprising intimacy with the other. The intimacy seems metaphorical, a result of fortuitous similarities between terms that belong to different and unconnected discourses, Incan and Jewish. But metaphors, we know, sometimes win their shock effect by losing their memory of historical connection. They become metaphors when the metonymic moment is forgotten. And forgetting is just what the Spanish empire demanded of culturally complicated subjects such as the Incan prince and the Jewish "aristocrat." But these "mosaic" subjects preferred not to forget their pre-Hispanic pride. They were therefore related, not through stories of presumed continuity of Israel's lost tribes that were supposedly being found in America where they still dressed, ate, and prayed like Christianity's forebears, but through a shared history of Spanish reconquest, consolidation, and new conquests.[4] "Comenzaron las conquistas de indios acabada la de los moros, porque siempre guerreasen españoles contra infieles" (The conquest of Indians began

---

4. The Dominican friar Gregorio García was convinced of the continuity, as was Fray Diego Duran. But Father Acosta rejected the theory vehemently and categorically, which is a sure sign, as Rolena Adorno points out, of its lasting and far-flung grip on the popular mind (Adorno 1988: 63).

with the conquest of Moors finished, so that the Spaniards would always make war against infidels), in López de Gómara's (1979 [1552]: 8) famous formulation. It was a univocal story of forced inclusions and simplifications that produced some wonderfully dissonant, or dialogic, refusals to be simple.

If Garcilaso's choice of material for his writerly apprenticeship can be called circumstantial, perhaps the circumstances of Spain's estranged sons vibrate with overdetermined resonance. The Inca's enduring *Traduzión* (1590) was the first document to bear the mestizo's newly coined and culturally compound signature, a name no less complicating than Hebreo's label of intimate foreignness from Spain. Why Hebreo, of all people, should have provided the mestizo with a master text was a question from the very beginning, as Garcilaso records in the second part of his history: Don Francisco Murillo of Córdoba asked how the Antarctic Indian could presume to translate the Italian treatise.

One very good reason is the book's content. I mentioned its Neoplatonic ideas about the basic universality of all cults and about a perfectible world created by love. Logically, and through dialogic probing, the book coordinates the competing codes of classical, Christian, and Jewish philosophy as useful versions and developments of one accommodating truth. The challenge that the *Dialogues* sets and meets is to appreciate the interlocking allegorical meanings of disparate traditions. A good translator, in other words, need not have divided loyalties; he can weave among them. Some of Hebreo's sources must have surprised certain Jewish readers, despite the attractions Christianity displayed for Kabbalists. In fact, his inclusion of John the Baptist along with Enoch and Elijah as immortal souls (Hebreo 1947 [1590]: 320) evidently amazed some readers enough to make them assume that Hebreo was no longer what his name said, that the man must finally have converted. It certainly surprised a scribe of Ibn Yahiya's early Spanish translation, writing the Spanish in Hebrew characters as the Sephardim usually did; it surprised him enough to assume that John was there because of a Christian interpolation (an opinion Carl Gebhardt would share [1934: 271]). The scribe therefore excluded Saint John from the list, as did the early translation into Hebrew by Rabbi Yosef Baruch of Urbino (Dorman 1983: 128). It is a wonder that exception wasn't taken to what precedes the Baptist in Hebreo's text: I mean the trinitarian logic of dialectical thinking that coordinates between the one truth and a three-part movement of the intelligence that begins with unity, develops apparent contradictions, and returns to coherence (Hebreo 1947 [1590]: 292). At the same time, Philón finds authority in the sacred scriptures which are synonymous with Mosaic law (ibid.: e.g., 153, 156, 158, 173). Through the zigzagging, though, *Mosaic* begins to work like a pun, pointing backward to an exclusive relationship between God and his particular people, and forward to a universal design made of many peoples.

The Neoplatonic and universalizing ideas in Hebreo's book surely pleased Garcilaso enormously. Enrique Pupo-Walker (1982) mapped out the Neoplatonic ground that attracted Garcilaso to Hebreo's ideas, but downplayed, as had José Durand (1950: 161) and Aurelio Miró Quesada (1971: 121), the translation's literary significance as a mere warm-up exercise for Garcilaso's original works. Later, Susana Jákfalvi-Leiva argued that translation, between codes and between cultures, is precisely the art that Garcilaso would exercise throughout his career; the *Diálogos de amor* are not an excisable appendix to his literary corpus, but are instead its very heart (1984: 14). Sabine MacCormack would concur, calling Hebreo's philosophy an Ariadne's thread that would soon lead Garcilaso through the labyrinth of competing histories of Peru; she sees his entire career as commentator on indigenous religion as a long development of the pre-Christian apologetics learned from León (1991: 332). Garcilaso, the humanist, was quite naturally in his company, agrees Margarita Zamora, for linguistic and philosophical reasons; she shows that the two outsiders were inside a humanistic culture that valued ethnically marked experts for their authenticating knowledge, even when those marks might mean a political liability (Zamora 1988: 58–60). These rereadings suggest that style was Hebreo's most lasting lesson. Garcilaso's training through translation is by now a standard signpost for criticism, yet the question of style is often merely remarked on and passed by. I want to tarry there.

Style, in Garcilaso's case, means even more than philosophical probing and linguistic legitimation. What exactly did Hebreo's text offer the Inca in terms of technique? If the target language for Garcilaso's translation practice was Spanish, any other foreign book might have provided opportunities for cultivating Castilian flair. But Hebreo's book must have caught Garcilaso's attention for a range of reasons, technique being among them. Under-studied as it is, Hebreo's technique was perhaps the main attraction for Garcilaso. At the very least, whether or not he modeled some of his own maneuvers on the *Diálogos,* they offer Garcilaso's readers a telling repository of those repeatable techniques. Hebreo had the imitable manner of a man on the move.

Hebreo was a storehouse of ideas for Garcilaso, but he was more than that. He was also a poignant Hebraic figure for a new Christian's peregrination and passion, yet this doesn't exhaust his significance for Garcilaso. Hebreo was more even than a pre-text for translation between equally legitimate languages and lores. He was also a modern writer about cultures of antiquity. Despite his sometimes tortured Tuscan prose, Hebreo managed to produce a chatty style that brought celestial love down to earth and circled it back again.

Beginning with either textual interpretation, or circumstantial information, many readers have already noticed more than one coincidence between the Inca and the Jew. As if responding to Murillo's early and ill-humored taunt about what possible connection there could be between an Antarctic Indian and an Italian master, a chorus of commentators answers with all sorts of connections. To mention something of the range of readings, to which I add my own piece about their practice of wise maneuvering around epistemologically loaded positionalities, is to remember how frankly surprising the combination can still seem. For example, in an exhaustively historical and comparatist introduction to his own 1983 Hebrew translation of the *Dialogues,* Menachem Dorman is evidently moved by the unforeseen parallels between the Abravanel and the Inca. Other Spanish versions simply don't compare in accuracy or in elegance with the 1590 *Traduzión,* nor do the French or Latin translations of the period. Dorman may have had no notice of Garcilaso before, and yet the spiritual affinity with Abravanel is unmistakable. The "new (world) Christian" and the Jewish humanist were treading the same interpretive and syncretic waters between Spain and the areas she both feared and disdained. Similar conclusions had already come from the Spanish-language critics mentioned above. For Hispanists, Hebreo is no surprise; not one of them stammers, even for a moment, with Dorman's sense of wonder. Don León has simply been a standard name in the Spanish canon ever since Marcelino Menéndez y Pelayo published his still authoritative *Historia de las ideas estéticas en España* (1883–1891). There, the Jewish philosopher occupies a good part of chapter 6 as a necessary name in the Spanish history of ideas. No matter that the man had to leave Spain (the country has always been too complicated to reduce its culture to one intolerant strain), or that he wrote in Italian (it is full of hispanisms, suggesting a Spanish pre-text), Hebreo is ours: so legislated the lasting historian of Spanish letters.

It was his style that probably did the most to seduce the Peruvian pupil. By style, I do not mean the uneven quality of Hebreo's language, a clumsy Tuscan that has nurtured endless speculations about an original manuscript in Spanish, Hebrew, or Latin.[5] Instead, style here refers

5. Dorman (1983) devotes a long section of his introduction to the inconclusive speculations about the *Dialogues'* original language, which I summarize here:

In 1871, F. Delitzsch didn't doubt that the 1535 Italian text was original, but he felt that the style suggested a nonnative speaker of Tuscan, thus agreeing with Benedetto Varchi (1503–65) that the style mars the work. Delitzsch reasoned that, given the popular everyday language of the dialogues, Hebreo would not have written them first in either Greek or Latin (Dorman 1983: 87).

The famed humanist Claudio Tolomei (1492–1555) had already wondered about the original language, comparing Hebreo's unfortunate style to the admirable clarity of Caesar and Cicero. The dialogues would have been even greater, wrote Tolomei, "if they were translated to Tuscan in a clear and a clean manner, as if the dialogues were translated into Tuscan from some other language" (ibid.: 88).

Carlos Montesa, who did the 1584 Spanish translation, thought that the original was in Latin (ibid.: 89); and Emanuel (Ben Yitzhak) Aboab agrees: "It was written in Latin even though by now it is translated into almost all the languages of Europe" (*Nomologia o discursos legales, compuestos por el virtuso Haham Rabi Emanuel Aboab de buena memoria estampados a costa y despeza de Manuel Avuhav, sus heredos, en el año de la creación 5389 [1629]*, 303. Aboab was born in 1555 in Oporto, Portugal, and spent time in Italy near the Abravanels) (cited in Dorman 1983: 90).

But Marcelino Menéndez y Pelayo, in 1891, was sure that Hebreo wrote in Spanish because of the many hispanisms in the first Italian publication. I Sonne agreed in 1928, pointing out that Abravanel never broke ties with Jews, and stayed mostly in cities with large Jewish populations, Napoli, Genoa, Venezia, Ferara, not Firenze or Roma (only at the end of his life). So Sonne comes to the same conclusion as did Tolomei, and reasons that the original must have been either in Spanish or Hebrew (ibid.: 92). Disagreement comes from Carlo Dionisotti in 1959, whose reading of the third Dialogue in manuscript, written in a Tuscan too modern to have been original, implies that Hebreo did not write in Italian, but probably in Hebrew (ibid.: 93). In that case, we can assume that he translated the book from Hebrew into Latin, the form found by publisher Mariano Lenzo of Sienna (ibid.: 94). Carl Gebhardt, in 1929, preferred the Spanish theory: no one denies the Spanish turns of phrase in the Italian (though Dionisotti ignores them). Spanish was not only his mother tongue, but also influenced the Italian of Naples, still in the Spanish orbit (Gebhardt 1934: 258; Dorman 1983: 94).

In any case, we *do not know* which language was in fact the original. Critics into Hebreo's peculiarly coy and flirtatious dialogical movement. The lesson about how to get ahead by sometimes stepping back may not have been entirely new to Garcilaso the ex-soldier, but its literary application was apparently just what he needed to initiate his writing career. The translator would be just as coy in the *Comentarios* as Hebreo was in philosophizing about love, maybe more so. He probably outdid his teacher's technique. He had to, because Garcilaso, unlike Hebreo, could not assume that knowledge or wisdom were already the objects of spiritual lust. From a Spanish perspective, at least, Incan glories, and surviving Incas themselves, may have been matters of relative indifference. Unlike Philón's declaration of feeling with the opening line of the *Dialogues:* "El conocerte, o Sophía! causa en mi amor y desseo" (Hebreo 1947 [1590]: 29) (Meeting you, O Sophía! awakens in me love and desire), the Inca begins his *Commentaries* with caveats and cautionary delays. Knowing his beloved arouses Hebreo's lover. But Garcilaso's reader knows next to nothing about Peru, and therefore cannot love his Andean interlocutor.

How will Garcilaso make us want him? A worthy disciple of his coy master, Garcilaso performed a kind of metaleptic reversal of feeling. He discovered that by stepping away from his reader he could induce love; by assuming our hunger for knowledge, he could supply it in small, appetizing portions. Just to be sure that we want it, he keeps full familiarity in view, but unreachable. After offering points of contact, he steps away, translates himself (literally moving from one place to another), waiting for us to make the next, predictably dependent, move. Garcilaso noticed that Hebreo had written for an active reader, one who would follow along, philosophizing with the author. If the same kind of reader is constructed in the *Comentarios,* it is one who knows how to follow; that is, how sufficiently to appreciate the complex trajectory of an expertly guided exploration so as not to hazard it alone.

Multiple pages of preliminary admonitions about the linguistic and historiographic foreignness of Peru warn readers about underestimated hazards. Finally, chapter 3 of *The Royal Commentaries* begins with "How the New World Was Discovered." The conventional heading promises familiar ground. Then the ground begins to shake: "In about 1484, to within a year or so, a pilot born in Huelva, in the county of Niebla, called

---

sist on their own preferences, and the competition testifies to the book's importance (Dorman 1983: 95).

Alonso Sánchez de Huelva, had a small ship" that was blown off course (Livermore 1966: 12).

What is this? It cannot be about America's discovery, can it? Who is this obscure Alonso who comes out of a foggy place literally known as Niebla, a mere merchant pushed and pulled against his will by natural forces from the Canaries to the Caribbean? Am I being told that America was discovered by mistake? And, as this version continues, barely alive back in Spain, the unknown victim of his own uncontrollable voyage is cared for and questioned—to death—by Columbus. How can this be? And why is this unanticipated and rather damaging, undignified story narrated in so straightforward, so deadpan and unapologetic a style? As if we didn't know better. Unless we're holding out for a Viking version of the discovery, a version that evidently didn't translate well into imperial Spanish, everyone knows that Columbus discovered America in 1492. We know how he and his men mounted three little ships with charmingly girlish names and then sailed to glory, thanks to the admiral's bold intelligence, and thanks also to Queen Isabel for deciding to take a chance on the daring man.[6]

Given what we know, then, we might have imagined that the title of Garcilaso's early chapter would introduce the standard facts in order to give the *Royal Commentaries* a conventional or formulaic beginning, and so to identify the chronicle within a century-long practice of writing histories, both official and independent, of the Indies. But Garcilaso is apparently after a different kind of validation, and a different relationship with his reader. Instead of fitting into the conventions, he operates alongside them, writing "commentaries" on other chronicles. And instead of flattering his readers with affirmations of what we know, this mestizo informant offers the kind of dangerous, supplementary information that destabilizes the very epistemological framework we had taken for granted. What do we know for sure about the discovery after reading Garcilaso? In fact, it is perfectly plausible that we know next to noth-

---

6. For a most provocative speculation on how the Queen succumbed, in a love-hate dilemma, to a man marked as a Jew and poised for deportation anyway see Alejo Carpentier's masterful novel about discovery and conquest, *El arpa y la sombra* (1979). For example, "During nights of intimacy, *Columba* that's what I called her when we were alone would promise me three caravels, ten caravels, fifty caravels, a hundred, all the caravels I wanted. But as soon as dawn broke the caravels vanished and I remained alone, walking in morning's light" (91; my translation).

ing, but that Columbus knew quite a lot about the New World before he sailed to "discover" it. "But if it had not been for the news that Alonso Sánchez de Huelva gave him he could not have promised so much and so exactly what he did promise merely out of his own imagination as a cosmographer" (ibid.: 14).

Many years later, in a 1979 novel, Alejo Carpentier would speculate about Columbus's contrition at the end of a life that exploited multiple sources of unacknowledged information — information gleaned from merchant maps and from rowdy bars where drunken salts would spice their talk with the unconventional details that couldn't have come from adventure books. A sailor on the southern coast of Spain would have to have been either deaf or indifferent, Carpentier concludes, not to have known about the New World. Columbus was neither hard of hearing nor unambitious. And even Garcilaso's contemporaries might have sensed that informed interest motivated him as much as daring did, given all the ignominious controversy about the "discoverer" 's rights to titles and privileges. Why not, then, imagine that a rather simple but resourceful Spanish sailor came out of the fog to show the way? Is there any reason to defend Columbus? Does it enhance Spain's glory to think that the credit goes to a Genovese opportunist of indefinite national loyalties, a man who had failed to convince the Portuguese princes to risk capital on what was probably still a vague project before 1484? Disappointed, Columbus left for Spain in that very year, when the Abravanels were escaping Portugal and Alonso was learning what would make Columbus a risk worth taking. "Like a wise man keeping the secret" of that information, Garcilaso explains that Columbus was also smart enough to report it "in confidence to certain persons who enjoyed great authority with the Catholic monarchs" (Livermore 1966: 14). Carpentier's Columbus ejaculates the empowering secret to a queen who had been condescending to her lover (Carpentier 1979: 93).

The point is not that the supplementary story about Alonso the sailor was unknown to other historians. Garcilaso does not, in fact, invent it. He says that the primary source is his father's conversations with comrade conquistadores. Apparently, the people in the business of discovery and conquest were wise to Columbus, because they could fill in some missing pieces of his simplified and self-serving account. But Garcilaso had other sources, too. He even cites one laconic mention of the sailor in Father José de Acosta's history of Peru. There were other mentions, too, all of them undeveloped versions in standard histories. Rumors of an unnamed precursor of Columbus appeared in Fernández de Oviedo's official history of 1535, where the story is almost parenthetical, like an unauthorized or apocryphal curiosity. Then, Francisco López de Gómara's equally official 1552 report favored the rumor, but failed to supply much corroborating detail. That is one reason Italy's contemporary Girolamo Benzoni rejected the tale as so much invidious Spanish chauvinism, designed to discredit a Genovese genius (Markham 1869–71: 24–6n). The controversy lasted at least until Washington Irving took sides with the admiral, and against Alonso, in his *Life of Columbus* (1828). But Garcilaso's intervention doesn't seem to take sides; it has a deliberately objective tone, as if the details were neither debatable nor potentially damaging. Where other historians used indefinite pronouns and vague timing to conjure up a character and a period, Garcilaso affirms his information with proper nouns and precise numbers. He identifies names, places, dates, and cargoes without losing his way among conjectures and speculations that can carry other historians off to unknowable conclusions, as Alonso was carried off his course. The Inca's concreteness has the effect of inverting assignations of rumor and truth. It underlines the anecdote and puts the standard story under erasure. With this sleight of hand, he also suggests that his own unsolicited expertise is superior to any official authority. Whatever other historians were guessing at, Garcilaso knows in detail; and whatever readers thought we knew starts to dissolve, from the beginning. Here is a local informant who will talk, if we relax our habitual posturing and learn to listen properly.

In an introductory "Word to the Reader," Garcilaso had already apprised us of the corrective nature of these "commentaries." They are intended to develop existing, but laconic, histories of Peru written by Spaniards who are dutifully cited, but who have an understandably limited knowledge of the country, compared to this native son of Cuzco. The "commentary" on Columbus is already a hint of the sabotage these additional details can wreak on standard histories. After the preliminary "Proemio," Garcilaso adds cautionary "Advertencias" about the language of Peru. Spaniards need to be cautioned, he explains, about particular phonetic and grammatical features of the general language imposed by the Incas throughout their empire, because the foreigners do not yet (nor can they possibly) know the language with a native's mastery. The Jesuit Father Blas Valera can be trusted, not so much because he is the author of a learned history in Latin, but because he is a mestizo local. Garcilaso refers respectfully, and often, to Valera's frayed and sometimes fragmentary pages. By contrast, not even the exemplary Jesuitical discipline and dedication of Acosta can compensate for his foreignness. Less careful practitioners have imagined that competence can be casual and incomplete—enough to evangelize, for example. But Garcilaso knew that compromises with competence lead to errors, both epistemological and evangelical (Garcilaso 1609: "Caution Prior to the Narration"). This mestizo master of his mother's tongue, the man who would be respected by Andalusia's admirable linguists before composing these commentaries, knew the ravages of getting words almost right. Inexpert translations were misshaping the memory of a glorious Incan past; they were perjuring reports of current practices in Peru, and they were mistaking the eloquent difference of the country by normalizing it in Spanish.[7] These were no less than historiographical sins. Just as seriously, inarticulate priests were moving Indians to laughter rather than to lofty feeling. A mistaken noun or a misused verb, uttered with the most saintly intention, were sure obstacles to the salvation of new souls. Snickering Incan subjects were used to associating more elegance and precision with authoritative discourse (ibid., pt. 1, bk. 2, chap. 3).

After these exhortations, chapters 1 and 2 keep delaying us, this time with moralizing detours into circumspection. The first chapter affirms God's universal creation in order to catch Christians as blasphemers if they mistake his holy unity for two, hierarchically organized worlds. The second chapter sets the limits of Garcilaso's own writing, in effect to counsel general modesty that refrains from speculating about geography (or anything else) before exploration advances. European readers may find some of Garcilaso's almost pedantic preambles about language and cultural differences to be plausible. He is evidently establishing his own, homegrown expertise in these first pages. They may even allow his righteous reminders about Catholic universality and about the necessarily slow progress of human understanding. But conceding our ignorance about Peru doesn't seem to be enough; leveling our differences with the mestizo before God and before natural science doesn't sufficiently

7. See Julio Ortega (1992: 374). After identifying a Peruvian fruit called *ussun* Garcilaso writes, "I mention this to avoid confusion between it and the Spanish plum," and Ortega glosses: "With this, he indicates the need to preserve differences and avoid referential vagueness. . . . One can see that the discourse of abundance, here practised in full, has substituted previous discourses, turning resemblance into eloquent difference."

humble us either. No. Garcilaso obviously tips the balance in his own favor when he demonstrates superior knowledge about Spanish history, and when he does so in such enviable Spanish style. Garcilaso's almost unequaled style in the period (some critics say that only Cervantes wrote better),[8] and his expertise in linguistic analyses, outperform readers on their own intellectual ground. "Yupanqui," he explains, "is a verb in the second person singular of the future imperfect in the indicative mood"; *ayusca* is a past participle; and Spaniards have entirely misunderstood the proper noun *Viracocha,* which could not possibly be a compound word meaning "sea of fat" because in combinations of nominative and genitive, the genitive always precedes (ibid., pt. 1, bk. 2, chap. 17; pt. 1, bk. 4, chap. 12; pt. 1, bk. 5, chap. 21). To the corrosive logic of the narrative supplement he adds the academic training of a European expert in linguistics and comparative historiography, until the reader can hardly hold on to any intellectual advantage over this socially marginal mestizo. The imbalance can be irksome, if not downright offensive. Even more annoying are his repeated delays of narrative information.

Why do we need to be held off for so long? Does Garcilaso imagine us to be incapable of judgment? Why dig so many moats around Incan information that we would drown if we presumed to cross over unattended? Are the moats meant to create a job for the local maker of interpretive locks? These would not be locks to keep us out, obviously, but the kind that regulate a flow and raise us, little by little, to a navigable level. And once readers get there, exactly what have we gotten? The native guide first floats us a story of dubious historical value, a tall tale about sailors that neither Oviedo nor any other Spanish historian knew enough about to authorize. The very next chapter, chapter 4, gives us the tragicomic "Just So" story of how Peru got its name: When the first Spaniards asked an Indian where they were, the unarmed informant, scared to death ("pasmado y abobado"), first fainted and then, sure that he was the blameless object of their insistent questioning, identified himself as Berú and pointed to the place where they found him, Pelú (river). Confusing one sound with another, as the Spaniards always did, they invented the misnomer *Perú* for the far-flung empire of four corners, Tahuantisuyu. "The Christians believed what they wanted to, imagining that the Indian

8. See, for example, González-Echevarría (1990: 44). But José Mazzotti has reminded me that this evaluation is based on late and stylistically adjusted reeditions, rather than on Garcilaso's first versions.

had understood them and had answered accordingly, as if he spoke Spanish like they did" (ibid., pt. 1, bk. 1, chap. 4; pt. 1, bk. 8, chap. 11).

It is one thing for Garcilaso to allege this sort of European arrogance and even ignorance about Incan matters in his preambles and throughout the text; he can logically claim authority about his own culture, as I said, whether or not that culture mattered much to Spanish readers. For centuries, they have noticed the self-authorizing gambit of the insider who makes cultural capital of his positionality. But it is quite another thing for the Inca to dismiss a foundation of European knowledge about the conquest in the Columbus chapter. There, his American authenticity was no advantage at all; in fact, it would disqualify him from academic debates about Spain by the same logic of local grounding that granted him expertise about Peru. Why should we concede any credibility to an Indian's story of the high seas that is mere hearsay for Spanish historians? The reason is simply that the story is plausible, as we admitted, and not easily dismissed. Its authoritative style demanded a hearing at least long enough to broaden official history beyond the cult of sudden heroes. The dangerous supplement has its own destabilizing logic; it undermines authority instead of substituting one master for another. Garcilaso may not become our expert, even if he effectively challenges others; but whether or not his story convinces its readers, its very objectivity of tone offers an alternative narration and keeps open the floodgates of interpretation and choice. Not only has the native guide argued for his inimitable expertise, in terms that would make any competition literally misguided, but this politically frail and economically precarious product of Spain's conquest has also managed to make us doubt whether we know anything at all, even the most basic information of a European tradition. By the end of chapter 3 (with its caveat on Columbus), and chapter 4 (about Spanish linguistic impertinence), a possibly presumptuous reader has been weakened by stages, the way an overbearing bull is bled into docility before the matador leads him gracefully into new paces. Perhaps now the reader may stoop to follow a skillful guide.

Do Garcilaso's authorizing strategies contradict one another? They certainly seem to. Can he logically affirm the knowledge that comes from a privileged insider's position on one page, and on the next destabilize the knowledge associated with tradition and power? No, not logically. But there is an advantage to shuttling from one tactic to another, an advantage that doesn't respond to limited questions about consistent argumentation. As if he were planting a clue to look elsewhere, Garcilaso tells a story that reads like a parable of misfired and insufficient questions, the kind of misguided interrogation that demands an inquiry beyond convention and into the unsolicited, supplementary "commentaries" that his book generally supplies. The story is about a murder investigation in which a *curaca* (a regional, non-Incan dignitary) supplied extra information to Spanish authorities. He overrode their limited procedure in the service of truth, since the facts of the case would have continued to escape the Spaniards if he responded only to the questions they thought to ask. "Saying one part and hiding another" would have amounted to a cover-up and a lie (ibid.: pt. 1, bk. 2, chap. 3). One lesson to take from here is that supplements are necessary, not ornamental. But another, less direct, message is that real informants can make surprisingly independent moves; they can slip into a controlling spot by inverting the hierarchy of Q and A. It may be more consistent to tailor answers to questions, but consistency is not always the chronicler's most effective technique. Sometimes chronic alternations of viewpoint and argument work better. The value of Garcilaso's shuttling between ethnic grounding and deconstructive displacement is, in short, strategic. He is difficult to catch, or to contain. This insures his authority, and agility, over his slightly disoriented and overwhelmed readers. If Garcilaso writes himself into a problem, he keeps on writing, so that even a critical reader comes away with enough countervailing information to be contaminated by complexity and doubt.

Permission for the practice, or an incitation, could have come from Hebreo's philosophical Sophía, if we take her taunts and instigations as a collection of narrative strategies that Garcilaso appropriated. He had other sources, certainly, for learning how to put one version of history under erasure by writing another; plenty of competing and contentious historians preceded him. To cite just two of the most familiar examples: Las Casas had countered Fernández de Oviedo's official disdain for dying Indians with the pious outrage of *History of the Indies* (written 1527–66); and Bernal Díaz's eyewitness testimony filled in López de Gómara's bureaucratic version (1552) of Mexico's conquest with a corrective *True History* (written in 1570; published in 1632). Sophía, on the other hand, is not a practitioner of corrosive commentary; instead, she is practically an instructor in its performance. Her few discursive gestures thematize a whole lifetime of lessons for Garcilaso, some of which might not have suited the other, venerable historians. Sophía instructs her interlocutor Philón to unsay, "desdezir," a mistake, if he has made one. (For

Emmanuel Lévinas, a twentieth-century philosopher of ethical erotics, anything that is said, thematized, and congealed must always be unsaid [1974: 7].) On second thought, she notices that her lover is so glib that his best way out of a discursive difficulty is to supplement it with more discourse; he can either erase or overwrite, either unsay or say more. "Ya puedes dezir lo que se te antojare, que segun veo, bien sabes el modo de rescatarte" (You can already say whatever you want, because as far as I can see, you're the master of rescuing yourself). In either case, she incites more talk. Did Sophía give Garcilaso some of the ideas for his unstoppable style? I am referring to three basic and characteristic strategies of Garcilaso's *Comentarios:* (1) supplementing; (2) unsaying; and (3) inciting expert talk. We have already seen something of the first, practically generic strategy; that is, adding comments and writing over standard histories. Second is the play between *dezir* and *desdezir,* a move and double move that writes and almost unwrites its own text. For example, Garcilaso will introduce an indigenous theme, advance toward giving it a Christian name, and then retreat a bit toward the first term.[9] Lest this procedure seem to traduce the truth, Garcilaso adduces the speculation of Spanish authors who shuttle between cult and religion. And then he steps back, just far enough to incite the reader's chase. He coyly drops the handy interpretive thread of *praeparatio evangelica* (Mazzotti 1993: 123) that has been sewing honest pagans into a Christian fabric; he drops

9. Here are a few of many instances:

The Incan cult of the Sun, of his consort the Moon, and of Pachacámac, the Maker of all things, is called idolatry (Garcilaso 1609: pt. 1, bk. 1, chap. 15), then called religion (or a compromising "vana religión" [ibid., pt. 1, bk. 4, chap. 1]), and again idolatry (or less categorically, "el culto divino de su idolatría" [ibid.]). Although the Moon is the mother of all Incas, they never adored her as a goddess (ibid., pt. 1, bk. 2, chap. 1). Is there an implied, and barbed, comparison here with Mariolotry, since the Incas only venerated their mother instead of worshiping her? On one page, the "virgins of the Sun [Son?]" are naively devoted to a pagan cult; on the next, they are translated into Christianized "nuns" (their aged superiors are abbesses), before the section ends with a reference, again, to wives of the sun (ibid., pt. 1, bk. 4, chap. 1). And *Raimi* sounds as impressive and solemn to Indians as Easter does to Christians (ibid., pt. 1, bk. 6, chap. 20), Garcilaso writes in the first chapter dedicated to the summer solstice festival; by the third chapter, after detailing the ritual sacrifice of lambs (more evocative of Deuteronomy or Numbers than of the New Testament), he fuses the comparison into a qualified substitution: the Incas celebrated "their Easter" by publicly roasting and distributing the meat (ibid., pt. 1, bk. 6, chap. 22).

it just long enough to make a reader stutter and bend down, perhaps, to recover the connection. "De lo que hemos dicho puede haber nacido lo que algunos españoles han querido afirmar, que comulgaban estos Incas y sus vasallos como los cristianos. Lo que entre ellos había hemos contado llanamente: aseméjalo cada uno a su gusto" (What we have said could have given rise to what some Spaniards have wanted to affirm, that these Incas and their vassals had Communion like the Christians. What was among them we have openly recounted: each can assimilate it to his liking) (Garcilaso 1609: pt. 1, bk. 6, chap. 22). Taste and judgment, the renaissance relativist knows, are often products of one's positionality. In Quitu, for example, roosters are said to chant "Atahuallpa" in mourning for the martyred king from that region; but in Cuzco, roosters (and rowdy children) shriek the name in mockery of Atahuallpa, murderer of his brother Huáscar, the legitimate Inca (ibid., pt. 1, bk. 9, chap. 23). "Cada uno dice de la feria como le va en ella" (Each tells of the fair how it went for him) (ibid.), is the homey Spanish proverb that Garcilaso's readers would have to recognize.

Third of the strategies mentioned is Garcilaso's sometimes studiously naive, nearly coquettish posture that beckons an affectionate interlocutor to speak more. The source of loving lore here is Garcilaso's Incan uncle, as it was Philón for Sophía. To make room for the speaker, an infantilized (feminized) Garcilaso wisely retreats at points from the insider's privilege that he usually assumes. It would have made him privy to secrets about Incan mummies that Spaniards could never know (ibid., pt. 1, bk. 5, chap. 29), for example; and it made him the overseer for Indians who couldn't trust the foreigners in business transactions (ibid., pt. 1, bk. 6, chap. 9). Garcilaso steps back occasionally to stay under his uncle's authority, and to dramatize how knowledge must submit to those who know more. The Hispanized nephew has, nevertheless, brought the baggage of his technical superiority to the questions he asks, perhaps as a figure for future and presumptive Spanish readers of the *Comentarios*. Cagey as ever, Garcilaso gives his uncle the floor, but keeps one foot forward, grounded in the lasting advantages of his own writerly craft that will preserve memory far better than the Inca's ephemeral techniques of knotting colored strings and streamlining stories for easy oral relays (ibid., pt. 1, bk. 1, chap. 15). Just as cagey, though, his uncle responds to the incitation with apparently endless detailed information, and with a royal indifference to the child's effrontery about memory needing script.

What possible advantage could anyone bring to a superior informant? (Livermore 1966: 41).

Many pages later, the boy will ask how so few Spaniards could have conquered so many Indians in a sophisticated Incan Empire. Garcilaso's slip into a Spanish positionality anticipates the obvious question for foreign readers already convinced of their own superior intelligence and prowess. The provocation incites a sarcastic response: Do you think that Spain could have conquered, the uncle sneers, if Peru hadn't anticipated the change in regime? Huaina Capác's last prophecy and exhortation "fueron más poderosas para nos sujetar y quitar nuestro Imperio que no las armas que tu padre y sus compañeros trajeron a esta tierra" (were more powerful in subjecting us and depriving us of our empire than the arms your father and his companions brought to this land) (Garcilo 1609, pt. 1, bk. 9, chap. 15). And when the youth practically packed off for Spain and, evidently thinking from that distance, wonders why his family is not mourning the death of Atahaullpa's son, the uncle turns on him, furious at the reckless mistaking of a traitor for a king (ibid., pt. 1, bk. 9, chap. 39).

The unsolicited supplements that undermine what we know, the recursive rhythm of translation from pagan to Catholic and back again, and the shifts in perspective from Iberia to the Andes, are some techniques for keeping a bullish reader dizzy and docile. Garcilaso has others, too. For example, he practically (re)moves the very ground from under us when he says that two distant provinces or cities can have the same name. (Go know that another Chelem really does exist.) If Spaniards attribute certain marriage practices to the Incas, it is because they confuse one province with its namesake (ibid., pt. 1, bk. 4, chap. 8). But how can they avoid confusion, if one place is called by another's name? Spaniards thought they were learning about cannibalism near Cuzco, Garcilaso corrects, because they were being told about a remote regional homonym during the primitive pre-Incan period (ibid., pt. 1, bk. 2, chap. 8). Provinces could share the same name, it seems, if they shared a professional mission. This is what happens in Rucana and Rucana, "ambas de un nombre" (both of the same name), two different places that provided royal bearers for the Inca (ibid., pt. 1, bk. 6, chap. 3). The geographic doubling that shuttles readers from one place to another blurs familiar information into disorienting double vision. The move may mean something more than a simple corrective to the epistemological limitations of a European identity principle. It may also be designed purposefully to disorient and to dizzy a reader. Unsure of how to step, an otherwise bullish traveler stays submissive and permits an agile guide to weave gracefully back and forth. If I am reading control out of this nominal doubling and displacement, it is because Garcilaso suggests as much in a passage that praises Incan political strategy. One winning tactic of political control was the *mítmac*, which amounted to shifting newly conquered populations from familiar territory to unknown parts (ibid., pt. 1, bk. 9, chap. 12). First the Inca's enemies lose the war, and then they are lost in a vast, unknowable empire that only the royal house can truly comprehend.

The bidirectional translations, the repeating place-names that send us coming and going, the alternating and almost equally pitched praise for Spaniards and for Incas, these are practically signatures of Garcilaso's style. An unkind observer might call him a "weaver," in the sense that Gonzalo Pizarro's merciless field marshal used the term *tejedor* to slander soldiers who went back and forth during the civil war between Pizarro's men and the Spanish crown.[10] Whether or not Garcilaso's father was such a warrior of wavering, or pragmatic, loyalties, the son's later military service to Spain was unimpeachable, if minor. His soldier's career, highlighted by a war against unruly moriscos, lasted only long enough to show that it was going nowhere. But his literary tribute of a lovingly detailed Incan world lasted a lifetime, and it surely increased the value of His Majesty's conquests. Once the Inca substituted his sword for a pen, he showed himself to be an expert weaver indeed. Without forsaking one side for the other, he alternated endlessly between languages and loyalties.

The alleged opportunism tarnished his reputation for a while, especially a generation ago when he was being unfavorably compared to other Andean chroniclers of the period, notably Guamán Poma de Ayala and Juan de Santacruz Pachacuti Yamqui, who were said to be more racially and culturally "authentic" than the Hispanized master of Castilian style.[11]

10. "Francisco de Carvajal, Gonzalo Pizarro's ruthless field marshal, liked to refer to those who changed allegiance during the civil war as *tejedores* (weavers) because they went back and forth. The weave of Garcilaso's *Comentarios* is so complex because his father was a weaver of sorts" (González-Echevarría 1990: 75).

11. Guamán Poma's *Nueva corónica* was first published in 1936, almost four centuries after it was written. The publication opened an entire field in Andean studies,

No wonder the Spaniards loved him; he pandered to their pride in over-powering Peru, militarily and culturally. Spanish contemporaries were, in fact, evidently impressed enough with his work to pass it through the Inquisitorial approvals and to publish it. But the Spaniards knew they had made a politically delicate decision by the time of Tupaq Amaru's rebellion in 1781. After that Garcilaso's book was banned in America. Some years later, the liberator San Martín remembered why: the *Commentaries* could teach Americans to be proud of a great indigenous civilization, and he was sure that a local printing of the work would stimulate the struggle for emancipation (Rojas 1943: 19, 20). A successful strategist himself, San Martín may have appreciated the virtues of Garcilaso's pragmatic parries with the powerful. Sometimes this means choosing when to be heroic. Certainly early Spanish historians had sometimes preferred discretion over daring (Garcilaso 1609, pt. 1, bk. 8, chap. 24). Garcilaso promises to be bolder, but evidently that didn't mean being foolhardy.

Philón Aunque no es de hombre virtuoso dezir mentira (puesto que fuesse provechosa), no por esso es de hombre prudente dezir la verdad, quando nos trae daño y peligro; que la verdad, que siendo dicha es dañosa, prudencia es callarla y temeridad hablarla.

(Philón: Although it is not for a virtuous man to tell a lie [just to seek advantage], this is not to say that a prudent man should tell the truth, when it will bring harm and danger; because a truth, which when told is hurtful, is prudently kept quiet and spoken with temerity.)   (Hebreo 1947 [1590]: 235–36)

The wise are not stupid, Sophía's philosophical lover explains. They neither welcome disaster nor mistake the negligence of basic needs for sanctity. It is more pious, obviously, to provide alms than needlessly to beg them (ibid.: 38–39).

Garcilaso was good at avoiding disaster, and at shoring up basic needs. As a weaver, doubling back and forth sometimes within the same sentence, he was prudently mending a torn text, rent between Spain and Peru, a fabric that could, potentially, protect him. Indians were expert at weaving together their own torn garments, Garcilaso tells us, and

---

that had generally contrasted the mestizo with the Indian. For recent examples of this tendency, see Wachtel 1973 and Seed 1991. See also Adorno 1992: 369–95.

they would laugh at the holes and clumsy stitching that scarred Spanish clothing (Garcilaso 1609: pt. 1, bk. 4, chap. 14). For Garcilaso, weaving was not so much turning coats, as composing a coat of many colors. The privilege of a doubly noble heritage that Garcilaso hoped to display by showing his complicating coloring was also, perhaps, a demonstration that racial and cultural threads are stubbornly colorfast. They don't easily bleed into an assimilated monochrome that could camouflage difference. Although a multicolored covering is not always a safe style of self-presentation, especially when it can provoke powerful Spanish brothers and offend the already damaged pride of Incan survivors, it suited him handsomely. Being the very style that could favor Garcilaso, he wove so beautifully complicated a text that brothers from both sides would want to see themselves in its flattering lines.

The lines crossed, but they never twisted into a synthetic mestizo unity. More and more, today's readings of Garcilaso's *mestizaje* are changing it from a composite term to an internally divided word. It is not only that his two worlds are finally irreconcilable, juxtaposed rather than fused, but that Garcilaso himself meant different things when he called himself mestizo, as Antonio Cornejo Polar explains: sometimes the word stood for his particular mix of noble blood, and at other times for the marginalization he shared with the misfits of both worlds (1989: 20). Garcilaso's work has sometimes been celebrated as an agenda for resolving cultural tensions, but his best readers (including Cornejo, Jákfalvi-Leiva, and Mazzotti) notice that the tensions persist unabated throughout the text.

Garcilaso locates himself both at the authentic root of American civilization and at the modernizing vanguard of European culture. Through an Incan creed that, like the Old Testament, delivered people from idolatry and prefigured salvation, Garcilaso is a native of the New World. (Huaina Cápac's personal testament condenses the story, when the dying Inca urges his empire to obey a superior civilization about to arrive [Garcilaso 1609: pt. 1, bk. 9, chap. 15].) Through his easy and elegant Spanish, sometimes replacing Blas Valera's worn Latin letters with modern speech (ibid.: pt. 1, bk. 9, chaps. 14, 23), Garcilaso stations himself inside the Crown's colonial enterprise. Spanish was the language of empire, just as grammarian Antonio de Nebrija had predicted in his 1492 prologue to the language's first manual. Christianity didn't need Spanish, as the Jesuits and other evangelizing orders knew very well from their work in

Latin and in several local languages.[12] But conquest did demand a unified code, comparable to the "general language" that the Incas imposed
in each newly conquered and capably controlled territory. It was not
the exclusive and elite language spoken among Incan royalty, but a consistent and uniform colloquial language. Spaniards might perfect their
own best tool of empire, Garcilaso suggests, by emulating that consistency. Instead, they corrupt the Andean general language by confusing
localisms with standard usage. What is one to expect from people whose
native language cannot decide to call a pepper either "ají" or "pimiento"?
(ibid., pt. 1, bk. 5, chap. 5).

Style, then, in Garcilaso is something different from the dialogic conventions of Hebreo's genre, which others have already appreciated. One
feature of dialogue is that it can drive an argument forward, and this
was obviously a handy frame for Garcilaso's long-term defense of his
trammeled rights. Yet, if the dialogic genre were Hebreo's main asset,
his translator might have chosen a more classic, Socratic-type dialogue
to drill on, one that sets an objective and presses on to win. Dialogue
need not, of course, be a genre for winning points; it can also explore
them, which is what Hebreo did and, as some have noticed, what Garcilaso learned from him. He learned to manipulate a bivocal figure for his
doubled identity, and thereby to frame his transactions and translations
from one world to another. Two voices engaged in understanding each
other, and the universal principles that affect them both, would indeed
be ideal vehicles for Garcilaso's crossover efforts from one position to
another. But neither the forensic force that one variety of the genre can
promise, nor the equalizing reciprocity that a different kind of dialogue
can represent, says much about the particular style that Hebreo practiced and that Garcilaso perfected.

Hebreo's dialogues don't drive; they ramble and circle. His interlocutors don't use each other as foils for reaching a truth that favors one
and dismisses the other; they amuse each other with intelligent talk and
probing questions. Philón talks. Sophía questions. One answer raises
more queries, and objections bring opportunities for more speculative
discourse. In fact, they never end; they only stop. Hebreo announced

12. Walter Mignolo has developed these observations, for example, in *Writing
without Words: Alternative Literacies in Mesoamerica and the Andes* (Boone and
Mignolo 1994: 292–313).

another conversation to follow his three-part work, but that final, fourth dialogue has never been found. Perhaps it was preempted by the unstable environment. Writing projects can get lost in geographic shuttles and political seesaws (Gebhardt 1934: 270). But the unfinished form is noteworthy for more than its possible traces of circumstance; it makes sense in a Neoplatonic treatise about the continuing process of perfecting the world. How could a final, grammatically "perfect" word be pronounced before the process is finished? Whatever Garcilaso may have learned about legal argumentation from these dialogues, it was not how to reach closure.

As for noticing the possibility of ideal reciprocity in the genre, its opportunities for translating from one position to the other, there is nothing of the sort in Hebreo. The translations between codes transpire only in Philón's voice. He develops classical myths into allegorical analogies with scripture; he follows the thread that ties human desire to universal love. Sophía tells us nothing, it seems. She just taunts the man, goads him on, keeps him chasing after explanations, and after her. To focus on the balance of voices in an open-ended dialogue like this one, as opposed to the Socratic sort, is to miss the particular style here. It is playful, or nervous; and the only balance it produces between the interlocutors is a balance of power. He has all the answers, but she keeps dodging any conclusive assent. Whatever legal and logical connections he can master, Philón is finally a slave to the law of desire.

No te puedo resistir, o Sophía! Quando pienso averte atajado todos los caminos de la huyda, te me vas por nueva senda. Conviene, pues, hazer lo que te plaze; y la principal razon es que soy amante y tu amada; a ti toca darme la ley, y a mi guardarla con execucion.

(I cannot resist you, O Sophía! When I think I have cut off all the paths of your flight, you escape through a new route. It makes sense, then, to do what pleases you; and the principal reason is that I am a lover and you are the beloved; it is up to you to give me the law, and up to me to keep and execute it.)   (Hebreo 1947 [1590]: 235)

Hebreo's most original lessons are in coquettish instability. Renaissance intellectuals could be responsive to women's physical and intellectual charms; certainly Hebreo was. He dedicated his book to Madonna Laudomia Forteguerri, and admired, along with everyone else, his captivating cousin Doña Benvenida Abravanel, the center of intellectual salons and spirited conversation, who married his younger brother Samuel. Guedella Ibn Yahiya, that first and almost forgotten Spanish translator of Hebreo's *Dialogues,* confessed that the book had changed his own misogynist mind and had inspired a short work he later wrote "In Praise of Women" (Dorman 1983: 123).

Coyly, but unmistakably, Sophía's lessons are thematized in Hebreo's book. Her loving quip about Philón's intellectual agility gives a name to his practice of unstoppable discoursing on knowledge. It is a stream that finds outlets from its own tight spots by daring to continue; "Ya puedes dezir lo que se te antojare, que segun veo, bien sabes el modo de rescatarte." Endless talk that solves the very problems it has created (as if problems were a desired opportunity to keep talk alive) and the slippery wisdom that keeps intelligence on the chase by subordinating knowledge to desire are Hebreo's basic elements of style. They describe the book's constant maneuvering between engagement and estrangement. Together, the lessons teach an inexhaustible logic of errancy that evidently inspired Garcilaso.[13] That the translator was attentive to the alternating rhythm of the book is clear from his comments in the prologue letter to Don Maximiliano of Austria: Hebreo did not write for passive readers, but "for those who would accompany him, philosophizing together" (Hebreo 1947 [1590]: 25). Garcilaso's very process of translation, in bits and pieces for his own recreation, suggests that Hebreo's almost playful rhythm of pursuit must have been at least as alluring as its philosophical conclusions about the ultimate coherence of competing systems of belief (ibid.: 23).

Hebreo was the master dialectician of desire, the model of a literary practice that urged correspondences and cast them as ever higher degrees of love. When Sophía wonders why desire shouldn't flag after the act of love is consummated, Philón answers, rakishly, that she obviously lacks experience in the matter. Desire of the flesh may be sated by contact with the flesh. But a lover's desire has no rest. When it is born of intellectual as well as corporeal attractions—like the multiple charms with which Peru could captivate her conqueror in Garcilaso's historical seductions—corporeal copulation frustrates the lovers more than it ful-

13. A similar observation, from the perspective of a doubled politics of identity, comes from Susana Jákfalvi-Leiva (1987).

fills them. Physical love is so limited a form of penetration that it only whets an appetite for a more complete union. Bodies are vehicles, but they get in the way (ibid.: 84).

Heretical as it sounds, the philosophical content of Hebreo's book sometimes seems beside the main point for his interlocutors, the point being simply to keep talking. The diachronic-dialogic frame shuttles a reader between what Emmanuel Lévinas would call the Saying and the Said, between responding to a lover's command and the always insufficient words that renew the command. That frame continually shows through the philosophical, synchronic, and thematizable meanings that Philón apparently masters.[14] And the diachrony, the proximity through time, is what keeps the lovers together. Philón and Sophía crave each other's conversational contact, they can't get enough of one another, because whichever tongue happens to be working (either the one between the arms or the one between the legs, in Philón's [porno]graphic analogy [Hebreo 1947 [1590]: 112] borrowed from *Sefer Yezira* [Kaplan, I: 4]), the limited and frustrating contact it makes with the beloved only goads desire. When Philón seems to have sewn up all the arguments, Sophía wisely points to a loose thread in a badly stitched text. The exasperated and exhilarated man in love concedes, and continues to talk.

Can it be merely casual that the dialogues do not end? The fragmentary form, as I mentioned, makes philosophical sense, since it participates in an unfinished Neoplatonic process of perfecting the world. But the form makes another kind of tactical sense, too. It gives an open-ended shape to the lesson of continuity in the dialogues, a lesson of avoiding closure, of maneuvering back and forth into the intellectual gaps that produce more talk and keep the lovers together. Philón's intellectual superiority is acknowledged in every one of Sophía's endless questions. I have admitted that he has all the ideas, all the explanations; he makes all the theological and philosophical connections between cultures. From either a cursory or a considered reading, it is clear that Philón's tongue is the source of information. He is also the more sublime lover, as a man who can use a nether tongue for giving love. "Ten pa-

---

14. "If, after the innumerable 'irrefutable' refutations which logical thought sets against it, skepticism has the gall to return (and it always returns as philosophy's illegitimate child), it is because in the contradiction which logic sees in it the 'at the same time' of the contradictories is missing, because a secret diachrony commands this ambiguous or enigmatic way of speaking, and because in general signification signifies beyond synchrony, beyond essence" (Lévinas 1974: 7).

ciencia, o Sophía!, que más perfectamente ama el varón, que da, que la hembra, que recibe" (Be patient, O Sophía!, because the man, who gives, loves more perfectly than the woman, who receives) (Hebreo 1947 [1590]: 189). And the capacity to engender both ideas and babies with a man's two tongues makes his "bilingual" love analogous to a parent's selfless love for a child and God's divine love for creation.

Sophía is, in fact, quite patient with his unflattering comparison between their levels of intelligence and generosity. Her advantage over him is entirely different. She is as wise as her name, Hebreo shows us repeatedly. How can that be? What virtue can she possibly have in a philosophical dialogue about love that casts her counterpart as the only expert? The answer is strategic, as I have been arguing: Sophía embodies the virtue and the wisdom of tactical evasion. She can humble a superior intellect by simply refusing to be overwhelmed. Sophía is ever on the alert for discursive lapses, those promising opportunities to talk and to stay, to safeguard, in Lévinas's vocabulary, the eroticized and ethical proximity of incomplete Saying from the cold and asocial finality of the Said.[15]

Although Philón is the uncontested giant of scholarship, the powerful mind that is heir to a privileged (male) birth and to a patrician education in perfectibility, pretty little Sophía can lead him by the nose. Like a delicate but dauntless choreographer of bulls, she is wisdom itself, perfecting the powerful intellect by engaging it in a continuing program of graceful exercise. Desire (Lévinas's ethics?) is what makes Philón submit; it weakens his will, constrains his self-confidence, and puts him to work. It would seem that Garcilaso learned to double as Sophía when he learned to maneuver around a privileged and powerful reader who could be taught to desire and to defer to the guide. As a student of both interlocutors, Garcilaso's seduction reaches an almost perverse level of refinement. It both offers satisfaction and undercuts it. Sophía's

15. Emmanuel Lévinas writes: "Saying is not a game. Antecedent to the verbal signs it conjugates, to the linguistic systems and the semantic glimmerings, a foreword preceding languages, it is the proximity of one to the other, the commitment of an approach, the one for the other, the very signifyingness of signification" (1974: 5); "Essence fills the said, or the epos, of the saying, but the saying, in its power of equivocation, that is, in the enigma whose secret it keeps, escapes the epos of essence that includes it and signifies beyond in a signification that hesitates between this beyond and the return to the epos of essence. This equivocation or enigma is an inalienable power in saying and a modality of transcendence" (ibid.: 9–10).

coy evasions and Philón's passionate pronouncements, her destabilizing questions and his intellectual reparations, both voices echo through one dialogic style. Garcilaso's characteristic shuttling and weaving (between viewpoints, languages, cults, and countries) not only unhinges any intellectual mooring a reader may have had. The destabilizing dialogue also makes Garcilaso the moving target of his reader's unsated desire. And insatiable desire, we know from Hebreo, is one sure sign of love.

REFERENCES

Adorno, Rolena
  1988 "El sujeto colonial y la construcción de la alteridad," *Revista de crítica literaria latinoamericana* Vol. 14(28): 55–68.
  1992 "El indio ladino en el Perú colonial," in *De palabra y obra en el Nuevo Mundo.* Vol. 1, *Imágenes interétnicas,* edited by M. León-Portilla, M. Gutiérrez-Estévez, G. H. Gossen, and J. Klor de Alva, 369–95 (Madrid: Siglo Veintiuno).
Boone, Elizabeth Hill, and Walter D. Mignolo, eds.
  1994 *Writing without Words: Alternative Literacies in Mesoamerica and the Andes* (Durham, NC: Duke University Press).
Carpentier, Alejo
  1979 *El arpa y la sombra* (Mexico: Siglo Veintiuno).
Cornejo Polar, Antonio
  1989 "Cinco respuestas en torno a Garcilaso," *Literaturas Andinas* 6(2): 19–27.
Dorman, Menachem, trans.
  1983 *Leone Ebreo (Giuda Abarbanel) Dialoghi d'amore, tradutione ebraica di Menachem Dorman* (Jerusalem: Bialik Institute).
Durand, José
  1950 "El Inca Garcilaso, historiador apasionado," *Cuadernos Americanos* 60 (6): 153–68.
Gaon, Salomon
  1993 *The Influence of the Catholic Theologian Alfonso Tostado on the Pentateuch Commentary of Isaac Abravanel* (Hoboken, N.J.: Ktav).
Garcilaso de la Vega, El Inca
  1590 *Traduzión del Yndio de los tres Diálogos de Amor de León Hebreo hecha de Italiano en Español por Garcilasso Ynga de la Vega* (Madrid: Casa de Pedro Madrigal).
  1605 *La Florida del Inca* (Lisbon: Pedro Crasbeeck).
  1609 *Los comentarios reales de los Incas/The Royal Commentaries of the Incas* (Lisbon: Pedro Crasbeeck).

Gebhardt, Carl
   1934 "León Hebreo: Su vida y su obra," *Revista de occidente* 12(32): 233–73.
González-Echevarría, Roberto
   1990 *Myth and Archive: A Theory of Latin American Narrative* (New York: Cambridge University Press).
Hebreo, León
   1947 [1590] *Diálogos de amor, traducción Inca Garcilaso de la Vega* (Buenos Aires: Austral).
Jákfalvi-Leiva, Susana
   1984 *Traducción, escritura y violencia colonizadora: Un estudio de la obra del Inca Garcilaso* (Syracuse, N.Y.: Maxwell School of Citizenship and Public Affairs).
   1987 "Errancia y (des)centralización lingüística en la cultura andina," *Discurso literario* 4: 357–65.
Lévinas, Emmanuel
   1974 *Otherwise than Being: Or, Beyond Essence,* translated by Alphonso Lingis (Dordrecht/Boston/London: Kluwer Academic Publishers).
Livermore, Harold V., trans.
   1966 *Royal Commentaries of the Incas, and General History of Peru, Part One by El Inca Garcilaso de la Vega* (Austin: University of Texas Press).
López de Gómara, Francisco
   1979 [1552] *Historia general de las Indias y vida Hernán Cortés* (Caracas: Biblioteca Ayacucho).
MacCormack, Sabine
   1991 *Religion in the Andes: Vision and Imagination in Early Colonial Peru* (Princeton: Princeton University Press).
Markham, Clements R., ed. and trans.
   1869–71 *First Part of the Royal Commentaries of the Yncas, by the Ynca Garcilasso de la Vega* (New York: Burt Franklin).
Mazzotti, José A.
   1993 "Una coralidad mestiza: Subtexto andino y discurso sincrético en los Comentarios reales del Inca Garcilaso de la Vega." Ph.D. diss., Princeton University.
Miró Quesada, Aurelio
   1971 *El Inca Garcilaso y otros estudios garcilasistas* (Madrid: Cultura Hispánicas).
Ortega, Julio
   1992 "The Discourse of Abundance," translated by Nicolás Wey Gómez, *American Literary History* 4: 369–85.
Pupo-Walker, Enrique
   1982 *Historia creación y profecía en los textos del Inca Garcilaso de la Vega* (Madrid: José Porrúa Turanzas).

Rojas, Ricardo

    1943 "Prólogo," in *Comentarios reales de los Incas,* edited by Angel Rosenblat (Buenos Aires: Emecé).

Roth, Cecil

    1937 "Introduction," in *Leone Ebreo, The Philosophy of Love,* translated by F. Friedeberg-Seeley and Jean H. Barnes, ix–xv (London: Soncino).

Seed, Patricia

    1991 "Failing to Marvel: Atahualpa's Encounter with the Letter," *Latin American Research Review* 26(1): 1–24.

Wachtel, Nathan

    1973 "Pensamiento salvaje y aculturación: El espacio y el tiempo en Felipe Guaman Poma de Ayala y el Inca Garcilaso de la Vega," in *Sociedad e ideología: Ensayos de historia y antropología andinas* (Lima: IEP).

Zamora, Margarita

    1988 *Language, Authority, and Indigenous History in the Comentarios reales de los Incas* (Cambridge: Cambridge University Press).

ALICIA BORINSKY

GOMBROWICZ'S TANGO:

AN ARGENTINE SNAPSHOT

I GREW UP IN A KIND OF JEWISH FAMILY not uncommon in Argentina. My parents, aunts, and uncles, Eastern Europeans with varying degrees of hostility toward countries that had spat them out and massacred those who stayed on, developed a nervous allegiance to a Buenos Aires that in many ways remained foreign and suspect. They participated in the cult of the city as a cosmopolitan cultural space bent on the pleasures of good food and high fashion while acknowledging its brutal tendency toward anti-Semitism with a fatalism brought on by the circumstances that had landed them there. The children of these immigrants were born into a secular, integrated society in constant financial crisis, toying with various modes of nationalistic expression and political activism. The overall feeling for this younger generation was, nevertheless, one of belonging to the place, not of being stranded like the numerous groups of older exiles consumed by nostalgia, such as the Spanish Republicans (the subjects of more than one joke) patiently waiting for Franco's death for their return to Spain.

With many others of my generation, I left Argentina during the dictatorships of the late sixties and experienced for myself the longing that had seemed so quaint and easy to parody in my parents and the numerous other groups: exiled Spanish Republicans who continued to harangue against Franco for decades; Russians agitating against the Red Peril; Nazis jealously guarding their sinister paraphernalia; Italian and Jewish anarchists and socialists discussing Peronism in terms of their own European pasts. I became part of a group that learned afresh what their parents had known: how to prepare one's bags not for a season, a short stay, but rather to select what would become the complete stock from a home that had become threatening. That first departure was for me unlike any other and even though, with circumstances changed, I return frequently now to an Argentina with a much altered political and social atmosphere, the length of the distance traveled on that first trip remains immeasurably distinct. I made up a list of indispensable items:

books I could not do without, musical recordings I was concerned I would not be able to find elsewhere, shoes to weather a climate I had never encountered. I developed an anxiety about the efficiency of the post office and an urgent need to find previously neglected manuscripts of my own work and translations I had made of others'. Those papers and objects, once located, made me realize that a choice had to be made since there was not enough room in the suitcases for everything. It all resulted in a feeling of loss, a sense that light as I had become I could go anywhere. None of this is rendered by the tame word *trip*. This was no trip; it was the change of a pace, the beginning of a way of being in the world not centered in the memory of a nurturing homeland. In the early seventies I met the Chilean writer José Donoso who, as we talked about the times we were living in, said that I was wrong not to write letters more frequently to my friends because I should realize that the post office was a writer's true homeland. This insight still accompanies me because changing addresses, long-distance friendships, the weave of foreignness and familiarity have become part of the way I see the world.

I have a long-standing fascination with writers and artists whose profiles are to be found in their peculiar displacement. A mere fragment of that list includes, for example, in Paris: Walter Benjamin, strolling in a city that is at the same time a writing pad, his persona by turns that of the Jew promising himself and his friend Gershom Scholem that he will, should, or might learn Hebrew, or that claimed by Marxists as a materialist, or that of the academic searching for help to get a teaching position in the United States; Julio Cortázar, whose uncannily upbeat grave in the Montparnasse cemetery stands as a de facto resolution of the conflict he enunciated in the pages of his novel *Hopscotch*[1] (1967) by calling one of its parts *Del lado de aquí* and the other *Del lado de allá*; and Jean Rhys, whose strolls and stays at Left Bank hotels helped her weave the character of the uprooted woman as an aimless poseur and outsider. Buenos Aires, London, towns and cities in the United States and Bra-

---

1. The novel suggests two readings: one that is linear and another that hops from chapter to chapter in an order given at the beginning. The division into two main parts (*Del lado de aquí,* From here; *Del lado de allá,* From there) alludes to Argentina and France. One of the epigraphs of the novel is by Jacques Vaché, who is quoted as saying in a letter to André Breton that nothing can annihilate a man more surely than the obligation of representing a country ("Rien ne vous tue un homme comme d'etre obligé de représenter un pays") (Cortázar 1967: 11).

zil become permanently temporary homes to writers such as Vladimir
Nabokov, Isaac Bashevis Singer, Witold Gombrowicz, Clarice Lispector,
and so many others who provide us with the textures and meanings of a
sense of distance intricate beyond maps.

The essay that follows is part of a book now in progress about contemporary writers and the culture of exile. The book focuses on trips without return, one-way tickets, whether biographically accurate or with the
precision rendered by fiction. The present excerpt considers the strange
destiny of Witold Gombrowicz, Polish writer in Argentina, as he becomes intertwined with the characters of tango lyrics.

TANGO OR THE CITY AS DEPARTURE

The architecture of Buenos Aires, with its mixed styles reminiscent of the
cities left behind by those who commissioned them or who longed for
places unknown to the builders, intrigues some and exasperates others.[2]
The very intermingling of periods, schools, and geographic locations
seems to bespeak a peculiar form of travel. Being in Buenos Aires might
be a mirage; we could be either there or in Madrid, Palermo, Paris, London. Buenos Aires is a city built with an architecture of quotations and
one's itineraries delineate arrivals of different groups and hopes for departure in a triumphant argument for decontextualization. The look of
Buenos Aires is distinct but borrowed. It is itself thanks to the power of
the derivations that compose it. Buenos Aires exists as a myth in tango, a
promise of exile enmeshed in the experience of love.

The streets of Buenos Aires are not fully traversed without a sense of
tango, with its implied choreography for encounters, disappointments,
and passions. Tango is a register for interpretation, a map that decodes

2. Antoine de Saint-Exupéry was in Buenos Aires in 1929 and was thoroughly
put off by the look of the city and the admiration for the French that he saw in
the *porteños* he met. Stacy Schiff says of his view of Buenos Aires: "Every well-
bred Argentine thought himself spiritually and culturally a Frenchman, but all her
love of France could not make Buenos Aires look like Paris. A house dating from
1890 was considered old; the city's architecture was a jumble of steel and concrete
New York–style skyscrapers, French-inspired *hotels particuliers,* and small colonial
homes, all piled atop one another" (Schiff 1994: 168). His reaction exemplifies the
strong impression, both negative and positive, that the city made and continues to
make on its visitors and inhabitants.

poses of characters in bars, praises certain street corners and neighborhoods, warns us of the dangers of downtown glitter, and laments that we
have been banned from the honest destinies behind the modest doors of
the one-story houses in the low-income areas of the city. It creates the
illusion that one does not die in vain because its stories give meaning to
resentment and orchestrate mistrust of the wealthy, of the collective, and
of love. Tango names a void, a lack, in its evocation of women, inscrib-
ing their role in love as a peculiar disappearing act.[3] As we turn to one
of the most celebrated examples of how a man falls for a woman, "Malevaje," we are told the story in the first person: "Te ví pasar tangueando
altanera / con un compás tan hondo y sensual / que no fue más que verte
y perder / la fe, el coraje y el ansia 'e luchar" (I saw you pass me by in a
tango step / so haughty / so deep / so sensual / that as soon as I saw you /
I lost my faith, courage, the urge to fight).[4] The male voice is addressing a woman who has mesmerized him; her sensuality has transformed
him. He went from being a swaggering rabble rouser to attending mass,
leaving his friends, losing, in fact, his way of life. The magnetism of the
woman as she defeats his male posturing by turning him into a lovesick
suitor is seen as a fall from grace. "Malevaje" understands manhood as
distinct from love. Being a man is staying with the boys in the rough,
knife-wielding neighborhoods where violence gains respect. By sheer
magnetism she has been able to turn him inside out. Her body, perfectly
attuned to the cadences of tango, suggests a path of pleasure exclusively
for two. No male friends. Not seeing his mother.

Tango teaches that a seductress, sinuous and promising but never
quite truthful, is always capable of altering the paradoxical harmony of
the violent male world. A man's success in conquering such a woman
is one with the deterioration of his life. In this sense, tango is deeply
suspicious of love, which is so frequently a maddening infatuation. "La
ingrata," the ungrateful, undeserving woman, may turn out to be a pros-

3. Borges went so far as to suggest that the true tango is womanless. He frequently
vindicated the tradition of tango as a dance between males, emphasizing the early
lyrics in which the main subjects are male knife fights. I think that he was mistaken
because those fights imply a strong presence of a woman triggering rivalry among
men, a subject that Borges raised in an exemplary manner in his short story "La
intrusa" (The female intruder) (1970).

4. The translations of tango lyrics are mine. Whenever I have not provided translations I have paraphrased or summarized the contents fully enough to enable the
reader to follow my argument.

titute or an adulteress, or may disappear from her lover's life, leaving him in debt and subject to ridicule from male friends who warned him of the dangers awaiting him. The lyrics of "Aquel tapado de armiño" (That ermine coat) tell of the state in which the jilted lover was left with an eloquence that has made the composition endure in the repertory for decades:

> Aquel tapado de armiño
> todo forrado en lamé
> que tu cuerpito abrigaba
> al salir del cabaret.
>
> Cuando pasate a mi lado,
> prendida a aquel gigoló
> aquel tapado de armiño
> ¡Cuánta pena me causó!

As he sees the woman coming out of the nightclub holding on to a gigolo and wearing an ermine coat that he is still paying for, the cost of the coat becomes a figure of his mistake. The woman's victim, he recalls the sacrifices he made to buy her that present even as she dons it for a life that humiliates his original hopes for their future. The woman in the ermine coat is no lady; she has left him to go out cavorting with sleazy nightclub characters. Here, as elsewhere in tango, the streets of the city provide a stage for glances, criticisms, betrayal and disapproval, or solidarity of friends and lovers. If the woman in "Malevaje," glanced at as she sashays by on the dance floor, promises an intensity of pleasure that she betrays by turning her man into a domesticated suitor, the sin of the one berated in "Aquel tapado de armiño" is the opposite: she goes from being a humble woman to delving into tango bars after she gets the coveted coat. The dance floor and the city are a writing pad on which the failures of love are inscribed and the mirages of infatuation forged.

Observing and being observed, the ones telling us their story are, at the same time, bringing us into the city; their love is intertwined with the streets and walking becomes a rehearsal of false starts and intermittent successes, a dance floor for tango. When they leave or are left, these characters are thrown back into the streets, their paths now traced by the wisdom of their stories.

Who are tango's good women, those deserving of love and loyalty? Mothers and sick sisters tend to be above reproach. One of Gardel's most celebrated renditions, entitled "Victoria," features a man who sings his joy (voicing victory) upon being left by his wife because he will be able to see his old friends again and go back to living with his mother ("volver a ver mis amigos/ vivir con mama otra vez"). Loyalty is found after love has already been defeated by the absence of one of the members of the couple; longing takes the form of circling around the pain of solitude. The preferred locale for telling the story is a table in a bar or a café or the lovers' home. Pascual Contursi wrote the most representative of these compositions, "Mi noche triste":

> Percanta que me amuraste
> en lo mejor de mi vida,
> dejándome el alma herida
> y espinas en el corazón,
> sabiendo que te quería
> que vos eras mi alegría
> y mi sueño abrasador,
> para mí ya no hay consuelo
> y por eso me encurdelo
> pa' olvidarme de tu amor

Jilted in the flower of his life, a drunk sitting by himself in a bar tells his story. The explanation for his deterioration is invariably the wound in-flicted by a woman. In this case, the evocation of what she has left behind is given in terms of the breakdown of the cozy domesticity of the room they shared, so that he is thrown into the streets unable to recover alone in their place. The departure of the "good" woman redefines the space in which the romance took place; longing for her is one with bemoan-ing the gloom of his surroundings. The serene harmony of the everyday, rather than anxiety at the sort of sexual harrassment practiced by the provocative *milonguera*,[5] is the mark of the worthwhile woman who is, nevertheless, bound to disappoint. While the departure of the unworthy objects of infatuation is a relief (although it is associated with moral and financial ruin), the loss of a good woman permeates every aspect of daily life. This is why the singer says that when he goes to sleep at night he

---

5. The *milonga* is a fast-paced and sensual dance that forms part of the tango tra-dition. The word also refers more generally to a party with dancing and alcohol. *Milonguera* is slang for a woman with a great deal of sexual appeal who is fond of nightlife.

leaves the door open so that she may come back in. He still brings home the little pastries she used to enjoy, and feels that the bed is angry at not having them both there:

> De noche cuando me acuesto,
> no puedo cerrar la puerta,
> porque dejándola abierta
> me hago ilusión que volvés.
> Siempre llevo bizcochitos
> pa' tomar con matecitos
> como si estuvieras vos,
> y si vieras la catrera
> cómo se pone cabrera
> cuando no nos ve a los dos.

The wealthy are regularly denounced by tango's populist lyrics. Men and women who dress up in fancy clothes and show off their money and jewels in nightclubs are shown to be fakes or mere parasites; *niños bien* (for men) and *pitucas* (for women) are the chosen definitions for these characters who abound in the city. The worthy woman of tango, then, is humble in appearance and her attributes offer an alternative to the nocturnal glitter and sexual density of the relationships between pimps and prostitutes. In this manner, missing the woman also betrays nostalgia for an original, uncomplicated relationship to reality in which money does not play the decisive role it does elsewhere. Descriptions of appearance become keys in defining the moral profiles of characters evoked by tango, creating a complicity with a listener who shares the judgments made by the singer in his confession. Thus, the shabby brown coat and hat of the departing María in the composition of that name are emblems of her kindness:

> Acaso te llamaras solamente María,
> no sé si eras el eco de una vieja canción,
> pero hace mucho, mucho fuiste hondamente mía
> sobre un paisaje triste, desmayado de amor.
>
> El otoño te trajo, mojando de agonía,
> tu sombrerito pobre y el tapado marrón.
> Eras como la calle de la melancolía
> que llovía ... llovía sobre mi corazón.

Perhaps her name was just María, the singer tells us; she might have been the echo of an old song, but he knows that she was deeply his a long time ago. The landscape was sad, rainy; María brought in by autumn with her humble clothes was just like the melancholy street raining on the singer's heart. María is, then, the medium through which an absent, humble young woman is woven into the landscape with the certainty of goodness lost. Her aura of moral uplift a result of her attire, she has left a wound that defines autumn as well as the streets in which she appeared.

Humble women and humble neighborhoods carry the ethical conviction of tango, providing a momentary way out from the betrayals of glitter. It is on those subjects that tango lyrics lose their sharp-edged sarcasm and skepticism and wish instead for the return of the one who holds a key to that particular harmonious state in which love, the good, and simple pleasures coexist.

Returning women, though, seen passing in the street years after the love affair is over, show that time has erased the beauty of youth, with traces that bespeak the misleading nature of all love. A ubiquitous lament is the one expressed as "y pensar que hace diez años fue mi locura / que llegué hasta la traición por tu hermosura / que esto que hoy es un cascajo fue la triste metedura / donde yo perdí el honor" (and to think that ten years ago I was crazy about her / that I went as far as betrayal for her beauty / and that which is today an empty shell / was the sad infatuation / for which I threw away my pride). Better not to come back, tango teaches us, because the drunk wallowing in his pain in a bar will be further disappointed by the looks of his beloved. The young woman who left her poor origins for the allure of money and nightlife is portrayed as heartless and ugly after her youth and innocence are snatched away by "la farra," the pleasures of the cabaret. Such is the lesson of Pascual Contursi's "Flor de fango" (Gutter flower), which tells the story, in lunfardo (Buenos Aires slang), of a beautiful girl who gives herself up at the age of fourteen to "las delicias de un gotán" (the indulgences of tango) and ends up losing herself night after night in the ongoing party, portrayed in contrast to the domesticity of her previous simple, worthy existence. She has been coaxed, like other women in tango tradition, into believing in love only to be left alone, old and disillusioned.

The repertoire of the early female tango singers, notably Rosita Quiroga, contained a number of compositions — of which "Maula" is among the better known — that addressed with insults a male lover who did not live up to his end of the couple's obligations. But it is the white slave trade of the first part of the century that provides the stories with which tango renders a woman's loss of her hopes.

The journey from Paris to Buenos Aires is a favorite subject for tango. Several compositions tell of the longing felt by those who are stranded in Paris, unable to return to the homeland, a subject which became popularized from the male exile's point of view by the movies of Carlos Gardel, whose renditions of "Mi Buenos Aires querido" (My beloved Buenos Aires) and "Anclao en París" (Stuck in Paris) continue to define the distance between Montmartre, the Latin Quarter, and Corrientes Avenue. For the women, though, nostalgia is felt in reverse. It is the French women, taken to Buenos Aires under false pretenses and made to work as prostitutes, who experience the loss of both their homeland and the men who seduced them. Enrique Cadícamo's "Madame Ivonne" portrays the destiny of such a character:

> Han pasao diez años que zarpó de Francia
> Mamausel Ivonne es hoy sólo Madam,
> la que al ver que todo quedó en la distancia
> con ojos muy tristes bebe su champán.
> Ya no es la papusa del Barrio Latino,
> ya no es la mistonga florcita de lis,
> Ya nada le queda ... ni aquel argentino
> que entre tango y mate la alzó de París.

Ivonne, ten years after having left France, has gone from being called Mademoiselle Ivonne to just *Madam* and is shown sipping champagne, looking sadly into the distance, no longer the pride of the Latin Quarter, with nothing left, not even that Argentine who between *mates* and tangos swept her away from Paris. Ivonne, a victim of love, joins the parade of the seduced and abandoned in Buenos Aires, another figure for the gallery of characters that tango offers as a definition of life in the city.

What does she want? Where is she going? (¿Qué pretende? ¿Adónde va?) asks the male voice in Homero Expósito's "Margo" as he portrays the return from Paris to Buenos Aires of Margo, now without faith, friends, or youth. Tired and mistaken, Margo did not understand her destiny:

> París
> era oscura y cantaba su tango feliz,
> sin pensar, ¡pobrecita!... que el viejo París
> se alimenta con el breve

fin brutal de una magnolia
entre la nieve.
Después,
otra vez Buenos Aires
y Margo otra vez sin amor y sin fe.

Margo should not have returned anywhere. Paris was no longer hers after the time she had spent away and Buenos Aires would only further undo any hopes of love or, for that matter, of anything else. Gone, forgotten, remembered and glimpsed again, the women sung by tango suffer from a wound that cannot be healed. The appearances that trigger love's entanglements endlessly deceive those they capture.

Returning is always a mistake because time does not heal but punishes. Tango tells us to study the faces, the clothes, the pride, and the defeat, the momentary triumphs as we walk in the city and to recognize those who have been lost or are about to leave; their names do not matter because their stories are already woven and repeated with other faces in the same streets. The princess in Rubén Darío's poem "Sonatina," whose mysterious sadness is presented against the aristocratic backdrop of a royalty nobody disputes, has given way to the itineraries of the urban novelist Roberto Arlt with his gallery of prostitutes, would-be inventors, thieves, and losers and to the tangos of Contursi so that a myth of distance may be constructed in the proximity of Buenos Aires neighborhoods.

Tango says that the distance between hope and fulfillment is unbridgeable. The very landscape of Buenos Aires has inscribed that distance in its architecture; the city's scattered stylistic allegiances seem triggered by a passion for other places. Its people sitting in cafés or bars and milling in the street are seen by tango as always waiting for or recovering from somebody's departure. Everything and everybody appears to be distant. Buenos Aires is a city of departures and yet it has the capacity to seduce, to make itself be missed, to instill the sense that that very skepticism about its own roots is a unique source of identity.

AN ARRIVAL: HOW FOREIGN CAN YOU BE?

Witold Gombrowicz went from Poland to Argentina in 1939, thinking that he was to pay a brief literary visit, but as the events of the war unfolded, he decided to stay, eventually being forced into a fight for survival in a country in which people did not recognize his name. He had undertaken the trip because of its literary interest, but pretty soon he had to struggle to make a reputation for himself. The arrival, the life-defining turn he took by not going back to Europe for more than two decades, became a source of conversation, self-justification, and writing. He spent a great deal of time in cafés, striving to overcome the shadow of anonymity cast by a not-excessively-hospitable city. He became a permanent fixture of some of those places, integrating himself into the city landscape with the battered coat in which he was photographed many times, an idiosyncratic character with an aristocratic but marginal existence.[6]

His journals (Gombrowicz 1989) bear witness to the feelings and reflections about distance and cultural rifts experienced by a man whose Spanish remained noticeably awkward throughout his life in Argentina. In 1946 the Cuban writer Virgilio Piñera met him in *El Rex,* one of several cafés in which Gombrowicz spent time with literary acquaintances. In his description of their encounter, Piñera tells how Gombrowicz treated him to a version of his arrival in Buenos Aires, a story that everyone else around the table knew already but that constituted the inevitable beginning of getting to know him. By then, he attributed his having stayed to a study of the South American soul he had initiated the night before the boat docked in Buenos Aires (Gombrowicz 1989: 72). The journey itself had been comfortable, even luxurious, with dinners at the captain's table and all the recognition due to a writer coming on a special visit. Gombrowicz liked to be addressed as "the count" even when he was in such monetary need that he would have to ask to be invited to dinner by friends he pretended to encounter by chance in the streets.

Silvina Ocampo, undeniably well-placed in the Argentine literary milieu, sister of the legendary Victoria who founded and supported *Sur,* one of the most influential literary magazines in Latin America, married to Adolfo Bioy Casares and close friend of Jorge Luis Borges, held a rather condescending and amused view of Gombrowicz as a character. *Sur* was silent about the publication of Gombrowicz's most important work, *Ferdydurke,* because, according to Silvina Ocampo, they simply did not like it (R. Gombrowicz 1984).[7] A dinner at her home that in-

---

6. A thoroughly compiled assortment of testimonies about his stay in Argentina may be found in Rita Gombrowicz, *Gombrowicz en Argentine, 1939–1963* (1984).

7. Milan Kundera says that *Ferdydurke,* which appeared in 1937, deserved the place accorded to Sartre's *La Nausée,* published one year later. "*Ferdydurke* a été

cluded Gombrowicz and Borges among other writers did not yield any contact between the two because neither of them enjoyed talking in public. Silvina Ocampo's account of Gombrowicz contains an imitation of his diction and faulty grammar as illustration of what she euphemistically called the differences between her circle and Gombrowicz (ibid.: 63). The most cosmopolitan writers of the country were also the most profoundly rooted in Argentine customs. Theirs was the best way of speaking the language, theirs the capacity to ridicule because of an accent or the manner in which Gombrowicz enjoyed wearing his shirt unbuttoned, just a bit too low for him to look right by the Buenos Aires standards of the group at that particular time. This is not to say, of course, that the extreme modernism of Gombrowicz's work would have pleased them had he sounded more vernacular; but his philosophical bent and theories about the role of writing could have allowed him to occupy a place similar to that of Macedonio Fernández, whom Borges touted as his master.[8]

Gombrowicz may not have made it into *Sur*, but he was held in admiration by groups of younger writers, some of whom revered him to the point of proselytism in the hope that *Ferdydurke* would be widely known and regarded as a way of looking at the world, not as a mere novel. The translation of the novel was in itself a testimony to the faithfulness Gombrowicz elicited in those people. A group of writers in a café, presided over by Virgilio Piñera, worked as a committee to translate the novel. The poet and essayist Adolfo de Obieta—son of the legendary Macedonio Fernández—initiated a subscription campaign to get the novel published. That group knew the importance of what Gombrowicz was doing, and rescued him from the isolation that he both cherished and wished to shatter. Gombrowicz wanted to be famous. One of his diary entries reflects on how mistaken Argentines were to hold Borges in such high

---

edité en 1937, un an avant *La Nausée*, mais, Gombrowicz inconnu, Sartre célèbre, *La Nausée* a pour ainsi dire confisqué, dans l'histoire du roman, la place due à Gombrowicz" (Kundera 1993: 293) (*Ferdydurke* was published in 1937, one year before *La Nausée*, but because Sartre was famous and Gombrowicz remained unknown, *La Nausée* took, in the history of the novel, the place due to Gombrowicz). English translation is mine.

8. It is coincidental that Adolfo de Obieta, who is now so carefully preserving the manuscripts of his father, Macedonio Fernández, also bestowed his generosity on Gombrowicz by making decisive efforts to publish *Ferdydurke* in Spanish.

regard, not recognizing that Gombrowicz was the better one to represent their nature:

They do not know that I am somewhat of a specialist in their main problem immaturity and that all of my literature is at home in it. It is paradoxical that in South America, Borges, abstract, exotic, not tied to their problems, is a luminary, but I have only a handful of readers. The paradox, which stops being a paradox when one reflects that they can show off Borges in Europe. Not me because I am a Pole. I am not *valor nacional.*   (Ibid.: 198)

He tested those around him in ways that gained him a reputation for arrogance. He acted as though he wanted to be alone but he did so in the very public space of the café so that his wish for aloofness would be widely known. One cannot help but be reminded of the paradoxes of privacy as developed by Derrida in *La Carte postale* (1980), when he insists that he writes in full view of everybody so that his wish for concealment might be understood and forge a secret. Gombrowicz did not want the invisibility of a foreigner; he wanted to be known as a writer and followed as a visionary, but he needed to establish a link that he could break time and again.

In a city and a country in love with the idea of the individual, he was an eccentric who played his role for others to see. Thus, his maneuvers at being set apart brought him into the fold and he became naturalized as part of the life of the cafés and *pensiones* (boarding houses) in which he spent his days when he was not working. His jobs were varied and obtained through acquaintances he had charmed into believing in his worth. He worked in a bank, with rather bad results, and taught classes to private groups on a number of subjects that seem trivial today, but that must have brought home to those involved in the discussions the originality with which Gombrowicz saw the everyday.

One of the leading informal philosophers of Buenos Aires, the tango lyricist Enrique Santos Discépolo,[9] says in one of his better-known compositions, "Cafetín de Buenos Aires" (Buenos Aires café): "en tu mezcla milagrosa de sabihondos y suicidas / yo aprendí filosofía / y la poesía cruel de no creer más en mí" (in your miraculous hodgepodge of know-it-alls and would-be suicides / I learned philosophy and / the cruel

9. Discépolo's tangos are regularly quoted by *porteños* to interpret daily situations. Both in the mainstream and in the intellectual milieu, his lyrics bridged the gap between popular and "high" culture long before it became fashionable to do so.

poetry of not believing in myself anymore). Gombrowicz joined the city as one of those café visionaries, uprooted, detached, willing to tell the story of his arrival for everybody to hear so that all might realize that he belonged or at least *had* belonged elsewhere.

When Virgilio Piñera tells of the way in which Gombrowicz recounted his arrival in Buenos Aires to those eager to become members of his circle, and suggests that it had the air of a rite of passage, he is only hinting at the importance that such an arrival had for Gombrowicz. It is in his novel *Trans-Atlantyk* (1994) that Gombrowicz weaves together his contradictory national and cosmopolitan wishes. The plot of *Trans-Atlantyk* completes the meaning of *Ferdydurke* and invites the reader to participate in the same rite of passage as Piñera. In Argentina he decided to write a novel that is modeled on an old Polish form, written in a stilted, recondite style. The tale is precisely that of the arrival by boat of a Polish writer, Gombrowicz, in Argentina. The characters, his efforts at survival, and the comedy of manners parallel his life without being closely auto-biographical. *Trans-Atlantyk* reads almost like marionette theater; its emphasis is not drawn from affect but from hyperbole, the transitions are not fluid but abrupt. Its humor is dark and threatening. And yet, without knowing it, Gombrowicz was associating himself with the powerful Spanish tradition of the *esperpento,* the freakish theater of Ramón del Valle Inclán, the dismissal of the realistic idea of self and literature of Macedonio Fernández, and the practice of the absurd of Ramón Gómez de la Serna. He wanted to write in a Polish uniquely his own due to its anachronism, and ended up being readable to the Spanish-speaking public because of its being part of a tradition of which he was not aware. Those around him, drawn to *Ferdydurke* and taken by the sheer energy and depth of his vision, retranslated not only in the literary sense his work and naturalized his presence in Argentina as a productive mistake. Conversation was at the root of this phenomenon. Without knowing Polish, a number of writers undertook the task of rendering *Ferdydurke* into Spanish with Gombrowicz's full collaboration. The translating was a formidable result of communion around a book. One can only imagine the discussions that ended up yielding this or that choice of words, the interpretations that were advanced in the effort to naturalize *Ferdy-durke.* This was Gombrowicz's welcome into the country, the assurance that he would not remain invisible. The friends and associates sought by the protagonist of *Trans-Atlantyk* materialized in the real-life admirers of *Ferdydurke.* In a recent conversation, the Argentine writer and psychoanalyst Carlos Bruck, one of the then-adolescents who felt the impact of *Ferdydurke*'s vision, told me how he made a trip to Tandil when Gombrowicz was living there to film him and to record the man he thought crucial to his own understanding of the world. Bruck's gravitation toward Gombrowicz as a person was not isolated; the faithfulness of those on the translating committee was matched by the readership in Argentina which, although small, found in this book its own language.

Ferdydurke was not only no longer foreign; it started to constitute the very texture of the experience of life in Buenos Aires and other Argentine cities. Its games of distancing, its remoteness and sarcasm, and the deliberate awkwardness of its flow became the touchstones of a way of being essential to shaping the lives of those who, not satisfied with the idea of *Ferdydurke* as a mere book, took it as a paradoxical program for action. In the meantime, Gombrowicz himself was being absorbed by the ethos of the place. Argentine popular culture surrounded him in the form of friends and admirers who shared a twin fascination with tango and his writing. Mariano Betelú, a graphic artist whose close friendship with Gombrowicz is noted in the *Diary*, drew portraits of the self-styled Polish aristocrat at the same time that he was developing what would constitute a lifelong interest in tango lyrics and scenes. Others, such as Ernesto Sábato, would go on to write about the origins and stories of tango.

Gombrowicz may not have been aware of the extent to which loss and longing are inscribed in tango, but in living the dual life of a foreign writer cut off from his original language and community, he was reproducing the situation ubiquitous in the genre that defined the sense of life in Buenos Aires. A café character himself, exuding the cult of chance encounters and a fatalistic sense of human nature, he had turned himself into an embodiment of the very thing others attempted to understand through their art and writing. Silvina Ocampo did not capture Gombrowicz in her imitation of his accent because the most telling aspect of his foreignness was not its awkwardness but the perfect fit it represented in Argentina.

FAR FROM THE HOMELAND

Gombrowicz experienced exile as an encounter with a persona he might not have known had he remained in Poland. His diaries explore the situation that his voyage to Argentina created for him as an apprenticeship. One of the entries is particularly clear about the impact of being cut off from his language and community:

Today I awakened in the delight of not knowing what a literary award is, that I do not know official honors, the caress of the public or critics, that I am not one of "ours," that I entered literature by force — arrogant and sneering. I am the self-made man of literature! Many moan and groan that they had difficult beginnings. But I made my debut three times (once before the war, in Poland; once in Argentina; and once in Polish in emigration) and none of these debuts spared me one ounce of humiliation.

I thank Almighty God he got me out of Poland when my literary situation began to improve and cast me onto American soil, into a foreign tongue, into isolation, into the freshness of anonymity, into a country richer in cows than in art. The ice of indifference conserves pride quite well.   (1989: 180–81)

The free-floating life of the café world in Tandil and Buenos Aires was not the public recognition that he felt he deserved. Although he noted time and again the blinding effects that official honors might have had on him, he remained acutely interested in the critical reception of his writing. The thought of Argentina as a backwater and of Poland as a land inhabited by deluded nationalists helped him to carve out for himself the persona of the lonely aristocratic writer. By being misunderstood, unknown, or disregarded, he achieved a measure of independence that he portrayed in a self-deprecatory manner: "In Tandil I am the most illustrious of men! No one equals me here! There are seventy thousand of them — seventy thousand inferiors. . . . I carry my head like a torch" (ibid.: 67). Provocation is at the root of Gombrowicz's writing; his thoughts on being an expatriate are part of the same continuum. The years spent in Argentina between 1939 and 1963 were the birth of Gombrowicz as a thinker of distance. Arrogance and mistrust of any efforts at national recognition of art and talent sustained him, even as they served to cut him off philosophically from any particular land. But Gombrowicz, who wanted nothing better than to speak to universal concerns, found his voice in an almost constant play with specific national geographical spaces. Poland and Argentina are determinant of his own understanding of his condition. Recognition — that is, the knowledge that one's readers speak one's own language, either in the narrow sense or in the broader sense of sharing and understanding one's thoughts — seemed to him both a proof of parochialism and a coveted reality. He wrote in an émigré journal in Paris and attempted to meet writers in Argentina, but considered himself a swaggering loner whose proof of excellence was the difference between the stature he merited and the relative anonymity he had.

Gombrowicz's literature has a staged feeling. His characters seem to parade on the page. The *Diary* captures that effect when Gombrowicz talks about himself. When he says that he carries his head like a torch, he stresses that he is there so that others may look at him in a certain way. His invisibility is a source of pride and, paradoxically, of the possibility of a successful spectacle. *Trans-Atlantyk* opens in a tone that exemplifies the theatrical aspect of his writing:

> I feel a need to relate here for Family, kin and friends of mine the beginning of these my adventures, now ten years old, in the Argentinian capital. Not that I ask anyone to have these old Noodles of mine, this Turnip (haply even raw), for in the Pewter bowl Thin, Wretched they are and, what is more, like wise Shaming, in the oil of my Sins, my Shames, these Groats of mine — oh, better not to heave it to the Mouth save for eternal Curse, for my Humiliation, on the perennial track of my Life and up that hard, wearisome Mountain of mine. (Gombrowicz 1994: 3)

He is not vying for intimacy. Gombrowicz eschewed the idea that art and literature were there for communication. This novel, loosely connected to his biography, recounts his arrival in Argentina as a parody in which poverty, hunger, unemployment, the glitter of the diplomatic world, and the life of the wealthy appear in the form of a laughable parade. As for himself: "I Walk, Walk, and he likewise there Walks, is Walking and the Devil, the Devil!" (ibid.: 36), he says. Indeed he walks, with his head like a torch telling what he sees in a nonparticipatory tone. Walking in order to let us know that the experience told is passing or a pursuit of anonymous contact, or just to see without attempting to understand, are ubiquitous in *Trans-Atlantyk* and in the *Diary*. Walking is the precondition for the narrator's superiority. He is there at the moment but he has the opportunity to walk away. Let's go on to something else, this is part of a fleeting reality, we are told. I shall walk and so will the reader.

The lightness of the experience of national borders given by the possibility of taking off on a voyage is part of Gombrowicz's sense of *walk*. If one can leave one's country not to return, everything else becomes a stop in an open itinerary. *Trans-Atlantyk* takes on at times the rhythm of a Lewis Carroll celebration:

In a flock they came and in a flock they Dance, hoopla, hoopla, fiddle dee dee, heels they spark, the whole house Fill so that into the Park it bursts. Chirp, chirp,

with his children in a chimney Mazur-cricket sits! And in the lake all the fishes
are a-sleeping. Kuling now, Kulig!

Caught Pann Zenon Panna Ludka, Whirled:

Beyond the wood, beyond the glen,
Danced Gosia with the mountain men!

Here servants rush about with food, with bottles, tables lay, there Gonzalo
gives commands, and coachmen, footmen peer through windows, and now the
whole house Booms so that into Meadows, into Fields is booming out! Let's
drink! Let's revel, have a drink, why do you not? And another! Hoopla, hoopla,
heigh, heigh, heigh!   (Ibid.: 116)

But this is not Alice's dream; it is Gombrowicz's rendition of a voyage
in which something irreversible has occurred. The voice that creates the
dance of the Polish revelers in Argentina communicates itself as artifice.
From the outset the novel lets us know that the arrival in Argentina is
to be rendered in a dark, humorous manner; thus the extreme vulnera-
bility of the narrator who tells us his adventure is made into a joke by his
own reluctance to take himself seriously. The characters he encounters
take on the consistency of playing-card figures. We sense that a game is
being unfolded here; the conviction that what we are reading is couched
in make-believe is not enough to allow us to walk back into the comforts
of intimacy.

The Polish characters are Polish in an anachronistically formal way,
and the Argentines, presented in snatches, show up in the streets of
Buenos Aires as though they were stepping in and out of a cartoon.
Banned from dialogue and everyday talk because of the farcical nature
of their voices, they join the narrator in announcing to us that what they
say is not for ordinary communication. Instead, they create the peculiar
isolation of the absurd.

An exile or voluntary expatriate, Gombrowicz regularly chose to avoid
the comforts of common sense that allow for the smooth, though mind-
less, flow of situations regarded as cordial. His prose reveals a preference
for an awkwardness already present in his interactions with people. His
Diary and the testimonies of friends and acquaintances tell of the many
situations in which he would press embarrassing personal encounters to
the limit, such as when somebody introduced him as a foreign, very well-
known writer but mispronounced his name, and he proceeded to quiz
her on its exact spelling as well as on which of his books she had actually
read. The contempt that he exuded for the Polish in *Trans-Atlantyk* was

matched by his sense of the pitiful comfort taken by Argentines in collective acts of self-congratulation. A banquet for the Argentine painter Raquel Forner—whom he did not like as an artist—and her husband on the occasion of their departure to receive an award in the United States caused him to reflect on the meaning of success within that community:

I saw them, painters, an entire body of them, talking, lashing each other with discourse, having a holiday. I observed them from the sidelines, from another table in the same restaurant. 'One can only wonder,' as people say. It is indeed strange to see how a mechanism of degradation becomes one of elevation in such circumstances. Each of these painters secretly scorned his colleagues because, well, an Argentinean brush is nothing compared with a Parisian brush—yet there, at the banquet, all together, affirming mutual honors, they became quite like a lion, altogether in one heap they became a paean to their own honor; and their table rang with praise, their table seemed momentous, even appealing, because of the number of persons participating in the act of self-elevation.   (Ibid.: 46)

Not *we,* not *our,* but *I* is his choice. He has nothing but scorn for the Argentine love of Paris and the need to have talent recognized there first in order even to see it among their own. Tango's good fate was that it had been successful in Paris and its integration in a place of prominence in Argentinian life was, at the same time, a testimony to a servile kind of kinship that Argentines felt for Paris. No matter that the stories of tango were about failed love encounters and betrayals. Their very existence was a triumph of the Argentine link to Europe. Gombrowicz, fascinated by the cult of the national as foreign, was also repelled by it. He would have liked to see both in Poland and in Argentina a self-reliance that rejected group identity in favor of individualism. The banquet for Raquel Forner exposed for him ease of celebration as one of the symptoms of group identity. Better the stridency of the lone aristocrat, the man without a country, than the hypocrisy of the heap.

When he left Argentina for Paris, Gombrowicz felt for the first time, or so it seemed to him, how important Argentina had been. Struck by the full weight of the years he had spent there, he felt free to recollect and to sense a loss in his departure. Although he was returning to Europe as a much better-recognized writer, and he was leaving what he had experienced in more than one respect as the hinterlands, his relationship to Paris was not one of admiration. The entries in his *Diary* show how ugly he found the French, how—as he had done before with the Argentines— he resented their orchestrated opinions about art and literature.

Intoxicated by the same feeling that Gardel expressed when singing about Buenos Aires from Paris, Gombrowicz annotates his disdain for the French and suggests a growing nostalgia for Argentina. Uncomfortable with the idea of cenacles, Gombrowicz would have liked, nevertheless, to be at the center of one. His corrosive look at the place where he ended up living until 1963 seems to have changed as soon as he left it. It is not hard to imagine that by the time he died in Paris, in 1969, he had become the kind of full-fledged, ill at ease, and reluctant Argentine-in-exile whose foreignness is exalted by tango.

REFERENCES

Borges, Jorge Luis
    1970 "La intrusa," in *El informe de Brodie*, 13–23 (Buenos Aires: Emecé).
Cortázar, Julio
    1967 *Hopscotch*, translated by Gregory Rabassa (New York: Random House).
Derrida, Jacques
    1980 *La Carte postale: De Socrate à Freud et au-del à* (Paris: Flammarion).
Gombrowicz, Rita
    1984 *Gombrowicz en Argentine, 1939–1963* (Paris: Denöel).
Gombrowicz, Witold
    1967 [1961] *Ferdydurke*, translated by Eric Mosbacher (New York: Grove).
    1989 *Diary*, translated by Lillian Vallee (Evanston: Northwestern University Press).
    1994 *Trans-Atlantyk*, translated by Carolyn French and Nina Karsov (New Haven: Yale University Press).
Kundera, Milan
    1993 *Les Testaments trahis* (Paris: Gallimard).
Schiff, Stacy
    1994 *Saint-Exupéry: A Biography* (New York: Knopf).

JACQUELINE CHÉNIEUX-GENDRON

SURREALISTS IN EXILE:

ANOTHER KIND OF RESISTANCE

WHO, AMONG THE SURREALISTS, and not only in World War II, was *not* in exile? Certainly some of the founding fathers of the movement in the 1920s and 1930s remained, with few exceptions, in their countries of origin: Aragon, René Char, Paul Eluard, Philippe Soupault, and Robert Desnos in France; René Magritte and Paul Nougé in Belgium; Marko Ristic in Yugoslavia. The majority of artists and writers went to France as voluntary exiles. Voyages of initiation, which were at the same time voyages of emigration, were at the heart of their experience. The surrealists were often *métèques* in the original sense of the word: "resident foreigners." That was the status the Athenians of classical Greece conferred on their resident aliens, who were accepted in the community though deprived of the right to vote—but the contemporary French slang pejorative connotation of the word is also relevant. The surrealist "métèques" traveled under the conjoined pressures of personal need and historical and sociological upheavals; in fact, often, the moment when they took on the status of "surrealist" corresponded to their arrival from another country.

Tristan Tzara went to Zurich from Romania to found Dada, in neutral Switzerland, in the middle of World War I; there he hoped to find a milieu that shared his hostility to the bourgeoisie and his scandalous pacifism. He then moved on to Paris to implant Dada and later to participate in the activities of Breton's group. Max Ernst, in the excitement of the affective encounters of the postwar period, responded with enthusiasm to Breton's invitation in May 1921 to come and show his collages in Paris; he left behind a conquered Germany, where the humiliations inflicted by the Allies were already working to incite revenge. Gisèle Prassinos belongs to a family of métèques who emigrated, when she was still a child, from the Greek community of Istanbul. Two or three others would become métèques once outside their country of origin: Wolfgang Paalen, a Viennese of Jewish origin, left Europe under Nazi pressure; André Breton and André Masson were exiles in New York during World War II, having fled the Nazi peril with the help of Varian Fry and the

Emergency Rescue Committee. After the war, Gherasim Luca fled Romanian socialism in 1952.

What did the surrealist "map of the world," published in a special issue of the journal *Variétés* in 1929, look like? The map shows the primary areas which magnetized surrealist thought: Oceania and the parts of America populated by American Indians, especially in the North. The Charlotte Islands and Alaska are swelled to exaggerated size with respect to the rest of their continent and to the other ones, in particular Europe, which are reduced to less than their proportionate surface areas.

What this map shows—one could even pencil them in—are the multiple circulatory movements between countries and continents that surrealism promoted and supported, making emigration a magnetic attraction, a voyage of initiation, or the reverse. Thus one could describe the curve of the initiatory voyage through the heart of Europe from Yugoslavia to Paris that Marko Ristic made in 1927; or that of Jacques Hérold in 1930, from Romania to Paris on the traces of his compatriot Brancusi; the sentimental journey undertaken by Enrico Donati, a nomad who was attracted to New York and who remained in that city from 1940 on; or the similar voyage undertaken thirty years earlier by Marcel Duchamp, who traveled back and forth between New York and Paris from then on; the voyage of initiation into primitivism that Michel Leiris made to Africa in 1933, those of Kurt Seligmann and Wolfgang Paalen after 1939 to the regions inhabited by American Indians, Paul Eluard's trip around the world in 1925 and Jacques Viot's some years later, the various wanderings of Leonora Carrington, which led from Great Britain to Mexico, passing through France, Spain, the United States. And many others.

Voyages of initiation, voyages of emigration: on the whole, one finds in both a positive idea of the voyage. At this point one must make a distinction between emigration and exile: emigration, whether collective or individual, defines the voyage which impels one to leave one's place of origin or birth, for whatever reasons, political or economic; exile, however, is an interior experience.

Any writer, as a poet, is exiled in language itself, in the language of communication; he creates a space in which he can write *his own* language. By definition, the situation of any artist is an interior exile. Strangeness can be of oneself, from inside one's own consciousness. Strangeness is a base of common experience, that of the inadequacy of language. It rebounds into the anxious search for those with whom communication becomes possible in spite of everything. In a state of self-loss, the exile searches for partners in exile, or for that which, in childhood, foreshadowed the exile to come.

I would like to advance the thesis that, however painful exile may have been for the surrealists, it was experienced nevertheless as a voyage of initiation—as if it were turned inside out, like the finger of a glove, into a voyage of magnetic attraction. This happened to the composer Kurt Weill when he went from Germany to the United States in 1935— there, he later said, he found his true homeland. One finds in surrealism neither the bewailing of or nostalgia for a lost paradise, nor the pain of double exile, from language and land, but the almost excessive response to an untenable position that was nevertheless maintained, politically and aesthetically.

I will discuss several examples of this complex position: Wolfgang Paalen in the United States and then in Mexico during World War II; Benjamin Péret in Mexico; and the French surrealists in New York during the same period. Refusal, challenge, and even a kind of bizarre self-righteousness define their positions, at a moment when all energies were turned toward the Resistance: theirs was an apolitical attitude, apparently, and was seen for that reason as scandalous. But one must take a closer look.

POLITICS: THE PARADOX OF A RESISTANCE THAT IS AT ONCE ANTIMILITARISTIC AND VIOLENTLY LIBERTARIAN

As an indication of the misunderstanding concerning the surrealists in exile, it is useful to note that as recently as 1992, when a colloquium organized by Antoine Compagnon was held at Columbia University on the subject of "The French in New York during the Second World War," the French press accorded it extensive coverage, but the surrealists' position was described in clichéd terms. Thus the journalist Michel Kajman of *Le Monde*, in an article dated April 18, cited the American journal *View* as a surrealist journal—a typical misunderstanding which my entire talk had been devoted to denouncing. I tried to show that *View* (founded in 1940 by Charles Henri Ford) was completely apolitical, whereas *V.V.V.* (founded in 1942 at Breton's instigation, with David Hare as editor) had a political purpose. What accounts for the misperception? I would suggest that in the French press's semidiplomatic celebration, where what was in question was the resistance to Nazism, it was easier not to look closely at these people who, in the middle of the war, had left France for their own protection[1] and had spent their time drawing up astrological themes, who hadn't been able to choose between Giraud and De Gaulle, and who had invented that useless and disturbing object, the "myth" of the *Grands Transparents* (Great Transparents), which I'll discuss further on.

The will to optimism at any price was never more flagrant—nor more shocking to some—than in that historical situation during World War II. Likewise, there was nothing more shocking than to express disgust with regard to *all* wars in the middle of a crusade, the crusade of the "free" French, who strove not only to reconquer their occupied country, but to destroy the very particular monster that was Nazism. The surrealists' political isolation in France after the war was the result of this misunderstanding.

For concrete examples, one can think first of the provocative object created by Marcel Duchamp for the front page of *Vogue*, celebrating the Fourth of July holiday. *Allegory of the Genre* can be read as the image of George Washington's noble face, superimposed upon the flag of the forty-eight states (*V.V.V.* 1944: 65–66). Perversely, however, it is also the contrary of a celebration, because the face of the founding father is composed of bloody bandages. When one looks at the image of Washington, what one sees is bandages. Here the nation is inseparably bound up with its wars: the glorified American Revolution, but also the less glorious Civil War, and—who knows?—the wars against the Indians as

1. Let me clarify that the political engagement of the surrealists during the 1920s and 1930s placed them first in line for attacks by the Pétain government, vaunting the values of family and fatherland. This engagement had consisted for Breton in the unstable interdependence of anarchist, then communist, and finally, Trotskyist thought. One can easily imagine the dramatic consequences of the inevitable arrests, had he remained in France. Former surrealists such as Aragon and Eluard, who in the 1930s had joined the French Communist Party, could soon rely on the support of a strong organization. That was not the situation of Breton and his friends. In Marseilles, in December 1940, Breton was arrested as a preventive measure on the occasion of a visit to the city by the chief of state. By then, the censor's hand was already exerting itself against the surrealists: Breton's *Anthology of Black Humor,* printed in April 1940, and the poem *Fata Morgana,* printed at the beginning of March 1941, had their publication delayed even before Breton's departure for the United States. For a detailed account of surrealist activity in New York, see Sawin 1995.

well. These bloody strips evoke a mild but inevitable reaction of disgust. The editors of *Vogue* made no mistake about it, and refused the cover. When the picture was published by the journal *V.V.V.*, the editors (one of whom was Marcel Duchamp), in order to avoid any misunderstanding, placed on the facing page a no less disturbing, though less directly violent, image signed by Matta, titled *Prince of the Blood*. George Washington was not purely and simply characterized as a prince of death, for the primary meaning of the phrase is "prince of the royal family." Ambiguity is nonetheless at the heart of this double page: even the War of Independence, one of the most justified, was not so clean. In that political context, who would not have understood the message that bad conscience is at the heart of every war?

Yet the New York surrealists' stand against Pétain and the Nazi government was clear as well: one need only reread a passage from the "Prolegomena to a Third Manifesto of Surrealism or Not," published in *V.V.V.* in 1942 and totally forgotten by commentators, which launches an extraordinary accusation against those who collaborated with the Nazis. Breton is speaking here, and the vigor of his tone, the mocking vulgarity, the evident sexual innuendos are extremely uncharacteristic of his writing: the passage is a pastiche of the newspaper published during France's Revolution of 1793–94 by the faction known as the *exagérés* or the *enragés* who, staking out a position to the left of the Committee of Public Safety (Robespierre and Saint-Just), met at the Club des Cordeliers. They published a fiery populist journal which served as the voice of the sansculottes, the artisans and day-workers: the newspaper of *Père Duchesne*. One may judge from the tone of Breton's text:

Il est bougrement dispos, le père Duchesne!
De quelque côté qu'il se tourne, au physique comme au mental, les mouffettes sont véritablement reines du pavé! Ces messieurs en uniforme de vieilles épluchures aux terrasses des cafés de Paris, le retour triomphal des cisterciens et des trappistes qui avaient dû prendre le train du bout de mon pied, les queues alphabétiques de grand matin dans les faubourgs dans l'espoir d'obtenir cinquante grammes de poumon de cheval, à charge de remettre ça vers midi pour deux topinambours pendant qu'avec de l'argent tu peux continuer tous les jours sans carte à t'en foutre plein la lampe chez Lapérouse, la République envoyée à la fonte pour que symboliquement ce que tu as voulu faire de mieux revienne te cracher sur la gueule, tout cela sous l'oeil jugé providentiel d'une moustache

gelée qui est d'ailleurs en train de passer la main dans l'ombre à une cravate de vomi, il faut avouer que ce n'est pas mal! Mais, foutre, ça ira, ça ira et ça ira encore. Je ne sais pas si vous connaissez cette belle étoffe rayée à trois sous le mètre, c'est même gratuit par temps de pluie, dans laquelle les sans-culottes roulaient leurs organes génitaux avec le bruit de la mer. Ça ne se portait plus beaucoup ces derniers temps mais, foutre, ça revient à la mode, ça va même revenir avec fureur. Dieu nous fait en ce moment des petits frères, ça va revenir avec le bruit de la mer. Et je vais te balayer cette raclure, de la porte de Saint-Ouen à la porte de Vanves et je te promets que cette fois on ne va pas me couper le sifflet au nom de l'Etre suprême et que tout cela ne s'opérera pas selon des codes si stricts et que le temps est venu de refuser de manger tous ces livres de jean-foutres qui t'enjoignent de rester chez toi sans écouter ta faim. Mais, foutre, regarde donc la rue, est-elle assez curieuse, assez équivoque, assez bien gardée et pourtant elle va être à toi, elle est magnifique!

(He's alive and kicking, Père Duchesne!

Whichever way he turns, whether toward the physical or the intellectual, the skunks are masters of the streets! These gentlemen sprawling on the café terraces of Paris, in uniforms stitched of old potato peel, the triumphant comeback of Cistercians and Trappists, whom I once dispatched with kicks in the pants, the early-morning alphabetic lines in the suburbs, with people standing in the hope of obtaining two ounces of horse lung, and ready to have another try at noon for two Jerusalem artichokes, while for money you can eat your damn fucking fill every day without a ration card at Lapérouse, the Republic sent back to the foundry, so that your best intentions return symbolically to spit in your face, all this under the allegedly providential eye of a frozen mustache [reference to Pétain], which lends a hand in the dark to a vomitous necktie [Pierre Laval, Pétain's minister], you have to admit, this is some fine mess! But, damn it fuck [*foutre*], *ça ira*, it's going to be OK, don't worry about it. I don't know whether you have heard of that solid, striped three-pennies-a-yard cloth, you get it for free during rainy weather, in which the *sans-culottes* rolled their genital organs, making a noise like the sea. It hasn't been worn much of late, but damn it fuck it's coming back into fashion, it will even come back with a furor! God is now making little brothers for us, it will come back with a noise like the sea. And I'm going to sweep away all that scum, from one end of Paris to the other, and I promise you that this time I won't be shut up in the name of the Supreme Being and that things won't go according to strict regulations and the time has come to refuse to eat all those books by fucking fools [*jean-foutres*] who order you to stay at home and not listen to your hunger. But damn it fuck, have a look at the street, is it interesting enough, shifty enough, watched enough, and yet it's going to be yours, it's magnificent!) (*Breton* 1942: 23–24)[2]

Especially remarkable here are the invectives directed against the Parisian police (*mouffettes*), who actively implemented the policies of Pétain; the invectives directed against the religious orders, several of which lent their support to the regime; the insulting contempt for those who profited from the black market, which recalls the diatribes of the sansculottes against the *accapareurs* (those who grow rich by illicitly selling goods). It is interesting to follow the circulation of signifiers alluding to sex: the queues in front of the shops in a time of scarcity is an ambivalent term (*queue* is French slang for penis), and if "s'en foutre plein la lampe" refers principally to eating well, the swearword *foutre* is too clearly repeated, notably in *jean-foutre,* for it not to be a call to eroticism in all its senses: eroticism is essentially linked to the surrealist consciousness of freedom. In this sense, one must pay particular attention to the call which closes the text: the call to the street is, metaphorically speaking, a call to popular revolt.[3]

Thus Breton pleads for the reconstruction of a libertarian and anarchist society. Whatever the historical roots of this anarchism (the political philosophy of Max Stirner, cited by Breton and his group, or that of Pierre-Joseph Proudhon, are more important for surrealist reflection than that of Bakunin and his communist anarchism), it is characterized by the rejection of the state and the demand for total justice, the principle of anarchist sensibility. No one has ever denied the political significance of this borderline position which incites revolt to empower the people, and of which "the Street" is the metaphorical expression. *La Rue,* or *The Street,* was the title of a 1950s journal which devoted a special "surrealist" issue to refuting the arguments presented by Albert Camus in his book *L'Homme révolté* (*The Rebel*) (*La Rue,* June 1952). Camus argued in favor of revolution as an organized political and social movement, to the detriment of revolt and its individualist inspiration, which he strongly condemned. The surrealists disagreed; but to call the position of André Breton and his friends in New York and Mexico apolitical (one thinks as well of Benjamin Péret's *The Dishonor of Poets,*

2. Breton's text appeared in *V.V.V.* in facing French and English versions. (We have modified the translation slightly.)

3. On the importance of the street in surrealist writings see Suleiman 1991.

published in 1945) is simply incorrect.[4] Libertarian spirit and anarchism *are* a political position. Denying this fact does away with the possibility of borderline positions in political philosophy. Liberty is an "intake of air," wrote Péret, quoting Breton, in the last pages of *The Dishonor of Poets* (Le Déshonneur des poètes) (1994 [1945]). The surrealists' position is untenable according to political logic (in the immediate and practical sense of the term); yet it is rigorous in terms of political philosophy. The surrealists cannot be accused of historical and political irresponsibility.

As concerns the position expressed by Duchamp's *Allegory of the Genre* and Breton's "Unexpected Return of Père Duchesne," the predominant idea is that even war against racism or Nazism must be fought with a bad conscience; it must not weaken the struggle, but on the contrary, must cause it to overflow into the street. An "indefensible position," defended by surrealism.

One must point out the parallel between this political position and the aesthetically "indefensible" position that Breton and Péret took up in opposition to the poetry of the French Resistance, represented by Eluard and Aragon. Exile thus appears to be the occasion for a resistance of a different order: resistance to compromise, the demand for even greater adherence to positions of principle.

In the small volume *The Dishonor of Poets,* which Benjamin Péret published in Mexico in 1945, the poet is, by definition, the one through whom dishonor comes to pass (*celui par qui le déshonneur arrive*). Moreover, a poem which takes liberty as its theme says less than a poem whose liberty of expression calls for Liberty in all its senses.

Any "poem" that exalts a "liberty" purposely left vague, when it is not decorated with religious or nationalist attributes, ceases first of all to be a poem, and furthermore, constitutes an obstacle to the total liberation of man, because it tricks him into showing him a "liberty" which hides new chains. (Péret 1994 [1945]: 12; translated by Andrew Eastman)

Poetry, Benjamin Péret affirms earlier in his essay, apprehends reality itself, and is the fixed point that Archimedes called for. The poet must be the bearer of dishonor, he must "pronounce words which are always sac-

4. *Mexico City: Poésie et révolution* (1945), reprinted in volume 7 of Péret 1994: 7–12. This provocatively titled pamphlet, published by friends of the author, was a response to the anthology of poets of the Resistance, titled *L'Honneur des poètes,* which appeared in France upon the Liberation. For a recent commentary, see Suzuki 1995.

rilegious and permanent blasphemies" in order to bring about a network of new signs, into which we may project our freedom.

The desire for freedom and the libertarian poetics of Péret are thus modeled on a very particular cybernetics: desire cannot be drawn according to simple geometrical models, with continuous lines and exponential values. Desire is resistance to the all-too-convenient attitude of immediate resistance, and in the final analysis, exile is one of the conditions of the emergence of desire.

Gradually, we have moved from an analysis of the political position of the surrealists in exile grouped around André Breton to an examination of the conditions of a poetics of exile.

POETICS: THE PARADOX OF A LYRICISM INSCRIBED IN THE VIOLENCE OF LANGUAGE

I would like to try to define the paradoxical lyricism that characterizes surrealist works, which critics rarely speak of except in terms of the sublime. It seems to me that this specific poetics applies to the situation of exile the discoveries of the attitude of opposition in which the surrealists entrenched themselves from the 1920s on. There is thus little difference between the poetics of the 1940s and surrealist poetics in general. The surrealists were well-versed in opposing everybody and everything by any means. Their poetics of a lyricism where utterance is violence is the opposite of lyrical effusion.

Surrealist poetics is commonly identified with lyrical expression. And in fact, the "vanishing point" of surrealist writing is determined by the intention of *seeing* and *making* [others] *see:* witness the surrealists' overriding interest in the *image*. This was already for Longinus the major objective of the writer of the "heights" (*Peri hypsous*, translated through the tradition as the *Treatise on the Sublime*):

In addition, young man, images also contribute to boldness and greatness of address and courtroom pleading; thus some speak of making pictures: though every sort of conception which gives birth to a speech or writing (no matter how it affects the soul) is commonly called an image, it has now become the vogue to use the word whenever, as a result of enthusiasm and emotion, you think you are gazing at what you are describing and you set it in the sight of those who hear you. (Longinus 1985: 87)

André Breton refers in similar fashion to the aesthetic and ethical concerns that motivated him, in diverse areas: in the "Letter to Ecusette de Noireuil," written to his newborn daughter in 1936, he refers to his own constant ethical concern:

J'ai parlé d'un certain 'point sublime' dans la montagne. Il ne fut jamais question de m'établir à demeure en ce point. Il eût d'ailleurs, à partir de là, cessé d'être sublime et j'eusse, moi, cessé d'être un homme. Faute de raisonnablement m'y fixer, je ne m'en suis du moins jamais écarté jusqu'à le perdre de vue, jusqu'à ne plus pouvoir le montrer. J'avais choisi d'être ce guide, je m'étais astreint en conséquence à ne pas démériter de la puissance qui, dans la direction de l'amour éternel, m'avait fait *voir* et accordé le privilège plus rare de *faire voir*.

(I have spoken of a certain "sublime point" on the mountain. It was never a question of establishing my dwelling on this point. It would, moreover, from then on, have ceased to be sublime and I should, myself, have ceased to be a person. Unable reasonably to dwell there, I have nevertheless never gone so far from it as to lose it from view, as to not be able to point it out. I had chosen to be this guide, and therefore I had forced myself not to be unworthy of the power which, in the direction of eternal love, had made me *see* and granted me the still rarer privilege of *making others see*.)   (Breton 1992 [1937]: 780, 1987: 114)[5]

When, in 1925 and 1926, Breton began to define a surrealist aesthetic, he referred in the same way to a certain "point," "very high above any mountain," from which one would *see*, in a flash, and would *make* "see." The result would be to show several paintings, created with this principle in mind:

Longtemps, je pense, les hommes éprouveront le besoin de remonter jusqu'à ses véritables sources le fleuve magique qui s'écoule de leurs yeux, baignant dans la même ombre hallucinatoire les choses qui sont et celles qui ne sont pas. Sans toujours bien savoir à qui ils en doivent la troublante découverte ils placeront une de ces sources au-dessus de toute montagne. La région où se condensent les vapeurs charmantes de ce qu'ils ne connaissent pas encore et de ce qu'ils vont aimer, cette région leur apparaîtra dans un éclair... Alors, s'il reste au monde, à travers

5. Breton had not previously used the term *sublime point,* but spoke instead of a "point within the mind" in the *Second Manifesto of Surrealism in 1930.* Vera's French translation of Hegel's *Phenomenology of Mind* uses the term *point extrême* to refer to the point where contradictions cease to be perceived.

le désordre du vain et de l'obscur, une seule apparence de résolution parfaite, de réduction idéale à un point de tout ce qui a bien voulu se proposer et s'imposer à nous à l'époque lointaine de notre vie, je ne demande pas mieux que ce soient les vingt ou trente tableaux dont nous avons fait les seule rivages heureux de notre pensée, heureux sans y penser, heureux qu'après tout il y ait des rivages.

(For a long time, I think, men will feel the need to return straight to the veritable springs of the magic river which streams from their eyes, bathing those things which are and those which are not in the same hallucinatory shadow. Without always knowing to whom they owe the troubling discovery, they will place one of these springs above any mountain. The region where the enchanting vapors are condensed of what they do not yet know and what they are going to love will appear to them in a flash of lightning. . . So, if there remains in the world, across the disorder of the vain and the obscure, a single appearance of perfect resolution, of ideal reduction to a single point of everything that sought to propose itself and impose itself on us at a distant epoch of our lives, I ask no better than that it be the twenty or thirty paintings which we have made the only happy shores of our thought happy without thinking about it, happy that after all there are shores.) (Breton 1965 [1926]: 7. translated by Marti Hohmann)

One could follow the thread of the sublime throughout Breton's works, starting with the *Second Manifesto of Surrealism* of 1929. It is interesting to note that when in 1937–38 he set himself to defining "black humor," he borrowed his definition of humor from Freud, who insisted on man's capacity to detach himself from suffering *through speech,* and thus to "sublimate" suffering. The French translation of Freud's essay emphasizes this by rendering the German *Grossartiges und Erhebendes* as "sublime":

Like wit and the comic, humour has in it a liberating element. But it has also something fine and elevating [*Grossartiges und Erhebendes,* Fr.: *sublime*] . . . what is fine [*Grossartiges,* Fr.: *sublime*] about it is the triumph of narcissism, the ego's victorious assertion of its own invulnerability. The ego refuses to be hurt by exterior realities . . . moreover, it shows that these [realities] can themselves become occasions for affording it pleasure.   (Freud 1950 [1927]: 216–17)

Breton's lively interest in the mechanisms of Freudian "sublimation" seems to me to derive from these preoccupations: is it not a question of *seeing* and *making others* see the trigger mechanism which tips the balance from neurosis to creation? But one must keep in mind that this interest in the sublime is merely theoretical and thematic, embodied in declarations of intention. The study of the poetic texts and manuscripts leads us to the more specific conclusion that writing and the signifier play a central role in this paradoxical lyricism.

Martinique, Snake Charmer (Martinique, charmeuse de serpents) (1972 [1943–44]) is a text, sometimes narrative but more often lyrical, which describes André Masson's and André Breton's fascinating encounter with the Caribbean tropics during their forced stopover in Martinique en route to exile in New York in 1941. One of the eight short prose poems written by Breton, to which he gave the general title "Trembling Pins," is titled "For Madame Suzanne Césaire" (wife of the great Martinique poet Aimé Césaire, whom Breton first met at that time). This title appeared only in the second version of the poem, which was copied on a postcard, like all the other poems of the series. (The poems went through three manuscript versions.)[6] The strangeness of the system resides in the use of the postcards conserved with this set of manuscripts, on the backs of which Breton recopied the poems. The postcard is thus a sort of mediant around which the prose poems take form: each poem was copied out on a separate card. The individualization of the poems on the cards gave rise to the systematic use of titles, previously lacking for several of the poems.

One is first attracted to the writing on the backs of the cards and its evident lyricism. The perfect plenitude that Breton encountered in the tropics (one thinks of the dazzled pages published in *Minotaure* and reprinted in *L'Amour fou*) sets the signifiers in motion around the impressions of the five senses, as though in these magical places one could encounter the four elements in their natural state.

Let's take a moment to think about the function of the postcard, which is obviously not that of a missive actually sent or even worthy of being sent, since it is part of a conserved set of manuscripts. First, it designates the implied reader, the symbolic addressee of the text. Second, it indicates the point by which the text is anchored to the "real world," because one can turn it over and find on the other side one of those poor and touching images typical of 1930s postcards. Third, the postcard limits the world, miniaturizes it within a narrow, old-fashioned space. But it is

6. The poems were published for the first time in numbers two and three of the review *Hémispheres* (1943–44), edited by Yvan Goll. The text as published is identical to the final manuscript versions. I would like to thank Barbara Lekastas for her help when I went to see the manuscript in the library at Hofstra University, of which she is the curator.

essential here, as in certain games of chance, to *turn over* the cards: between front and back the imaginative dimension of the real comes into play, in enigmatic relation with the words.

In this regard it is interesting to note that the other side of "Pour Madame Suzanne Césaire" contains a picture representing the Madame River. One needn't wonder which came first, the interest in a river called *Madame* or the meeting with Suzanne Césaire: what is at work here is an effect of the signifier. In the same way the expression "les Grands Transparents" invites one to imagine the impalpable forms surrounding us whose magnetic power directs us like pawns on a chessboard.[7] The last page of the catalog of the exhibition *First Papers of Surrealism* held in New York in 1942 shows an engraving with the same title by the hermeticist Michel Maïr, representing a giant (*grand*) whose belly holds a child (*transparent*): at once great and transparent, this androgynous being is sufficient to its own procreation. Whether these "rebus effects" depend on the passage from signifier to form, or from form to signifier, Breton's writing remains within the paradoxical lyricism I am trying to define. It is obvious as well that the Great Transparents are also the *parents* in a *trance,* figures in the primal scene which psychoanalysis invites us to recognize. There is a double play of signifiers in this play on forms.

Exile reinforces the tension of a mode of thinking intent on *suggesting,* without describing or narrating, within a paradoxical lyricism which strives to define the exigency for the subject to find his *poetic site.* Breton's "Great Transparents" is pure temptation for the mind of the reader. Entirely constructed around words such as *perhaps* and *for example,*[8] this short text invites us to give full scope to intellectual "speculation." And here, the speculative imagination is indistinguishable from the poetic imagination, since the text works at a degree of generality in

7. This fable is located at the end of "Prolegomena to a Third Manifesto of Surrealism or Not" (Breton 1942: 25–26). It begins as follows: "Man is perhaps not the center, the focus of the universe. One may go so far as to believe that there exist above him, on the animal level, beings whose behavior is as alien to him as his own must be to the day-fly or the whale."

8. As in this passage: "Man is *perhaps* not the center, the focus of the universe. One *may* go so far as to believe. . . . It is not doubtful that the largest *speculative* field lends itself to this idea. . . . Around us circulate perhaps beings who are built following the same plan as ourselves, but who are different, men, for example, whose body tissues [albumines] would be straight [droites]. Thus spoke Emile Duclaux, the former director of the Institut Pasteur (1840–1904)" (Breton 1942: 25–26).

which the poet Novalis is cited as witness along with William James and a former director of the Institut Pasteur in Paris. In this famous text, exile reinforces the lesson of the 1930 text "Il y aura une fois," in which Breton, voluntarily confusing aesthetics and ethics, invites us not to distrust "the practical virtue of imagination" and to search instead for a poetic site where language is necessarily inventive: "Place the mind in the position which . . . seems the most favorable poetically," so that the poet knows only how to say "Once upon a time, there will be" (Breton 1966 [1932]: 105).[9]

Breton's exile in the early 1940s is particularly rich in this kind of explicit formulation, at once poetic and dealing with poetics. A final example: in the text "Genèse et perspective artistique du surréalisme" — his contribution to the catalog of the exhibition *Art of This Century*, organized by Peggy Guggenheim in October 1942 — Breton returns to the notion of automatism in order to give it, at last, a satisfying definition. This definition is analogical, yet rich, because it consists in comparing the gesture of automatism to a bird building its nest, or to the complex elaboration of a musical melody.[10] Now in Breton, the comparison is rational and functions as a demonstration. The bird's nest building corresponds to finalized instinctive behavior, rather than to the primal urge with which automatism seemed to be associated in Breton's thinking in the 1920s. Here one is quite close to the "purposiveness without purpose" which Kant considered to be the goal of the work of art. In this definition by analogy, I read an emphasis, at the level of the subject, on rhythmic tension and on the effort to link the Imaginary with the Symbolic, according to the meaning Lacan attributes to those terms.[11]

Thus for the surrealists, political freedom and a free poetic form (link-

9. Originally published in the journal *Le Surréalisme au service de la Révolution* (July 1930), this text was reprinted in 1932 as the preface to the poetry volume *Le Revolver à cheveux blancs* (Breton 1966 [1932]).

10. In "Le Surréalisme et la peinture" (1965 [1926]: 68), Breton notes: "One has been moved to compare the construction of a bird's nest to the beginning of a melody which tends toward a certain characteristic ending. . . . I contend that automatic writing, as well as speaking, is the only mode of expression which fully satisfies the eye and the ear in realizing rhythmic unity (as appreciable in drawing and the automatic text as in the melody or the nest)" (translated by Marti Hohmann).

11. I give a more detailed reading of pages 68–70 of "Le Surréalisme et la peinture" (Breton 1965 [1926]) in my essay "L'Image chez Breton peut-elle faire effet de théorie?" (Chénieux-Gendron 1995).

ing the Imaginary to the Symbolic) go hand in hand. In *Le Déshonneur des poètes,* Péret attacked Aragon and Eluard for trying to separate these two kinds of freedom.

CONCLUSION: EXILE REINFORCES THE SUBJECT'S SELF-REFLECTIVE ACTIVITY

I conclude this overview with the following observation: self-analysis is built on the foundation of a lucid exile. One could reread the remarks I have just made about André Breton's thinking in the 1940s in light of this observation. I prefer, rather, to take a look at the journal Wolfgang Paalen kept during his trip to the northwest coast of the United States and to British Columbia in 1939, and the related writings he published in the early 1940s.[12] For Paalen, exile reinforces the conviction that "life" confirms the earlier discoveries of his sensibility. This experience is first of all an illusion of recognition, in which the past has already expressed the present, but in which everything comes to resemble everything, since dead trees cannot be distinguished from totem poles:

Journal:
The landscape resembles more and more surprisingly that of my paintings; here are the great forests of my dreams, the great forests of North America that I always wanted to see.   (Paalen 1994: 16)

Fairy tale forests; natural totem poles; burnt trees of which nothing remains but the bark marked off like crocodile skin.   (Ibid.: 19)

DYN:
Finally I see them other than in a dream, the great forests of North America. The "Lands of Silence" as the Indians say, the pylons of all the silence of the New World, the tops of the trees where the nets of the sky soak and dry. (Ibid.: 39)

At that time [in 1937] I had just painted a painting for which the title *Totemic Landscape of My Childhood* seemed to impose itself on me. Shortly afterwards I

12. Christian Kloyber, who is responsible for Wolfgang Paalen's archives, has very generously allowed me to publish this journal, written directly in French by the Austrian painter and thinker, along with the text of the unfinished book *Paysage totémique,* which Paalen wrote between 1939 and 1942 and which first appeared in several installments in his review *DYN.* These texts appear as "Voyage Nord-Ouest" in Paalen 1994: 11–32.

came into possession of one of those objects I had so desired for a long time, a model of a totem pole, the fine handiwork of Haida Indians carved in a piece of black argilite. But no one was able to tell me much about the legendary Queen Charlotte Islands, British Columbia, or Vancouver Island, much less well known than the center of Africa, or about what was left of those famous tribes of warriors and magnificent sculptors. (Ibid.: 46)

Above all, the trip to the heart of the forest makes it possible to confront ancestral fears, the "fear with the green grasshopper throat" (ibid.: 41), and to resuscitate other, more fully accepted terrors: the terror of the childhood encounter with a vulture, at the side of a lake (ibid.: 49); the terror of the adolescent in the face of his younger brothers, visceral enemies (ibid.: 43).

Exile, here, is clearly far from euphoric: magnetic attraction and initiation should not be confused with euphoria. Exile, for the surrealists, involves the retreat of a psychological subject into a past encountered in its violent tension, the retreat of a linguistic subject into the tension of writing, the retreat of political consciousness into a resistance to facile solutions, which are those of all summary analyses. Such was surrealist exile.

TRANSLATED BY ANDREW EASTMAN

REFERENCES

Breton, André
    1942 "Prolegomena to a Third Manifesto of Surrealism or Not," *V.V.V.* 1: 18–26.
    1965 [1926] "Le Surréalisme et la peinture," *La Révolution surréaliste* (New York: Arno).
    1966 [1932] *Le Revolver à cheveux blancs* (Paris: Gallimard).
    1972 [1943–44] *Martinique, charmeuse de serpents* (Paris: Jean-Jacques Pauvert).
    1987 *Mad Love,* translated by Mary Ann Caws (Lincoln: University of Nebraska Press).
    1992 [1937] *L'Amour fou* in *Oeuvres complètes,* 2: (Paris: Gallimard).
Chénieux-Gendron, Jacqueline
    1990 *Surrealism* (New York: Columbia University Press).
    1995 "L'Image chez Breton peut-elle faire effet de théorie?" *Revue des sciences humaines* 237: 77–95.
Freud, Sigmund
    1950 [1927] "Humour," in *Collected Papers,* translated by James Strachey, 5: 215–21 (London: Hogarth).

La Rue

1952 "Revolte sur mesure" (June, special issue).

Longinus

1985 *On the Sublime,* translated by James A. Arieti and John M. Crossett (New York: Edwin Mellen).

Paalen, Wolfgang

1994 "Voyage Nord-Ouest," *Pleine marge* 20: 11–50.

Péret, Benjamin

1994 [1945] *Le Déshonneur des poètes,* in *Oeuvres complètes,* 7: 7–12 (Paris: J. Corti).

Sawin, Martica

1995 *Surrealism in Exile and the Beginning of the New York School* (Cambridge, MA: MIT Press).

Suleiman, Susan Rubin

1991 "Between the Street and the Salon: The Dilemma of Surrealist Politics in the 1930s," *Visual Anthropology Review* 7(1): 39–50.

Suzuki, Masao

1995 "Le *Déshonneur des poètes:* Benjamin Péret et la theorie surrealiste du signe," *Pleine marge* 21: 111–17.

JANET BERGSTROM

JEAN RENOIR'S RETURN TO FRANCE

How we have waited for this return from exile! We have been ingenious in finding excuses for his delay, persuaded that for Renoir, no less than for ourselves,
there could be no question. War had made him leave, peace should bring him
back to us. We were almost amazed not to find him with the cinema division of
the army when it landed.

ANDRÉ BAZIN, "Renoir français"

WHEN ANDRÉ BAZIN WROTE THESE LINES, he knew he was premature in signaling Jean Renoir's return from Hollywood, for in December 1951 Renoir was only in Paris briefly in connection with the new film
he was making in Rome. It was in Italy, not France, that he was about
to shoot the Franco-Italian coproduction, *The Golden Coach*.[1] Bazin referred to Renoir's delay with tact. We can imagine that he hoped the special Renoir issue of the *Cahiers du Cinéma* (January 1952) he had organized would help convince the director that the evolution of his work
had finally been understood in his native country and the time was right
for him to come back to live in France and make his career there again.[2]

Bazin's contribution, "Renoir français," provided a thoughtful appreciation of Renoir's career, including his American films, which had re-

This research was inspired by the opening of the Jean Renoir Collection at
UCLA. I would like to thank Brigitte Kueppers, Head of Arts—Special Collections, for her generous cooperation. I would like to thank Olivier Dehors, Bibliothèque de l'Image, Cinémathèque Française and Emmanuelle Toulet, Bibliothèque
de l'Arsenal, Paris. I owe a special debt to Alexander Sesonske for making available
to me his manuscripts on two of Renoir's American films. I hope he can be persuaded to publish them. Translations are my own unless otherwise noted. Some of
the published translations have been modified slightly.

1. The title is in English because Renoir considered the English-language version
to be the definitive one. The film was also released in French and Italian versions.

2. This was the first time an issue of *Cahiers du Cinéma* had been devoted to a
single director. Part of Bazin's essay, "Renoir Français," was published in Bazin 1973
[1971]. The first section, from which I draw several citations, was omitted from the
book, which was compiled by Truffaut after Bazin's premature death. I consider this
omission to be consistent with Truffaut's ahistorical critical perspective.

ceived a cold welcome in France. But the heart of the essay was devoted to demonstrating, with his characteristic, quiet eloquence, the axiom Bazin wished to prove: that Renoir was as necessary for French cinema as France was for Renoir's cinematic art. He pointed out that Renoir's approach to filmmaking, unlike René Clair's, was fundamentally at odds with the way films were made in Hollywood. Other than Renoir, Clair and Julien Duvivier were the only French directors who had spent the war years in America. Clair and Duvivier returned in 1945; Renoir did not. How strange that the most French of French filmmakers should elect to remain in a country where he was not able to fulfill his potential as an artist. "Unlike René Clair, everything about the man and his work seemed to stand in contradiction to the American cinema: their attitude to film production, the style of their films. Renoir represented *the* French cinema: the best of its artisanal methods, the opportunities for improvisation, its very disorder. His collaborators' stories all confirmed that he needed total freedom to work with the inspiration of the moment; his most wonderful achievements emerged during the heat of the action thanks to the moral ambience he knew how to inspire in his co-workers" (Bazin 1952: 9–10).

To remind his readers of Renoir's convictions about his national and artistic identity before he left for Hollywood in 1940 (and perhaps to remind Jean Renoir himself), Bazin quoted several lines from an essay Renoir had published in December 1938. That was the month *La Bête humaine* was released; Renoir was working on the script for *La Règle du jeu*: "I know that I am French and that I must work in an absolutely national vein. . . . I had not yet learned that, even more than by his race, man is shaped by the soil that nourishes him, by the living conditions that fashion his body and his mind, and by the countryside that parades before his eyes day in and day out. I did not yet know that a Frenchman, living in France, drinking red wine and eating Brie cheese against gray Parisian vistas, can only create a work of merit if he draws on the traditions of people who have lived as he has" (Bazin 1973 [1971]: 158, 151–52). Before describing the unique qualities of Renoir's work in France, Bazin followed these words of 1938 (which were to be repeated countless times by other critics) with an appeal that was hardly neutral: "Renoir should make contact again with French soil in order to recover his strength and his distinction" (Bazin 1952: 10). As we will see, Georges Sadoul, one of the most consistently intelligent supporters of Renoir's work throughout the 1930s, will make a similar statement worded even more strongly in

Figure 1 Jean and Alain Renoir on the set of *La Règle du jeu*, 1939. Printed with permission of UCLA Arts Library Special Collections, Jean Renoir Papers.

1955 in his review of *French Cancan*, the first film Renoir was to make in France after the war.

What some, like Bazin, saw as a loss or a paradox, others felt as a betrayal. How could the very director whose films had been indispensable for the creation of a distinctively French national cinema in the 1930s, the man Sadoul characterized as "the most French of the pre-war film-makers" (1972 [1965]: 213), have turned his back on his native country and the way of life that provided the basis for his most inspired work?

Renoir had made important films during the 1920s, but it was throughout the 1930s, with the new dimension of sound, that his films stood out as brilliant, if sometimes ominous, signs of their time, even though many films now considered classics were not understood when they were released. And it was during this turbulent decade that French cinema came into its own through a form of social, "poetic" realism (Andrew 1995). Renoir's films provided the best cinematic index to French society during those years, from the economic depression of the early 1930s (*La Chienne, Boudu sauvé des eaux, Toni*) through the rise and fall of the Popular Front (*Le Crime de M. Lange, La Vie est à nous, La Grande Illusion, La Marseillaise, La Bête humaine*) up to the very eve of war (*La Règle du jeu*). Although Renoir kept his distance from party affiliations, his films showed a strong social and political sensitivity to the inequities of class structures in France and a sympathy for the working class. *La Vie est à nous* was commissioned by the French Communist Party, and *La Marseillaise* was financed through the CGT, the national trade union.

During the 1930s, Renoir, a genial, intelligent, sociable man, lived in the midst of a left-wing social and political environment. He described those days as follows: "Militant leftists at the time of *La Vie est à nous* were sincerely disinterested people. They were French, with all that means in terms of failings and good points. They had no Russian mysticism or Mediterranean bombast. They were open-minded realists of various leanings, but they were still French. I felt comfortable with them, and we all loved the same popular songs and the same red wine" (quoted in Bertin 1991 [1986]: 121). Marguerite Houllé (credited as Marguerite Renoir after 1932), Renoir's common-law wife and his editor throughout this period (1929–39), and her family were active in the Communist Party (Beylie 1975: 107 n. 17; Bertin 1991 [1986]: 167–68). Through them, Renoir met the Party's leader, Maurice Thorez, and invited him to the Renoir family home in southern France. Thorez asked him to be the "lay godfather" of one of his sons (Bertin 1991 [1986]: 124). Renoir was close to Prévert's Groupe Octobre, too, with whom he made *Le Crime de M. Lange*. Between March 1937 and November 1938, Renoir contributed over sixty columns to the left-wing paper *Ce Soir*.[3]

As a filmmaker, by the 1930s Renoir had learned how to create a sense of spontaneity that disguised classical, rigorously symmetrical struc-

3. The essays were reprinted in Renoir 1974a; for a summary see Faulkner 1979: 191–92.

tures. He experimented with actors and technicians throughout the decade to find ways to stage the social reality of his day according to its own unique idiom: the way people spoke, the way they wore their clothes, the way they looked at one another, their movements, their silences, their music, their milieus. In *Ce Soir* in February 1938, Renoir called for the return of three important directors who had left France: "I am going to allow myself to close these lines with an appeal to our great comrades who, discouraged by the situation here, have gone to work elsewhere. René Clair in England, Feyder in Germany, Duvivier in America. Have they found what they were looking for? I doubt it. If they can, let them come back home to us. French cinema needs them" (Renoir 1974a: 153). This was precisely the way Bazin addressed Renoir in "Renoir français."

In 1954, two years after Bazin's appeal, Renoir did come back to France to direct *French Cancan*. But his return was equivocal. Although Renoir was to make six more films in his native country (*French Cancan* [1955]; *Elena et les hommes* [1956]; *Le Déjeuner sur l'herbe* [1959]; *Le Testament du Dr. Cordelier* [1961]; *Le Caporal épinglé* [1962]; *Le Petit Théâtre de Jean Renoir* [1970]), he never again made France his home. During his prolonged absence, Renoir had become an American citizen. Although he came to France from time to time, he lived most of his life after 1940 in Los Angeles, where he died in 1979. The way he spoke about his work as a filmmaker had changed considerably, especially after his experience in India making *The River*. In 1952 he wrote that he believed he could sense the mood of his contemporaries as he had been able to do in 1938. But in 1952 it was no longer a question of France or even of America: Renoir had come to regard himself as a citizen of the world: "When I made *La Règle du jeu*, I knew what I was doing. I knew the malaise eating at my contemporaries. That doesn't mean that I knew how to present a clear idea of it in my film. But I was guided by my instinct. . . . I have found the same kind of certainty with *The River*. I felt the desire to touch my neighbor, whom today I believe to be more or less the entire world" (Renoir 1952: 8).

In 1969 Renoir's delay in returning to France after the war was the subject of a concise, astute book by François Poulle, *Renoir 1938 ou Jean Renoir pour rien?* By that time, one could measure the distance not only between Renoir's French and American films, but between those he had made in France before and after World War II. In 1969 Renoir was seventy-five years old and near the end of his career. It was more obvious that a major shift in his orientation had taken place in the United

States. Poulle asked the question directly: "Why didn't he come back in 1945, like Clair or Duvivier? . . . Why did Jean Renoir, specifically, spend those ten years far away from France? The difference between *La Règle du jeu* and *French Cancan* is not simply a difference in style. Between the ages of forty-two and sixty, the man must have changed completely: in his political and artistic ideas, in his way of seeing the world and the cinema and, in fact, in his way of being a man before his fellow citizens. And the country, too, of course, must have changed; but was that ever in doubt?" When Renoir returned "he no longer belonged to us: he had stopped being a citizen and a witness in order to become a sage" (1969: 68). By the end of his study, Poulle's initial question has given way to a more insistent one: "Why did a French filmmaker named Jean Renoir stop making films that bore witness to their time?" (ibid.: 123).

I believe that anyone who studies Renoir's career is bound to come back to these fundamental questions. His films from the 1930s still make a lasting impression "because of their sensuality, their almost tactile sensitivity to the appearance of this French universe" (Bazin 1952: 13). The universe Bazin meant was not eternal nor was it limited to surface appearances. It had changed by the time Renoir returned. For his part, Renoir was no longer working in the realist mode he had helped define in the 1930s. Even if we can never know all the factors that went into Renoir's change between 1939 and 1954, we can come closer today to the paradoxes of national identity he experienced during the period leading up to *French Cancan*. We can see from documents that do bear witness to their time (personal and business correspondence, contemporary interviews and essays, memoirs) that, particularly after 1946, in some sense Renoir felt he belonged to two national cinemas and in some sense he was an outsider to both.

My essay deliberately maintains the emphasis on French cinema as a distinctive national cinema that runs throughout the materials I consulted (this is seen in moral as well as aesthetic terms), in contrast to the argument frequently voiced today that the long-standing dominance and influence of American films in France had rendered "French cinema" an illusion long before the 1930s. Renoir's relationship to French cinema was almost always put in terms of his relationship to France by himself as much as by others. I have cited many contemporary voices that express urgency and sometimes perplexity with far greater force than any modern summary could do.

Documentation available to us today makes it possible to reconstruct more precisely the great difficulties and complications Renoir faced when he decided to try to live and work in Hollywood, in other words, the context within which he gave up his 1930s realist mode of representation. We can even show with a fair degree of certainty when and why this happened, even if the choices Renoir made in America were not inevitable and we cannot factor in all the personal elements of his decisions. But we cannot begin to answer these questions or understand the impact that changing national cinemas had on Renoir and his work unless we begin by asking why Renoir left France in the first place. From there, we will follow a number of turning points in his career up to the release of *French Cancan* in France, which marks the end of our investigation.

My conclusions are staggered throughout this essay, but I will briefly summarize those that most directly concern Renoir's return to France. I believe that Renoir's prolonged absence from France after the war made his eventual return more conflicted than it would otherwise have been and ultimately influenced him to make a film whose principle ambition would be to minimize his risks and guarantee him success in the eyes of the French public and film industry so that he could continue to make films in France or international coproductions with French financial participation. Without wishing to offend any of Renoir's admirers — I am certainly one of them — and without wishing to take anything away from the pleasure Renoir took in designing *French Cancan* for Technicolor, in working with his actors, and in evoking the physical vitality of the dancers on the screen, I cannot help but see *French Cancan* as a betrayal of the intelligent, socially evocative, photogenic filmmaking Renoir had excelled in before the war, a mode of filmmaking steeped in the visual traditions of silent cinema. Moreover, because *French Cancan* was set in the artistic milieu of Montmartre during the Belle Epoque, the film performed a double regression, both personal and social, that allowed Renoir to return through fiction to the period and locale of his childhood and the innocence it represented for him, as well as the innocence of France before the Occupation. But this innocence rings hollow, especially when correlated with a third aspect of Renoir's regression in *French Cancan,* his retrograde representation of male-female relationships. Perhaps it is not fair to hold Renoir responsible for so much after reviewing the confusing, contradictory, and possibly traumatic experiences in filmmaking and national identity that he experienced between the 1930s and the 1950s. Yet it is simply a fact that the cinema, and not only French cinema, lost a lot when Renoir abandoned the direction he had pursued with so much conviction during the 1930s in France.

1939: THE FAILURE OF *LA RÈGLE DU JEU*

The fact remains that the failure of *La Règle du jeu* depressed me so much that I resolved either to give up the cinema or to leave France.

JEAN RENOIR, My Life and My Films

In the light of the critical status of *La Règle du jeu* today, it is difficult to comprehend that the film was a disaster with the critics and the public when it was released in July 1939. But Renoir's conflicted attitude about returning to France after World War II cannot be understood without taking into account his bitter disappointment at the hostile French reaction to this film he had put so much of himself into and staked so much of his future on.

In November 1938, Renoir had set up a production company, La Nouvelle Edition Française (NEF), with his brother Claude and three other partners. *La Règle du jeu* was the NEF's first venture Renoir was fulfilling a dream in creating his own production and distribution company, like Marcel Pagnol, who had coproduced *Toni* in 1934 with his company near Marseilles and allowed Renoir to use his equipment, facilities, and technical crew. The press reported that Renoir planned to buy a first-run theater (*une grande salle d'exclusivité*) that would showcase the films produced by his company and Pagnol's (Esnault 1965: 7–8; Gauteur 1974: 54).[4]

Since the 1920s, Renoir had wanted to make films as a family business, perhaps a little like the cooperative in *Le Crime de M. Lange*. In a letter to one of his partners a month before *La Règle du jeu* was released, he outlined a much more ambitious plan. What he had in mind was a French version of United Artists, the company formed by Charlie Chaplin, D. W. Griffith, Mary Pickford, and Douglas Fairbanks in 1919 to gain autonomy from the Hollywood studios: "We will be confronted with other stages in the development of the NEF: the planning and ac-

4. George Cravenne, *Paris-Soir,* December 6, 1938; Claude Renoir Sr., *Le Nouveau Film,* February 11, 1939 (quoted in Gauteur 1974).

quisition of our own technical facilities, which means at least what is needed for filming and recording sound, the planning of a workplace in North Africa, which is even more necessary as filming in color requires a lot of light, and finally bringing together new producers willing to make films with us. . . . Don't forget that in creating the NEF, my far-off goal was to form something like a French 'United Artists,' that is to say, a much larger and more fair-minded business than the kind that exists simply for distribution" (Renoir 1994: 59).[5] The American documentary filmmaker Robert Flaherty was already interested in joining them, and Renoir intended to speak to Duvivier about it. As he had done before, Renoir was working with members of his family on *La Règle du jeu:* his younger brother Claude was production director; his son Alain (from his marriage to his first star, Catherine Hessling) was assistant cinematographer; and Marguerite Renoir was the editor. In an interview in January 1939, Renoir spoke confidently about his plans: he and his partners "got along like the five fingers of a hand. I will make two films a year, and I'll be able to keep my crew: de Bretagne, the sound engineer; Bachelet, the cameraman; Lourié, the designer, and the others" (Bussot 1939: 184). Renoir himself was responsible for writing, directing, producing, and playing one of the main characters, Octave.[6] The new production company provided independence within the comforting environment of a large family. It represented both a financial investment and an investment in a dream. It was the failure of the latter that proved devastating.

By late 1938 when he began work on *La Règle du jeu,* Renoir wanted to move away from the model of realism he had used in *La Bête humaine,* even though that film had been extremely successful. Zola's naturalism remained an important point of reference for Renoir throughout his life, but he had come to believe that one aspect of his narrative strategy was artificial. Renoir had followed Zola, he said, in organizing the narrative around a single dramatic line that followed an individual who had a unique destiny, like the heros of Greek tragedy. "I should say that [*La Bête humaine*] departed a little from my usual practice, because I emphasized characters who are virtually unknown to me in order to be faithful to Zola's novel. The people I know almost always identify with their class, while these characters are like heroes, singled out by destiny. . . . Despite

5. Letter to Camille François, June 1, 1939. Renoir's ambition to make a film in color would have to wait until *The River.*

6. Renoir, Karl Koch, and André Zwobada were credited as co-writers.

everything, because I wanted the characters to have a certain class definition, I insisted on the exact, pictorial description of their gestures, habits
and manners . . . , which added a documentary aspect to the drama" (Renoir 1938b).

In *La Règle du jeu,* Renoir wanted to make a film that did not carry a
specific message and did not conform to traditional genre expectations.
He wanted to experiment with juxtaposing different genres, which he felt
was truer to life. He changed the conception of the hero radically, in part
by increasing the number of important characters so that no one of them
would carry the action or the moral attitude of the film. It was his intention to ground each of his characters in a specific time and place, and
to make their actions a function of their lived history. Class distinctions
were part of this history; each character occupied a specific place within
the social hierarchy the film presented. To an interviewer two months
before the film's premiere on July 7, 1939, Renoir replied:

What do my characters represent? It would be wrong to try to decipher their
symbolic meaning, or to find the themes of social satire in *La Règle.* These characters are simple human beings, neither good nor bad, and every one of them
is a function of his condition, his milieu, his past. Nora Gregor is the foreign
woman in a country that is not hers. Roland Toutain is even more complex: he is
the impotent hero, that singular character of our day who devotes all his energy
to action, and when he is not in action he becomes a child. Paulette Dubost is
feminine kindness itself and Mila Parély is the woman who leads a fierce but
legitimate battle against the woman she wants to dispossess. All these characters — and Carette, the anarchist *bricoleur,* Gaston Modot, game-keeper and slave
to duty, myself — gravitate around Dalio, who is the pivot of the action and the
only one who dominates because of his intelligence. Every one of them has reasons for their actions, and these reasons are respectable. They follow "the rules
of the game." And the game, like life, is sometimes comic, sometimes dramatic.
(Renoir 1939: 52–53)

As it turned out, all the new elements that Renoir worked hard to integrate into this complex social tableau confused and alienated critics as
well as the public. Historians tell us that *La Règle du jeu* was banned
along with several other films soon after its release because it was judged
to be demoralizing at a time when France, on the brink of war, could not
afford to have its citizens watching films that seemed defeatist (Jeancolas
1983: 280). But critics expressed other reasons for their hostility. No one
doubted Renoir's great talent. But either the film had gotten away from

him or, as many believed, he must have deliberately chosen to make a film that they would not know how to interpret. Why hadn't he made another film like *La Grande Illusion* or *La Bête humaine*?

What was Jean Renoir's intention? That is a question I kept asking myself as I left this strange spectacle. A satirical comedy like the ones that made Frank Capra's fortune? But this laborious fantasy with its heavy dialogue is just the opposite of irony. A comedy of manners? But whose manners, since these characters don't belong to any known social species? A drama? The intrigue is carried out in such a juvenile fashion that this hypothesis cannot be correct.   (de Coquet 1939)[7]

Why hadn't Renoir made it clear who the sympathetic characters were? The film seemed to go haywire as soon as the costume party began. Was it a comedy or a tragedy?

All this commotion is entertaining, but it becomes disturbing. We realize we are two-thirds into the film and we know nothing about the main characters. . . . These pursuits involving four or five couples through sumptuous drawing rooms, with fairground music, are extraordinary pieces of cinema. But Mr. Renoir's virtuosity has run away with him. These characters are nothing more than mannequins with sound. The sense of truth has abandoned him. . . . This is no longer drama or farce or satire, but a night of drunkenness in which women are no longer in control of themselves and someone is killed stupidly. Mr. Renoir lost his footing because he wanted to mix too many situations, intentions and genres. (Vinneuil [Rebatet] 1939)[8]

Renoir never forgot the pain he experienced witnessing audiences around him react against his film. He didn't have to read about it, he could feel it. He seemed to be caught completely off guard. The few favorable reviews were drowned out by the loud voices of the people who reacted as if Renoir had offended them intentionally. Renoir described this later in his autobiography:

I depicted pleasant, sympathetic characters, but showed them in a society in the process of disintegration. They were defeated at the outset, like Stahremberg and

7. Many other reviewers express the same opinions on these points. See the Renoir clippings files in the Jean Renoir Collection, UCLA; the Cinémathèque Française; and the Bibliothèque de l'Arsenal.

8. The complete essay from which Gauteur's excerpts are drawn is one of the longest, most intelligent reviews of this film, despite the author's notorious right-wing political views.

his peasants.[9] The audience recognized them. The truth is they recognized themselves. People who commit suicide do not like to do it in front of witnesses. I was utterly dumbfounded when it became apparent that the film, which I wanted to be pleasant, rubbed most people the wrong way. It was a resounding flop. The film was greeted with a kind of hatred. Despite a few favorable reviews, the public regarded it as a personal insult. . . . At every screening I attended I could feel the unanimous disapproval of the audience. . . . The fact remains that the failure of La Règle du jeu depressed me so much that I resolved either to give up the cinema or to leave France.   (Renoir 1974b: 172–73)

We know that Renoir did not give up the cinema. It is less well known how, in the interval between Paris in July 1939 and Hollywood in January 1941, another chapter of Renoir's life was played out between France and Italy. On July 14, only a week after the premiere of La Règle du jeu, the press announced that Renoir had agreed to direct La Tosca in Italy (Renoir 1984: 13). On August 10, 1939, Renoir went to Rome to begin work, accompanied by his old friend and collaborator, Karl Koch, and Dido Freire, who had been script supervisor on La Règle du jeu and would later become his wife. But his stay was cut short by the war in Europe. Renoir was called back to France at the beginning of September when the general mobilization was declared. He entered the army in the Service Cinématographique. This was the beginning of the waiting war, the "drôle de guerre" that lasted until the German army took the offensive on May 10, 1940. In the meantime, Renoir, now a lieutenant, was sent back to Italy to resume work on La Tosca as part of France's short-lived diplomatic effort to maintain Italian neutrality. But he only had time to finish the script and the first few shots when, in early June, he was advised to leave the country.[10] Italy was about to enter the war on Germany's side. Renoir reached Paris, found his son, Alain, who was in the military, lost him again in the general confusion, and then joined the exodus from the city. On June 14, the German army entered the capital. Eight million French people were on the road. Among them, headed south, were Renoir, Dido Freire, and Renoir's childhood friend Paul Cézanne Jr. and his family, with a load of Cézanne's canvases in their car. They camped in a

9. Nora Gregor, who plays Christine, was the wife of the Austrian Prince Stahremberg. The couple had been driven into exile by the Nazi annexation of Austria.

10. The film was completed by Karl Koch, coauthor of the script, who was German. After La Tosca, Koch and his wife, Lotte Reininger, the famous silhouette animator, emigrated to London.

barn in a small town and waited to see what would happen, hanging the paintings around them for moral support (Bertin 1991 [1986]: 167–78; Renoir 1984: 15–16, 1994: 70). This exodus brought Renoir one step closer to leaving Europe.

France was not Germany. Renoir's extended family and most of his contemporaries in the film industry remained in the country during the war. At first it seemed that Renoir would stay with them. On August 6, now at his family's home in the unoccupied zone near Nice, he wrote to Robert Flaherty, who was urging him to come to the United States, that he was unable to leave because he was still under contract to make *La Tosca*. And besides, "I am thinking about our French cinema, which is in such a state of confusion after our disaster. . . . I would be ashamed to walk out on my compatriots when everything is going badly" (Renoir 1984: 16). According to Renoir's biographers, soon after this he received visits from people representing Nazi cultural affairs who spoke to him about making films for "la nouvelle France." Renoir felt that if he remained in France he would be faced with an impossible dilemma: working for the Nazis or refusing their offer seemed out of the question. The situation terrified him. While Renoir was trying to decide what to do, Dido Freire and Flaherty went ahead with preparations for departure, obtaining official permissions and a contract from Twentieth Century-Fox. Finally, Renoir himself made a trip to Vichy on September 2 to obtain authorization for his departure. Renoir's papers were in order in Washington as well as Vichy by September 18, 1940. Renoir did not burn his bridges behind him, and he could look ahead to a certain amount of economic security: he had permission to leave France to make a film in the United States.

Renoir's route to America was circuitous, uncertain, and slow, like that of many other émigrés, but by January 10, 1941, he had arrived in Hollywood. He was forty-six years old. He did not speak English. At the top of his career in France, despite a temporary setback, he had left his family and many people dear to him whom he had known since childhood. As an "auteur" who was used to writing, directing, producing, occasionally acting, and, as he put it, doing a little of everything, who had built up relationships with excellent writers, technicians, and actors who understood how he worked, Renoir now found himself in an environment in which his producer controlled almost all the decisions that had previously been his. How confident Renoir had been before the release of *La Règle du jeu* when he stated: "The first generation of the cinema belonged to the producers; the second, to the directors; now the third has appeared, which belongs to the authors" (quoted in Esnault 1965: 7).

HOW HARD IT WAS TO ADAPT

To understand how hard it was for Renoir to consider returning to France to live in 1945, one has to realize how he had to struggle to function within his new environment. As he wrote to Paulette Renoir, the wife of his brother Claude, on February 27, 1942: "It has been too difficult for me to learn English and adapt myself to American techniques to give up the fruits of all this labor at the very moment when certain possibilities seem to be opening up in front of me" (Renoir 1984: 98). Once in Hollywood, the kind of success Renoir wanted always seemed to be right around the corner.

One has to admire Renoir's optimism in the face of great obstacles. He had an unusual assistant in Freire, who acted as his interpreter on the set as well as in everyday life. But for an actor's director like Renoir, not being able to communicate directly in his own language was an enormous handicap. He could not rely on his charming, subtle manner of speaking in French to encourage his actors to improve their performances. More fundamentally, he didn't have an ear for American English, which meant that he could not tell whether the rhythm and intonation of the dialogue sounded authentic to him. This factor alone was enough to prevent him from working successfully in the realist mode that was so powerful in his French films. Renoir wasn't in a position to find American equivalents for other crucial components of his French realist style either: the sure evocation of characters by their milieus and habits. Yet it is evident from the abundant documentation on his first film, *Swamp Water,* that Renoir tried hard to continue working in his realist mode and to convey the authenticity of the contemporary and even regional American idiom (Sesonske 1982). The odds were against him.

The fact that he couldn't communicate in English had other important consequences: he couldn't establish enough of a rapport with his technicians, especially his cinematographer and art director, to get around the studio hierarchy and a rigid division of labor that was utterly foreign to him. He felt isolated. Unlike the German émigrés, Renoir was not used to working in a studio system. Whereas Fritz Lang used the evenings to map out the shots he would film the next day, Renoir liked to decide how he would set up his shots in the mornings as he walked around the set and discussed the possibilities with his crew. Georges Sadoul described Renoir's style of direction after a visit to the set of *La Règle du jeu* in 1939: "Renoir is not a man who begins directing a film with a script in which every detail has been finalized. Of course, his scenes have been prepared and worked on, but the details are modified as he goes along. Every morning Renoir organizes what he is going to do that day with his assistants, and the dialogue is finalized only after it has been worked through with the actors. Depending on how Dalio or Modot see their roles, their words and movements will be modified during the rehearsals in a spirit of cordial collaboration" (Sadoul 1979: 41).

For a man who had spent over fifteen years making films in this way, Renoir's first American film was a severe test. *Swamp Water* was dominated by its producer, Darryl F. Zanuck. For the studios, time meant money, and Renoir worked too slowly for Zanuck, as he made clear in his memos. Zanuck's objections and advice document with precision what Renoir was trying to do on the set and how he was blocked.

July 30, 1941

Dear Renoir:

. . . 1. You are wasting entirely too much time on non-essential details in your background.

2. You are moving your camera around too much on the dolly or on tracks.

3. You should not play scenes two different ways as you did the sequences on the porch in yesterday's rushes. You should decide upon which way you are going to play it and then follow through without compromise.

4. You are worrying too much about background, atmosphere and elements which will not be important in the finished film.

5. The dolly shot of the sheriff in front of the store took over two hours to get in the camera. It isn't worth it.

6. In order to make up time and keep on schedule and budget, it is essential for you to concentrate your attention on the important scenes featuring the principal actors, and on the other scenes find ways and means of covering them as quickly and efficiently as you can.

7. You used four different angles to get over the action with the sheriff on the porch. This could have been covered with one or two angles at the most.

8. The rushes that I have seen in the last two days should have been shot in one day. . . . I regret that it is necessary for me to be stern in this matter, but after reviewing the budget it is easy to read the handwriting on the wall and see that we

are headed toward a price on this picture that we will never be able to get back unless radical change is made at once. D.F.Z.

Aug. 2, 1941

The Camera Report shows that most of the wasted time is because of lack of decision on camera angles. Renoir will give an angle to the cameraman at night that he is going to shoot the following morning, and then when he arrives and the set is all lined up, he has changed his mind. This, of course, can continue to cost us a fortune. D.F.Z.

Aug. 8, 1941

Dear Renoir:

The daily working report shows that a tremendous amount of time is spent each day on discussions. These are things that should be settled the night before so that when you get on the set you know what you are going to do, and go after it. In closing, I want you to know that I am behind you and I am going to see you through on the picture—but, by the same token, I expect you to play ball my way. D.F.Z.   (Behlmer 1993: 51-54)

Renoir's perspective was different. He described his new job in a letter to his brother Claude on May 26, 1941: "The director's job here is reduced to saying OK. You don't decide on the shot breakdown or write the dialogue; a dialogue director directs the actors; the set designer is treated with great deference and so is the cinematographer" (Renoir 1984: 45-46). On July 20, he added, referring to Zanuck: "If I tell you that he personally selected the ties and the buttons for the shirts my characters will wear, I think you will have understood what I mean" (ibid.: 69-70). Renoir summed up his experience in a letter to Dudley Nichols, who wrote the original screenplay that Zanuck changed extensively: "It is useless to tire oneself out trying to present the scenes according to a personal conception, for everything is decided by Zanuck, and when the rushes don't conform to his ideas, he has the scenes reshot. I'm afraid you will be disappointed in *Swamp Water*. I ask you not to judge my work in America from this film, which will be Mr. Zanuck's and not mine" (Renoir 1994: 107-8). Despite everything, *Swamp Water* was a commercial success. But Renoir reacted to this experience by trying to work outside the studios on independent productions that would give him more freedom. This quest would turn out to be only moderately successful.

Renoir did not begin his American career by abandoning his version of realism—not by choice anyway. Nor did he abandon his sense of political commitment to his native country: he took concrete steps to help France from abroad. Alexander Sesonske's important commentaries on Renoir's correspondence from the 1940s in *Lettres d'Amérique* tell us that already in February 1941 he provided assistance for French radio broadcasts originating in Los Angeles, and in 1942 he wrote several letters offering his services as a filmmaker to the American war effort (Renoir 1984: 107–8).[11] Although these letters did not have immediate results, the next two films Renoir would make were directly aimed at winning American support for the French people: *This Land Is Mine* (1943), an independent feature that he coproduced and cowrote with Dudley Nichols, and *Salute to France* (1944), an educational/propaganda film made for the Office of War Information to accompany the Allied landing in northern France.

The production history of *This Land Is Mine* shows how much opposition Renoir faced in his attempt to continue the style he had developed during the 1930s in France. He lost several key decisions about how he wanted to shoot the film, decisions which may, in fact, have marked the turning point in his career. Renoir's lack of confidence in his understanding of American business, the American idiom, and the American public may have caused him to back down and agree to compromise in a way that turned out to have far more serious consequences for his filmmaking than his compromises in France, where Renoir had learned how to influence and work with the alternatives his producers proposed (for the French experience, see Tesson 1992a, 1992b, 1993).

Renoir wanted to continue working with long takes and composition in depth (shots of long duration in which two or three picture planes could be in focus simultaneously, the kind of composition that Orson Welles became known for); this time, it was not the studio (RKO) but his friend, Dudley Nichols, in his role as coproducer, who took the first step in preventing Renoir from working in the style he had realized so brilliantly in *La Règle du jeu* and that he had already been working toward in his silent films. Nichols refused to allow Renoir to open the film with a complicated tracking shot using a crane. According to Eugene Lourié, Renoir's production designer, Renoir reacted strongly, too strongly, to

---

11. *Lettres d'Amérique*, a selection of Renoir's letters from the 1940s, is an invaluable resource not only because of the richness of the material but because of Alexander Sesonske's presentations and notes. Sesonske studied Renoir's papers before they were donated to UCLA and discussed them with Renoir and his wife, Dido. I am greatly indebted to his meticulous, intelligent work.

Nichols's interference and cut every tracking shot from the film (Lourié 1985: 77). This decision changed the film's style completely. Sesonske documents this with some amazing figures that compare the final film with *La Règle du jeu*. *This Land Is Mine* is ten minutes shorter than *La Règle du jeu*, but it has over two hundred additional shots. There is camera movement in half of the 336 shots of *La Règle du jeu*, while the camera moves in only one-sixth of the 550 shots in *This Land Is Mine*, and "most of these are small reframing adjustments." Five shots in *This Land Is Mine* last more than one minute, but there is significant camera movement in only one of them. The longest shot—ninety-five seconds—is static: Albert's (Charles Laughton's) address to the courtroom. Most scenes are broken down into many short shots edited in the Hollywood continuity style. Almost two-thirds of the shots are less than ten seconds long; almost one-third are less than five seconds. In *La Règle du jeu* (excluding the central scene of the hunt), half the shots are seventeen seconds or longer; fifteen shots are one minute or longer. Sesonske's study of the production history shows that Renoir did not intend to move away from the shooting style of his earlier film. "His notes from July suggest a style similar to that of *La Règle du jeu* and the script, though it includes several scenes omitted from the film, lists only 369 shots. One scene described in a single shot in the script takes 32 shots in the film" (Sesonske n.d. a: 98).

Another noticeable difference had to do with verisimilitude. According to the introduction to the published screenplay, the authors (although only Nichols was credited) had deliberately chosen not to specify the film's location: it takes place "somewhere in Europe. . . . The locale is symbolic of all occupied countries and hence resembles no one precisely. Neither sets nor manners should be too foreign" (Nichols 1943: 834). Yet a number of details point to France, not the least of which is Albert's long recitation from the Declaration of the Rights of Man in the courtroom scene. Renoir considered the film's central theme to be collaboration, meaning the enemy inside France (*l'ennemi à domicile*) (Sesonske n.d. a: 85). According to Sesonske, RKO was responsible for excising references to France because the studio was worried about anti-French public opinion. Many Americans believed that France's quick capitulation meant that all French people, except for those who followed de Gaulle, were collaborating with the enemy. Perhaps for the same reason, the studio did not allow Renoir to construct sets that would have let him re-create a believable portrait of the country or even of Europe as he knew it. Instead he had to use leftovers from the 1939 version of *The Hunchback of Notre Dame* (ibid.: 77–78; Lourié 1985: 76–77). Unlike his earlier films, *This Land Is Mine* did not evoke an authentic milieu of any kind. On the contrary, it seems barren and cold. The characters are one-dimensional and rather strident at times.

While general opinion has it that Renoir abandoned his sense of class politics when he left France, a letter written on September 13, 1942, to his son Alain indicated otherwise. "I have finished writing the scenario I have done with Dudley Nichols for Laughton. We are delighted. It is very violent and shows, I hope clearly, that certain European leaders have preferred to see the Nazis penetrate their own country rather than grant some advantages to the workers. It is the story of collaboration, conscious or not, honest or dishonest, that we are trying to explain" (quoted in Sesonske n.d. a: 77; Renoir 1994: 138). There is a strong affinity between this description and Renoir's sharp juxtaposition of class interests in *La Marseillaise*. But by the time *This Land Is Mine* was finished, the violence as well as the representation of class differences had become homogenized into blandness.[12]

In summary, there were too many areas in which Renoir, still the newcomer, understandably lacked experience and deferred to the Americans. He lacked confidence in his ability to communicate with an American audience about the problem of French collaboration and the resistance to it inside the country itself. Understandably again, Renoir felt he could not afford to take a chance because, for him, the importance of *This Land Is Mine* would be measured by its effectiveness as pro-French propaganda. He deferred to Nichols's toughness in his role as producer because he was not in a position to estimate how much his methods would cost under the American system of unionized workers and working hours. Both he and Nichols had a personal financial stake in the film. Renoir feared failure for professional reasons, too. Sesonske believes that he thought Dudley Nichols saved his career by making it possible for him to direct this film. For the same reasons, Renoir agreed to major editing

12. In his essay, Sesonske gives many more examples of important aspects of the script that were either omitted in shooting or eliminated during the long process of editing. He provides an excellent analysis of the film's formal structures, demonstrating that the message Renoir wanted to convey was still present, if less forcefully than Renoir had intended, not only in the dialogue but through symmetrical structural patterns despite the radical changes in the conceptualization and eventual presentation of his *mise en scène*.

concessions (Sesonske n.d. a: 80, 83). Despite all these handicaps, there is good evidence that *This Land Is Mine* was a success for its intended audience, and that, in America, the film did help to accomplish the strategic, political goals Renoir had set for himself. Still, it represented a radical departure from his previous work.

One cannot help but conclude that at some point in the production of *This Land Is Mine* or immediately afterward in the film commissioned by the OWI, *Salute to France,* which spiraled even more radically out of Renoir's control (Sesonske n.d. b), Renoir began to internalize the interdictions of the studio system. In an interview with Jacques Rivette and François Truffaut in April 1954, Renoir described the rationale for some of the concessions he had made.

But in the large studios — once again for financial reasons; when a product is expensive, you must be sure it will satisfy the client — the only method is a secure method, and that is why you have to have shots, reaction shots, master shots, medium shots, so that with just a few retakes you can make almost another film if the editing doesn't work. I never did that. I did do it in *This Land is Mine* because the stakes were too high. . . . I therefore had a great responsibility, and so I adopted the mind-set of a large studio that wants to be very cautious, but for different reasons. I composed the film carefully; I wrote a shooting script as if it were a commercial film, so that if need be I could change it during the editing, and with the help of previews, I could find the correct dosage to produce the desired effect on the public I wanted to influence.   (Renoir 1989 [1979]: 17–18)

In Hollywood Renoir was no longer able to work as a writer-director within a system he understood and could influence effectively. None of his American films were as fully integrated, conceptually and technically, as his works of the 1930s.

FRANCE OR AMERICA?

Throughout the 1940s Renoir's correspondence showed that he believed he could still learn to juggle the elements to his advantage and make an unqualified success in America using the methods he had developed in France. He did not want to leave Hollywood at a point when he was not likely to be called back. The question of returning to France was raised continually in Renoir's letters. It began almost as soon as he arrived in Hollywood. Much earlier than one might expect, Renoir indicated that he might remain in the United States permanently. On February 27, 1942, he wrote to his sister-in-law, Paulette Renoir, that his future was in Hollywood. "I will certainly come back to France, whether to spend some time there or to make films. But my future is here. Whatever difficulties I have encountered in Hollywood and still face, I remain convinced that the people in the film industry here are more honest and open than all of those I knew in France" (Renoir 1984: 98).

Rather than planning his return to France, Renoir spent a great deal of effort trying to persuade his family to come to California. After a year of persistent letters and intercessions by personal emissaries, he succeeded in bringing over his son, Alain, despite obstacles of every kind. Alain was of prime military age and, moreover, he had a mind of his own. Renoir's correspondence to his son and to friends abroad who might assist him shows that often Alain did not respond to his letters, and he did not keep his father informed of his whereabouts (Jean Renoir Collection, UCLA). When Alain finally arrived in New York in December 1941 (like his father, he could not speak English), Renoir convinced him to enlist in the American army rather than sign up with the Free French and ship out for North Africa. Alain spent the war years fighting in the Pacific theater.

Renoir encouraged his brother Claude to come to Hollywood with his family, where he hoped to find work for him. On May 28, 1942, in a letter about Claude's visa, he told him that he had requested his own citizenship papers. Renoir did not want to be a refugee in America. "You may want to know a little more about America before deciding to make the kind of move that amounts to emigrating. As for myself, I have made my decision. I have requested my preliminary papers for becoming an American. In three years I will be a citizen of this country. My decision has nothing to do with the present circumstances. It is simply that I feel more at ease in this big country than in narrow Europe. Alain is like me; he doesn't think of himself as a refugee but as an American" (Renoir 1984: 102). He likewise encouraged his older brother Pierre to come as well as his nephew Claude (Pierre's son, who had been his cinematographer) and his friend Louis Jouvet. Gabrielle Slade, his father's model, his childhood nurse, and the woman Renoir said had most influenced his life, moved next door; the two families created a common garden that resembled southern France. It was with Slade's assistance that Renoir was finally able to write the book about his father that he had planned for many years. After the war Renoir had the belongings he considered really important, things that had belonged to his parents and the cherished portrait his father had painted of him as a child, *Le Chasseur*, shipped to him from France (Renoir 1984: 242–43).

During the night of November 7–8, 1942, American troops landed in French North Africa and faced armed resistance from Vichy troops. By November 11, the Americans were nearly in control of Morocco and Algeria. The Vichy government broke diplomatic relations with the United States. To protect southern France from an Allied invasion, German troops crossed the line of demarcation that separated the northern zone from the "free zone" and occupied the entire country (Azéma 1979: 277–81; Paxton 1972: 280–81). Mail services were cut off between France and the United States until the spring of 1945. When the mail began to flow again, it was slow and unreliable. Renoir wrote many letters that spring to reestablish contact with his family and his closest friends to try to find out where they were and what had happened to them during that long period of worried uncertainty. Summarizing his work in Hollywood with characteristic, down-to-earth honesty, Renoir described his lack of real success considering what he had hoped to accomplish. Yet he still believed he had a better chance to make good films there than in France. From early 1942 until December 1945, when Alain finally returned to California, Renoir's letters showed that he was constantly preoccupied with his son's safety and his whereabouts. In response to many letters asking him to come back to France, Renoir replied that he couldn't risk being away when Alain came home.

Renoir had another serious reason for staying away from France in 1945. According to French law, Renoir was still legally married to Catherine Hessling. The couple had been separated since 1932, but Renoir had only begun divorce proceedings in California in August 1942. When communications with France were cut off several months later, the divorce had not yet been finalized. As a result, it was not recognized in France after the war, although it was official in the United States. Renoir and Dido Freire were married in February 1944. Hessling learned of this and threatened to have Renoir arrested as a bigamist when he came back to France. Her threats were taken seriously. A protracted legal battle ensued which was not decided in Renoir's favor until June 1949.

Renoir's correspondence during the months in which he was making contact again with his family and friends in France put other matters into relief that directly concerned his attitude in 1945 and 1946 toward his own national cinema. "The drama for me was that the elements which had hitherto constituted my life were changing, so that I was in danger of becoming as much of an outsider on the Place Pigalle as on Sunset Boulevard" (Renoir 1974b: 245). In 1945 Renoir decided to begin work on another American film, *Woman on the Beach*.

Renoir wanted to remain in America long enough to make an unqualified success. That would give him the option of returning to Hollywood later. On February 14, 1946, he replied to a proposal for a French film production from Sam Siritzky, a film distributor and theater owner whose father had saved *La Chienne* in 1931 with a brilliant reverse psychology advertising scheme. "I don't want to return to my country without having made a really, really successful film that would secure my place in Hollywood even if I come back to France to work. This is in my interest as well as in the interest of French cinema. The day when I will have made a film in Hollywood that corresponds in value and importance to what *La Grande Illusion* represented in France nearly ten years ago, on that day I will consider that the task I set myself has been accomplished and I have the right to begin something else" (Renoir 1984: 211). He expressed these concerns somewhat differently to Paul Cézanne Jr. on April 5, 1946. He did not want to be thought of as just another émigré: "Little by little I hope to be able to recreate the conditions that would allow me to make an absolutely personal film. I already did it when I made *The Southerner*, but that was a low-budget film. I would like to do that with a more important production. Then I think that I could return to France without feeling that my stay in Hollywood had been a last resort, a kind of refuge for an emigré" (ibid.: 214).

Besides this, in the intervening years he had become estranged from France: "All my imagination has been used up trying to represent to myself, throughout the war, what could be happening on the other side, that other side where you, most of your friends and mine had to remain" (ibid.: 224). This is how he put it in a letter to Charles Spaak, cowriter of *La Grande Illusion,* on May 10, 1946. A few days later he wrote to his nephew Claude Renoir Jr.: "Since the war ended, my ideas have been very confused. They are barely beginning to become clear and I don't think that if I went to Paris now, I would have anything worthwhile to offer a producer. I probably have more ideas which could apply to America, and that is why I want to try to make a good film here, taken from a personal story" (ibid.: 229; Renoir 1994: 177).

RENOIR'S COMEBACK IN ABSENTIA

"Ah, si nous avions Jean Renoir!"

If he didn't return to France in person in 1945, Renoir's correspondence showed he was making a comeback in absentia. His earlier films were being revived with great appreciation and sometimes renewed scandal in ciné-clubs, and his films from the late 1930s were being re-released in commercial theaters. Renoir's name was in the air. On September 26, *La Règle du Jeu* was released again.[13] On October 15, his old friend Pierre Lestringuez wrote to Renoir: "Right now, they think of you as a god of the cinema, paternal and genial, omnipotent and truculent, and everywhere . . . they are sighing: 'If only we had Jean Renoir!' " (Renoir 1984: 199–200). In a letter from his brother Claude, written on October 22, Renoir was told that the film had just been banned again. "People were getting into fights leaving the theater. There's a film that doesn't leave the audience indifferent" (ibid.: 199). But in May 1946, Lestringuez reported that *La Règle du jeu* had found a new life: "Suddenly people understood what had not been explained" (ibid.: 209). *La Grande Illusion* was released during August and September 1946, edited somewhat to comply with postwar censorship, and was a huge success (ibid.: 209).[14] *La Bête humaine* was playing in several cinemas. *Une partie de campagne,* which Renoir had abandoned in 1936, had been completed as a short film in his absence thanks to producer Pierre Braunberger's inspired suggestions. The film was presented at Cannes in 1946 and drew excellent reviews (Bertin 1991 [1986]: 231). A number of offers came to Renoir from France.

Unfortunately, the news from France was not destined to remain so positive. The situation was reversed dramatically when Renoir's American films were released. The reviews were unsympathetic and uncomprehending. The first to be released was a badly dubbed version of *This Land Is Mine* in July 1946. Dubbing was anathema to Renoir. (He had written a long letter on this subject to the actor Pierre Blanchar, President of the Comité de libération du cinéma, in December 1944. He felt the future and integrity of French cinema were at stake in the postwar debate about dubbing [Renoir 1984: 163–65].) The film was violently at-

13. There is confusion and some controversy about which version was released (Faulkner 1995).

14. For an explanation of the censorship issues, see Renoir 1984: 222.

tacked as unrealistic and an insult to those who had lived through the dark years of the Occupation. Some took the opportunity to say that Renoir had taken the easy way out by going to Hollywood. Renoir reacted strongly and emotionally to this news about a film that he had made specifically to persuade Americans, who were cut off from France in every way at the time, that they should support the French people. In a letter to his brother Claude on July 26, he wrote:

I read in a Hollywood newspaper that *This Land Is Mine* was very badly received in Paris because the subject of the resistance was treated in an unorthodox way in the film. I won't hide from you how unpleasant this news is to me. It wasn't easy for me to insist on a subject of this kind at a time when everything French was considered to be the enemy in America. It seemed to me that my primary duty was to explain to Americans through the medium of film, which is "my medium," that anti-Nazi feelings existed in occupied Europe. I believe I succeeded and I had proof from many letters written by soldiers. . . . I think . . . that RKO was wrong to release a film that was topical in 1942. But that doesn't change the fact that, if what I read is true, I am not prepared to forget the deep pain this lack of understanding by my fellow countrymen has caused me. I told you at the beginning of my letter I felt a great desire to stay here. This incident can only reinforce my desire not to go where I will find men whose heroism during the war forces my admiration but whose susceptibility seems regrettable to me. (Renoir 1984: 238, 1994: 183)

Perhaps Renoir had also been caught off guard because, in addition to letters from soldiers and American citizens, he had received appreciative letters and telegrams from French émigrés, including Louis Jouvet, who had seen the film in Uruguay (Jean Renoir Collection, UCLA). But these French spectators, like Renoir, were displaced. Pierre Lestringuez, who had participated with Renoir on his films since his earliest efforts in 1924, attempted to make him understand the point of view from France. Lestringuez underscored the distance between the country that Renoir had left and the realities of postwar conflicts about the representation of its recent past which Renoir had not experienced. "Despite all its good qualities, *This Land Is Mine* doesn't give the impression of that realism in depth and poetic truth without symbols to which you have accustomed us. And then, we have lived too long under the occupation, which was 100% more oppressive than you could have shown it" (Renoir 1984: 102). Even *The Southerner,* which Renoir considered to be his best American film (the National Board of Review named it third best film of the year and Renoir best director, and it won the prize for best film at the Venice Biennale in 1946), was booed when it premiered in France at the prestigious Festival Indépendant du Film Maudit at Biarritz in 1949 (Andrew 1978: 155–56).

Renoir's son returned to California in December 1945. Renoir learned that his divorce was official in France in June 1949. Yet, even after these reasons for staying away from France had been eliminated, he did not set foot in his native country until six months later, on November 21, 1949, and then for only thirty-six hours. He had been working on *The River* in India, using Technicolor equipment and labs based in London. It was during his first brief trip to Paris from London that Renoir met and was interviewed by André Bazin.[15] After *The River* was finished, Renoir and Dido must have stopped in Paris briefly in May or June 1950, judging from a letter written to Claude Renoir Jr. in June (Bertin 1991 [1986]: 258). According to Bertin, Renoir moved back to Paris in May 1951 to resume his film career "with no specific project in mind" (ibid.: 260). But his correspondence from March and April shows that *The Golden Coach* with Anna Magnani had already been planned for Italy before he left the United States (Renoir 1994: 263, 269). Renoir was in Paris only three times in 1951: from May 8 to May 17, when he left for Rome to work on *The Golden Coach*;[16] from June 29 to July 19, to cast the French actors for the film; and from November 19 to December 2, to see a medical specialist following an accident that had reopened his old leg wound from World War I and once again raised fears of amputation (Renoir 1984, 1994). This last was the trip Bazin referred to in the remarks that opened this essay.

When *The Golden Coach* was released in France, the press reaction was negative. The hostility was absent, yet as with *La Règle du jeu*, critics complained there were too many characters and the action was hard to follow. *The Golden Coach* was about spectacle, yes, but what else did

15. Sesonske's account in *Lettres d'Amérique* and Bertin's account differ slightly, but one obtains a fairly clear picture from Renoir's voluminous correspondence. See Jean Renoir Collection, UCLA, in addition to the two published books of correspondence (Renoir 1984, 1994). Bazin's interview, published in *Écran français*, was called "Author of *Grand Illusion* Has Not Lost Confidence in Creative Freedom."

16. On May 10, he wrote to Dido from Paris that the real reason for being there was to become informed about current French film production. Contrary to Bertin's account, Dido joined him later in Italy (Renoir 1994). The interview Bazin did on this occasion appeared in *Radio-TV-Film* (Bertin 1991 [1986]: 262–63).

Renoir have on his mind? Why did the film look so artificial? Not that the film was rejected by everyone: by now, Renoir had won over the new cadre following Bazin's lead, most notably Truffaut and Rivette.[17]

I would argue that Renoir's delay and the subsequent phases of his return by proxy (the positive reaction to the re-release of his 1930s films and the negative reaction to the French release of his American films) complicated the decisions he would make about his return movie and his return to France. Bazin had said that the war had made Renoir leave, so the end of the war should bring him back. But, at this point, it is safe to say that the war wasn't the only reason Renoir left France.

FRENCH CANCAN: RENOIR'S RETURN

French Cancan corresponded to my great desire to make a film in a very French spirit that could make contact again between us easy, that would be an enjoyable bridge between French audiences and myself. I felt the public was very close to me, but I wanted to make sure.

JEAN RENOIR, May 1954

Was Renoir really that confident? He had good reason to be apprehensive about a direct encounter with the French public.[18] I believe Renoir did not want to risk jeopardizing his return to filmmaking in France with another film that might confuse and alienate critics and the public as *La Règle du jeu* had done in 1939, as his American films had done, and as *The Golden Coach* had done most recently in 1952. With *French Cancan* I believe that Renoir wanted to make a film that was simple, clear, positive, and self-evidently French. All this he achieved. We have the right to ask what was at stake in the simplicity he opted for.

The public and his longtime supporters would have been happiest to see a return to Renoir's 1930s realist mode. However, Renoir was no

17. Truffaut named his production company Les Films du Carosse as an homage to *The Golden Coach* (Le Carosse d'or) and the man who made it.

18. Two years had passed since Renoir had made a film, *The Golden Coach*. On March 12, 1955 (*French Cancan* had been shot but not yet released), *Orvet,* a play written and directed by Renoir starring Leslie Caron, premiered at the Théâtre de la Renaissance in Paris. According to Bertin, critics were reticent (1991 [1986]: 289–90). According to others, they expressed negative views more actively.

longer working in that mode or thinking along those lines. In 1954 he was
sixty years old. He had not lived in France for fifteen years. He had not
experienced the German occupation or the deep conflicts in the country
that had followed (Rousso 1991 [1987]). In 1946 he had wanted to bring
his brother Claude and Claude's son to Los Angeles to work with him on
a script about the French Resistance: they had been active participants
and they knew the contemporary situation in France. That project did
not work out. By 1954 this kind of subject was no longer on his mind.
Renoir went back to an even earlier period than World War II or the
1930s. He set his film in the Belle Epoque, France's age of innocence before the Great War. In his autobiography, Renoir explained his decision
in 1946 to make a film unrelated to France (instead, he made *Woman on
the Beach*): "It was natural that I should look for themes having nothing
to do with a fatherland that was no longer itself. I had a horror of sentimental images of pre-war France" (Renoir 1974b: 246). By 1954 he had
evidently changed his mind.

French Cancan is about the impresario Charles Zidler, called here
Danglard (played by Jean Gabin), who created the Moulin Rouge in 1889
and in so doing invented the modern French music hall. Zidler succeeded in attracting the bourgeoisie, a new clientele who would pay high
prices to mingle safely with the colorful residents of Montmartre, especially the dancers. The plot of *French Cancan* turns on Danglard's relationships with three women. His longtime mistress and star performer,
a belly dancer called La Belle Abesse, obtains financial backing for him
from a German capitalist, Baron Walter, who supports her. Danglard begins construction of the Moulin Rouge. In search of talent he finds Nini
(Françoise Arnoul), a laundress, and offers her mother money to allow
her daughter to become a cancan dancer. Nini becomes Danglard's mistress. When La Belle Abesse finds out, she has Baron Walter withdraw
from the project. Work on the Moulin Rouge stops. A Russian prince
falls in love with Nini and, after attempting suicide when she refuses him,
he gives her the money for the Moulin Rouge. On the opening night,
the crowd comes, the show moves along smoothly, and the main event,
the cancan, is about to be announced when Nini catches sight of Danglard kissing the singer Esther Georges, another of his discoveries. Visibly
shocked and hurt, Nini retreats to her dressing room and refuses to
dance (she is the star attraction) unless Danglard agrees to remain faithful to her. Danglard declares his independence from all women and his

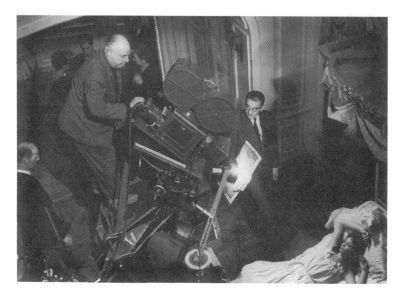

Figure 2 *French Cancan* (Jean Renoir, Françoise Arnoul). Printed with permission of UCLA Arts Library Special Collections, Jean Renoir Papers.

dedication to spectacle. Nini gives in. The cancan begins. The show is wildly successful.

French Cancan recalled the colors, the simplicity, and the *joie de vivre* of Montmartre in the Belle Epoque as seen by the Impressionists, especially Auguste Renoir in his paintings of the Moulin de la Galette. In all these respects, it was very different from John Huston's *Moulin Rouge,* a recent success in France and the United States, which focused on the tortured psyche of Toulouse-Lautrec. Over and over again, *French Cancan* was called a fresco. Critics proclaimed that the son had made a film worthy of his father. The film was openly theatrical. One could see its relationship to *The Golden Coach,* but without that film's difficulties: both celebrated spectacle. It ended with an ecstatic ten-minute cancan that filled the screen with colors and vitality that no critic failed to praise. The dancers burst through the crowd, crisscrossing the floor with provocative, acrobatic movements and shrieks of pleasure. By the end, a united community prevailed as the haunting melody that Renoir himself had written (the "Complainte de la Butte") returned to the soundtrack and everyone sang or hummed the song. Jean Gabin's presence evoked his roles in Renoir's 1930s films, and the press hailed the reunion of the two men. Gabin was paired with Françoise Arnoul, a young star who created a link between two postwar generations. *French Cancan* was meant to be a celebration of Renoir's return to France. He offered it as a gift to the French public, who responded exactly in the way he had hoped. It was a huge popular success, and so was Renoir's return.

Critics reviewed *French Cancan* in terms of Renoir's renewed relationship to France and French cinema. Here are two examples, inflected somewhat differently, from the dozens one could cite.

Those who followed Renoir's efforts to master a craft from the beginning . . . didn't hide the disappointment he inflicted on them with his work in America, in India, in Italy. . . . His first French film, after 16 years away from France was awaited with apprehension by those who wished him a better success than some aesthetes gave him for the brilliant improvisations of *La Règle du jeu* or *The Golden Coach*. But in making contact again with his native soil, Jean Renoir has instantly recovered that sense of life that characterizes his best films. We recognize in *French Cancan* all the qualities that we admire in *Toni, La Bête humaine, La Marseillaise.* . . . If you go to the Orangerie to see "The Boatsmans' Luncheon" by Auguste Renoir, you will see that Jean is the worthy successor of his father. (Charensol 1955)

After a long exile in Hollywood, after the new research he carried out in *The River* and *The Golden Coach,* Jean Renoir marks his return to the French sources of his inspiration in a dazzling manner. . . . The French public will not be disappointed: under the flounces of the *belle époque,* under the kindness and exuberance of this *French Cancan,* it is really France that has just found Renoir again. And through this new contact with his country's heart, Renoir has recovered his youth. In marking his return to our studios with this dazzling display of fireworks, Jean Renoir has brought great hope to our cinema, our culture, and our people. (Monjo 1955)

In *Arts* Truffaut (1955) summarized the film's strengths: its unprecedented use of color; Renoir's evocation of Degas when the girls are training to become dancers; and the cancan finale.

But *French Cancan* also contained darker elements that connected it with dominant tendencies in postwar French cinema: (1) a flight into the past to escape the Franco-French conflicts (*la guerre franco-française*) that resulted from the Occupation and were intensified by the war in Algeria; (2) a retrograde depiction of sexual politics and a fairy-tale representation of class relationships. To take the second point first, there were a few critics who expressed reservations about the new Renoir.

Something fundamental had changed in his representation of class and sex roles.

Josette Daix's long review in *Les Lettres Françaises* was full of praise for Renoir's talents but, unlike other reviewers, she did not hesitate to criticize his representation of sexual difference. Daix raised important issues that others chose to ignore and that Renoir's commentators still ignore to this day. Referring to the scene in which Nini's mother virtually sells her daughter to Danglard, and then Nini runs to her fiancé, the baker, to prepare herself for her new job by losing her virginity, Daix commented: "In spite of Françoise Arnoul's gentle manner and all the effort she makes to give this scene some discretion, the sequence has a vulgarity that is rather shocking and pointless. . . . One cannot help but think about the discretion [Renoir] used when he made *Une partie de campagne* and the suggestive power the kiss had then. . . . When one has become a great director, one doesn't really have the right to become just a good filmmaker" (1955).

A week later, *Les Lettres Françaises* published a second long essay on *French Cancan* by Georges Sadoul. Sadoul began by reminding his compatriots "for those who may have forgotten it—that there are few men to whom French cinema owes more than to Jean Renoir" (1955). Sadoul described how the films Renoir made during the 1930s were crucial in giving life to a specifically French national cinema.

Renoir reached the height of his art . . . between 1930 and 1940, and contributed more than anyone else (unless it might be René Clair) to restore to our cinema the international prestige it had lost in 1914. He attained his apogee because, better than anyone else, he expressed the mood of his day. His art was then deeply impregnated by the movement of the Popular Front. One can understand nothing of his greatness by studying his films without reference to the developments in society, to the popular struggles of the years 1933–1939, not only *La Vie est à nous* and *La Marseillaise* (masterpieces misunderstood by some), but *Toni*, *La Grand Illusion*, *Le Crime de M. Lange*, *Une partie de campagne*, *La Bête humaine*, *La Règle du jeu* (masterpieces recognized by all). The liaison of the great creator with his nation and his people was conscious, willed and sought after. One can see that from the articles he published in 1938 in *Le Point* which had a universal educational value that extended beyond the expression of Renoir's personality.   (Ibid.)

Like others, Sadoul praised the "extraordinary final ballet" and Renoir's use of color and rhythm. Moreover, he argued that the film provided several important critiques: Danglard's plan showed the beginning of the contemporary Parisian "package tour" industry, especially as marketed to Anglo-Saxons. Renoir showed that it was the financiers represented by Baron Walter, not the middlemen like Danglard, who would reap the profits and that France needed foreigners to function economically—at the beginning for investment capital and later as clients.

Sadoul expressed reservations, however, about other aspects of *French Cancan*'s representation of class: for one thing, presenting the future Czar of Russia as a selfless, virtuous Prince Charming. More fundamentally, an easy populism pervaded the film that didn't ring true. Renoir's portrait of Montmartre and its laundresses was so lovely that one couldn't believe "the girls would leap at the chance to escape misery by becoming dancers" (ibid.). Nor is it for the sake of art that Nini follows Danglard, but because she believes she has agreed to become his mistress. "We witness the beginning of *Nana* (not written by Zola) without Renoir ever criticizing this natural course of events. For Danglard, Montmartre's working girls are a reservoir of future prostitutes. The laundresses of *French Cancan* are, one sees, very far from the laundresses of *Monsieur Lange*. The entire distance between solidarity and venality" (ibid.).

There was more at stake than a good or bad review: Sadoul was calling on Renoir to rejoin the French people and bear witness to his time once again, if it was not too late. He ended his essay with passion and hope. "Is it possible that [Renoir's] generosity did not mature into kindness but turned to bitterness? That he now sees the world with the cynical eye of this Baron Walter whom he detests? In 1955, one could not paint the France of 1880 exactly like the best creators of this period, de Maupassant in *La Maison Tellier* or Zola in *L'Assommoir*. Because he didn't want to understand this, Renoir did not give us, in *French Cancan*, a film that equals his masterpieces of 1934–1939. Let him quickly recover all his courage and lucidity. One cannot be fully French today if one misrecognizes or despises our people" (ibid.). However, being "fully French" again was not Renoir's primary motive in making films in France after the war.

Daix and Sadoul anticipate a contemporary feminist perspective. I would like to add to their comments by drawing attention to Renoir's *mise en scène* of sexual difference: that is, his specific choices in cinematic staging. Nini discovers her lover's infidelity (his betrayal) just before she is about to debut in the cancan finale. In the broad, open space backstage, she sees Danglard and the singer, Esther Georges, embrace pas-sionately, and she hears Esther echo her own words: "I will be with you forever." Nini, shocked and in tears, makes her presence known to the couple and then retreats to her dressing room. As the crowd shouts for Nini, she insists that she will not perform. Finally, she tells Danglard that she will not dance unless he agrees to remain faithful to her.

Everyone knows that Jean Gabin was famous for his obligatory "scene of rage" in his 1930s films. In *French Cancan*, Renoir allowed Gabin's ex-plosion to be triggered by Nini's refusal to take her place in the cancan. Danglard/Gabin, it should be emphasized, by making it clear that he has taken a new lover so publicly and in the middle of the show, has undercut not only the young woman who has shown him nothing but tenderness, affection, and support throughout the film, but his star dancer moments before she is about to perform in public for the first time in her life. (La Belle Abesse rushes to Nini's defense: "I hope you haven't cheated on a good girl like Nini.") In a rage, Danglard shouts his defiance at Nini in a manner that is relentlessly sarcastic and needlessly cruel. In fact, although Gabin's acting is rather stolid throughout, it is the only scene in the film in which he abandons every pretense of charm and nuance. His "rage" is mechanical, as if it were not addressed to a person at all. Throughout this scene, Renoir's visual rhetoric shows Nini alone in the frame while the reverse shots show the troupe gathered tightly around Danglard. Here is a sample of his oratory (stage directions are italicized):

My poor Nini, it's a lover you want? Telegraph [Prince] Alexander. You will never find a better one. A husband? All you have to do is whistle and Paolo [the baker] will come running at a gallop. . . . You know what I do. I make you, and her [*pointing to La Belle Abesse*], and her [*pointing to Esther*]! There were others before and there will be others tomorrow. [*hard*] You want Danglard? Does it matter what you want . . . or what I want? You think that counts for anything? [*noise of the audience in the other room*] It's what they want that counts.   ("M. Renoir, Version anglaise," Jean Renoir Collection, UCLA)

"I make you, and her, and her . . ." For most of the film, we have seen Danglard as Nini's lover, as she has. We witness his betrayal from her point of view. From one minute to the next, we see Nini fall from happy excitement to humiliation. As the scene is staged, Danglard tells her off harshly in front of everyone, photographed in such a way as to isolate Nini visually and tacitly to position the entire troupe against her. Nini is made to feel that she is the only one not playing by the rules of the game.

Let's not be mistaken. Danglard's cold fury is not motivated by his conviction that putting on the show to please the audience is the only thing that counts in life. He explodes because Nini tries to hold him accountable for his sexual exploits. In effect, Danglard is shouting that he is entitled to his harem, because the public needs him to have it so that he can produce better and better spectacles for them. It is the women who draw the public; Danglard discovers them, makes them work to realize their talent, and gives them a place to perform. He is the capitalist; the women are his capital. Not only that, Danglard's women are willing to pay by any means necessary to support him throughout most of the film, before the Moulin Rouge has been built and he is penniless and, for a while, bedridden with a broken leg.

Where earlier in the film, we have dialogue to support Renoir's critique of the role of foreign capital and the transformation of Montmartre into a tourist attraction, here there is nothing . . . for the simple reason that the male prerogative is taken as a natural given. It is entirely possible that Françoise Arnoul, enacting the role of Nini, indicated more depth of feeling—her affectionate manner, her desire not to hurt the other men who love her, her pain in watching Danglard with his new lover—than Renoir intended, with the kind of psychological realism Renoir said he deplored, but that can be seen throughout his 1930s films. But then, the film moves quickly from Danglard's callous triumph backstage to the amazing performance of the cancan that concludes the film and is designed to wipe out that memory and absorb everyone in the vibrant rhythm of the spectacle. The implication is that the ends justify the means.

In response to those who would argue that Renoir has anticipated the contradictions in this dynamic and inscribed them as a critique of existing social/sexual relations, I would point out that not only the dialogue but also the way this scene is staged invites complicity, not critique. Gabin's speech was reproduced in its entirety as one of the best in the film in at least three places (*Cahiers du Cinéma* [Renoir 1955], *Cinéma 55* [1954], Pierre Leprohon's *Jean Renoir* [1971 {1967}]), without comment and without any indication of the context. Truffaut, in his review, described Danglard's relationship to women as if it were something he understood from personal experience: "Danglard devotes his life to the music hall, discovers young female talents, dancers or singers, and 'makes' them stars. He becomes, for a while, their lover and they become exclusive, possessive, jealous, capricious and insupportable" (Truffaut

1955). There is only one woman in the film who is portrayed as "capricious and insupportable," and that is La Belle Abesse, not Nini and not Esther Georges. If Renoir seems to have created Danglard in his own image in a number of noticeable respects (his age, his trade, even his leg injury), it is important not to confuse self-reflexivity with a critique. In the end Danglard has manipulated Nini into doing exactly what he wants: she will dance, and she will let him have other lovers. "Love of the *métier*" seems to give the *metteur en scène* carte blanche, and to cancel the need for an environment based on mutual respect and understanding. The show turns out to be a heartless endeavor. Danglard doesn't even watch the cancan: listening from another room, he is the puppet master who has already programmed every movement and can see the dance better in his mind than as part of the audience. If he is represented visually as an outsider, he is still the one in control. His spectacle has created an artificial community.

Critics have frequently equated the ending of *French Cancan* with that of *The Golden Coach,* but they are fundamentally different. *The Golden Coach* ends with a speech that affirms spectacle over life, but it is the actress Camilla (Anna Magnani) who delivers it on a stage, in a bittersweet performance directed toward the film audience (the camera), not an impresario who "makes" performers. She decides to give up her three suitors and remain with the troupe. The decision is her own. She speaks of her suitors with warmth and regret. The manager of the troupe, Danglard's counterpart, is a benign, elderly man who reminds her gently from the wings that her real love is performing for an audience, and it is their love she needs in return. Compared to Magnani, Gabin, who keeps three lovers rather than give them up, is smug and too sure of himself. His performance of male prerogatives is enacted in the real space backstage and is strictly functional: the show must go on. Lest one think Gabin had lost his best qualities as an actor, remember his role in Max Ophuls's *Le Plaisir* in 1952, where he moved and spoke with the nuanced sensuality of his best 1930s films, and the lighting and framing (the cornerstone of Renoir's great talent for photogenic images in the 1930s) were as soft and modulated as if the film had been made then. The same year as *French Cancan,* Gabin played an elegant, aging gangster with understated charm and warmth in *Touchez-pas au grisbi,* directed by the man who had been Renoir's understudy in the 1930s, Jacques Becker.

Renoir's choice of a vehicle for his return to filmmaking in France can be seen within a much broader framework which gave it an important resonance in 1955. I would suggest that the Moulin Rouge as mobilized by Renoir in *French Cancan* functions as a *lieu de mémoire* in the sense described by Pierre Nora (1989 [1984]): it is a specific site to which memory attaches, which can be invoked differently according to changing social and symbolic needs. The Moulin Rouge served a mythic function in two ways in *French Cancan* and, in doing so, marked a double regression, both personal and social. The Moulin Rouge was invoked as a screen memory in the Freudian sense, masking the traumas of postwar France by going back to an untroubled age of youth and innocence for both Renoir and France. The film created an innocent image of Renoir's childhood days in Montmartre, before his conflicts about national and professional identity. At the same time, it represented an image of France (Paris as synecdoche for the nation) before the violent paradigm shift that the Great War forced on the country and its people, and that Renoir never stopped using as a point of reference. Moreover, in its implicit allusions to the Impressionist painters through the connection with Renoir's father, the film invoked the French tradition of artistic and cultural superiority, which had not been tainted by the Occupation. *French Cancan* participated in the postwar avoidance of speaking about Vichy and its aftermath: it is one of many postwar French films set in the Belle Epoque.

I would argue, further, that *French Cancan* served as a screen for Renoir's troubled relationship to the representation of sexual difference. The Moulin Rouge, as a fabled site of spectacle, facilitated a displacement from a narrative centered around the opacity and complexity of male-female relationships (as in *Une partie de campagne*) to a story about Spectacle (the origin of the Moulin Rouge standing in for other kinds of spectacle, including the cinema), in which human relationships can be absorbed and forgotten in a whirling finale. Although Renoir's representation of women was never unproblematic, a topic that has received scant attention, it too had changed during his years in America. The celebration of the cancan in this film could not be more distant from Renoir's avant-garde *Nana* in 1926, in which the final cancan was a frenetic dance of death, Nana's last performance that led to her descent into hallucinations brought on by smallpox. Was it just a coincidence that *Nana* had premiered at the Moulin-Rouge cinema?[19] Did Renoir recognize the irony represented by this strange return in his career and his life?

19. "*Nana* was given a terrific world *première* for which I had prepared the way with a riot of publicity. The walls of Paris were covered with posters of Catherine

In *French Cancan* we find an unexpected link between 1939 and 1955: Renoir ended up doing exactly what had been asked of him after *La Règle du jeu*. On September 2, 1939, the day before France declared war on Germany, the trade journal *La Cinématographie française* published an appeal to producers and directors:

ATTENTION PRODUCERS! MAKE HEALTHY, OPTIMISTIC FILMS! A number of important films, among them films that have won honors, have been banned. This is no longer the time to make demoralizing films. We must make films that are healthy, optimistic and constructive. Carné, Chenal and Renoir have to change genres. French producers and directors will know how to follow our leaders to make up for the past. They will give us films of light, courage and happiness.   (Quoted in Jeancolas 1983: 281)

Wasn't this the recipe for *French Cancan?* It seems to me an even stranger turn of events that Renoir needed to go back to France to make the kind of American success he so much wanted, for *French Cancan* would qualify as a perfectly respectable Hollywood film. To journalists who asked him in 1955 which country he preferred, Renoir replied: "I belong to the nationality of the spectacle" (Fabre 1955).

REFERENCES

Andrew, Dudley
    1978 *André Bazin* (New York: Oxford University Press).
    1995 *Mists of Regret: Culture and Sensibility in Classic French Film* (Princeton: Princeton University Press).
Azéma, Jean-Pierre
    1979 *De Munich à la Libération, 1938–1944* (Paris: Seuil).
Bazin, André
    1952 "Renoir français," *Cahiers du cinéma* 8: 9–29.
    1973 [1971] *Jean Renoir,* edited by François Truffaut, translated by W. W. Halsey II and William H. Simon (New York: Delta).
Behlmer, Rudy, ed.
    1993 *Memo from Darryl F. Zanuck: The Golden Years at Twentieth Century-Fox* (New York: Grove).

Hessling, and the press heralded the event with a fanfare of trumpets. I had hired the big hall of the Moulin Rouge, together with its excellent orchestra" (Renoir 1974b: 84).

Bertin, Célia

1991 [1986] *Jean Renoir: A Life in Pictures*, translated by Mireille Muellner and Leonard Muellner (Baltimore: Johns Hopkins University Press).

Beylie, Claude

1975 "L'Oeuvre de Jean Renoir: Cinéma, Télévision, Radio," *Cinéma d'Aujourd'hui* nouvelle série 2 (May–June).

Bussot, Marguerite

1939 "Before *The Rules of the Game:* An Interview with Jean Renoir," *Pour vous* (January 25), in Bazin 1973 [1971]: 183–86.

Charensol, Georges

1955 *"French Cancan," Les Nouvelles Littéraires* (May 5). Collection Cinémathèque Française. *Cinéma 55*

1954 "Extrait du découpage de French-Cancan" (December): 47–49.

Daix, Josette

1955 "Un faux Renoir: *French Cancan* de Jean Renoir," *Les Lettres Françaises* (May 12). Collection Cinémathèque Française.

de Coquet, James

1939 *Le Figaro*, July 12, in Gauteur 1974: 60.

Esnault, Philippe

1965 "Le Jeu de la vérité," *L'Avant-scène du Cinéma* 52: 7–15.

Fabre, Jacqueline

1955 *Libération* (May 6). Jean Renoir Collection, UCLA.

Faulkner, Christopher

1979 *Jean Renoir: A Guide to References and Resources* (Boston: G. K. Hall).

1995 "They Had Their Reasons: Un-Restoring *La Règle du jeu.*" Paper presented at the annual meeting of the Society for Cinema Studies, New York City.

Gauteur, Claude

1974 *"La Règle du jeu* et la critique en 1936," *Anthologie du Cinéma* 282: 45–75.

Jeancolas, Jean-Pierre

1983 *Quinze ans d'années trente: Le cinéma français, 1929–1944* (Paris: Stock).

Leprohon, Pierre

1971 [1967] *Jean Renoir*, translated by Brigid Elsen (New York: Crown).

Lourié, Eugene

1985 *My Work in Films* (New York: Harcourt Brace Jovanovich).

Monjo, Armand

1955 *"French Cancan* de Jean Renoir," *L'Humanité* (May 4). Collection Cinémathèque Française.

Nichols, Dudley

1943 *"This Land Is Mine"* in *Twenty Best Film Plays,* edited by John Gassner and Dudley Nichols, 833–74 (New York: Crown).

Nora, Pierre

    1989 [1984] "Between Memory and History: *Les Lieux de Mémoire,*" *Representations* 26: 7–25.

Paxton, Robert O.

    1972 *Vichy France: Old Guard and New Order, 1940–1944* (New York: Columbia University Press).

Poulle, François

    1969 *Renoir 1938 ou Jean Renoir pour rien? Enquête sur un cinéaste* (Paris: Éditions du Cerf).

Renoir, Jean

    1938a *Ce Soir* (February 17), in Renoir 1974a: 153.

    1938b *Ce Soir* (October 7), in Gauteur 1974: 57.

    1938c "Souvenirs," *Le Point* (December); translated as "Memories" in Bazin 1973 [1971]: 149–58.

    1939 Interview with Nino Frank, *Pour Vous* (May 24), in Gauteur 1974: 52–53.

    1952 "On me demande," *Cahiers du Cinéma* 8: 5–8.

    1955 "French Cancan (Extraits)," *Cahiers du Cinéma* 47 (May 1955): 9–10.

    1974a *Écrits, 1926–1971,* edited by Claude Gauteur (Paris: Pierre Belfond).

    1974b *My Life and My Films,* translated by Norman Denny (New York: Atheneum).

    1984 *Lettres d'Amérique,* presented by Dido Renoir and Alexander Sesonske, introduction and notes by Alexander Sesonske, translated by Annie Wiart (Paris: Presses de la Renaissance).

    1989 [1979] *Renoir on Renoir: Interviews, Essays, and Remarks,* translated by Carol Volk (New York: Cambridge University Press). This is a translation of *Jean Renoir: Entretiens et propos* (Paris: Éditions de l'Etoile Cahiers du Cinéma).

    1994 *Jean Renoir: Letters,* edited by David Thompson and Lorraine LoBianco, translated by Craig Carlson, Natasha Arnoldi, and Michael Wells (London: Faber and Faber).

Rousso, Henry

    1991 [1987] *The Vichy Syndrome: History and Memory in France since 1944,* translated by Arthur Goldhammer (Cambridge, MA: Harvard University Press).

Sadoul, Georges

    1955 "*French Cancan,*" *Les Lettres françaises* (May 19). Collection Cinémathèque Française.

    1972 [1965] *Dictionary of Film makers,* translated, edited, and updated by Peter Morris (Berkeley: University of California Press).

    1979 *Chroniques du cinéma français: Écrits 1, 1939–1967,* edited and annotated by Bernard Eisenschitz (Paris: Union Générale d'Éditions).

Sesonske, Alexander

1982 "Jean Renoir in Georgia: *Swamp Water*," *Georgia Review:* 24–66.

n.d. a *"This Land Is Mine":* 73–106 (unpublished manuscript).

n.d. b "1944: *A Salute to France*": 107–125 (unpublished manuscript).

Tesson, Charles

1992a "La Production de *Toni:* La Règle et l'esprit," *Cinémathèque* 1: 45–58.

1992b "La Production de *Toni:* La Règle et l'esprit (2)," *Cinémathèque* 2: 84–97.

1993 "La Production de *Toni:* La Règle et l'esprit (3)," *Cinémathèque* 3: 36–46.

Truffaut, François

1955 *"French Cancan," Arts,* May 4.

Vinneuil, François [Lucien Rebatet]

1939 *L'Action française,* July 7, in Gauteur 1974: 61.

ERNST VAN ALPHEN

A MASTER OF AMAZEMENT:

ARMANDO'S SELF-CHOSEN EXILE

The words exodus and exile indicate a positive relation with exteriority, whose exigency invites us not to be content with what is proper to us (that is, with our power to assimilate everything, to identify everything, to bring everything back to our I).

MAURICE BLANCHOT, "Being Jewish"

IN HIS BOOK *Krijgsgewoel* (Warbustle) (1986), the Dutch artist, poet, novelist, and filmmaker Armando comments on his writing and art practice:

Langzamerhand ben ik gaan begrijpen dat je niet moet schrijven of schilderen wat je weet. Je zou datgene moeten schrijven of schilderen wat zich tussen het weten en begrijpen verbergt. Een kleine aanduiding, een wenk, is mogelijk, een vermoeden, meer niet, en dat is heel wat.

(Little by little I began to understand that one should not write or paint the things one knows. One should write or paint that which hides itself between knowing and understanding. A little mark, a wink is possible, a suspicion, no more, and that is already a lot.)   (1986: 161)[1]

This remark can be read as the motivation of the theme that haunts all of his work: Armando is obsessed with the past of the Second World War. While the past as such — every past — hides itself, the destruction of which this particular portion of the past consists is extremely hard to understand, especially in its most sinister practice which has become the center and symbol of that war: the Holocaust.

But Armando's preference for what hides itself between knowing and understanding is more than just an indication of his theme. It is at the

I wrote this essay in July 1994 during my stay at the Bellagio Study and Conference Centre. I am deeply grateful to the Rockefeller Foundation for the exceptional hospitality I enjoyed at the Centre.

1. All translations from Dutch are my own.

same time an epistemological attitude or mode. It implies a method of how one can get to know that which cannot, or can hardly, be known or understood. His self-reflexive remark formulates how he has to proceed in order to get in touch with what can never be identified, or pinned down.

Let me briefly characterize his procedure in making his art. Armando takes a willfully subjective stance that he draws from his past. He is permanently in the situation of a witness of aggressive power and destruction. This position has an autobiographical background. During the war he was a young boy. He grew up in the vicinity of the Amersfoort concentration camp, in the middle of Holland, not far from Utrecht. The immediate surroundings of this camp were his playground. Without being a direct victim of the war or the Holocaust, he was a witness of both. Without ever having seen the absoluteness of the destruction that went on there, somehow he felt it. He was confronted with its symptoms.

Starting from this autobiographical position of a young witness-without-understanding, Armando surrounds or encircles the historical events of this wartime destruction in such a way that practically all historical and geographical location remains unclear. He uses a violent strategy of "annexation and isolation" to represent a history without narrative plot, without a beginning, ending, or development, without a clear distribution of roles. Although the Second World War is a historical event, Armando's representation of it is paradoxically antinarrative. He represents history not as a sequence of events, but through the isolation and repetition of moments or situations. His work seems to fight against the meaningful continuity produced by plot. When he commemorates history, Armando meets narrative practice with suspicion. This is so because the mechanisms of narrativity constitute a coherence, one of development and continuity, that is radically alien to the "reality" of the experience of the present.[2]

Armando's work seeks to drive the absolute uniqueness of traumatic war experiences home to us. The very fact that the war, especially the Holocaust, is unique, so incomparable for those who were there, entails specific consequences for the manner in which it can be represented, including the nonnarrative nature of that representation. Its uniqueness

2. I have analyzed in detail how Armando develops a new language with a structure of its own, in order to protect the uniqueness of World War II against oblivion (van Alphen 1993).

implies that tropes based on similarity between two things, like comparison and metaphor, are by definition inadequate. For claiming similarity takes away that which makes the experience unique, automatically unspeakable, and overwhelms it with similarity to something else. The uniqueness of war, and especially of Holocaust experiences, must be indicated through other devices.

Armando develops a consistently *indexical* language. According to Pierce, the indexical sign is based on contiguity or continuity between the sign and that for which it stands. Armando "circles" the unique and unspeakable aspect of the war by speaking or visually representing what is juxtaposed to it, what touches it. He gives shape, not to the violence, death, destruction, but to what was there around them. Like a footprint, which is a silent witness of the presence of a human being, the signs which constitute Armando's work are indexical traces of the incomparable experiences of death and destruction. His work suggests or "touches" phenomena without ever formulating or describing them.

But his procedure for getting in touch with what cannot be known involves more. He had to exile himself from the place where he witnessed the past he wants to understand. In the 1970s he moved to Berlin, where he lives now "surrounded by the enemy," to use his own words. The question I want to address in this essay is: What does Armando's self-chosen exile have to do with his artistic practice? Or, to reverse the question, why is the situation of exile productive for this particular practice of art?

REPORTS FROM ABROAD

To answer this question I will focus on three of Armando's books, a selection of which will soon appear in English: *Uit Berlijn* (From Berlin) (1982), *Machthebbers* (People in power) (1983), and *Krijgsgewoel*.[3] These books meant a breakthrough in Armando's literary reputation. While he was already much respected as a visual artist, until the publication of these three books his literary reputation was quite controversial. His poetry and short stories were misunderstood. His obsession with the war and with violence was seen by the Dutch audience as an irresponsible and childish flirtation. It was alleged to be the pose of an adolescent

3. An English translation of a selection of these three books was published in 1995 by Reaktion Books of London.

fascinated by war, which could hardly be taken seriously. His book of interviews with former Dutch members of the SS, *The SS-ers: Dutch Volunteers in the Second World War* (1990 [1967]), caused an outcry of indignation. Armando and his cointerviewer, Hans Sleutelaar, were even accused of being in sympathy with the interviewed SS-ers. The three new books demonstrated the seriousness of his project beyond any doubt, and earned him a much wider audience.

These three books consist of short texts written in Berlin and originally published in the Dutch newspaper *NRC-Handelsblad*. All the texts can be read as reports by somebody who lives abroad. In more than half of them the speaking voice is Armando's: he tells about astonishing events that have happened to him in this German city where he is an alien, and he reports on seemingly insignificant situations that are somehow remarkable to him. In the two later books some of the texts tell about situations or events that happened to him during short trips to Italy, Austria, and California. There, too, he encountered situations that seem to him worthy to stop and dwell on.

These autobiographical texts alternate, however, with short fragments of speech of the inhabitants of Berlin. Each time, four or five of these fragments together form short chapters, always having the same title: "flarden," which means literally "rags" or "scraps." The word used is ambiguous in a significant way. In Dutch one speaks of the "scraps" of a conversation, indicating a fragment or part of a conversation one happens on or overhears. But the word also refers to the "wisps of a cloud," for instance, when a cloud has been dispersed or fragmented by the wind. In both meanings, the noun implies flimsiness, incompleteness, transience, and chance.

Armando seems to quote directly from conversations he may have had or overheard. He does not identify his source, or the situation of speech. He identifies the speakers only with the labels "man" or "woman." After the identification of the voices, their speech follows in direct discourse.

In all these fragments of speech, the war can be heard. It is exactly the great variety of the ways in which the war is referred to that makes these texts so strong and disturbing. In some of the fragments it is suggested that nothing has changed in Germany, that "the Germans" have learned nothing from the war they started and lost. Others make you realize that German civilians were also victims of the war. This awareness, however, never leads to a relativizing of Germany's responsibility for the war, as some revisionist historians would have it. On the contrary: if it is true that even the aggressor's own conationals were victimized, then the evil of this war becomes even worse. All the "scraps" leave the impression that the war is far from over.

The situation in which these "scraps" are uttered remains unclear. This lack of clarity, as it turns out, is a crucial element of Armando's discourse of exile. At first sight the composition of the books suggests the situation of a conversation. Chapters with a first-person narrator alternate with chapters that present "second-person" speech, in which the speaker addresses the former first person as "you" (*U*, the form of politeness). This has the appearance of an alternate account by each of the two parties. According to one possible narrative of the war, this organization of chapters alternating between the view of the war victim, an inhabitant of one of the occupied countries, and the view of the perpetrator, embodied by unidentified Germans, evokes an ideal of integrated memory.

This appearance is misleading, however. For one thing, the first-person reports are not addressed to the German speakers of the "scraps" but to the people back home in the Netherlands. In the second place, the speech situation of the "scraps," uttered "in the second person," deceptively suggests a dialogue between Armando the "reporter" and the speaking German who says "you." The addressee, however, is not identified and is not necessarily Armando. The title of the fragments, "scraps," indicates that these bits of speech are ready made, "found," overheard fragments that the subject, again, sends home like a postcard.[4]

THE IMPORTANCE OF BEING NOT-AT-HOME

The text entitled "Night" can be read as a *mise en abîme*[5] of the exiled position from which Armando speaks in the three books. In this text, he reflects on what his residence in Berlin means for his artistic calling:

Soms vraag ik me af wat doe ik hier. Waarom ga ik niet in een hol of grot wonen, met vriendelijke dieren, die proviand voor mij halen. Maar nee, ik ben hier, mid-

---

4. In his visual work of the seventies Armando often made use of postcards. He is, however, not so much interested in the visual images on the postcards as in the past world from which they stem. He uses postcards as leftovers, as indexes, of an irretrievable past. I have discussed these works in my essay "Touching Death" (van Alphen 1993).

5. For an explanation of the term, see Bal (1985).

den in de nacht. Want schoon is het kunstenaarsleven, maar de tol is hoog, laat dat je gezegd wezen, de tol is hoog.

Ik wandel alsof ik luister. Wat zich hier verstopt, verbergt, besef je dat? Natuurlijk, je zult geen enkel spoor ontdekken, maar het gaat om de <u>poging,</u> zullen we maar zeggen. Waar het om gaat is een vorm te vinden voor deze poging: vormgeving van de poging van de onmacht. Er is iets aan de hand.

(Sometimes I ask myself what I am doing here. Why do I not go to live in a cave or grotto, with friendly animals, who get provisions for me? But no, I am here, in the middle of the night. For the life of the artist is beautiful, but the toll is heavy; just hear this, you: the toll is heavy.

I stroll as if I listened. All that hides, conceals itself here, do you realize that? Of course, you will never discover a trace, but the only thing that matters is the *attempt,* let's put it that way. What matters is to find a form for this attempt: the forming of the attempt, forming of the impotence. Something is going on.) (1982: 164)

Armando makes it clear that there is nothing specific to be found or traced in Berlin. It is his mode of being in that alien city that matters. What is important is not the object that can potentially be found there, but the attempt at discovering something. It is his attitude of being which is transformed by the state of exile.

This transformation is due to the special need that occurs in this state: the artist in exile is forced to relate to phenomena outside her/himself. Armando's discourse remains on this side of knowledge and answers. He writes a little further on:

Maar wat kan ik in deze stad anders doen dan nadenken over andermans waaiende geheimen. Wie weet waait de dood wel mee. Je meester proberen te maken van vermommingen. Maar waarom, waarom toch. . . . Hij [de kunstenaar] vertoeft veel te vaak in z'n zelfgeschapen spelonken en hij licht zichself bij met een zwak kaarsje, dat het tegen de onbarmhartige tocht moet afleggen. Hij moet zo nu en dan waarlijk dolen en dat is geen pretje.

(What else can I do in this city but try to think about other people's blowing secrets? Who knows, perhaps death blows along with them. Trying to master disguises. But why, why then. . . . He [the artist] dwells much too often in his self-made caverns and he gives himself light with a faint candle, which is defeated by the merciless expedition. From time to time he must truly wander around and that is no fun.) (Ibid.: 165)

The phrase "blowing secrets" is related to the keyword "scraps." Secrets are not "facts" that can be found out; they just fly by like a light breeze. And yet, thinking about those flying fragments is all the artist can do in the foreign city. Death blows along if he is lucky. Secrets are hidden in disguises and although they have no substance, the disguises that are "in touch" with the secrets can perhaps be mastered. The passage is a lamentation, an elegy on the lack of substance as the telos of his quest. But that negativity is the absolute condition for his exile to become a source of creation.

It is crucial for Armando that the exiled condition does not lead to a new or second home. That which can be gained by being in exile gets lost when the new city or country becomes a place where one dwells and feels truly at home. The place to which Armando has exiled himself is not allowed to become a new cave in which he can hide. Caves, for all their poverty and darkness, still offer a dwelling place, in the dark of night, in a time "before." The temptation of the cave dweller is also lamented, in a tone that stays just on this side of the lyrical outburst of elegy.[6] "It is no fun" to maintain the necessity to wander. "Night" articulates negatively all the temptations, all the borders or corners of the exilic condition that put him in danger of dwelling.

This taboo against establishing himself anywhere, even outside of civilization, explains the writing subject's interest in former inhabitants of the houses in Berlin to which he is invited. In the text titled "Grosz-bürgerlich" in *People in Power,* he talks about this curiosity. Entering a private home in Berlin, he wants to ask the following questions of the person who lives there now: "Ik zou zo graag willen weten wie hier woonden en hoe ze woonden, how zag het eruit in 1912 of 1926 of 1934 of 1941, wat werd hier gezegd, hoe rook het hier, dat zou ik so graag willen weten. Maar ik neem aan, dat u dat niet weet. Ik merk het al, het inter-esseert u niet eens" (I would like to know who has lived here and how they have lived here, how did it look in 1912 or 1926 or 1934 or 1941, what was being said here, how did it smell here, I am so eager to know all this. But I suppose you don't know it. Oh I see, it doesn't even interest you) (1983: 15). The unknowable past of these houses makes it impossible for him to feel at home in any of them. But that is exactly what he wants. For

6. For a theory of elegy as an interdiscursive genre with a long tradition, see Ra-mazani (1994).

he needs to be alienated from himself. This is a precondition for getting in touch with the past he is looking for.

Armando is not even able to feel at home in the houses he himself has inhabited. When, full of admiration, he describes the kind of majestic bourgeois house of the Berlin upper middle class (the type of house one calls a *groszbürgerliche Wohnung*) he confesses the following:

Ik heb al in menig Berlijns huis gewoond, ook in deze huizenpracht, maar ik heb snel moeten toegeven, dat het nooit je eigen kamers worden, al zou je zo'n huis kunnen kopen: je zit in *hun* kamer. Maar de loense gloed van hun interieurs zie ik niet, hun stemmen hoor ik niet, ze dringen nauwelijks tot me door, hoe ik me ook inspan. Een onhoudbare toestand.

(I had already lived in several Berlin houses, also in this kind of beauty, but I soon had to admit that they would never become my own rooms, not even if I were able to buy such a house: I am sitting in *their* room, but I don't see the cross-eyed shine of their interiors, I don't hear their voices, they don't reach me, whatever I try. An untenable situation.)   (Ibid.: 15–16; emphasis in original)

Armando does not regret that he did not feel at home in the houses where he lived. On the contrary, his only regret is that it did not help. He has problems with the fact that while he was living in *"their"* rooms and did not feel at home, he still was not able to trace "them" there. He is confronted with his inability to get in touch with the past he tries to understand.

But as he travels and wanders, it becomes more and more difficult for Armando to exile himself to places where he can feel alien. One of the effects of modernity is that the differences between places are erased. In the text entitled "Heinrich," he recounts a trip he made to the German city Kiel. The rebuilding of this city after the war has made it interchangeable with any other twentieth-century city. Contemporary Kiel evokes the following meditation in Armando:

Bekijk je oude ansichtkaarten van even voor de oorlog, dan zie je duidelijk *buitenland,* namelijk een echte Duitse stad met schonkige huizen. Als je voor de oorlog als huurling in vreemde landen kwam, wist je niet wat je overkwam, alles was inderdaad *vreemd,* alles vol geheimen, en dat gaf, mij althans, een groot gevoel van tevredenheid. . . . Nu ziet iedereen er bijna gelijk uit. Niet dat ze gelijk *zijn,* maar het lijkt zo. Weinig nationale kenmerken nog. Of zou zou dat bevordelijk voor de vrede zijn.

(When you look at old postcards of just before the war, then you see *abroadness*, that is to say, you see a real German city with bony houses. Before the war, when you came as a hireling to foreign countries, you didn't know what was happening to you, everything was really *strange*, everything full of secrets, and that gave you, me at least, a great feeling of satisfaction. . . . Now, everybody looks almost similar. Not that they *are* similar, but it seems so. Only a few national characteristics are left. Or would that be conducive to peace?)   (1982: 160–61; emphasis in original)

The past is a foreign country, indeed, but the question is whether one can reverse that saying. Armando regrets that foreign places are becoming less and less strange, as if thereby a past gets lost. Do foreign countries have features similar to those of the past Armando wants to retrieve?

This passage strikes an almost nostalgic note. One is led to believe that his disappointment arises from an unfulfilled desire for the exotic. As in the overtones of elegy in the previous case, here he appeals to the recognition of a genre he toys with, only to reject it emphatically. The craving for estrangement alludes to a form of travel literature.[7] But this enables him to stake out the difference from that romantic genre. For Armando's project, travel writing is not adequate because he is not engaged in sampling "abroadness" in order to meet and "catalog" as many different places and peoples as possible. In contrast to travel writing, the confrontation with "strangeness" and difference is not satisfying as such; he does not want to be amazed and astonished as a goal in itself. Travel is not exile; at the end of the journey is homecoming, a homecoming Armando needs to cut off.

Another genre Armando is interdiscursively engaged in rejecting is ethnography.[8] Again, at first sight it might appear as though his interest in dissimilar places is ethnographically motivated. Like ethnographers, his motivations are epistemological, but both the knowledge pursued and the mode of producing it are different. The ethnographer wants to get to know and ultimately *understand* the otherness of different cultures. The feeling of amazement and astonishment is then only a symptom of the confrontational nature of the encounter with otherness. The

---

7. On travel literature, see Mary Louise Pratt (1992) and Gananath Obeyesekere (1992).

8. Good surveys of the problems inherent in ethnography can be found in Fabian 1983, Clifford 1988, and Sperber 1982.

next step of the epistemological procedure is to follow the right method-ology in order to reach understanding and document it.

As if to "discuss" this possibility openly, Armando's discourse does show some features that support a reading of his work as ethnographic. Often he uses expressions like "a doubtful observation," "an important observation" as if he were carrying out a scientific project. He distances himself from the observed otherness, so that he can reach "objective" understanding. The question is, is he really interested in the object or event that causes his astonishment, or does his astonishment serve another purpose? At second glance, in fact, he shows astonishment with-out any pretense of scientific or scholarly ambitions. The distance im-plied by his scientific discourse alternates, moreover, with moments in which he is engaged with what he sees. But this engagement is not an at-tempt to merge; instead, the objective is to experience the distance ever more sharply. In this sense he positions himself against ethnography. He does not want to know the object and set himself up for astonishment as a way toward that knowledge; on the contrary, he approaches objects that will produce the astonishment he needs to experience.

EXILE AS VOCATION

If Armando's interest in abroadness is neither a lamentation of home-lessness nor a fascination with the exotic, nor the epistemological drive of an ethnographer toward the understanding of otherness, the meaning of his interest in strangeness, abroadness, in the difference of otherness, must lie elsewhere. The text "Being Jewish" by Maurice Blanchot will help me to formulate Armando's position in relation to what astonishes him. In this essay Blanchot tries to formulate the difference of being Jew-ish. He wants to find an alternative to conceptions in which the Jew is no more than a product of the other's gaze. In order to rearticulate Jewish-ness he decides not to focus on Jewish thought or Jewish truth but on the Jewish experience. He proposes that Judaism is able to take on meaning for Jews in relation to the idea of exodus and exile.

The experience of being Jewish exists "through exile and through the initiative that is exodus, so that the experience of strangeness may af-firm itself close at hand as an irreducible relation" (1993 [1967]: 125). The "experience of strangeness" is the relevant concept for my purpose. Blanchot makes it clear that the idea of strangeness is the qualification and the consequence of a relation, not a feature of an object. Exile and exodus become a vocation as soon as one begins to see the relation of strangeness as an adequate relation in which to exist. Uprooting becomes a requirement, because it is the only way of positioning oneself "in relation to," instead of as part of, origin-bound identities. For Blanchot, the Jew is someone who relates to the origin, not by dwelling, but by distancing himself from it. Separation and uprooting are the acts in which the truth of origin can be found:

If being Jewish is being destined to dispersion — just as it is a call to a sojourn without place, just as it ruins every fixed relation of force with *one* individual, *one* group, or *one* state — it is because dispersion, faced with the exigency of the whole, also clears the way for a different exigency and finally forbids the temptation of Unity-Identity. (Ibid.: 125–26)

In Blanchot's writing, the experience of being Jewish becomes more and more emblematic of an epistemological mode. He is not only speaking about the self-identity of a group of people as an experience, but also about the identity of experience as the basis of truth. According to this epistemology, the truth is not to be pursued by trying to identify and *place* it, as traditional ethnographers do. Instead, one needs to engage a relation, a "conversation" with what one is not part of and what one cannot understand, but *not* with the purpose of understanding it.

In Blanchot's thinking, the notions "conversation" and "speech" are crucial. But the features he ascribes to speech in the context of conversation are again emblematic for the epistemological mode he favors. Normally, speech is seen as *mediating* something that precedes it. Speech has an origin, and this origin is the subject of speech. In contrast, Blanchot teaches us that the origin of speech is constituted while speaking. It is the event of speaking and the act by which one relates to "others" while one speaks that give speech its origin. Blanchot argues:

Speaking inaugurates an original relation in which the terms involved do not have to atone for this relation or disavow themselves in favour of a measure supposed to be common; they rather ask and are accorded reception precisely by reason of that which they do not have in common. To speak to someone is to accept not introducing him into the system of things or of beings to be known; it is to recognize him as unknown and to receive him as foreign without obliging him to break with his difference. Speech in this sense, is the promised land where exile fulfils itself in sojourn since it is not a matter of being at home there but of being always Outside, engaged in a movement wherein the Foreign offers itself, yet without disavowing itself.   (Ibid.: 128)

Blanchot posits the object of speech no longer inside speech, as its topic, but facing it, as its addressee and partner in conversation. One does not speak *about* what cannot be known or pinned down, one speaks with it. One tries to get "in touch."

In this way of thinking, exile becomes the precondition of a pursuit of knowledge that does not try to mediate, but to touch knowledge. This epistemology makes use of language not because of its referential capacities, but for language's ability to constitute subjectivity. This is in line with Benveniste's (1966) view that the essence of language is not in reference but in subjectivity, defined as relational and contrastive. The key to reaching knowledge in this language is the use of deixis: terms, like the personal pronouns *I* and *you,* whose content is cosubstantial with the situation of language use. Deixis requires presence; its semiotic mode is the index. Exile as a relation pursues difference, not substance, as knowledge. The exilic condition of the Jews makes "being Jewish" into the emblem of the subject who is able to perform this epistemology.

It is of course somewhat problematic for a non-Jew to idealize the "exilic condition" of the Jew. For Jews the exilic condition is much more than an epistemological mode of pursuing knowledge: it is a historical reality. I assume that many Jews who live the reality of exile have little patience with Blanchot's idealization. The French philosopher Jean-François Lyotard seems to be more self-conscious concerning the problems of idealizing the situation of Jews. In his essay "the jews" (1990 [1988]), Lyotard therefore provocatively associates the problem of what he calls "the unrepresentable and the unforgettable" with "the jews," a name that is always plural, in quotation marks, and in lower case. "The jews," he claims, refers neither to a nation, nor to a political, philosophical, or religious figure or subject. It is neither a concept nor a representation of any specific people as such.

Although Lyotard clearly avoids idealization, his is a *metaphorical* notion of Jewishness. "The jews" should therefore not be confused with real Jews. However, as David Caroll argues in his introduction to Lyotard's essay, the name "the jews" obviously cannot be separated completely from real Jews either, for it is real Jews who have always paid, through conversion, expulsion, assimilation, and finally extermination, for what Lyotard calls the repeated dismissal of the appeal or ethical demand associated with the name "the jews" (1990 [1988]: xii).

Indeed, metaphors are motivated, and must be held accountable for that motivation. In full awareness of that problematic, I would like to endorse Blanchot's idealizing reading of exile, yet not as the condition which ontologically characterizes "being Jewish," but as an epistemological attitude. This attitude is not unrelated to Jews because it has been imposed on many of them as an unintended side effect of the sociopolitical situation of exile which was intentionally inflicted on them. Yet this relation is obviously partial, and does not cover an ontological similarity.

Armando, who is not a Jew, is very "jewish" in the way he approaches things he does not know or understand. He exiled himself to Berlin in order to be in the epistemological situation of being Outside. He is not so much interested in understanding the former German enemy. He knows all too well that he is not able to understand this agent of destruction. It is also naive to think that the enemy can be found in Germany. Armando expresses his annoyance with people who think that he has exiled himself to Berlin in order to come across the enemy in his contacts with that city's inhabitants:

Een ongeduldige winkelier, een norse postbode, een halsstarrige ambtenaar, een kwaadaardige buurvrouw, is dat de vijand? Dacht van niet. Zo eenvoudig zit de vijand niet in elkaar. De vijand leeft toch meer in het verborgene. Dat heeft ie me tenminste beloofd, de vijand. Hij verstopt zich liever, af en toe mag je een glimps van 'm zien, en dan weet je niet eens zeker of ie het wel is. Ik mag 'm wel de vijand. Ineens is ie er, dat doet vertrouwd aan als ie er is. Wat zouden we zonder de vijand moeten beginnen. Niets.

(An impatient shopkeeper, a grumpy postman, a stubborn clerk, an evil woman next door, is that the enemy? I don't think so. The enemy is not that simple. The enemy lives more in secrecy. That is what he has promised me. He prefers to hide himself, only once in a while can you catch a glimpse of him, and even then you are not sure if it was really him. I like him, the enemy. Suddenly he is there. It seems very familiar to me, when he is there. What would we do without the enemy. Nothing.)   (1983: 50)

Instead of trying to get to know the enemy, then, Armando wants to live the condition of the speaking subject-unable-to-know. But what exactly does that condition imply? Although he is not after the enemy, it is important for his artistic project to have a glimpse of him now and then. Not in order to get a better understanding of him, but in order to have an experience of astonishment and amazement.

Writing about his situation as an artist in exile, he casually formulates the core of his creativity:

Maar je moet ook weten, als je niet geheel onnozel bent, dat je hier in een ander land bent, waar niemand op je zit te wachten. En je moet ook weten, dat je een *produkt* maakt, zwartgallige hangsels, waar eveneens niemand op zit te wachten. Integendeel. Het heeft weinig zin om je daarover te beklagen en toch zijn er die dat doen, ik verbaas me daar iedere keer weer over, want slechts in het vebazen ben ik een meester.

(You must also realize, unless you are totally green, that you are here in a foreign country, in which nobody is waiting for you. And you must also realize that you are making a *product,* those bilious hanging things, which again nobody is waiting for. On the contrary. It makes no sense to complain about that, and yet there are many who do that. Again and again I am amazed about that, because I am only a master in amazement.)   (Ibid.: 51; Emphasis in original)

Armando is a master in amazement. His literary as well as his visual works are representations of amazement. And his exiled condition is a precondition for the possibility of being astonished.

It is important to note, however, that the origin from which he has exiled himself is not "Dutchness." On the contrary, he cannot stand Holland. He never went into exile from the Netherlands. He sees it as a privilege not to live there. He feels totally alienated from Dutch culture. It is a culture in which you are constantly "waylaid by unwieldy noise." He has expressed his abhorrence of the Dutch national identity tersely. According to Armando, the Dutch rule of life is the following: "I am loud, therefore I am" (1982: 110). Leaving the Netherlands was no exile for him, but an escape.

Instead, he has exiled himself from the *primal scene*[9] observed in

9. When I use the term *primal scene,* I don't use it in the strict psychoanalytic sense, indicating a scene of sexual intercourse between the parents which the child observes, or infers on the basis of certain indications, or fantasies (Laplanche and Pontalis 1980 [1973]: 335). I call the concentration camp scenes witnessed by Armando *primal* because they function as the basis for all his later observations and experiences.

his boyhood playground during the Second World War: the immediate vicinity of the Amersfoort concentration camp. In this primal scene, elements of aggression and destruction are entangled with elements of boyish adventures. This primal scene is the scene he is not able to grasp, to know or understand. He had to exile himself from the spot where the primal scene took place: his primal watching. This exile was necessary in order to be able to approach the scene. Exile is the unavoidable detour back "home" to the past.

In the text entitled "Hassle," in *Warbustle*, Armando describes moments in which the primal scene of Amersfoort is traced while he is living in Berlin:

Het gebeurt wel eens dat ik midden in deze hardhandige stad plotseling de hei ruik. Dat is natuurlijk maar verbeelding, toch ruik ik duidelijk de hei. Dan komen de herinneringen: knarsende grintpaden en vrolijke familieleden. De hijgende vijand ook, die daar ronddoolde om te oefenen, hij moest, hij kon niet anders. De kruiddamp. De dorst. De verborgen wapens, de resten van uniformen en de speurtocht naar soldatenlaarzen. Buit. Roof. De dreiging. En de geuren van de namiddag, het versterven. De vermoeide zon. De galm.

(It happens sometimes that in the middle of this rough city I suddenly smell the moor. Of course it is only imagination, yet I really smell the moor. Then memories come: crunching gravel paths and merry family members. Also the gasping enemy, who roved thereabout, exercising, he had to, he couldn't do anything else. The gunpowder smoke. The thirst. The hidden weapons, the remains of uniforms and the search for military boots. Loot. Plunder. The threat. And the smells of the late afternoon, the dying out. The weary sun. The boom.)   (1986: 91)

This retrieval of the past through literal displacement is articulated through the evocation of a kind of discourse that belongs to Armando's own past in its "pastness." For in this passage Armando mixes elements of the discourse of boys' adventure books with the reality of the war he witnessed, in expressions like "the gasping enemy, who roved thereabout, exercising." This is yet another discursive allusion to a genre he subsequently rejects.

Of course, one could argue that this allusion to boys' adventure books is autobiographically motivated. The frame which enabled him to bestow meaning on the events of the war was offered by his boyhood reading. It turns his witnessing of the concentration camp into an exciting adventure. But this hybrid discourse produces an indispensable yet provisional effect. It seduces the reader with the promise of romanticized adventures. The camp and the war are becoming the objects of an improper fascination. But since the plot and the closure of the adventure story are missing, the reader is stuck with a glimpse of adventure that is just enough to pull her in. One is lured into the realm of destruction without getting the means of escaping. Hence, this adventure, like the one-way trip, leads you away with a false promise but fails to bring you back "home."

Once pulled out, one gets stuck, exiled like the writing subject. Hence, the reader is forced to go along with the writer into this pointless exile. Armando has to displace himself in space in order to reach a destination not in space but in time. He must get in touch with the past he needs to safeguard from oblivion. Thanks to this mechanism, he is able to trace his primal scene in the middle of Berlin. His search for the past is not carried out by trying to retrieve the past or by capturing it in involuntary memories, in the manner of Proust, but through "respatialization." He has to displace, to exile, himself in order to keep in touch with his primal scene.

It is therefore not necessary to displace oneself to Germany. Other places would do. Armando recounts a trip to England which had the same effect. Visiting Norfolk on the east coast of England, the point of departure for British warplanes on their flights to bomb Berlin, he sees in his differential experience of space his boyhood surroundings as they were but are now irretrievably lost: "Engeland is een land waar je van alles te binnen schiet. Oja, dat was bij ons ook, waarom is dat in Nederland op geniepige, zo niet gluiperige wijze verdwenen" (England is a country where all kinds of things occur to you. O yes, we had that also, why has that disappeared in the Netherlands in such a sneaky, if not skulking way) (1982: 173). Again, the wording recalls adventure: sneaky, skulking; danger and guilt are part of simple, banal details. He tries to get in touch with his primal scene of the past by using expressions which displace the attention from what has happened to *how* it has disappeared. In this displacement of attention the war returns, because the expressions he uses for describing changes in time are not arbitrary. They depict the enemy. The expressions suggest that the enemy was not only responsible for what happened in the past, but also for the fact that this past is going to disappear into oblivion. The enemy manifests itself in the passing of time. It is elusiveness that the past and the enemy have in common, and that turns the past into the enemy. That's why the passing of time can be described as sneaky and skulking.

Armando's displacement in space has yet other possibilities for re-
trieving the past. Although Germany is not the only place that enables
him to get in touch with the events that took place at his playground,
the place of exile is not arbitrary. It must have certain features. In the
text entitled "Prey," he tells of his admiration for Peggy Guggenheim.
Already in 1948 she knew where she wanted to live: in Venice. Armando
is not able to choose among cities like Berlin, Paris, Munich, Rome, New
York, or even an island like Tahiti. Although he is not able to settle down
somewhere permanently, he knows very well what kind of qualities the
cities have among which he cannot choose.

Mijn voorkeur gaat uit naar een omgeving met bouwwerken die op hoge benen
staan, ik hou van de brede trappen, de hoge wanden, de fiere zuilen, de trotse
zalen, de bordessen, zelfs van de metopen en architraven en meer van die onder-
delen. Ik ben minder geschikt voor het veilige kleine en genoeglijke, ik ben niet
zo erg voor het kleingoed. Liever het monumentale, liever de paleizen en de on-
deraardse gewelven.

(I have a preference for environments with buildings which stand on high legs,
I love wide stairs, high walls, high-spirited columns, proud halls, steps, even the
metopes and architraves and more of those elements. I am less suited for safe
smallness and pleasantness, I am not very much in favor of tiny things (runts).
Rather the monumental, rather the palaces and the underground arches.) (1986:
201)

The features he ascribes to the kinds of buildings he likes are features
that belonged to the enemy: high legs, proud, high-spirited, broad.
These features lead to fascination and astonishment. In these buildings
he is confronted with the strangeness of difference, which reminds him
of his astonishment before the enemy. Armando wants to live in and between buildings that evoke the same feelings of astonishment that were
evoked in him while witnessing the war. He prefers buildings endowed
with the qualities of the enemy. The spaces to which he exiles himself
are metaphors for the enemy and for the destructive past this enemy
set in motion. The intimidation and astonishment he feels in front of
monumental buildings reenact the astonishment he once experienced as
a witness of events caused by the enemy. He reenacts situations in which
he feels astonished, but not as a second effort to understand the cause of
astonishment.

Armando's exile to enemy-like places is a directed return of the past in the form of a spatial encounter with it. Not having been able to understand his primal scene at the moment he witnessed it, he looks for places or spots in which this failure of understanding is reenacted. However, Armando knows too well that the past he has witnessed can never be thoroughly understood. His epistemological attitude consists of besieging the past with the awareness that the past will never be surrendered or understood. Knowing the unknowable means, then, being in touch with it, having an ongoing conversation, not about it, but with it. Or to use Blanchot's way of putting it, Armando does not try to identify or place the past; instead, he enters into a relation with it.

The past's elusiveness makes it threatening and renders the urge to know the past more acute. Exile is Armando's weapon against the past as enemy and the enemy of the past. He displaces himself in space in order to reach his destination in time. In exile he is not able to master his amazement, so that he has to pursue his vocation of being a master in amazement. Going into exile is his artifice, which produces experiences of astonishment. In exile he is exposed to abroadness in all its forms. In the form of the "scraps" of speech, in which the past he has witnessed elsewhere is evoked in surprising ways; in the form of houses where the enemy has lived without leaving any traces, but without supplying the possibility of feeling at home; in the form of monumental buildings and streets. In the moments of astonishment in exile Armando does not understand the past — on the contrary — but he keeps alive the effect the past has had on him. This reenactment of astonishment is a way of talking back to the past, an effort to keep in touch.

REFERENCES

Alphen, Ernst van
   1993 "Touching Death," in *Death and Representation,* edited by Sarah Webster Goodwin and Elisabeth Bronfen, 29–50 (Baltimore: Johns Hopkins University Press).
Armando
   1982 *Uit Berlijn* (Amsterdam: Bezige Bij).
   1983 *Machthebbers: Verslagen uit Berlijn en Toscane* (Amsterdam: Bezige Bij).
   1986 *Krijgsgewoel* (Amsterdam, Bezige Bij).
Armando and Hans Sleutelaar, eds.
   1990 [1967] *De SS-ers. Nederlandse vrijwilleigers in de tweede wereldoorlog* (Amsterdam: Bezige Bij).

Bal, Mieke

> 1985 *Narratology: Introduction to the Theory of Narrative,* translated by Christine van Boheemen (Toronto: University of Toronto Press).

Benveniste, Emile

> 1966 *Problèmes de linguistique générale* (Paris: Gallimard). Reprinted as *Problems in General Linguistics,* translated by Mary Elizabeth Meek (Coral Gables, FL: University of Miami Press, 1971).

> 1970 "L'Appareil formelle de l'énonciation," *Langage* 17: 12–18.

Blanchot, Maurice

> 1993 [1967] "Being Jewish," in *The Infinite Conversation,* translation and foreword by Susan Hanson, 123–30 (Minneapolis: University of Minnesota Press).

Clifford, James

> 1988 *The Predicament of Culture: Twentieth-Century Ethnography, Literature, and Art* (Cambridge, MA: Harvard University Press).

Fabian, Johannes

> 1983 *Time and the Other: How Anthropology Makes Its Object* (New York: Columbia University Press).

Laplanche, J. and Pontalis, J. B.

> 1980 [1973] *The Language of Psycho-Analysis,* translated by Donald Nicholson-Smith (London: Hogarth).

Lyotard, Jean-François

> 1990 [1988] *Heidegger and "the jews,"* translated by Andreas Michel and Mark S. Roberts, introduced by David Caroll (Minneapolis: University of Minnesota Press).

Obeyesekere, Gananath

> 1992 *The Apotheosis of Captain Cook: European Mythmaking in the Pacific* (Princeton: Princeton University Press).

Pratt, Mary Louise

> 1992 *Imperial Eyes: Travel Writing and Transculturation* (London: Routledge).

Ramazani, Jahan

> 1994 *The Poetry of Mourning: The Modern Elegy from Hardy To Heaney* (Chicago: University of Chicago Press).

Sperber, Dan

> 1982 "Ethnographie interprétative et anthropologie théorique," in *Le Savoir des anthropologues* 13–48 (Paris: Hermann).

OUTSIDERS

SVETLANA BOYM

ESTRANGEMENT AS A LIFESTYLE:

SHKLOVSKY AND BRODSKY

THE WORD *nostalgia* comes from two Greek roots—*nostos* (home) and
algia (longing)—yet this composite word did not originate in ancient
Greece. It is only pseudo-Greek, or nostalgically Greek. The nostalgic
disorder was first diagnosed by seventeenth-century Swiss doctors and
detected in mercenary soldiers (Lowenthal 1985: 11).[1] This contagious
modern disease of homesickness—*la maladie du pays*—was treated in a
seventeenth-century scientific manner with leeches, hypnotic emulsions,
opium, and a trip to the Alps. Nostalgia was not regarded as destiny,
nor as part of the human condition, but only as a passing malaise. In
the nineteenth century, the geographic longing was superseded by the
historical one; maladie du pays turned into *mal du siècle*, but the two
ailments shared many symptoms.

I will not suggest a therapy for nostalgia, but only its provisional
classification. Affectionately parodying Roman Jakobson's theory of the
two types of aphasia, one could speak of two types of nostalgia. The first
one stresses nostos, emphasizing the return to that mythical place somewhere on the island of Utopia, with classical porticos, where the "greater
patria" has to be rebuilt. This nostalgia is reconstructive and collective.
The second type puts the emphasis on algia, and does not pretend to rebuild the mythical place called home; it is "enamoured of distance, not
of the referent itself" (Stewart 1984: 145). This nostalgia is ironic, fragmentary, and singular. If utopian nostalgia sees exile, in all the literal
and metaphorical senses of the word, as a definite fall from grace that
should be corrected, ironic nostalgia accepts (if it does not enjoy) the
paradoxes of exile and displacement. Estrangement, both as an artistic device and as a way of life, is part and parcel of ironic nostalgia. Its
nostos could exist in the plural as geographical, political, and aesthetic
homes. This essay is a part of my investigation of twentieth-century ideas

---

1. I am grateful to Paul Holdengraber for sharing with me the origins of *nostalgia*.
On *la maladie du pays* and *mal du siècle* see also Levin 1966: 62–81 and Jankélévich
1974.

about home — from metaphorical, transcendental homelessness to literal loss of home and the relationship between home and nationhood, home and culture, homesickness and the sickness of being home.

Benedict Anderson in *Imagined Communities* (1991 [1983]) suggests a connection between the history of the nation and individual biography: both are seen as narratives of identity and personhood that sprang from oblivion, estrangement, and loss of the memory of home. In a lyrical passage, Anderson draws on a developmental metaphor of the adolescent who wishes to forget childhood and the adult who desires to reinvent it by looking at an old photo of a child who supposedly resembles him or her.[2] Anderson proposes thinking about nationalism anthropologically (in the order of kinship, religion, or culture), rather than ideologically (in the order of liberalism and fascism). (One could also examine liberalism and fascism anthropologically to see what kinds of imagined communities they promote.) What is important for the national imagination is not history, but biography, not scientific facts, but collective myths. However, Anderson treats "biography" merely as a popular nineteenth-century genre, a confessional narrative that "begins with the circumstances of parents and grandparents." What he leaves out are the stories of internal and external exiles, misfits and mixed bloods who offer digressions and detours from the mythical biography of a nation. The story of their consciousness does not begin at home, but rather with their departure from home. In fact, many modernist autobiographies written in the twentieth century problematize the three roots of the word *auto-bio-graphy* — self, life, and writing — by resisting a coherent narrative of identity, for they refuse to allow the life of a single individual to be subsumed in the destiny of a collective. Instead of curing alienation — which is what the imagined community of the nation proposes — they use alienation itself as a personal antibiotic against the ancestral disease of home in order to reimagine it, offering us new ways of thinking about home, politics, and culture. Modernist texts have no place in Anderson's account of the national literary imagination.[3]

2. "How many thousand days passed between infancy and early adulthood vanish beyond direct recall! How strange it is to need another's help to learn that this naked baby in the yellowish photograph sprawled happily on the rug or cot is you!" (Anderson 1991 [1983]: 204).

3. What characterizes the imagined community of nations in Anderson's account is a desire for the nonarbitrariness of the sign, and a search for a sacred or pri-

My examples will be two stories of modern exiles and authors of un-conventional modernist autobiographies—Victor Shklovsky and Joseph Brodsky. Both addressed estrangement and nostalgia, and both, at differ-ent historical moments, left Soviet Russia. For Shklovsky this departure turns out to be a round-trip: from his Berlin exile back to the father-land, where he is forced to become a "spiritual exile," to denounce the formalist theories of estrangement, and then to practice them between the lines. Brodsky, on the other hand, is forced to leave Soviet Russia to become a naturalized American. Yet he never leaves his poetic home of an imagined Leningradian classicism and the boundaries of the time-less poetic empire. The two stories are not antipodes, but two different bifurcations of cultural fate, two reflections on the fate of Russian mod-ernism and its imagined communities. They reveal a twisted relation-ship between creativity and unfreedom, art and compromise, theoretical practice and physical survival. The autobiographical narratives of these two theorists and practitioners of estrangement share one reference—the Marxist-Leninist slogan that became an ideological commonplace and a cliché of Soviet everyday life: "Material being determines con-sciousness." This slogan revises Hegelian alienation and emphasizes the primacy of matter over spirit. The two exiled writers use this ideological commonplace to narrate their own stories of how material existence re-lates to consciousness.

Estrangement here will be seen as both an artistic device and a way of life. I will not only address the poetics of exile, but also the notions of exilic self-fashioning and arts of survival. Exile cannot be treated as a mere metaphor—otherwise one could fall into the somewhat facile argu-ment that every intellectual is always already a "spiritual exile." Rather, it is the other way around: actual experience of exile offers an ultimate test to the writer's metaphors and theories of estrangement. The myth of the prodigal son returning to his fatherland, forgiven but never for-gotten, is rewritten throughout these texts, without its happy traditional denouement.

Yet the modern disease of nostalgia, even when its symptoms are hid-den, has many side effects. The home that one leaves and "a home away

vate language proper to that community. But isn't this desire for nonarbitrariness of the sign exactly what Roman Jakobson defined as poetry? What is, then, the re-lationship between the nonconsanguineous poetic community and the community imagined by cultural nationalism?

from home," which one creates, sometimes have more in common than one would like to admit. A portable home away from home, which an émigré ferociously guards, preserves an imprint of his or her cultural motherland. The exiles might be bilingual, but rarely can they get rid of an accent. A few misplaced prepositions, a few missing articles, definite or indefinite, betray the syntax of the mother tongue. While in the traditional biography of the imagined community of a nation exiles are the ones who "lost their souls," in the postmodern story exiles embody the dream of "mad polyphony, for which every language is a foreign one" (Scarpetta 1981; Todorov 1992: 16–26). In contrast to those alternatives, which offer either a claustrophobia of strictly guarded borders or a metaphorical euphoria of their total dissolution, my modern parables tell of painstaking journeys that celebrate the limited practices of estrangement and also reveal the many defense mechanisms against polyphonic madness, not allowing us to turn foreignness into another euphoric poetic and theoretical trope.

External exile from Soviet Russia has additional complications, aside from the obvious political dangers. In the tradition of Russian philosophy from Chaadaev to Berdiaev, transcendental homelessness is seen not as a feature of modernist consciousness, but as a part of Russian national identity. Metaphorical exile (usually away from the transient, everyday existence) is a prerequisite for the wanderings of the "Russian soul"; as a result, actual exile from Mother Russia is viewed as unprecedented cultural betrayal. For a writer, it is more than just a betrayal; it is a heresy. After the nineteenth century, literature became a form of Russian civic religion. Yet the cosmopolitan ideal of a "republic of letters" is foreign to Russian culture. Rather, there is a Russian empire of letters, and the writer is a subject of that empire. Hence exile is a cultural transgression that threatens a writer's very survival, both physical and spiritual.

VICTOR SHKLOVSKY AND THE POETICS OF UNFREEDOM

Victor Shklovsky, best known in the West as one of the founding fathers of Russian formalism and the theorist of estrangement (*ostranenie*), was briefly a member of the Socialist Revolutionary Party and in 1918 voted for the restoration of the short-lived Russian Constitutional Assembly. In 1922, during the show trial of Socialist Revolutionaries, Shklovsky was denounced by an informer and had to flee the country to avoid imprisonment (Sheldon 1977: vii). Having narrowly escaped arrest, the writer found himself in Berlin, where he began to compose a series of unconventional autobiographical texts — *The Sentimental Journey*, an account of Shklovsky's trials and tribulations during the Civil War, and *Zoo; or, Letters Not about Love*, an ironic epistolary romance based on the author's correspondence with Elsa Triolet. The theorist's epistolary love is unrequited; the only letter to which he receives a positive response is the last. This last letter, however, is no longer addressed to a woman but to the Central Committee of the Communist Party. Here Shklovsky begs to be allowed to return to Russia: "I cannot live in Berlin. I am bound by my entire way of life, by all my habits [vsem bytom i navykami] to the Russia of today. . . . My nostalgia [*toska*] in Berlin is as bitter as carbide dust" (1990: 346).[4] Is there a connection between this old-fashioned nostalgia and the theory of estrangement, or do they contradict each other?

The theory of estrangement is often seen as an artistic declaration of independence, the declaration of art's autonomy from the everyday. Yet in Shklovsky's "Art as a Device" (1917), estrangement appears more as a device of mediation between art and life.[5] By making things strange, the artist does not simply displace them from an everyday context into an artistic framework; he also helps to "return sensation" to life itself, to reinvent the world, to experience it anew. Estrangement is what makes art artistic, but by the same token, it makes everyday life lively, or worth living. It appears that Shklovsky's "Art as a Device" harbors the romantic and avant-garde dream of a reverse mimesis: everyday life can be redeemed if it imitates art, not the other way around. So the device of estrangement could both *define* and *defy* the autonomy of art.

Tracing the genealogy of estrangement, Shklovsky also questions the autonomy and unity of the "national language." Ostranenie means more than distancing and making strange; it is also dislocation, *depaysement*. *Stran* is the root of the Russian word for country — *strana*. Shklovsky claims that according to Aristotle, "poetic language" has to have the character of a foreign language (*chuzhezemnyi*): "For the Assyrians it was Sumerian, Latin for medieval poetry, Arabism in literary Persian, old Bulgarian as a foundation of the Russian literary language" (Shklov-

4. I use Richard Sheldon's translations with slight modifications. For an interesting account of irony and eroticism in Shklovsky see Steiner 1985: 27–44.

5. See Striedter 1989, Erlich 1981, and Steiner 1984. On the connection between the theory of estrangement and romantic aesthetics see Todorov 1985: 130–48.

sky 1929: 21; my translation). He goes on to say that Pushkin and Tolstoy used Russian almost as a foreign language for the French-speaking Russian nobility. Hence, the early theory of estrangement already questioned the idea of language as organic and, in the Russian context, the strict opposition of Russia and the West.

Now that formalism and structuralism are often perceived as safely old-fashioned, we could defamiliarize some of the critical clichés about language, the autonomy of art, and art as a device. In fact, early modernist theories of language developed in response to the reemergence of neoromantic nationalism. In the least-quoted chapter of Saussure's *Course in General Linguistics*, he writes that the sign is not organically motivated, that there is no connection between language and blood (1966: 222–23). The Saussurian sign is motivated only by cultural convention. Conceived on the eve of World War I, this kind of structural linguistics or poetics of estrangement presented an alternative to official patriotism and suggested different ways to create imagined communities.

Shklovsky does not follow Anderson's proposed model of autobiography, yet nostalgia for an imagined community and reflection on estrangement and exile are his central preoccupations. *Letters Not about Love* are, of course, letters about love and an example of a modernist exilic lover's discourse in the paradoxical style of literary montage. Alya, the "new Eloise" of the formalist lover, prohibits him from speaking about love and begs him to discuss his literary theory instead. Shklovsky presents himself as a biographer and theorist against his will. The letters promise not to speak about love, yet they break many promises. They both fictionalize and resist fictionalization. The text could be compared to some theoretico-autobiographical writings of Walter Benjamin, like *One-Way Street* and *Moscow Diary*, dedicated to or addressed to the Latvian actress and writer Asja Lacis who eludes and escapes him.[6] In Shklovsky's account, his unrequited love for Alya mirrors his relations

6. The difference being, of course, that "Alya" writes back and Shklovsky publishes her letters verbatim. Ironically, Maxim Gorky, while praising Shklovsky's fictionalized epistolary autobiography, particularly appreciated Alya's letters. Hence, she inspired him to speak about literature, instead of love, and he, in turn, directly or indirectly, inspired her to become a novelist. Shklovsky's aesthetic (and pathetic) framing of her letters took them out of the everyday context and rendered them literary, encouraging their author, Elsa Triolet, to become a writer of fiction.

with Berlin. He never ceases to dramatize the irredeemable cultural difference between them, presenting Alya as "a woman of European, rather than Russian culture." In fact, they both come from a very similar background of Western-oriented urban intelligentsia.[7]

It turns out that the theory of estrangement and actual exile do not necessarily go together. Berlin, where Shklovsky found himself in 1922, might seem to be an ideal place for the modernist critic. (Shklovsky was one-quarter German but did not speak the language.) It was the center of the German avant-garde, frequented by many Russian and European artists, where the paths of Bely, Berdiaev, Nabokov, Kandinsky, and others might have crossed. Yet Shklovsky perceives the safe haven of West European everyday existence (which, for an impoverished émigré, was hardly very comfortable) as a major threat to his survival as an intellectual and as a Russian theorist and practitioner of estrangement. In one of his letters to Alya, he describes the "literary environment" of the exiled formalists. The protagonists are Roman Jakobson and Peter Bogatyrev, the latter the author of a pioneering formalist analysis of costume and marionette theater.

Europe breaks us, we are hot-tempered here, we take everything seriously. . . . Roman took Peter to the restaurant; Peter sat surrounded by the windows that were not scratched, in the midst of all kinds of food, wine and women. He began to cry. He couldn't take it any more. Everyday life [*byt*] here defrosts us. We don't need it. . . . But then again, for the creation of parallellisms, anything goes. (Shklovsky 1990 [1923]: 297)

European everyday life could be fine for an artistic device, but not for living. Shklovsky proudly proclaims that he will not exchange his craft (that of a literary theorist) for the European suit, as if the two were incompatible and one could not practice formalist theory and wear a decent suit.

While Shklovsky's letters are about allegories of the homelessness of a Russian intellectual, Alya's are often about domesticity and intimate

---

7. Later their fates radically diverged, revealing many more political and literary ironies. Unlike Shklovsky, Elsa did not return to Russia. She emigrated to France and married Louis Aragon, who was then still a surrealist. When Shklovsky was forced to denounce formalism in the Soviet Union and many fellow supporters of leftist art were executed or forced into silence, she would become a great supporter of the Stalinist Soviet Union in France.

relationships with her surroundings, which are not defined in national terms at all. In fact, the opening line of her first letter is the exact opposite of Shklovsky's Berlin nostalgia: "I settled comfortably [*uzhilas'*] in my new apartment" (ibid.). But it is precisely her comfort that makes her epistolary lover uncomfortable: "I don't complain about you, Alya. But you are too much of a woman. . . . In the store a woman flirts with things. She loves everything. This psychology is European" (ibid.: 306). The modernist lover is jealous of her flirtation with foreign things. It appears that the woman-expatriate loves her foreign dress, while her male counterpart cannot fit into a European suit.

Shklovsky's Russian Berlin is compared to the realm of shadows, a Hades of sorts. Real life is elsewhere. In Shklovsky's Russian Berlin "there is no force of gravitation, no movement. Russian Berlin does not go anywhere; it does not have a destiny." He writes: "We are refugees. Not even refugees, but fugitives [*vybezhentsy*] and now we are 'house-sitters.' [*sidel'tsy*]" (ibid.: 318). Unwittingly, Shklovsky repeats here some of the clichés reiterated by several generations of Russian intellectuals and travelers in Western Europe from the eighteenth to the twentieth century—Westernizers and Slavophiles, philosophers of the Russian idea and, surprisingly, formalists. European culture is identified with "a petit bourgeois ideal of a little house and a cup of cabbage soup, a dress for the daughter and school for the son" (Herzen 1986 [1865]: 353–56). "Western mercantile civilization" is seen as a stable culture that celebrates the cult of things and domesticity, while Russia is the land of "transcendental homelessness," where *byt* (everyday existence) is opposed to *bytie* (spiritual, revolutionary, or poetic being). The utopian communal home of the future can be built only in the land of spiritual homelessness. Estrangement might well be a device in art and life, but it has to signify culturally. In *The Sentimental Journey* Shklovsky remarks that, after the revolution, Russian life nearly turned into art (1990 [1923]: 271).[8] Perhaps he realized that in Europe the dream of reverse mimesis would never come true because, for better or for worse, everyday life would remain everyday life, no more and no less. It would not yield to the Russian artistic device. Shklovsky's romantic and avant-garde conception of aesthetics relies on the high prestige of art, and its intimate link to the conception of national identity. In this intellectual tradition "Russia" is not merely a geographical or ethnic unity but an imagined community

8. Shklovsky here refers to his conversation with Boris Eikhenbaum.

of fellow intellectuals and artists for whom art is a civic religion, even if its rituals became modernist. In his imagined Europe, the Russian theorist feels himself as another lost émigré with imperfect table manners.

In the last letter of *Zoo*, addressed to the Central Committee of the Communist Party of the Soviet Union, Shklovsky declares that the addressee of his prior correspondence, Alya, was not a real person, but only "a realization of a metaphor." The "woman of European culture" is killed into fiction. But the vertiginous ironies and metamorphoses of the text leave us wondering whether the "Central Committee of the Communist Party" is also only a metaphor. But the writer had to restrain his literary games once he returned from exile to his estranged motherland.

In his postexilic text, *Third Factory* (1977 [1926]), Shklovsky proposes not to speak about estrangement, but rather to theorize about unfreedom. He tries to think of unfreedom not as the opposite of creative activity, but as its necessary precondition. He proposes to demonstrate that most great literature from Cervantes to Dostoevsky was created under the circumstances of unfreedom — understood in the broad sense of social, political, and economic restrictions. The Marxist dictum that was turned into a Soviet commonplace is creatively rewritten by Shklovsky: "Material being determines consciousness but conscience remains unsettled" (Shklovsky 1926: 15).[9] This unsettled consciousness is dramatized throughout the text.

Third Factory opens with an anecdote about Mark Twain, who wrote letters in duplicate: the first one was destined for his addressee and the second for the writer's private archive. In the second letter he recorded what he really thought. This is perhaps the earliest formulation of Soviet doublespeak. It will become a foundational fiction of the Soviet intelligentsia — the Aesopian language, the way of reading between the lines and understanding one another with half-words. Between the 1930s and the 1980s, this language would bind together the imagined community of Soviet intelligentsia.

The key formalist idea of "laying bare the device" has a paradoxical history in the Soviet context. After the revolution and civil war, defamiliarization turned into a fact of life, while the everyday manner of existence and the maintenance of bare essentials became exotic. More-

---

9. Two different Russian words are used *soznanie* in the first case and *sovest'* in the second. *Sovest'* is distinctly Russian moral consciousness, while *soznanie* is connected to knowledge and rationality.

over, the practice of aesthetic estrangement had become politically suspect. In her diary of 1927, Lidiia Ginzburg (literary critic and Shklovsky's student) observed: "The merry times of the laying bare the device have passed (leaving us a real writer—Shklovsky). Now is the time when one has to hide the device as far as one can" (1989: 59; my translation).

Shklovsky constructs his new autobiographical venture as a montage of anecdotes and aphorisms whose multiple ironies do not allow the reader to establish a single stable meaning. It could be read as an enactment of political, personal, and artistic compromise. In the text, amusing and impersonal storytelling alternates with private confessions intended for some imaginary "gentle reader," followed by shrill declarations to the "comrade government" that from now on is perceived as the writer's permanent addressee. One no longer needs to address letters to the "comrade government"; "the comrade government reads them anyway."

Third Factory discusses three kinds of home, not all of which would be subjects of nostalgia. Shklovsky's metaphor for home is not organic but rather productionist: home is one of the "factories." The first factory is childhood and school, the second is the formalist Circle OPOYAZ, and the third is, literally, the Third Factory of State Cinema Studios, where Shklovsky was officially employed, but it also stands for postrevolutionary Soviet life. The first factory—childhood and school—are hardly idealized. Shklovsky declares his mixed blood and eclectic middle-class background, with German, Russian, and Jewish grandparents, and undermines the familiar Russian trope of the happy childhood and the lost Eden, as it is represented in Aksakov, Tolstoi, and others. There is no family garden, no idyllic estate in the countryside; instead, Shklovsky's family purchased a *dacha*; a small vacation place that put them permanently in debt. In the first factory the child felt quite displaced; later he was thrown out of schools and universities; thus he could be placed on the same list with Lukács, Benjamin, Barthes, and other celebrated twentieth-century theorists who never completed their doctoral dissertations.

It is the "second factory," the formalist circle, that became Shklovsky's true home and most beloved imagined community that he missed in Berlin. He is particularly nostalgic for the early years of OPOYAZ, the home of continuous conversation, collaborative work, friendship, and the collective intellectual labor of theoretical estrangement. By the mid-1920s the formalists were under attack on all sides by Marxists and traditionalists, whom Shklovsky called the makers of "red restoration." Among other things, formalists and constructivists were accused of being "capitalists and spiritual émigrés." So the exile returns to his homeland only to be called a "spiritual émigré"—one of the worst insults in the Soviet Russian context. The third factory of the Soviet fatherland did not embrace its formalist prodigal son. To describe the current situation of the formalist "second factory," Shklovsky tells a story about the "Flax Factory" in the chapter "On the Freedom of Art."

> Flax. This is no advertisement, I'm not employed at the Flax Center these days. At the moment I am more interested in pitch. In tapping trees to death. That is how turpentine is obtained.
>
> From the tree's point of view, it is ritual murder.
>
> The same with flax.
>
> Flax, if it had a voice, would shriek as it's being processed. It is taken by head and jerked from the ground. By the root. It is sown thickly oppressed, so that it will be not vigorous but puny.
>
> Flax requires oppression. . . .
>
> I want freedom.
>
> But if I get it, I'll go look for unfreedom at the hands of a woman and a publisher. (Shklovsky 1977 [1926]: 45)

The flax factory offers an interesting allegory. The author tries to persuade himself that the difference between freedom and unfreedom is only a matter of point of view, yet one thing clearly emerges from this painful, ironic tour de force: his "conscience remains unsettled" and very aware of the "shrieks and jerks" in the process of social production and the adaptation to "oppression." At the end of Shklovsky's postexilic autobiography, the "third factory" turns from an object of study into the author's judge:

> Take me, third factory of life!
>
> But don't put me in the wrong guild.
>
> Whatever happens, though, I have some insurance: good health. So far, my heart has borne even the things I haven't described. It has not broken; it has not enlarged.   (Ibid.: 98)

What might strike us in this quotation is a gradual slippage of images. The "Third Factory," which initially referred to a specific Soviet institution, has become a metaphor: first, for early Stalinist Soviet life, and then for life as such. Is Shklovsky's theoretical autobiography an avant-garde twist on the old Russian romantic drama of art and life? Or is it a political allegory of the specific Soviet transformation of intellectual life? Shklovsky the ironist gives us two versions of the story: the first turns unfreedom (like estrangement before it) into a device and a precondition for art making, not exclusive to the Soviet context. The second turns estrangement from an artistic device into a technique for survival in the Soviet Russia of the late 1920s. *Third Factory* is not only about literary production; it is also about the "production" of the Soviet intellectual.

Shklovsky's two autobiographical texts end with a series of "ostensible surrenders." Yet in spite of continuous attacks on his work and the official demands of narrative and ideological coherence, the devices of Shklovsky's texts remain almost unchanged. In his textual practices Shklovsky never betrays the "second factory." He remains the great theorist-storyteller who, like Walter Benjamin, speaks in elaborate parables, full of self-contradiction, in a unique style of Russian formalist baroque. Shklovsky's two "surrenders" could also be read as affirmations of the invisible exilic retreat of an ironist and a theorist. This exilic retreat between the tortured lines could only be carved through the secret rituals of the nearly extinct "formalist guild."

Nadezhda Mandel'shtam commented on Shklovsky's work in the actual "Third Factory of the Goskino — State Cinema": "Among the writers declared outside the law — not openly but hiddenly, as they always did in our country, was Shklovsky. He hid in the Film Factory the way Jews in Hungary hid in the Catholic monasteries" (Mandel'shtam 1972: 271). The comparison with Jews hiding during World War II appears anachronistic yet strikingly appropriate. Jews figure prominently in Shklovsky's parables and anecdotes, especially in *The Sentimental Journey*. There is a story about the pogrom his grandmother experienced and a story of a young Jewish artist trying hard to adapt to the violence of Red Army life and to become Soviet rather than Jewish — only to be insulted constantly as a "Jew." In *Third Factory* there is a strange refrain, "Forget the Jews." In his chapter about his fellow ex-formalist Osip Brik, Shklovsky writes:

Every year on a certain day, the Jews stand at the table with staff in hand —
signifying their readiness to leave.
Forget the Jews.
Let us leave.   (Shklovsky 1977 [1926]: 34)

The ritual celebration of exile (possibly a reference to Passover) is evoked by Shklovsky in passing as an obsessive memory. He was not a

practicing Jew and the Jews would soon be forgotten, or rather eliminated, from Soviet literature. (The word *Jew*, in fact, would appear in
print only very rarely after the late 1940s.) But those "forgotten Jews"
would continue to haunt the writer who would no longer be able to leave
and perform his exilic ritual.

The theorist of unfreedom became a persona non grata for the thirty
years following the publication of *Third Factory*. He was forced publicly to denounce formalism, but was still accused of being a spiritual
émigré and later a rootless cosmopolitan — for his essay "South West" on
the literature of Odessa and its Western connections. He was lucky to
avoid arrest and the tragic fate of many of his contemporaries and fellow
formalists and constructivists. Rehabilitated and published again in the
1960s, Shklovsky inspired the next generation of intellectuals who appreciated his ironic *salto mortale*. While Shklovsky's formalist years were
forgotten together with the word, traces of his subversive cultural memory persisted. Did the formalist Orpheus ever remember the journey
into the Hades of Russian Berlin? Or was actual exile not really a way out
at that time? Perhaps he could have theorized the market of unfreedom
with Adorno, or become an American academic like Roman Jakobson.
But responsible theorists should not speculate about unrealized twists of
plot. They only try to see how fiction is made, not how life is made.

BRODSKY: POETICS OF LENINGRAD CLASSICISM

Brodsky's cultural fate might appear to be the opposite of Shklovsky's;
he was perceived as a kind of cultural martyr, arrested by the KGB, sent
to prison, and later forced into exile. And here his poetic fate makes
a radical swing: from a poet of the resistance he turns into a poet of
the establishment in the United States, a poet laureate and a Nobel
prizewinner.

From Shklovsky's letters not about love we move to Brodsky's autobiography that is not about life: "A writer's biography is in his twists of
language" (Brodsky 1986: 3). Moreover, in Brodsky's case, his autobiography was in the twist of a foreign language, since his autobiographical
essays were written in English. From the outset, Brodsky defies the idea
of the conventional "developmental" biography that served as a model
for Anderson. He seeks a different temporality and a logic that does not
conform to calendar chronology or conventional developmental narra-

tives. Brodsky reveals that his first significant memory is the discovery of the "art of estrangement":

I remember, for instance, that when I was about ten or eleven it occurred to me that Marx's dictum that "existence conditions consciousness" was true only for as long as it takes consciousness to acquire the art of estrangement; thereafter, consciousness is on its own and can both condition and ignore the existence. (1986: 3)

"Art of estrangement" became a dissident art; in the Soviet artistic context of the 1960s, estrangement represented a resistance to sovietization. The Marxist slogan shaped several generations of Soviet dissidents of alienation; yet the ghost of that Soviet "material existence" that Brodsky ritually exorcises from his poetics leaves its traces throughout his oeuvre. If, in Shklovsky, the homeland was a factory, in Brodsky it is an empire—a First, Second, or Third Rome and its "eternal" classical poetics.

This classical poetics, however, has a distinct local color. There are two key architectural metaphors in Brodsky—the "room and a half" and the "Greek portico." The former refers to Leningrad's interiors—its crowded communal apartments. The latter evokes Leningradian–Saint Petersburgian imperial façades. Brodsky writes in the essay dedicated to one of his favorite poets, Osip Mandel'shtam:

Civilization is the sum total of different cultures animated by a common spiritual numerator, and its main vehicle—speaking both literally and metaphorically—is translation. The wandering of a Greek portico into the latitude of tundra is a translation.   (Ibid.: 139) [10]

"Civilization" in Brodsky is not merely a canon but a way of translation and transmission of memory. The Greek portico is reinvented by the "all-Union homeless" poet, Osip Mandel'shtam, who once was a "little Jewish boy with a heart full of iambic pentameters." This Greek portico is not merely a classical foundation, but a wandering structure. It is linked to a particular "nostalgia for world culture"—to use Mandel'shtam's term—that characterized Petersburg–Leningrad dissident poetry throughout

10. Since Brodsky's autobiographical writings are largely about the autobiography of consciousness and the art of estrangement, they are closely linked to his essays on other poets—Mandel'shtam, Tsvetaeva, and Auden among them. For an examination of Brodsky's metaphor of exile as a poetic palimpsest see Bethea 1994 and Loseff and Polukhina 1990.

the Soviet period, offering the dream of an alternative cosmopolitan transhistorical community where the poet does not feel claustrophobic or confined. Nostalgia here is of a second type; Mandel'shtam never wished to reconstruct this "world culture, but only to evoke it" (ibid.: 143).

In Brodsky's view, Russian poetic language was a survivalist mnemonic device, the preservation of an alternative space of cultural memory. The only home a homeless postrevolutionary poet had was a poetic one, where classical metrics and stanzas were pillars of memory, *Omnea Mea mecum porto*. The poet carries his portable home made of Leningradian hexameter like a snail in its shell; it is this home that he guards like a patriotic vigilante. "The exile," writes Brodsky, "slows down one's stylistic evolution. . . . it makes a writer more conservative" (1988: 18). This explains Brodsky's defensive attitudes toward what he calls "language of the street"; poetic language for him is not decorum but a foundation of his portable homeland.[11]

At the turn of the century, the search for lost classicism was strikingly prominent among modern writers and philosophers, many of whom came from assimilated Jewish backgrounds in countries far removed from classical civilization itself. It is as if the only homesickness they experienced was metaphorical — for the home that they and their countrymen never really had. Young Georg Lukács repeats Novalis's notion whereby philosophy is "really a homesickness. . . . It is the urge to be at home everywhere," that is, a nostalgia for a certain Greek Eden that cannot be rebuilt (Lukács 1971: 29). The classical metaphors of the displaced modernist writers display various degrees of destruction. For Walter Benjamin, for instance, the important thing was not the golden age of antiquity when the sky was starry and the temples were still intact, but the historical ruin that preserves the layers of time. Brodsky's classical portico is of the Age of Empire. It is defensively classical; ruin, the embodiment of imperfection and incompletion, is not his metaphor.

---

11. Brodsky advances the somewhat paradoxical proposition that in Russia, "if only for purely ethnographic reasons," classical or traditional metric form should not be regarded merely as provincial atavism. In his view, "Russian poetry has set an example of moral purity and firmness which to no small degree has been reflected in the preservation of the so called classical form without any damage to content" (1988: 143). This is hardly an antimodernist divorce of form and content but rather an affirmation of a certain cultural specificity that affects our understanding of what "form" is.

Brodsky's nostalgia pertains not only to the forms of Russian poetic classicism but also to the ways of reading and inhabiting literature, those sacred cultural practices of literary resistance that were so dear to him in his youth. Like Shklovsky, Brodsky has his own imagined community of Leningrad friends that he warmly evokes in his essay. It is a kind of elegy to the postwar generation that made ethical choices "based not so much on immediate reality as on moral standards derived from fiction":

Nobody knew literature and history better than these people, nobody could write in Russian better than they, nobody despised our times more profoundly. For these characters civilization meant more than daily bread and a nightly hug. This wasn't, as it might seem, another lost generation. This was the only genera-tion of Russians that had found itself, for whom Giotto and Mandelshtam were more imperative than their own personal destinies. Poorly dressed but somehow still elegant . . . they still retained their love for the non-existent (or existing only in their balding heads) thing called "civilization." Hopelessly cut off from the rest of the world, they thought that at least that world was like themselves; now they know that it is like others, only better dressed. As I write this, I close my eyes and almost see them in their dilapidated kitchens, holding glasses in their hands, with ironic grimaces across their faces. "There, there..." They grin. Liberté, Egalité, Fraternité... Why does nobody add Culture?"   (1988: 30)

This is an eccentric community of 1960s Leningradian "spiritual exiles" who nostalgically worship fictional "civilization" in their cramped communal kitchens. Rebelling against the imposed collectivity of Soviet everyday life, they created a community of their own, carving extra dimensions in Brodsky's "room and a half." For them, the works of Giotto and Mandel'shtam were not merely works of art but sacred fetishes of the imagined community. Mandel'shtam emerged from the yellowish pages of handwritten samizdat poems that were published very selectively in the early 1970s and immediately became the hottest items on the black market. Since virtually none of those Leningradian inter-nal exiles was able to travel, Giotto became known from reproductions, particularly from the Polish or East German edition of the Classics of World Art. Those books had a special status, aura, and "Western" smell. Yet, the Classics of World Art were not merely regarded as foreign ob-jects; they were images of the other world framed by a Leningrad looking glass, inspiring mirages on the rippling surface of the Neva. In retrospect, the little world of the kitchen community might appear to be nostalgic or even endearingly heroic, but it is also rather claustrophobic. Having outgrown this imagined community, the poet is nonetheless frequently homesick.

In Brodsky's view, the poet is a private person par excellence, yet it appears that this uncompromising dream of aesthetic privacy has its foundations in that heroic dissident moment of the 1970s (Brodsky 1994: 466). Alexander Herzen (1986 [1865]) has insightfully remarked that for an exile historical time often stops at the moment of leaving the mother country; that moment forever remains the privileged point of departure. Although he was the same age as Dmitrii Prigov and other conceptualist poets, Brodsky appears to belong to a different poetic generation; he never places the poetic language within ironic question marks and does not offer us a theater of comic poetic impostors and graphomaniacs playing with cultural myths. Brodsky is not a postmodern poet; he is rather a nostalgic modernist. His mode of modernist classicism has its own Leningradian local color, despite its global aspirations. It is precisely this nostalgic provincialism (in the best sense of the word) that makes it poetic. That Leningradian intimacy in poetic intonation permeates Brodsky's Russian works. In the English versions of his poems this quality is lost; the poet occasionally translates himself into the solemn rhythms of British and American modernists.

Brodsky's poetic home rests on the nostalgic foundation of the Leningrad kitchen community and is adorned with Mandel'shtam's wandering "Greek portico in the latitude of tundra," a feature of exilic classicism. So where did the poet emigrate and how is the "other world" to which he came different from that "other world" that he imagined in the kichen communities of his youth?

In "Lullaby of Cape Cod" Brodsky writes:

Like a despotic Sheik, who can be untrue
to his vast seraglio and multiple desires
only with a harem altogether new,
varied and numerous, I have switched Empires.

(1980: 108)

Not only is the poet compared to a sheik, but both his old country and his adopted country are described as "Empires," always with a capital *E*. One is safer for the everyday survival of a poet, while the other used to be more hospitable to the survival of poetry. Analogy is one of Brodsky's favorite devices. In *Less Than One* he writes: "A school is a factory is a poem is a prison is academia is boredom, with flashes of panic" (1986:

17). The empire is empire is empire with flashes of poetic insight and outbursts of nostalgia.

Imperial consciousness is part of the cultural baggage that the poet carries with him. There is no way to be exiled from the empire; the empire is, in fact, conducive to poetry. The poet is not looking for a liberal republic of letters: like Shklovsky, Brodsky is fascinated by unfreedom. For him, unfreedom is a fact of life (a strange poetic revision of Soviet Marxism, Roman stoicism in Russian translation, and the proverbial Russian fatalism). The "eternal law" of the empire is internalized and naturalized. In Shklovsky's work Soviet life was equated with life itself; in Brodsky's, the laws of empire are equated with laws as such. Empire is not a choice, it is a fate. Although the biographies of our two writers are quite different, it seems to me that their art of estrangement is not sufficiently estranged from fundamental Russian cultural myths.

In Brodsky's world if one dreams of waking up outside the empire, one quickly discovers that one has only awakened inside another dream:

> If suddenly you walk on grass turned stone
> and think its marble handsomer than green,
> or see at play a nymph and a faun that seem
> happier in bronze than in any dream
> let your walking stick fall from your weary hand,
> you're in The Empire, my friend.
>
> (Brodsky 1994: 284)

The Empire in Brodsky is laid out like a Borgesian labyrinth; you might imagine yourself emerging on the other side of the extreme polarity, but the polarities easily exchange roles, the hero can turn into a traitor, the executioner into a victim. Brodsky naturalized the Russian and Soviet cultural duel and also the mutual dependency of the tyrant and the poet. This is a threat to the poet's survival but at the same time it ensures the quasi-religious prestige of culture. For Brodsky, changing countries is easier than altering one's poetic style and system of aesthetic beliefs.

Yet Brodsky's poetic "eternal return" to the classical labyrinths is also about a nonreturn to the poet's actual motherland. It is no wonder that, in his autobiographical text, which is more an autobiography of consciousness than of life, Brodsky records two formative *prises de conscience*, or awakenings of consciousness. The first one was a discovery of the art of estrangement, and the second was the embarrassment of national identity. If the first awakening of consciousness is seen as a revelation of artistic truth, the embarrassment of origin is the acknowledgment of the first lie:

The real history of consciousness starts with one's first lie. I happened to remember mine. It was in a school library when I had to fill out an application for membership. The fifth blank was, of course, "nationality." I was seven years old and knew very well that I was a Jew, but I told the attendant that I didn't know. With a dubious glee she suggested that I go home and ask my parents. . . . I was ashamed of the word "Jew" itself—in Russian *yevrei*—regardless of its connotations. (Brodsky 1986: 8)

Indeed, in the Soviet Union of the late 1940s and early 1950s, anti-Semitism was not only popular and government sponsored; it was also linguistic. The word *Jew* became virtually unprintable and enjoyed the status of a cultural obscenity. Brodsky's art of estrangement and his early embarrassment of origins are interconnected. The unpronounceable Russian word *yevrei*, shameful for a seven-year-old boy, is recovered (redeemed) in the English word *Jew*, printed in thousands of copies by the established American poet. For Brodsky, the switch to writing in English is not merely a poetic catastrophe signifying the loss of a mother tongue, but also a way of transferring and preserving cultural memory. Translation plays such an important role in his work. Poetry is a vehicle for memory, lines are rails of "public transportation," and metaphor (from the Greek *metaphorein*) is a transfer of meanings.

Nomadism and translation are key concepts in Brodsky's recent reflection on the fate of European Jews in the twentieth century. He ponders the lessons of survivors and the reasons why so many Jews stayed in Nazi Germany despite all signs of disaster. (In Stalin's Russia, unlike in Germany before 1939, leaving the country was not an option [see Brodsky [1993: 64].) The nomadic impulse, estrangement, and exilic ritual offer another chance of escaping the fate of a passive victim on the grand historical scene of the crime. " 'Scatter,' said the Almighty to his chosen people, and at least for a while they did"—these lines become the leitmotif of the essay (ibid.). The figure of the Jew in Brodsky is similar to that of Shklovsky. It is a wandering ghost on the margins of their texts; it haunted several generations of secular and assimilated Soviet Jews who sought neither traditional nor Zionist ways and for whom, after the 1930s, the Jewish tradition was simply unavailable. Brodsky's Jew is a nomad; in the best possible circumstances, he manages to remain faithful to the diasporic predicament. The diasporic Jew seeks not the promised land but only a temporary home. It seems that for Brodsky the art of nomadism is a commemoration of those for whom exile was unavailable (or inconceivable) — those who made the tragic mistake of putting down roots in Germany and preferred not to take a chance and leave. Hence the art of estrangement offers a survival kit. As for exile, it is not just a misfortune — it is also a cultural luxury.

It comes as no surprise that Brodsky's most personal text, "In a Room and a Half," dedicated to the memory of his parents, is written in English — a language his parents did not know. It was composed shortly after their deaths in 1985, when the Soviet government refused to grant the poet an entry visa to attend their funerals. Brodsky writes:

I write this in English because I want to grant them a margin of freedom; the margin of freedom whose width depends on the numbers of those who may be willing to read this. I want Maria Volpert and Alexander Brodsky to acquire reality under a foreign code of conscience, I want English verbs of motion to describe their movements. This won't resurrect them, but English grammar may at least prove to be a better escape route from the chimneys of the state crematorium than Russian. . . . May English then house my dead. In Russian I am prepared to read, write verses or letters. For Maria Volpert and Alexander Brodsky, though, English offers a better semblance of afterlife, maybe the only one there is, save my very self. And as far as the latter is concerned, writing this in this language is like doing those dishes; it's therapeutic.   (1986: 461)

Some things could only be written in a foreign language; they are not lost in translation, but conceived by it. Foreign verbs of motion could be the only ways of transporting the ashes of familial memory. After all, a foreign language is like art — an alternative reality, a potential world. Once it is discovered, one can no longer go back to monolinguistic existence. When exiles return "back home" they occasionally discover that there is nothing homey back there and that one feels more at home in the comfortable exilic retreat that one has learned to inhabit. The exilic state has become familiar, and it is the experience of returning to the country of birth that might become defamiliarizing. One shouldn't ask writers-in-exile whether they plan to go back. It is condescending and presumes that the biography of a nation carries more weight than the biography of a writer and his or her alternative imagined community. To return, as in the case of Shklovsky, could be experienced as a second exile, claustrophic rather than liberating, unless, of course, one's vocation is the poetics of unfreedom.

Nation, ethnicity, blood is not the only foundation for imagining home and community. Modernist writers are not entirely cured of homesickness, but their "home" is impure in material and eclectic in style—be it a style of formalist baroque or Leningradian classicism.

REFERENCES

Anderson, Benedict
    1991 [1983] *Imagined Communities: Reflections on the Origin and Spread of Nationalism* (London: Verso).
Bethea, David
    1994 *Joseph Brodsky and the Creation of Exile* (Princeton, NJ: Princeton University Press).
Brodsky, Joseph
    1980 *A Part of Speech* (New York: Farrar, Straus, and Giroux).
    1986 *Less Than One* (New York: Farrar, Straus, and Giroux).
    1988 "The Condition We Call Exile," *New York Review of Books.*
    1993 "Profile of Clio," *New Republic.*
    1994 *Izbrannye stikhotvoreniia; Nobel Prize Speech* (Moscow: Panorama).
Erlich, Victor
    1981 *Russian Formalism: History, Doctrine* (New Haven, CT: Yale University Press).
Ginzburg, Lidiia
    1989 *Chelovek za pis'mennym stolom* (Leningrad: Stovetskii pisatel').
Herzen, Alexander
    1986 [1865] *Sochineniia v dvukh tomakh* (Moscow: Mysl').
Jankélévitch, Vladimir
    1974 *L'Irreversible et la nostalgie* (Paris: Flammarion).
Levin, Harry
    1966 "Literature in Exile," in *Refractions: Essays in Comparative Literature*, 62–81 (London: Oxford University Press).
Loseff, Lev, and Valentina Polukhina, eds.
    1990 *Brodsky's Poetics and Aesthetics* (London: St. Martin's).
Lowenthal, David
    1985 *The Past Is a Foreign Country* (Cambridge: Cambridge University Press).
Lukács, Georg
    1971 *The Theory of the Novel*, translated by Anna Bostock (Cambridge: MIT Press).

Mandel'shtam, Nadezhda

    1972 *Kniga vtoraia* (Paris: YMKA).

de Saussure, Ferdinand

    1966 *Course in General Linguistics*, edited by Charles Bally and Albert Seche-
haye, translated by Wade Baskin (New York: McGraw-Hill).

Scarpetta, Guy

    1981 *Eloge du cosmopolitisme* (Paris: Grasset).

Sheldon, Richard

    1977 "Victor Shklovsky and the Device of Ostensible Surrender," in Shklovsky
1990.

Shklovsky, Victor

    1929 "Iskusstvo kak priem" [Art as a Device], in *O teorii prozy* (Moscow:
Federatsiia).

    1977 [1926] *Third Factory* [*Tret'ia fabrika*], translated by Richard Sheldon
(Ann Arbor, MI: Ardis).

    1990 [1923] *Sentimental Journey: Zoo, or, Letters Not about Love* [Sentimen-
tal'noe puteshestvie: Zoo ili pis'ma ne o liubvi], translated by Richard
Sheldon (Ann Arbor, MI: Ardis).

Steiner, Peter

    1984 *Russian Formalism: A Metapoetics* (Ithaca, NY: Cornell University Press).

    1985 "The Praxis of Irony in Viktor Shklovsky's *Zoo*," in *Russian Formalism: A
Retrospective Glance: A Festschrift in Honor of Victor Erlich*, edited by Robert
Louis Jackson and Stephen Rudy (New Haven, CT: Yale Center for Interna-
tional and Area Studies).

Stewart, Susan

    1984 *On Longing: Narratives of the Miniature, the Gigantic, the Souvenir, the
Collection* (Baltimore, MD: Johns Hopkins University Press).

Striedter, Jurij

    1989 *Literary Structure, Evolution, and Value: Russian Formalism and Czech
Structuralism Reconsidered* (Cambridge, MA: Harvard University Press).

Todorov, Tzvetan

    1985 "Poetic Language: The Russian Formalists," in Steiner 1985.

    1992 "Bilingualism, Dialogism, and Schizophrenia," *New Formations* 17.

JOHN NEUBAUER

BAKHTIN VERSUS LUKÁCS: INSCRIPTIONS OF

HOMELESSNESS IN THEORIES OF THE NOVEL

The form of the novel is, like no other one, an expression of transcendental
homelessness
LUKÁCS, Die Theorie des Romans[1]

The novel begins by presuming a verbal and semantic decentering of the ideological world, a certain linguistic homelessness of literary consciousness
BAKHTIN, The Dialogic Imagination

THE TWO MOST comprehensive theories of the novel in our century
are infused with notions of homelessness that relate the two theories to
each other and to the various forms of exile their authors had to endure. In Lukács's case, the experience of homelessness included literal
exiles in Austria, Germany, and the Soviet Union, two longer periods
of ostracization within Communist Hungary, and a brief deportation to
Romania after the Hungarian Revolution of 1956; Bakhtin was banished
to Kazakhstan, and though the banishment was lifted some four years
later, it was only at the very end of his life that he could settle in Moscow.

These experiences profoundly marked Lukács's and Bakhtin's thought,
but they were not the first source of the homelessness they ascribe
to the novel. Lukács's "transcendental homelessness" (*transzendentale
Obdachlosigkeit*) appears in the article version of his theory of the novel
in 1916, prior to his exile years, while Bakhtin's (1975: 178) notion of
a "linguistic homelessness" (*jazykovaia bespriiutnost'*) harks back to
Lukács's essay rather than to his own banishment. "Homelessness" enters
Bakhtin's discourse, wholly in keeping with his theory, "in a dialogue as
a living rejoinder" to Lukács, and it is "shaped in dialogic interaction
with an alien word that is already in the object" (Bakhtin 1981: 279).

In preparing this article I received help from many people. I wish to express my
special thanks to S. G. Bocharov (Moscow), Margarida Llosa (Porto), László Sziklai
(Budapest), and Willem Weststeijn (Amsterdam).

1. My translation. Unless noted in the bibliography, all further translations in this
essay are mine.

By tracing the inscriptions of homelessness and exile in the novelistic theories of Lukács and Bakhtin, I do not intend to demonstrate their dependence on the experience of exile. Rather, I wish to indicate a more complex network among experience, thought, and the intellectual stance of the two thinkers. After all, Lukács landed in exile precisely because he attempted to overcome his youthful sense of "transcendental homelessness" by joining the Communist Party and its ideology, whereas Bakhtin's dialogical reaction to Lukács's theory cannot be explained by the fact that he was banished by the very power that granted a home to his exiled Hungarian colleague. If, as I intend to show, Bakhtin developed his theory of the novel by refiguring *transcendental* homelessness into *linguistic* homelessness, this was primarily because by disposition he was more willing and able to live in "permanent exile," without a sheltering community, than Lukács.

Tracing dialogical reinscriptions of exile and homelessness from Lukács's first essay on the novel through his Marxist texts from the mid-1930s (Lukács 1934, 1935) to Bakhtin's writings is made difficult, however, by the fact that Lukács was unaware of Bakhtin,[2] and Bakhtin carried out his dialogue with the idealist and the Marxist Lukács largely "silently," without naming his partner. The historical dialogue between Lukács and Bakhtin was one-sided and sotto voce; my reconstruction of it will necessarily go beyond the actual words spoken.

1

In Lukács's *Die Theorie des Romans* (1963 [1916]) exile means a double banishment: from a transcendental *Heimat* and from ancient Greece, where the transcendental became immanent in social formations. Like Goethe's Iphigenie — whose yearning for "the land of the Greeks" on the

2. Lukács's published works contain no reference to Bakhtin. He probably did not know Bakhtin's 1929 book on Dostoevsky. He may have become familiar with Bakhtin's study of Rabelais (1963) or some of his other writings in the later 1960s, but by that time he was concerned with other matters. According to László Sziklai, Director of the Lukács archives at the Hungarian Academy of Science, there are no references to Bakhtin in Lukács's unpublished notes and correspondence. Lukács seldom and reluctantly read professional texts in Russian, although he acquired the ability to do so; he did not read literature in Russian (Sziklai 1994).

shores of exile became the expression of a uniquely German *Heimweh* —
the author of *Die Theorie des Romans* believes that in ancient Greece the
social relations of individuals in the family and the state were substantial
because they were "more general, more 'philosophical,' closer and more
intimately related to the archetypal Heimat" (ibid.: 26).

But, following Hegel, Lukács believes that the security of the Greek
world became suffocating for later ages: "We can no longer breathe
in a closed world" (ibid.: 27). The transcendental shelteredness of the
Homeric epic gave way to the novel, the epic "of a world abandoned by
god" (ibid.: 87). *Don Quixote* signals that the Christian god has absented
himself from the world and that individuals have begun to find sense and
substance only in their "nowhere indigenous soul" (ibid.: 103).

Lukács adopts from Hegel the notion that the novel is the epic of a
prosaic and bourgeois world (Hegel 1965 [1862], 2: 452), without sharing
Hegel's ultimately optimistic vision. History, for Hegel, is a march of
the human spirit homeward. The arts, having reached their apogee in
classical Greece, become increasingly less capable of expressing the self-
sufficient spirit; they become problematic precisely because reality turns
unproblematic (Lukács 1963 [1916]: 12). For Lukács, however, the trauma
of World War I reproblematized reality. The crisis of the arts became an
index of the spirit's general alienation. Homelessness in the novel came
to indicate that the world itself was out of joint.

In a more technical respect, Lukács relies on Goethe's and Schiller's
idea (jointly formulated in 1798) that the dramatic poet represents an
event as "totally present" (*vollkommen gegenwärtig*), whereas the epic
poet tells it as "totally past" (*vollkommen vergangen*) (Goethe 1986: 126).
The epic singer has no relation to the past events of his songs. Lukács
concurs (1963 [1916]: 125) but contrasts the epic with the novel rather
than with drama, and he understands Goethe and Schiller to mean that
the epic knows no change: Nestor is old, Helen beautiful, Agamemnon
powerful. They do, of course, know of aging and death, but they experience the passing of time within "the blessed timelessness of the divine
world." The epic world "is stationary and to be overseen at a single
glance" (ibid.). The novel, whose constitutive principle is temporality,
emerges once this timeless Heimat fades. Novelistic action becomes a
fight against time, its temporality revealing transcendental homelessness.

2

German philosophy, romanticism, and Goethe were also the intellectual Heimat of the young Bakhtin (see Tihanov 1995b), though he cared little for Hegel's "monologic" dialectics (Bakhtin 1986: 162). Given Bakhtin's intellectual background and voracious appetite for reading, Lukács's essay was bound to come to his attention. Indeed, he had such high regard for it that he even started to translate it in the early 1920s. He had to stop when Lukács, who had meanwhile become a Marxist, refused to permit the publication of his idealist essay.[3]

The surprising ending of *Die Theorie des Romans* provides a first opportunity to explore the two writers' divergent perspectives on shared topics. Having dwelled on the modern predicament in the novels of Goethe, Tolstoy, and others, Lukács unexpectedly suggests that the epic may reemerge in a new form (1963 [1916]: 157) even if reality remains fragmented. The new epoch, of which Tolstoy offers only glimpses, emerges as a "simply seen reality" in the works of Dostoevsky, which *Die Theorie des Romans* no longer regards as novels. Dostoevsky belongs "to the new world," though only a future formal analysis can decide whether he merely anticipates or already represents its Homer or Dante (ibid.: 157–58). A seldom reprinted footnote of the first, article version of the essay reveals that this formal analysis was Lukács's unaccomplished agenda: the essay was originally intended to be the introductory chapter of a book on Dostoevsky.[4]

In fact, it was Bakhtin who carried out Lukács's plan of formally analyzing Dostoevsky's novels, albeit by turning Lukács upside down: in Bakhtin's view, Dostoevsky did not revive the epic by going *beyond* the novel, but instead *renewed* the novel by fully exploiting its potential. Accordingly, Bakhtin resolutely refrained from linking Dostoevsky's innovations to a new dawn in the human condition, and he gave little

---

3. Bakhtin mentioned this to S. G. Bocharov in conversations (Bocharov 1995).

4. Lukács claims that the project remained incomplete because he had to enter military service, but this is only part of the story. The notes and schemas for the project, which miraculously emerged from a bank safe in Heidelberg after Lukács's death (Lukács 1985), indicate that he struggled with internal problems. See Jung 1989: 66–70.

attention to their social and historical circumstances—a matter that is usually overlooked by those who celebrate Bakhtin as a "contextualist" critic. The foreword to the 1929 edition, which was not reprinted in the 1963 edition, states that he "had to exclude all historical problems," for the analysis was based on his conviction "that every literary work is *internally and immanently* sociological" (1984: 275–76; my emphasis).[5]

As if answering Lukács, Bakhtin rejected B. M. Engelhardt's dialectical and Hegelian approach by noting that in Dostoevsky's novels there was no "evolution of a unified spirit; in fact there is no evolution, no growth in general" (ibid.: 26). Instead,

> Semantic material is always given to the hero's consciousness all at once and in its entirety. . . . That internal ideological struggle which the hero wages is a struggle for a choice among already available semantic possibilities, whose quantity remains almost unchanged throughout the entire novel. . . . Almost no evolution of thought takes place under the influence of new material, new points of view. (Ibid.: 239; see also 240)

Thus Bakhtin finds in Dostoevsky's open and dialogical novels heroes who resemble the unchanging heroes of Lukács's totally past and closed epic poems. Imposing a dialectical scheme on them would bring the "simultaneous coexistence" of dialogic voices to a closure. That Dostoevsky *did* seek closure is a matter that Bakhtin tended to gloss over.

5. Bakhtin's attempts to link Dostoevsky's art to capitalism are tenuous. In the first edition, he agreed with Kaus (1923) that "Dostoevsky is the most decisive, consistent, and implacable singer of capitalist man," and added that "the polyphonic novel could indeed have been realized only in the capitalist era" (Bakhtin 1984: 19ff.). The revised version states that Dostoevsky's "consistent carnivalization of dialogue" proved "remarkably productive as a means for capturing in art the developing relationships under capitalism," for capitalism, like Socrates, "brings together people and ideas" on the market square (ibid.: 167; see also 288). As the analogy with Socrates suggests, this hardly leads to concrete socioeconomic analyses. The closest that Bakhtin comes (in works published under his own name) to a socio-Marxist interpretation of literature is in the prefaces he wrote (in 1929) to Tolstoy's dramas and to his *Resurrection* (Morson and Emerson 1989: 227–57; cf. Shukman 1989: 137–48). However, he attached no significance to these articles later.

3

Lukács had been in Austrian and German exile for a decade by the time Bakhtin's book on Dostoevsky appeared in 1929.[6] Ironically, it was exile and conversion to Marxism that led him to abandon the notion of metaphysical homelessness—indeed, to avoid all explicit references to *Die Theorie des Romans*, even if his work retained its general structure. Erasing exile became part of Lukács's strategy after 1933 to make the Soviet Union, his place of spiritual and physical exile, into a limited sort of Heimat.

For Lukács, this Jewish-German-Marxist thinker with intellectual roots in Germany, Hungary never was a true home. Like Béla Balázs, Arnold Hauser, Karl Mannheim, and other members of the now legendary Sunday circle that he led during World War I, Lukács was an assimilated Jew who had no ties to the Jewish tradition, yet who never fully integrated into a society that supported massive waves of nationalism and anti-Semitism during his lifetime (Gluck 1985: 8f.). When he had to flee to Vienna for his participation in the unsuccessful Communist revolution of 1919,[7] he reconfigured his German intellectual Heimat by breaking with the idealist tradition and embracing a Hegelian Marxism. However, the fruit of that reorientation, his *Geschichte und Klassenbewußtsein* (1923), was severely criticized by Marxists, and Lukács soon repudiated it as well. A second, decisive reorientation occurred in 1929–31 when, during a stay at the Marx-Engels Institute of Moscow, he became deeply impressed by Marx's *Economic and Philosophic Manuscripts of 1844*, and by Marx's and Engels's aesthetic writings that Michail A. Lifshitz was in the process of editing at the institute. When Lukács had to flee from Germany to Moscow in 1933, he started to collaborate with Lifshitz (Lukács 1963 [1916]: 11f.; 1968: 11; 1974: 9–10, 13–14, 38–40) on a reconstruction of Marx's and Engels's aesthetics: "We were the first to speak of a specific Marxist aesthetics, as opposed to this or that aesthetics which would complete the Marxist system" (Lukács 1983: 86).

This Marxist aesthetics was directed against Trotsky and Plekhanov,

---

6. Bakhtin was arrested on December 24, 1928. Through the intervention of friends, his sentence of ten years in a gulag was converted to exile in Kustanai, northwest Kazakhstan (Clark and Holquist 1984: 254).

7. On Lukács's exile years in Austria and Germany see Congdon 1991: 45–99.

the powerful organization of proletarian writers RAPP (Lukács 1968: 10), and the "vulgar sociology" in literary scholarship that claimed that writers could not escape the ideology of their class. Lukács's ideological and institutional base became the inner circle of the journal *Literaturny Kritik*, which included Lifshitz, Elena Usevich, and Vladimir Romanovich Grib (ibid.: 11; 1983: 96f.).

Much less is known about Lukács's involvement with the *Literaturny Kritik* and the ambiguous position of this journal within the Soviet power structure than about his polemics with the German exile community concerning expressionism and modernism. He justifiably stressed later that the journal's Marxist aesthetics opposed Stalinist demands for purely propagandistic literature, but he tended to gloss over the fact that its attacks on RAPP aided that group's suppression under Stalin and that in 1934 the journal enthusiastically supported the first Congress of the Stalinist All-Union Federation of Soviet Writers, where Andrey Zhdanov announced the dogma of "socialist realism" (Scott 1977 [1935]: 7-12). Pavel Fyodorovich Yudin—organizer of the congress, a favorite of Stalin, and a member of the Party's Central Committee—was a friend of Usevich and a patron of the journal, whose editor in chief he became in May 1933 (Ermolaev 1977 [1963]: 142). Although *Literaturny Kritik* was finally closed down in 1940, none of its editors fell victim to the purges, and Lukács himself was only briefly arrested (Lukács 1983: 96–97, 100, 180; 1968: 11f.).

This is the political background of the discussions on Lukács's revised, now Marxist theory of the novel that were held on the initiative of the *Literaturny Kritik* at the Communist Academy in Moscow on December 20 and 28, 1934 and January 3, 1935. Lukács's presentation was subsequently published in the *Literaturny Kritik* and served as a basis for his article on the novel in the *Literaturnaia enciklopedia*, which appeared in the same year (Lukács 1935).[8] All of these texts became available to Bakhtin in his exile and played a key role in formulating his own theory of the novel.

---

8. A stenographic record of Lukács's presentation and the subsequent discussion was published in the *Literaturny Kritik* (Lukács 1934; Strada 1976). It differs in several respects from Lukács's German notes for the presentation (Lukács 1981), but the deviation does not seem to be tendentious. The final encyclopedia article (Lukács 1935) is longer, but it retains the structure of the presentation and introduces no new ideas.

Lukács's Marxist restatement of *Die Theorie des Romans* retains the Hegelian juxtaposition of epic and novel, although it jettisons the notion of transcendental homelessless and marginalizes the epic. According to his new central contention, "It is in the novel that the specific contradictions of bourgeois society are represented in the most adequate and most typical manner. The contradictions of capitalist society provide thus the key for the understanding of the novel as genre" (Lukács 1974: 63; the last sentence is not in Strada 1976). Hence Lukács attempts to synchronize the epochs of the novel with a Marxist history of "the great phases in the history of the classes and of class struggle" (Strada 1976: 10–11): the novel is "in statu nascendi" when bourgeois society is born (ibid.: 11); it disintegrates into naturalist objectivism and modernist subjectivism when capitalism enters its final, imperialist phase (ibid.: 15).

Following the line adopted at the All-Union Congress of Soviet Writers, Lukács now claims that the revolutionary struggles of the proletariat "necessarily" open the possibility of portraying workers as positive heroes, leading to the revival of epic treatments, though not to the return of the "old epic" itself (ibid.: 15f.).

The ensuing debate pitted the editors of the *Literaturny Kritik* against a handful of opponents led by V. F. Pereverzev (Strada 1976: 36–44, 57–63, 65), who had already been attacked as a "vulgar sociologist" (Ermolaev 1977: 93–99). Pereverzev was actually unhappy with the surgical separation of epic and novel according to societal forms. He suggested that Petronius's *Satyricon*, Apuleius's *Golden Ass*, and other Roman books were prebourgeois novels (Strada 1976: 39–40) and that Camoes, Tasso, Milton, and Klopstock could well be seen as epic poets of the bourgeoisie's "heroic" ascendancy (ibid.: 41). Concerning methodology, Pereverzev insisted that historians start with concrete facts and work from there inductively. Although Marx laid the foundation of "scientific" history, his remarks on aesthetics and literary history were occasional and "axiomatic" (ibid.: 63f.). Whether, as Marx wrote, Voltaire's *Henriade* demonstrated the impossibility of a bourgeois heroic epic was still to be investigated. Marx had no theory of the novel, and Lukács's abstract, ahistorical, and deductive construction would have displeased him (ibid.: 65).

This hit at the very heart of Lukács's and Lifshitz's project. Responding swiftly and ruthlessly, the editors of *Literaturny Kritik* proclaimed that questioning Lukács's theory of the novel amounted to an attack on Marxism itself. Pereverzev's methodological objections to reliance on authority (ibid.: 39) showed that he was no Marxist. Some respondents attempted to answer Pereverzev's historical objections, but most simply branded him a "Pereverzist" and a "Menshevist" (ibid.: 45, 48–50), disregarding his vigorous protests (ibid.: 63, 90–91). His intimidated supporters rushed to demonstrate their political correctness by accusing the stenographers of having misunderstood them (ibid.: 85, 89). One by one they did penance by lashing out at Pereverzev with appropriate quotations from the Marxist authorities.

Summarizing the discussion, Lifshitz reasserted that empirical history without Marxist foundations was no history at all (ibid.: 109–25), and Lukács chimed in by denying the possibility that Marxists' remarks could be occasional or axiomatic: "For us, the utterances of Marx, Engels, Lenin and Stalin about literature and art are inseparable from their whole system, are a cornerstone for our scientific work, are the sure practical guide of our research" (quoted in ibid.: 128).

Lukács thus declared that his place of exile, the Soviet Union, was to become the home of the future epic novel, and he thereby acquired for himself social, institutional, and political space. Refashioning his Hegelianism into a Marxist discourse flavored with quotations from Lenin and Stalin, he adopted what Bakhtin was to call the "authoritative word" and converted exile into a seat of power.[9] The *Literaturny Kritik*, his power base, won the day, and Pereverzev was ostracized. In 1938 he was deported, and he was released only in 1956, in the same year, ironically, that Lukács was briefly banished to Romania for his participation in the Hungarian revolutions. Of course, Lukács cannot be blamed for Pereverzev's deportation, but he played a key role in his sinister stigmatization at the 1934 meeting.

4

The Moscow discussion of Lukács's theory of the novel indicates both the general climate and the specific points to which Bakhtin responded. His banishment to Kustanai, Kazakhstan, officially ended on August 4, 1934, just a few months before the debates at the Moscow Academy took

9. The success was remarkable in view of Lukács's poor Russian. One discussant called Lukács's style of presentation unsuited "for our public" (Strada 1976: 20). On Lukács's exile years in Moscow see Sziklai 1986.

place, but Bakhtin stayed on because he was not allowed to resettle in Leningrad or Moscow. In Kazakhstan he wrote in 1934–35 his *Discourse in the Novel*, which so sharply deviated from the views then dominant in Moscow that it could not be published.

Discourse in the Novel went beyond the book on Dostoevsky, in part by introducing some important new concepts, among them "heteroglossia" and the opposing terms "authoritative" and "internally persuasive" discourse (Bakhtin 1981: 342ff.). I suggest that these new terms, as well as the essay's long historical section entitled "The Two Stylistic Lines of Development in the European Novel" (ibid.: 366–422), responded to the Moscow discussions without explicitly naming them.

Heteroglossia is the dialogic coexistence of dialects, jargons, social speech types, and professional and other discourses. For Bakhtin, the life of a language is a perpetual struggle between centripetal institutional forces that strive for standardization and language's inherent centrifugal tendency to diversify and fragment, thereby producing a linguistic and ideological heteroglossia. By introducing this term, Bakhtin set himself in opposition to the dogma that was proclaimed at the All-Union Congress of Soviet Writers in August 1934, which served to create a monologic "all-Union" literature, in spite of its lip service to ethnic and national pluralism. As reported by the *Literaturny Kritik* from the Congress: "All the literatures of the Soviet Union's national republics were united by a singleness of aspiration, singleness of ideas, singleness of aim. Soviet literature is an all-Union literature" (Scott 1977 [1935]: 9). The dogma of socialist realism, the ideological underpinning of this unity, was inscribed into the Federation's bylaws (ibid.: 21).

Bakhtin's notion of heteroglossia could have been used to write, in opposition to both Lukács and the "vulgar sociologists," an alternative social history of the novel. Since heteroglossia was said to enter the novel by means of *"another's speech in another's language*, serving to express authorial intentions but in a refracted way" (Bakhtin 1981: 324), it could have become a "hinge" between social and literary history, providing a correlation between specific historical forms of the novel and the concrete state that heteroglossia assumed in the embedding culture.

Yet, for all its interest in history, *Discourse in the Novel* makes little use of this opportunity. Its theoretical sections (ibid.: 301–31) are essentially ahistorical, whereas the lengthy historical section speaks of two *stylistic* lines of development (ibid.: 366–422) and therefore reads like an *internalist* answer to Lukács's history. As I shall show later, Bakhtin's subsequent essays on the history of the novel are based on similar text-immanent materials.

All this results in curious discrepancies. On the one hand, heteroglossia is so central to Bakhtin's theory and formal analysis of the novel that he defines the latter as "a diversity of social speech types . . . and a diversity of individual voices, artistically organized" (ibid.: 262). On the other hand, heteroglossia is quite marginal in Bakhtin's *historical* treatments. In spite of the assertion that language is always "heteroglot from top to bottom" (ibid.: 291), heteroglossia becomes important for Bakhtin paradoxically just when it is partially or fully absent. Such is the case with prehistoric myth-dominated societies that produce epics (ibid.: 369) and with authoritarian modern societies that partly suppress heteroglossia and permit only monological novels. It is within this framework that Bakhtin enters into a double dialogue with Lukács, challenging both his idealist-Hegelian and his Marxist views.

In looking at myth-dominated cultures, Bakhtin redefines some key ideas from Lukács's *Die Theorie des Romans* by shifting their meaning. Bakhtin's prehistoric cultures are preheteroglossic, for they are monolithically held together by a central national myth. But if, for Lukács, this myth provides a transcendental shelter within which the epic can flourish, for Bakhtin it is a linguistic and ideological straitjacket which, like Rousseau's state of nature in Derrida's interpretation, is always already in the process of disintegration, decentering, passing into a state of heteroglossia that Bakhtin welcomes as an emancipation from monoglossic bondage:

This verbal-ideological decentering will occur only when a national culture loses its sealed-off and self-sufficient character, when it becomes conscious of itself as only one among *other* cultures and languages. It is this knowledge that will sap the roots of a mythological feeling for language. . . . What inevitably happens is a decay and collapse of the religious, political and ideological authority connected with that language. (Ibid.: 370)

These are the conditions under which the novel is born. To Lukács's melancholy thesis that the form of the novel is "an expression of transcendental homelessness" (Lukács 1963 [1916]: 35), Bakhtin replies: "The novel begins by presuming a verbal and semantic decentering of the ideological world, a certain linguistic homelessness of literary consciousness" (1981: 367). The "germs of novelistic prose" appear "in the poly- and heteroglot world of the Hellenistic era, in Imperial Rome and during the disintegration and collapse of the church-directed centralization of discourse and ideology in the Middle Ages" (ibid.: 370).[10] Hence "homelessness" means, for Bakhtin, losing one's "feeling for language as myth" and "absolute form of thought." It is the "fundamental liberation" from "the hegemony of a single and unitary language" (ibid.: 367) that leads to the novel's development.

The hegemonic domination of myth in prehistoric cultures corresponds to the rule of what Bakhtin calls hieratic and undialogized "authoritative" discourse in modern dictatorships (ibid.: 341–48). An "authoritative" discourse organizes around itself a great many other discourses that are allowed to interpret it, praise it, and apply it, but that cannot induce changes within it, for such a discourse is semantically "static and dead." An authoritative discourse is thus a dogma that demands "unconditional allegiance"; it is "indissolubly fused with its authority—with political power, an institution, a person—and it stands and falls together with that authority" (ibid.: 343). Since it is hostile to dialogic double-voicing and "hybrid" narrative constructions (ibid.: 344), it permits only epic and monologic novels. As if replying to Zhdanov's demand that Soviet literature become tendentious "for in an epoch of class struggle there is not and cannot be a literature which is not class literature" (Scott 1977 [1935]: 21), Bakhtin claims that novelists ought to be linguistically and ideologically homeless: "It is as if the author has no language of his own, but does possess his own style, his own organic and unitary law governing the way he plays with languages and the way his own real semantic and expressive intentions are refracted within them" (Bakhtin 1981: 311).[11]

Bakhtin somewhat optimistically and naively assumed that the collapse of such an authoritative discourse would automatically lead to dialogic novels, that

10. Lukács's "transzendentale Obdachlosigkeit" becomes Bakhtin's "jazykovaia bespriiutnost" (Bakhtin 1981: 367).

11. It must be acknowledged that Bakhtin immediately, if vaguely, qualifies the radicalism of this statement: "Of course this play with languages (and frequently the complete absence of a direct discourse of his own) in no sense degrades the general, deep-seated intentionality, the overarching ideological conceptualization of the work as a whole" (1981: 311). It may be possible to link this tension between dialogism and intentionality in Bakhtin (see Grüttemeier 1993) with that "triumph of realism" that Lukács adopted from Engels and directed against overtly propagandistic literature.

in modern times, the flowering of the novel is always connected with a disintegration of stable verbal-ideological systems and with an intensification and intentionalization of speech diversity that are counterposed to the previously reigning stable systems.   (Ibid.: 370–71)

It comes as no surprise that this thinly veiled condemnation of the Stalinist dogma that seized power in the literary discussions of 1934–35 could not be published until the dogma became "decentered."[12]

5

According to Sergey Bocharov, the editor of Bakhtin's papers, the Bakhtin archives contain summaries of two articles that Lukács published in the *Literaturny Kritik* in 1935, on Engels and on problems of the historical novel. Moreover, Bakhtin's papers include polemical notes against the theory of the novel that Lukács formulated in the 1930s. Bakhtin disagrees with Lukács's Hegelian view that the novel is a bourgeois epic, in part because it ignores the folkloric origins of the novel. The unnamed target of Bakhtin's theory of the novel is Lukács (Bocharov 1995).

Though Bakhtin's notes on Lukács are not yet published, we can reconstruct further dimensions of his critique from two essays on the novel that he wrote a few years after *Discourse in the Novel*, namely "Epic and Novel" (Bakhtin 1981: 3–40) and "From the Prehistory of Novelistic Discourse" (ibid.: 41–83). The very titles indicate that Bakhtin addresses here Lukácsian questions about the history of the novel, and several scholars have already noted the connection, though they do not explore the dialogue systematically.[13]

We may distinguish in these essays two elements of Bakhtin's anti-Lukácsian agenda. The first is nothing less than a substantiation of Pereverzev's claim that the novel has prebourgeois roots in the literature of antiquity. Indeed, the historical part of *Discourse in the Novel* had already included Apuleius and Petronius, precisely the authors whom

12. That Bakhtin did not associate authoritative discourse with Nazi dictatorship may indicate that he wanted to implicate Stalin's Soviet Union as well. I doubt that *Discourse in the Novel* was written to pave Bakhtin's way back into academic life or publishing (Clark and Holquist 1984: 268).

13. See Aucouturier 1983, Cases 1985, Holquist 1990: 73–77, Tihanov 1995a, and Prévost 1973.

Pereverzev had cited as cases negating Lukács's claim that the novel was a bourgeois genre (ibid.: 371, 372, 375, 385). The essay on the prehistory of novelistic discourse substantiated the suggestion with amazing erudition and massive documentation.

The second part of Bakhtin's response to Lukács, contained in the essay "Epic and Novel" (ibid.: 3–40),[14] is directed against *Die Theorie des Romans* rather than the Marxist Lukács. Following Lukács, Bakhtin adopts Goethe's and Schiller's characterization that epics speak of a past that is *vollkommen vergangen*. Bakhtin's expression, "absolute past" (*absoljutnoe proshloe*) (ibid.: 13; Bakhtin 1975: 456), indicates both that the singers are at an infinite temporal distance from their subject matter, and that they sing *sub specie aeternitatis* about "utterly finished" events from a valorized and reverently represented national past, in a language that is utterly different from contemporary discourse (Bakhtin 1981: 13–17). Furthermore, the epic as genre is itself from the "absolute past," for we come upon it as an "already completely finished, a congealed and half-moribund genre" (ibid.: 14). Epic- and myth-dominated societies are thereby pushed back into prehistoric time, so that the novel's "prehistory" can coincide with the dawn of history rather than the beginnings of the bourgeoisie.

While Bakhtin thus extends the novel's temporal life far back into history, he telescopes it internally by claiming that it eliminates epic distance and "contemporizes" the epic world in diverse ways: through parodies and travesties (ibid.: 21), by turning to an unfinished, still changing contemporary reality (ibid.: 22, 27), and, above all, by overcoming reverence. The language of depiction "now lies on the same plane as the 'depicted' language of the hero, and may enter into dialogic relations and hybrid combinations with it" (ibid.: 27ff.).

Whereas *Die Theorie des Romans* laments the passing of epic timelessness, "Epic and Novel" delights in overcoming an unchangeable national myth through temporality. Accordingly, Lukács and Bakhtin assign different values to irony, parody, and satire. For Lukács, as for Hegel, irony is a "negative Mysticism in godless times" (Lukács 1963 [1916]: 90), "a self-annihilation" (*Selbstaufhebung*) of an extreme subjectivity (ibid.: 93). Bakhtin, following Friedrich Schlegel, valorizes Socratic irony as a "new type of prose heroization" (Bakhtin 1981: 24). The displacement of

14. Some aspects of the essay "Forms of Time and of the Chronotope in the Novel" (written in 1937–38; Bakhtin 1981: 84–258) are also relevant.

the heroic epic by novelistic irony and parody is a joyous emancipation, a playful subversion of power, official language, and official thought. Popular spoken language, dialogue, and laughter constitute a system of "Socratic degradations" that combine with a "serious, lofty and for the first time truly free investigation of the world, of man and of human thought" (ibid.: 25). For Lukács, in turn, all great novels are pervaded by an adult melancholy, a mourning for the lost Heimat of childhood (1963 [1916]: 83, 85–87). Novelistic "heterogeneity" signals alienation for Lukács (ibid.: 83, 109, 141), but is a source of creativity and freedom for Bakhtin.

What one may call Bakhtin's "carnivalization" of Lukács is also evident when he restates the conflict that Lukács perceives between novelistic characters and their worlds. From the heterogeneity of soul and world Lukács derives two paradigms for the modern novel, depending on whether the soul is wider or narrower than its world (ibid.: 96). Obviously following Lukács, Bakhtin notes that characters may be greater than their fate or less than their condition (Bakhtin 1981: 37), and he even states that the hero's inadequacy to his situation is a "basic internal theme" of the novel. But larger-than-life characters are future-oriented for Bakhtin, and represent "unrealized potential and unrealized demands" (ibid.), whereas for Lukács they represent a prototypical nineteenth-century withdrawal from the world, a "most desperate self-defense" undertaken in light of the insight that realizing oneself in the world is hopeless and humiliating (Lukács 1963 [1916]: 116). Here, as elsewhere, Bakhtin converts Lukács's idealist melancholy into promise.

6

Lukács characterized his return to Hungary in 1945 as a "homecoming in the true sense" (1983: 166), but home soon became a place of internal intellectual exile, when László Rajk was executed as part of the purges that swept the Soviet satellites in 1948–49 and Lukács was viciously attacked by his former student József Révai for his lack of interest in socialist literature. During the Hungarian revolution of 1956, Lukács briefly and reluctantly returned to politics as Minister of Education and the Arts. After the suppression of the revolution he was first briefly interned in Romania, and then subjected to another lengthy internal intellectual isolation, which ended only a few years before his death in 1971. A year later Bakhtin, who was rediscovered and partially rehabilitated in the 1960s, could finally move to Moscow, where he lived until his death in 1975.

Lukács and Bakhtin thus represent different paradigms for thinking about exile and coping with its experience. Romantic Heimweh led Lukács to embrace Communism as his new mythology and ideological Heimat, which demanded that he enter the arena of politics, in which he never quite felt at home. And thus he often found himself in a double homelessness. As Béla Balázs noted in his diary when their ways parted in the Austrian exile: "He was born to be a quiet scholar, a lonely sage, a seer of eternal things, and not to make inquiries in coffeeshops about people who embezzled stolen party funds, not even to follow the daily stream of our ephemeral politics and to want to sway the masses— he, who does *not speak* his own *language*, when more than ten people understand him. His language is one of a terrible banishment; he is truly homeless because he has lost his spiritual home" (quoted in Karádi and Vezér 1985: 121). Although Lukács occasionally opposed the "authoritative" voice in politics, he adopted key tenets of the dogma and made his compromises because he wanted to believe that Communism would ultimately overcome alienation. Ironically, this led him to condemn his modernist fellow exiles (including Joyce), with the exception of Thomas Mann.

Bakhtin, though he could finally settle in Moscow, was a "permanent exile." For him, homelessness was a condition of intellectual freedom and the dialogic novel. As a modern prodigal son, he refused to resubmit to patriarchal power, preferring the *Geworfenheit* of exile to the *Geborgenheit* of unitary society. But ultimately his faith in the promise of intellectual freedom was no less romantic than Lukács's Heimweh, for he didn't quite realize (or didn't want to realize) to what extent his liberal utopia is time and again subverted by those who cannot live without a Heimat.

REFERENCES

Aucouturier, Michel
1983 "The Theory of the Novel in Russia in the 1930s: Lukács and Bakhtin," in *The Russian Novel from Pushkin to Pasternak*, edited by John Garrard, 227–40 (New Haven, CT: Yale University Press).
Bakhtin, M. M.
1929 *Problemy tvorchestva Dostoevskogo* (Leningrad: Priboi).

1975 *Voprosy literatury i estetiki: Issledovaniia raznykh let*, edited by S. G. Bocharov (Moscow: Khudozhestvennaia literatura).

1981 *The Dialogic Imagination*, translated by Caryl Emerson and Michael Holquist, edited by Michael Holquist (Austin: University of Texas Press).

1984 *Problems of Dostoevsky's Poetics*, edited and translated by Caryl Emerson, introduction by Wayne Booth (Minneapolis: University of Minnesota Press).

1986 *Speech Genres and Other Late Essays*, translated by Vern W. McGee, edited by Caryl Emerson and Michael Holquist (Austin: University of Texas Press).

Bocharov, S. G.

1995 Letter to author, January 22.

Cases, Cesare

1985 "La teoria del romanzo in Lukács e in Bachtin," in *Su Lukács*, 110–21 (Torino: Einaudi).

Clark, Katerina, and Michael Holquist

1984 *Mikhail Bakhtin* (Cambridge, MA: Belknap Press of Harvard University Press).

Congdon, Lee

1991 *Exile and Social Thought: Hungarian Intellectuals in Germany and Austria, 1919–1933* (Princeton, NJ: Princeton University Press).

Ermolaev, Herman

1977 [1963] *Soviet Literary Theories, 1917–34: The Genesis of Socialist Realism* (New York: Octagon).

Gluck, Mary

1985 *Georg Lukács and His Generation, 1900–1918* (Cambridge, MA: Harvard University Press).

Goethe, Johann Wolfgang von

1986 "Über epische und dramatische Dichtung von Goethe und Schiller," in *Sämtliche Werke*, 4.2: 126–28 (Munich: Hanser).

Grüttemeier, Ralf

1993 "Dialogizität und Intentionalität bei Bachtin." *Deutsche Vierteljahrsschrift für Literaturwissenschaft und Geistesgeschichte* 67: 764–83.

Hegel, Georg Wilhelm Friedrich

1965 [1842] *Ästhetik*, 2 vols. (Frankfurt am Main: Europäische Verlaganstalt).

Holquist, Michael

1990 *Dialogism: Bakhtin and His World* (London: Routledge).

Jung, Werner

1989 *Georg Lukács* (Stuttgart: Metzler).

Karádi, Éva, and Erzsébet Vezér, eds.

1985 *Georg Lukács, Karl Mannheim und der Sonntagskreis* (Frankfurt am Main: Sendler).

Kaus, Otto

1923 *Dostojewski und sein Schicksal* (Berlin: Laub).

Lukács, Georg

    1916 "Die Theorie des Romans," *Zeitschrift der Ästhetik und der allgemeinen Kunstwissenschaft* 11: 225–71, 390–431.

    1923 *Geschichte und Klassenbewusstsein* (Berlin, Malik).

    1934 "Problemy teorii romana" [Problems in the theory of the novel], *Literaturny Kritik* 2: 214–49, 3: 231–54.

    1935 "Roman kak burzhuaznaia epopeia" [The novel as bourgeois epos], *Literaturnaia enciklopedia* [Literary encyclopedia] (Moscow) 9: 795–831.

    1963 [1916] *Die Theorie des Romans* (Neuwied: Luchterhand).

    1968 *Müvészet és társadalom* (Budapest: Corvina).

    1974 *Écrits de Moscou*, edited and translated by Claude Prévost (Paris: Editions Sociales).

    1981 *Moskauer Schriften: Zur Literaturtheorie und Literaturpolitik, 1934–1940* (Frankfurt: Sendler).

    1983 *Record of a Life: An Autobiographical Sketch*, edited by István Eörsi, translated by Rodney Livingstone (London: Verso).

    1985 *Dostojewski: Notizen und Entwürfe*, edited by J. C. Nyiri (Budapest: Akadémiai Kiadó).

Morson, Gary Saul, and Caryl Emerson, eds.

    1989 *Rethinking Bakhtin: Extensions and Challenges* (Evanston, IL: Northwestern University Press).

    1990 *Mikhail Bakhtin: Creation of a Prosaics* (Stanford, CA: Stanford University Press).

Prévost, Claude

    1973 Présentation for Bakhtin's "Épopée et roman," *Recherches internationales à la lumière du marxisme*, no. 76: 1–4.

Scott, H. G., ed.

    1977 [1935] *Soviet Writers' Congress 1934: The Debate on Socialist Realism and Modernism in the Soviet Union* (London: Lawrence and Wishart).

Shukman, Ann

    1989 "Bakhtin's Tolstoy Prefaces," in Morson and Emerson 1989: 137–68.

Strada, Vittorio

    1976 *György Lukács, Michail Bachtin e altri: Problemi di teoria del romanzo. Metodologia letteraria e dialettica storica* (Turin: Einaudi).

Sziklai, László

    1986 *Georg Lukács und seine Zeit, 1930–1945* (Wien: Hermann Böhlaus Nachf.).

    1994 Letter to the author, November 9.

Tihanov, Galin

    1995a "Bakhtin, Lukács and Literary Genre." *Slovo: A Journal of Contemporary Russian and East European Affairs* 8 (2): 44–52.

    1995b "Bakhtin, Lukács and German Romanticism: The Case with Epic and Irony." Synopsis in *Materials of the Seventh International Bakhtin Conference*, 1: 203–15 (Moscow: Moscow State Pedagogical University).

NANCY HUSTON

ROMAIN GARY: A FOREIGN BODY IN

FRENCH LITERATURE

DESPITE HIS HUGE and continuing popularity in France, Romain Gary is not part of the "canon" of postwar French literature. And despite his familiarity with American culture and language (six of his books were written directly in English), he has been virtually obliterated from the memory of North America.

Who was Romain Gary? What I think, after having, over the past year, passionately plowed through virtually all the books written by and about him in French (some thirty-five volumes in all), is that he was not only one of the great writers of this century, but also one of its most unusual and impressive human beings. And what I shall attempt to convince you of is the apparently incredible fact that he gradually came to think of and shape his life as if it were the Second Coming. Romain Gary was a self-anointed, self-appointed, self-resurrected and, ultimately, self-crucified Messiah.

Quite disconcertingly, instead of revealing himself a little more with every page I read, every fact I gleaned about him, Gary seemed to disappear progressively, a bit like the Cheshire Cat. Not only did his life and work teem with contradictions of every sort but, in addition, he was an inveterate, shameless, and highly gifted liar. It soon became clear to me that the question he embodied was that of *identity*, in the most mathematical sense of the term, that is, being one, coinciding with oneself. He did everything in his power to confound and confuse us, to throw us simultaneously on and off the scent, to pull us into a dizzying dance of identities that pulverizes all possible points of reference and, ultimately, compels us to ask ourselves the same question he asked himself every minute of every day: did Romain Gary really exist? The incomprehension into which he plunges us gradually takes on the aura of a philosophy.

Is there a single irrefutable statement that can be made about him?

This text is adapted from my book *Tombeau de Romain Gary* (1995).

He was born. That much is certain. (*Je suis né*, as Georges Perec entitled one of his unfinished books.) There is no problem about the date, at least if one takes into account the slight disparity of the Orthodox calendar: he entered this world on May 8, 1914. His place of birth, however, is already problematic. According to all his biographers, Gary was born in Moscow; but he himself always firmly declared the event to have taken place in Poland. "From what I've been told, we were on our way from Moscow to Paris so my mother could give birth . . . and I was born in a small clinic next to the Polish Theater of Vilnius, but I wonder if it wasn't simply to excuse herself for not having given birth to me in France" [D'après ce qu'on m'a dit, nous allions de Moscou à Paris pour que ma mère accouche. . . . et je suis né dans une petite clinique à côté du théâtre polonais de Wilno, parce que ma mère se sentait dit-elle mal, elle a dû s'arrêter à Wilno, mais je me demande si ce n'était pas tout simplement pour s'excuser auprès de moi de ne pas m'avoir fait naître en France] (1973a).[1]

To be born in the middle of a trip—en route—like Jesus. Next to a theater, yet. A nativity play . . . with a spotlight in lieu of the blazing star? Why not?

As for his father's identity, if his mother Nina knew it, she guarded her secret as jealously as the Virgin Mary guarded hers. He may have been a passing lover. He may (and Gary favored this hypothesis without ever being able to confirm it) have been Ivan Mosjukin, the greatest Russian silent movie actor. He may also, after all, have been Lebja Kacew, Nina's second husband, whose name Gary was to bear for thirty years . . . We have no choice but to resign ourselves, as Gary had no choice but to resign *him*self, to the fact that the circumstances of his conception will forever be shrouded in mystery.

A good beginning. Bastardy. No one ever saw the slightest trace of Jesus' father, either. Gary was well on his way to becoming a legend.

"My mother," he would explain in 1973, "was pretty legendary. By that I mean that she was pretty good at fabricating legends." Moreover, he goes on, she was "affected by an illness quite common in Europe at the time . . . : galloping Francophilia, a Joan-of-Arcism typical of Eastern European Jews in particular" [Ma mère était assez légendaire: je veux dire qu'elle était assez fortiche pour fabriquer des légendes. . . .

---

1. All translations from the French are mine unless otherwise indicated.

elle était atteinte de cette maladie dont était atteinte souvent l'Europe à l'époque . . . : la francophilie galopante, Jeanne d'Arcisme typique notamment des juifs d'Europe de l'Est] (ibid). Gary inherited both of these traits from his mother: Francophilia and the lust for legend making.

Was she even Jewish? Once again, there is no ready answer. In public Gary enjoyed boasting that she was, but in private Nina's spectacularly authentic, shtetlizing, Yiddishophone Judaism often shriveled down to one-fourth. Gary himself, when asked if he was Jewish, would say, "If people want me to be, I don't mind." Nearly everyone did want him to be—starting, no doubt, with the Poles of Vilnius and Warsaw among whom he lived between the ages of three and fourteen. With a name like Kacew, it was unavoidable: he was considered a Jew, called a Jew, treated like a Jew, so to all intents and purposes he was one, despite the fact that Nina had him baptized a Catholic and regularly blessed by Orthodox priests. (Jesus wasn't a very kosher Catholic either.) And given that Gary ardently identified with everyone and everything that suffered, he was hardly going to pass up *that* opportunity.

Much later, he was furious when the Israelis refused to include him in their *Who's Who in World Jewry*. "The Germans," he said, "had broader views" [Les Allemands avaient des vues plus larges] (1974a: 169).

The only roots to which Gary laid claim, insistently and consistently, were those which bespoke the lifestyle Nina had embraced *against* the Mosaic tradition of her family in Koursk: the world of gypsies, traveling actors and acrobats, nomadic entertainers. He was rooted, in other words, in uprootedness. Far from home? He was homeless.

What about his name? *Comment s'appelait-il*? For once, the reflexive nature of this verb in French is wholly appropriate: he called himself, named himself, baptized and rebaptized himself ceaselessly. Nothing was stable, nothing remained in place, not even his "Christian" name because the name Nina had chosen for him was . . . *Roman*. Not *Romain*, but *Roman*—a popular name in the countries of Central Europe, where it also designates (as it does in French) a literary genre. This is also the name which appears on his French naturalization documents of 1935. Roman.

As for his surname . . . Well, he was called *Kacew* just as Jesus was called *Son of Joseph*, that is, falsely. And the "Gary" he finally settled on much later is, like "Christ," less a patronym than a cipher. *Christ* means "the anointed." *Gari*, in Russian, is the imperative form of the verb to burn. "Burn!"—an order he was to comply with throughout his life, all the way to *Ajar*, ember. He also called himself *Ajar*.

"Names, you know . . . ," Emile Ajar would write in 1976, "nothing but pseudonyms" [Les noms, vous savez . . . tous des pseudonymes"] (1976: 75). And it is true all of us bear false names, only we don't know it. A young couple sits down to discuss the possible names of the child they are expecting. They don't really believe in it yet; they *make*-believe. They draw up lists. They get a kick out of it a bit like novelists mulling over possible names for their characters. The child is the hero of an as-yet-unwritten play.

In Gary's case, the young couple comprised not his mother and his father but his mother and himself. Together, they sought the perfect name for the hero of this Roman that was to be his life. They talked over possible patronyms for the famous writer to whom they planned to give birth. "Alexandre Natal, Armande de la Torre, Terral, Vasco de la Fernaye . . . It went on that way," says Gary in his autobiographical work *Promesse de l'aube* [Promise at dawn], "for pages and pages. After each list of names, we would look at each other and shake our heads. No, that wouldn't do—that wouldn't do at all" [Alexandre Natal, Armande la Torre, Terral, Vasco de la Fernaye . . . Cela continuait ainsi pendant des pages et des pages. Après chaque chapelet de noms, nous nous regardions, et nous hochions tous deux la tête. Ce n'était pas ça— ce n'était pas ça du tout]. The problem, Gary adds, was that "no name, however beautiful and resonant, seemed worthy of what I wanted to accomplish for her" [aucun nom, aussi beau et retentissant fût-il, ne me paraissait à la hauteur de ce que j'aurais voulu accomplir pour elle] (1960a: 32).

Clearly, the first key to Gary's nonidentity can be found in this bottomless debt he had contracted to his mother. Nina had given up, for his sake, her career as an actress (it matters little that the career was a mediocre one). She had moved with him to Vilnius, then to Warsaw, and finally to Nice, working tirelessly and selflessly, sewing hats, running a hotel, selling jewelry, always for him, despite her declining health, her diabetes, her fatigue. . . . In impoverished circumstances but with endless wealth of imagination, Nina had striven to create the legend of Roman and, in return, Roman would strive throughout his life to redeem the suffering she had endured.

Is it really as simple as that? Might not this utterly self-sacrificial, despoiled Nina be, at least in part, a character invented by Romain Gary?

Of course we shall never know; all we have at our disposal is the son's testimony. But even if the real Nina were only half as altruistic as the legendary one, hers would still be an extreme, not to say pathological, case of maternal cannibalism.

"You'll be a great French writer, you'll be Victor Hugo, Chateaubriand, Gabriele d'Annunzio, ambassador of France," she whispered into his ear, night after night in Warsaw, to take their minds off the dire straits in which they found themselves. And Gary called this love? "*You'll be*"? Yes. Gary called this love; and indeed this would become his very definition of love. Nina implanted in his brain once and for all the singular conviction that *loving people means inventing them*. And the enchantment worked. They were no longer hungry; they were happy. Dreams were infinitely more powerful than, and preferable to, reality.

When at last they arrived in France — a decisive turning point, Nina's first major victory — Roman was fourteen years old. What language did he speak? His mother tongue, of course, which is to say a probably quite appalling mixture, by now, of Russian, Yiddish, and Polish, spiced with the French that was the dialect of their daydreaming *à deux*. In order to become a great French writer and ambassador, Roman would need to master the language of his new country to perfection. He set himself to the task, and succeeded.

One of his favorite jokes, in later life, was the one about the chameleon. You put it on blue cloth, it turns blue. You put it on red cloth, it turns red. You put it on green cloth, it turns green. You put it on Scotch plaid, it goes crazy. "Personally," Gary liked to say, after having run through the multiple national and cultural roots forming the Scotch plaid on which his mother had placed him, "if I wasn't made schizophrenic by this experience, it is thanks to literary creation" [si je n'ai pas été schizophréné par cette expérience, c'est grâce à la création littéraire] (1973a). This remains to be seen.

The years went by. Roman passed his baccalaureate at the lycée of Nice, moved to Paris to study law, published his first short stories. Occasionally he sent Nina other people's stories and told her he'd published them under a pseudonym because he didn't think them worthy of his gift. She rejoiced to see her predictions coming true. As of the early 1930s, having realized the serious threat that the rise of the German Nazi Party represented to Europe, Nina decided that the savior of France would be none other than her son, the Russian-Polish-Jewish bastard Roman Kacew. So Roman obediently joined the Air Force, trained as a bombing pilot, and readied himself for the worst. And when France collapsed in 1940, it was again Nina who—as of June 15, three days before de Gaulle—called for the forces of Free France to unite. And her Roman departed—first for Africa, then for England—and spent the next five years fighting with the Lorraine squadron, under the orders of Charles de Gaulle and Nina Kacew. Hang in there, said his mother's letters, month after month. Be strong, resist. We'll win out in the end. France will be victorious, thanks to you . . .

And it did not suffice to be a military hero: no, all of Nina's hopes had to be fulfilled simultaneously—time was running out, her health was failing, and Gary still had not proved to her he was Victor Hugo. So, as of 1942, he also undertook to write—quick, quick—a great novel. A powerful, pessimistic novel to which he gave the supremely sarcastic title of *Education européenne* (1956 [1944]).

As of this very first book, the structural traits and dominant themes that would characterize all of Gary's works are present. *Education européenne* is about the war—specifically, about the struggle of the Polish Resistance fighters against the occupying German forces in the winter of 1942–43. Yet despite the fact that as he was writing this story Gary himself was fighting the Germans, *Education européenne* is anything but a partisan, nationalistic, Manichaean novel. Indeed, the longer he fought, the more allergic Gary grew to everything that resembled heroism: his book is a sort of anti-Bildungsroman in the course of which Janek, the fourteen-year-old main character, reluctantly learns to kill. Each episode explores a different irony of the war, and cumulatively these ironies are tragic (some partisans turn out to be evil, or some Germans good; a man gives up his life for love of a woman who is betraying him with the enemy, and so forth). But the most painful contradiction of all, and the one destined to become a leitmotif of Gary's life and work, was the following: that art—and in particular the art of novel writing, the fact of storytelling per se—while it represents the only ray of hope amid all the horrors humanity inflicts upon itself, is also indissociable from, and even dependent on, these horrors.

All at once Janek was afraid. He was afraid of death. A German bullet, cold or hunger—and he would disappear before his soul could drink from this Grail. This human Grail that was created in massacre and misprision, with the sweat of the brow, with tears of blood, in great anguish of body and spirit, under the anger or the aloofness of the skies, by the incomparable toil of these human ants who had contrived in their brief span of aching life to engender beauty that should outlast milleniums.

[Et soudain Janek eut peur, il eut peur de la mort. Une balle allemande, le froid, la faim, et il disparaitrait avant d'avoir bu dans son ame le graal humain, crée dans la peste et dans la haine, dans les massacres et le mépris, à la sueur de leur front et au prix de leurs larmes de sang, dans la grande souffrance du corps et de l'esprit, dans la colère ou l'indifference du ciel, la labeur incomparable de ces fourmis humaines, qui ont su, en quelques années de vie miserable, créer de la beauté pour des millénaires.]   (1956 [1944]: 106)[2]

Gary was already profoundly divided against himself. He could not give up art—the idealistic search for meaning, beauty, and grandeur— without betraying his mother's hopes, which he held sacred; and yet he could not, as was Nina's wont, simply ignore reality. Thus he oscillated continually between idealism and cynicism, seeking at once to vindicate his mother and to get rid of her. And the method he hit upon to re- solve this dilemma was gently to sabotage his own work: to ensure that the illusions he spun were always slightly imperfect, that we could always glimpse the strings of the puppets he was manipulating. This art of self-sabotage affected each book taken individually, as well as his opus as a whole (especially in the beginning, when there was a strik- ing tendency for each of his excellent and popularly successful books to be followed immediately—and in effect attacked—by a verbose piece of grotesquery). "Men make up pretty stories and then they go off and die for them" [Les hommes se racontent de jolies histoires et puis ils se font tuer pour elles], says one of the Resistance fighters in *Educa- tion européenne* (1956 [1944]: 74).[3] At all costs, Gary wanted to prevent his stories from being too "pretty" and thus conducive to new acts of heroism.

2. Interestingly, in the revised 1960 English version of the novel, titled *Noth- ing Important Ever Dies*, this insight was watered down—whether by Gary himself or by his editor, we shall probably never know—into a banal opposition between art and evil. "He would disappear from this earth before he could receive from the hands and souls of men all the beauty that they had achieved against all odds . . . , answering the cruel challenge of death by creating beauty that shall outlast millenniums!" (1960b: 148; no translator mentioned).

3. Absent from the original version of the novel, this passage is turned around as

The year 1944 marked both the completion of his first novel and the liberation of France; Gary was lauded left and right; a British publisher printed an English translation of *Education européenne*, titled *Forest of Anger* (1944), and the French version was accepted by Calmann Lévy; Gary was Compagnon de la Libération, he had his arms full of laurels, and also — on one of his arms — a lovely British fiancée named Lesley Blanch. He rushed to Nice to lay all of these honors at Nina's feet . . . only to learn that she had been dead for more than two years. The 250 letters he had received since then had been written in advance and entrusted to one of her friends, with the understanding that she would continue mailing them to Romain one at a time, so that his courage should not falter.

Actually, this is not true. It is a moving story, and Gary was to go on telling it for the rest of his life, relishing the emotional response of his audience. The fact is that he received a telegram informing him of Nina's death in 1942, and the letters she wrote to him in the last months of her life — polyglot scribblings in a student's notebook — were never sent. Be this as it may, the unavoidable, unbearable, unedulcorable truth — the one Gary would never be able to change — was that Nina had died knowing nothing of his triumphs. From this point onward, he decided to occupy an absurd position, to exhaust himself in the performance of a literally impossible task: fulfilling the wishes of a dead person. Nina would haunt him all his life, living inside of him, judging him, giving him advice; she was, in his own words, his "inner witness" [témoin intérieur]. Others have called her his dybbuk.

When the war came to an end in 1945, Gary was decorated by de Gaulle himself with the Cross of the Liberation; he married Lesley Blanch; *Education européenne* received the prestigious Prix des Critiques and became an instant best-seller. Gary's sudden fame was impressive, but it was also acutely guilt provoking, for all his successes seemed to be based on misunderstandings. As far as his military medals went, Gary knew he was less deserving of them than his dead comrades: he was one of the five survivors among the original two hundred combatants of the Lorraine squadron — "one of the last coat-racks you could still hang a decoration on" [un des derniers porte-manteaux sur lesquels on pouvait

---

well in the later English version so that its message, rather than glancingly ironic, becomes banal: "Everything man believes in, and dies for, always ends up by becoming just one more little fairy-tale" (1960b: 57).

accrocher des décorations], as he put it (1973a). The person to whom he had dedicated his literary glory was also dead. As for his marriage, he had fallen in love with Lesley Blanch because she embodied his opposite: she was blonde and brilliant, British and bourgeoise. She, on the other hand, had fallen in love with him because he was . . . Russian! Blanch was a Slavophile, and though Gary did his best to convince her he was French—a great French writer and military hero—she would have none of it. She served him salted pickles in bed and made him drink strong tea through sugar cubes, and he had to admit that he loved these things. You are Russian, she told him, and what you write is part of the great Russian literary tradition, from Gogol to Tolstoy. Gary felt flattered, but uncomfortable. To complicate matters further, as he could not bear listening to his wife's French (which was fluent but imperfect), he insisted she teach him English. Before long, thanks to Lesley's pedagogy and to his own chameleonesque nature, he was as at home in this, his fourth, language as a native Anglophone. His identity had fissured a little more.

It would have been possible at this point, in 1945, for Romain Gary to settle down in Paris, play the role of feted author to the hilt, and live a relatively cushy Left-Bank-intellectual-and-artist's sort of life. Instead, turning his back on ego basking and on the sort of togetherness proffered him by the literary milieu—remembering also, perhaps, his mother's *other* prophecy, "you will be ambassador of France"—he entered the diplomatic service and took off, with his wife and his dreams, for Sofia. Then Berne. Then New York. La Paz. Los Angeles.

How could Gary have felt at ease on the terrace of Le Flore or La Coupole, next to Sartre and de Beauvoir? How could he have taken seriously the debates then raging in the auditorium of La Mutualité or in the pages of *Les Temps modernes*? He was not of the same cloth as the French intelligentsia, and he refused to embrace the convenient identity of "Resistance writer" the latter offered him. His origins were upheaval: the Russian Revolution, the devastation and atrocities of World War I, years of wandering, poverty, hunger. It was unthinkable for him to take refuge beneath reassuring labels, or to endorse the then-fashionable Marxist rhetoric. So he split.

Yet another split.

The diplomatic career, to which he would devote fifteen years (from 1946 to 1961), was damaging to Romain Gary in two ways. In the first place, it hurt his image: whereas the mysterious young author of *Education européenne* had been acceptable in the eyes of Paris's literary elite, the representative of de Gaulle's government would be systematically re-jected as "reactionary" and "rightist." Sartre, de Beauvoir, and Duras refused so much as to shake his hand. And although Gary feigned indif-ference, and repeatedly explained that his only political stance consisted of defending individual and human rights under all circumstances, he was profoundly affected by the Left's rejection of him.

The second way in which diplomacy harmed Gary was by forcing him to betray, regularly and with a smile, just those democratic and human-istic values he most cherished. As of his first post in Bulgaria, he was required to attend a formal dinner with the very men who, that same morning, had put to death his friend Petkov, leader of the Agrarian Party. Worse yet were the 1950s, which Gary spent in New York as France's spokesman to the United Nations, justifying his country's official views on colonialism, which were often violently at odds with his own.

If Gary chose to pursue his career as a diplomat nonetheless, it was perhaps because it was a perpetual reminder of his status as a nomad, an unbelonger. He *wanted* to be "mal dans sa peau" — he was *not* in his skin, and he needed not only to confirm but constantly to exacerbate this malaise, the friction between himself and the world, himself and the language he spoke, himself and . . . life. "I have problems with my skin because it isn't mine," Emile Ajar would write in *Pseudo*. "I want to be-come planetary" [J'ai des problèmes avec ma peau, parce que ce n'est pas la mienne. . . . Je me découvrais planétaire] (1976: 10–11). The fact of living abroad — and later, when he at last returned to settle down in Paris, the fact of traveling compulsively all over the globe — reassured him as to his basic nonidentity.

Conversely, he himself would become a source of friction: an irritat-ing, obstinate germ, a "foreign body in French literature" [corps étranger dans la littérature française] (as he once said) (1974a: 258): irreducible, unclassifiable, unassimilable. And as soon as there was a risk of integra-tion — as soon as the French establishment claimed him as one of their own — he repeated the gesture of flight. Just as the Prix des Critiques had sent him dashing off to Sofia, the Prix Goncourt he won in 1956 for his novel *Les Racines du ciel* [The roots of heaven] incited him to . . . write in English! You'll never catch up with me, never pin me down, I'll never be where/who/what you expect.

At the beginning of the 1960s, Gary's life underwent a profound trans-formation, partly because of *Promesse de l'aube*, the autobiographical work which was to freeze the legend of Nina once and for all, and partly because of Jean Seberg.

Gary was now serving as French consul in Los Angeles, frequenting the Hollywood scene with great assiduity. He began writing *Promesse* (held by many to be his masterpiece) in the course of a trip to Mexico with his wife. Lesley Blanch says (and her testimony is valuable) that by the time the book was finished, Gary's character had "changed": he had become, she says, "a different person. Not happier, but more arrogant. After that, he no longer owed anything to anyone" [quelqu'un d'autre. Pas plus heureux, mais plus arrogant. Apres ça, il ne devait plus rien à personne] (Blanch 1993).

If *Promise at Dawn* had this liberating effect on Gary, it was clearly because it allowed him to pay Nina back in kind: to do to her exactly what she had done to him, namely, turn her into a literary character. Page after heartwrenching page, Gary delivers his mother up to the public in all her excess, sometimes all her ridicule — just as, when he was little, she had so often humiliated him by boasting to neighbors about his glorious future. *Promise at Dawn* is an act of revenge, but it is also a monument: part of the son's debt to his mother had been repaid, and Gary must indeed have felt unburdened. In a sense, this book marks his second birth as a writer.

The novels of this period were also influenced by the presence in Gary's life of the American actress Jean Seberg. Born and raised in a Protestant family in Iowa, Seberg had been catapulted to fame by Otto Preminger and Jean-Luc Godard; she entered Gary's life in December 1959, when she was twenty and he forty-five. Unlike Lesley Blanch who, like Gary himself, spent her time traveling to exotic lands, laughing at human foibles, and writing best-sellers, Jean was pure, naive, and infinitely idealistic.

Gary abandoned Lesley's aristocratic, British-accented English to espouse Jean's American twang. He did his best to espouse her political convictions as well, but found this considerably more difficult. As a privileged white woman, Jean suffered from a sense of generalized guilt that incited her to take up the causes of all the underprivileged groups in American society, especially the Black Panther Party. This syndrome, while it did not inspire Gary's sympathy, inspired a number of characters for his novels — in particular the young Iowan heroine of *The Talent Scout* (1961), whose bad social conscience leads her to become the mistress of a grotesque, ferocious (but native) Latin American dictator. A few years later, the Black Panthers' shameless exploitation of Jean's money and energy, and their increasingly invasive presence in the living room of the French consul in Los Angeles, would serve as a backdrop for one of Gary's best books—perhaps one of the best books ever written on the subject of racial strife in America: *White Dog* (1971).

In France Gary was famous, but still, he felt, held in insufficiently high esteem. The type of literature he believed in had gone out of style. The war—in which, unlike Gary, the great majority of French writers had not fought, but which they had watched, helpless and incredulous, lending an occasional hand to the Resistance while pursuing their brilliant careers in the de-Semitized publishing world—had had a paralyzing effect on the French imagination. Not only had Auschwitz and Hiroshima been literally *unimaginable* events, but the role France had played in the war had been ambiguous to say the least: unlike any other Western European country, it was at once victim and perpetrator, humiliated and heroic, vanquished and victorious. And now it was bogged down in its colonial wars—first in Vietnam, then in Algeria—using methods of interrogation that many found distressingly reminiscent of those of the Nazis. There was a great deal of guilt in the air in France during the postwar decades, and what guilt tends to engender is not great art, but rather hypertrophied hope and rage, peremptory declarations and dangerous utopias.

The war, moreover, had annihilated the already tenuous faith of French writers in the virtue of plots and characters. Malraux, Sartre, and Camus had progressively abandoned the novel for theater or theory; Ionesco was blithely declaring people to be rhinoceroses, whereas Gary was still convinced that elephants were people; Beckett—though like Gary a bilingual writer in exile—was exploring a solipsistic Unnameable totally at odds with Gary's own; and as for Bataille's verbal glorification of death-imbued erotica, it amounted in Gary's eyes to "touche-pipi posthume" (1974a: 47).[4]

Pour Sganarelle (1965), a vibrant defense of the novel form and Gary's only attempt at literary theory, shows how very alone and bitter he was feeling at the time. The effort probably only worsened his aloneness and bitterness, for the book was a total flop. Gary's mother had promised him he'd be the star player in the game of French literature; now no one wanted to play anymore, and he was left standing with the ball. Both

---

4. *Touche-pipi* is the children's game equivalent to our "playing doctor."

"French" and "literature" had turned out to be something very different from the enchanted castles Nina had described to him in Warsaw. This hilarious passage on Sartre, from *Pour Sganarelle*, is an illustration of Gary's now intense ambivalence toward the two:

I love Sartre almost physically: I like to think of him in his era, the one in which he was born, dressing gown, nightcap, writing plume and candle, scratching away, while his servant-mistress screeches about his soup getting cold or his debt collector being at the door. Like Malraux's (very nineteenth century), Sartre's physique is not modern; it is redolent of Diderot, Descartes, the Encyclopedia, castles, humanism. I see him leaving the eighteenth for the seventeenth—the seventeenth century, I mean—to give his lesson in Rhetorics to the young de Gaulle, and finishing his existence as castle librarian, writing his treatise on Metempsychosis and occasionally galloping down the hall after a maid who defends herself with a broom. This is the grand tradition. I feel the same tender affection for him as for the physique of de Gaulle, and for the same reasons: my Francophilia is nourished by these medallion profiles on the covers of the Garnier Classics. All they are lacking is the wigs. This is France, the great, the traditional France—my how beautiful, my how permanent, my how still-there it is, and how my Cossack's soul rejoices to be allowed in, to sniff around and wag its tail and get a piece of the patrimony: there's real cultural treasure stored up here, real History, and it feels so good, so unspeakably good to be *chez soi*, to have learned about one's spiritual home at school and then be able to enter it on tiptoe, hat in hand, ass in air, and gaze at the family portraits, our ancestors the Gaulois—it's so good! You're accepted, allowed to join in, you can yell "French Algeria" and "Independent Algeria" with conviction—that, too, is French; that, too, is part of the French right to liberty—you have not been lied to, it really does exist, you can touch it, the family portraits are extraordinarily lifelike, those truly are de Gaulle's nose and ears, minus the wig and armor, that really is Sartre, Rameau's nephew, and—look, look!—they're not even anti-Semitic! What could be more beautiful?

[J'aime Sartre presque physiquement: je l'imagine souvent à son époque, celle qui l'a vu naître, robe de chambre, bonnet de nuit, plume d'oie et chandelle, en train de gratter, pendant que la servante maîtresse gueule que la soupe se refroidit ou que le créancier est venu réclamer ses écus. Comme celui de Malraux, très "dix-neuvième," ce n'est pas un physique moderne, ça vous sent son Diderot, son Descartes, l'Encyclopédie, le château, l'humanisme. Je le vois sortir du XVIIIe, pour se rendre au XVIIe—XVIIe siècle, je veux dire,—donner sa leçon de rhétorique au petit de Gaulle, et finissant sa vie bibliothécaire au château, écrivant son traité de Métempsycose, non sans pourchasser dans le couloir quelque soubrette qui se défendra à coups de balai. C'est de la grande tradition. J'ai pour lui la même douce affection que pour le physique de de Gaulle et pour les mêmes raisons: ma francophilie se nourrit de ces profils de médailles sur la couverture des classiques Garnier. Il ne leur manque que la perruque. C'est la France, la grande France traditionnelle, ah, que c'est beau, ah, que c'est permanent, ah, que c'est toujours là, ah, que mon âme de cosaque se réjouit d'être admise, de flairer, de remuer la queue, de jouir de son patrimoine: elle a acquis du bien, un trésor culturel, une Histoire, c'est si bon, si bon de se sentir chez soi, d'avoir appris son home spirituel en classe et de pouvoir ensuite y pénétrer sur la pointe des pieds, le chapeau à la main, le croupion en l'air, les portraits de famille, nos ancêtres les Gaulois, c'est si bon! Vous êtes accepté, autorisé à fournir, vous pouvez gueuler "Algérie française" et "Algérie indépendante" avec conviction — elle est aussi la France, elle a droit à la liberté française — on ne vous a pas menti, ça existe, on peut toucher, les portraits de famille ont une ressemblance extraordinaire, c'est tout à fait le nez et les oreilles de de Gaulle, la perruque et l'armure en moins, c'est tout à fait Sartre, le neveu de Rameau, et, voyez, ils ne sont même pas antisémites, que peut-il y avoir de plus beau?]   (1965: 101–2)

The theme of Jewishness, of which Gary had made relatively little in his novels up to this point, would increasingly haunt the books of his later years. A trip to Warsaw with Jean Seberg in 1966 was probably the turning point: in the middle of the crowd of tourists visiting the former ghetto, Gary fainted after having hallucinated the arm of a hidden Jew shaking its fist at him through a sewer grill. This incident inspired *La Danse de Gengis Cohn* (1966) [The dance of Genghis Cohn {1968a}], one of Gary's most dizzying literary achievements.

The novel begins as an allegory in the tradition of Gogol: the narrator Genghis Cohn, during his lifetime a Jewish comedian in Berlin, then Warsaw, was assassinated at Auschwitz. He has taken up residence for the past two decades in the mind of his German murderer (now a police commissioner) by the name of Schatz. The situation, if bizarre, is nevertheless recognizable: it is that of the dybbuk. Cohn torments Schatz by speaking through his mouth, or materializing suddenly in front of him at the most inappropriate moments. Gradually, however, identities begin to shift and merge, the protagonists apparently switch roles and at times it seems as if the Nazi were haunting the Jew, as if Schatz had brazenly taken up lodgings in poor Cohn's head.

Then, precisely halfway through the book, we come upon this passage worthy of Raymond Queneau: "Schatz grabs me by the arm. 'Let go of me, you idiot. Pork is forbidden us.' 'Cohn, this is no time to squabble. There's a guy out there who's trying to get rid of us.' 'What guy? Where?' 'We can't see him. *We're inside*'" [Schatz s'accroche à mon bras. — Lâchez-moi, imbécile. Le cochon nous est défendu. — Cohn, ce n'est pas le moment de nous disputer. Il y a là un type qui essaie de nous vider. — Quel type? Où ça? — Nous ne pouvons pas le voir. *Nous sommes dedans*] (1966: 147).

Obviously, the "guy" in question is the author of the novel we are in the process of reading. Gary's attempt to "get rid of" Schatz and Cohn reflects his hope, familiar to all novelists, of exorcising his demons by writing about them. Here, the characters are terrified at the prospect of their imminent liquidation; they start clutching onto each other for support. By the end of the book, the interweaving of the different narrative levels becomes inextricable and the story disintegrates entirely; we are left swimming in the muck of the writer's unconscious, amid corpses and masterpieces, barbed wire and Mozart, he-goats and Stradivarius violins — the flotsam and jetsam of Gary's two unreconcilable obsessions, art and suffering.

Social unrest and militancy were everywhere on the rise: race riots and political assassinations in the United States, and in France, the barricades of May 1968. French writers and intellectuals now began to sing the praises of Castro, Mao, and Malcolm X. It was fashionable to be revolutionary. But Gary, indefectible defender of the Philosophes on the one hand and *voyous* on the other, kept humming his tired old refrain: liberty, equality, fraternity, love, and laughter. He would probably have been listened to in the nineteenth century, and he might possibly make an impact on the twenty-first, but in the polemical decades in which he had the misfortune to be writing, his voice had a distinctly anachronistic ring. Just as in the 1950s he had refused to tout Russia as "the country of the Revolution" (where, at the price of a few little gulags today, tomorrow's "free man" was being forged), in the 1960s he shied away from facile celebrations of Black Power, Che Guevara, and the Little Red Book. While Sartre was cutely getting himself arrested for selling the Maoist rag *La Cause du peuple*, Gary satirized China's sickening cultural revolution in *La Tête coupable*. Thanks, perhaps, to his years at the United Nations, which had stripped him of his last illusions, he was pitilessly lucid in describing what happens when the oppressed and humiliated suddenly rise to power. Allergic to utopianism in all its forms, he was always prepared to believe the worst of his species.

In 1970, Gary lost his few remaining claims to identity. His marriage to Seberg fell apart in the course of a ghastly psychodrama involving Black Panthers, the FBI, drugs, and a dead baby. And in the midst of all this, Charles de Gaulle died. Gary found himself more alone than ever before. As usual, he wrote furiously to preserve his sanity—but now, for the first time, the madness that had always threatened him, the madness of inexistence, began to infect the writing itself. Having rejected all forms of social connection and having lost his important personal connections one after another, Gary's sense of his own existence was deeply disturbed. Might he not be the mere dream of some charlatan? The figment of some enchanter's imagination? The pure verbal invention of his mother?

Europa (1972) and *Les Enchanteurs* [The enchanters] (1973b) explore these questions with breathtaking literary brio. *Europa* in particular is a formal tour de force that makes the reader's head spin: all the artifices of literary technique are made visible, all the strings are ostentatiously pulled, and they end up tying knots in our imagination until we no longer know whom to believe, what to think, where we stand. Every character invents and dreams every other character; no narrative level can be taken as the one on which "events are really happening"; all the parts of the story reflect or echo all its other parts. The book's hero, Jean Danthès, is the French ambassador to Rome. Tortured by insomnia and hallucinations, he is struggling against "a tyrannical dependency . . . , the abominable sensation of being thought and even lived by someone else, in all likelihood his double, the one who did such a good job of hiding him, and whom he generally set up between himself and guilt" [tyrannique dépendance . . . , cette abominable sensation d'être pensé et même vécu par quelqu'un d'autre, selon toute vraisemblance son double, celui qui le cachait si bien et qu'il dressait entre lui-même et la culpabilité] (1972: 71).

The act of creation, Gary was becoming increasingly aware, meant playing with fire. ("Burn!") It was a Promethean gesture, a matter of life and death. Danthès's musings about imagination are no doubt analogous to Gary's own at the time: "An excess of facility in the immoderate use of the imagination eventually gave this admirable but sometimes dangerous faculty a strength that placed it in a situation of domination and even of autonomy, such that the instrument began, in turn, to manipulate the person who had forged it. This was all right as long as one remained aware of it — and on one's guard, so as not to allow oneself to be *invented*" [Un exces de facilité dans l'usage immodéré de l'imagination finnissait par conferer à cette admirable, mais parfois dangereuse faculté, une force qui tendait à la placer en situation et domination et comme d'autonomie, si bien que l'instrument se mettait à manipuler à son tour celui qui l'avait forgé. Ce n'était pas grave, à condition d'en prendre conscience, de s'en méfier, afin de ne pas se laisser *inventer*] (ibid.: 160).

Genghis Cohn, Europa, The Enchanters — all Gary's novels of this period are impressive for their sheer verbal energy, and for the complexity of their narrative structures. And yet, even in his most delirious passages, one senses that Gary was always a little too aware of what he was doing; a little too conscious (or self-conscious). He needed, somehow, to recover his lost innocence, *against* his own excess of intelligence; he could go no further in the crazy mirror game without becoming obscure or even opaque.

It was then that the entire situation shifted, and that, instead of continuing to explore the labyrinth of false appearances, Gary's work suddenly opened up to include his life. His novels could henceforth calm down and retrieve their linearity, for the locus of the complexity had been displaced. Instead of writing about a creator who manipulates characters who dream and invent one another, Gary *became*, in real life, this perverse God. He did this by dividing himself in two: the nameless body Romain Gary and the bodiless name Emile Ajar. At age fifty-nine, precisely Nina's age at her death, Gary hit upon this ingenious method not only of recovering his youth but of starting his career all over again. Engendered at the end of 1973, Ajar represents his third and final — pyrotechnical — birth as a writer.

Ajar means ember, and embers are not only what remains of a fire just before it goes out; they are also hotter than the flames themselves. Ajar gave Gary an unprecedented amount of literary energy: in all, writing *both* their works from this point onward, he would publish no fewer than twelve volumes of fiction in the final seven years of his life.

The miracle of Emile Ajar is that he exists, as a writer's voice, far more powerfully than does Romain Gary. Whereas it had always been possible instantly to recognize a sentence by Céline, Beckett, or Duras, Gary had written in such a huge number of styles — adopting, in his work as in his life, so many masks and costumes, churning out descriptions and dialogues, abrasive satire and lyrical philosophy with the same facility, in English and in French, spouting slang or precious rhetoric, assimilating and appropriating accents thanks to his chameleonic gifts—that it had never been possible to say of any sentence in particular, "That is pure Gary." Now, thanks to his literary virginity and his literal nonexistence, Ajar freed what Gary had always kept imprisoned, and the result was the invention of a language.

The first thing I have to tell you is that we lived in a seventh-floor walk-up and that for Madame Rosa, with all the pounds she had to lug around and only two legs, it was a real source of daily life. She reminded us about that every time she wasn't complaining about something else, because in addition she was Jewish. Her health wasn't so hot either and I can tell you right off the bat that she was one woman who deserved an elevator.

[La première chose que je peux vous dire c'est qu'on habitait au sixième à pied et que pour Madame Rosa, avec tous ces kilos qu'elle portait et seulement deux jambes, c'était une vraie source de vie quotidienne. . . . Elle nous le rappelait chaque fois qu'elle ne se plaignait pas d'autre part, car elle était également juive. Sa santé n'était pas bonne non plus et je peux vous dire aussi des le début que c'était une femme qui aurait merité un ascenseur.]   (1975: 9)

Of the hundreds of characters invented by Romain Gary—clowns and ambassadors, hippies and dictators, ecology activists and British aristocrats—none is as utterly believable as Madame Rosa, the heroine of La Vie devant soi [The life before us] (1975). This obese Jewish lady, a survivor of Auschwitz, looks after the children of prostitutes for a living and takes refuge, when she is frightened, in the basement hideout she calls her "Jewish hole." Throughout the novel, we see Madame Rosa only through the eyes of Momo, an illiterate Arab boy she has raised virtually since birth; and one of the joys of reading the book comes from the fact that the narrator is too young to grasp all the implications of what he sees and hears. Madame Rosa, at once admirable and pitiable, is the best symbol for humanity Gary ever created—"Madame Rosa, c'est moi," he could have declared, mimicking Flaubert. Like him, she is filled with tenderness and fear, ravaged by the hardships of her present life and the memories of her past—and, especially, aghast at her prospects for the future: living too long, watching helplessly as Time proceeds to skin her alive. The popular wisdom alluded to in the title ("you've got your whole life ahead of you") is in fact a curse.

Gary knew his life was now behind him. But, like one of his characters in *Les Têtes de Stéphanie*, "he still had a few good years ahead of him
and he wanted to have a spectacular end—a superb, bright red sunset . . .
An apotheosis" [Il avait encore quelques bonnes années devant lui et il
voulait les finir en beauté: un coucher de soleil rouge vif, superbe . . . Une
apothéose] (1974b: 246).[5]

When Emile Ajar's spectacular success required that he take on some
sort of physical existence, Gary did not hesitate to call on his cousin's
son, Paul Pavlowitch. Paul agreed to embody the phantom author, and
Gary proceeded, in the manner of an expert ventriloquist, to dictate
everything he was to say and do. Worse than Nina with himself as a
child, he forced Paul into total passivity and obedience, forbidding him
the least improvisation in the role he was making up for him as he went
along. Might he, yet again, have been acting out a symbolic revenge
against his mother? Perhaps, but what was at stake by now was more
than that, and it gradually became more than he could handle.

In 1975, Ajar won the Prix Goncourt for *La Vie devant soi* and, shortly
afterwards, a journalist revealed his "true" identity: Ajar was "really"
Paul Pavlowitch, Romain Gary's nephew! Because of the family tie between them, and also because Pavlowitch stayed with Gary when he
came to Paris, the press suspected the old pro of having lent the neophyte
a hand, if not of having actually written the book. Apoplectic with
rage, Gary denied paternity of the novel. And, to put a halt to rumors,
he wrote a book entitled *Pseudo*—an absolute literary hapax, signed
Emile Ajar, in which "I," ostensibly Paul Pavlowitch, explains why "I"
resorted to using a pseudonym. In this confession of a madman, "I"
also mercilessly attacks his uncle the famous writer (nicknamed "Tonton
Macoute") as a pretentious has-been with an insatiable craving for fame.
The book achieved its purpose of dissuading journalists from believing
that Gary and Ajar were the same person. They bowed to the obvious: it
was impossible.

And they were right—it *was* impossible. Gary was now residing in the
impossible.

The network of lies he had created gradually began to tighten around
him. Ajar was a hybrid; a motherless, Frankensteinian monster who had

5. *Les Têtes de Stéphanie* (1974b) was a fat page-turner Gary published under the
pseudonym Shatan Bogat and then admitted to having written, to throw people off
the scent of Emile Ajar, whose first hit, *Gross-Calin*, appeared later the same year.

no choice but to turn against his maker. Like a new dybbuk, he began to inhabit and dominate Gary's personality, dictating his words and behavior, just as Gary was dictating those of Pavlowitch. Moreover, Gary had now cornered himself in the role of imposter, which he dreaded more than anything else. This is why, far from laughing at his brilliant prank or gloating over his fabulous sales figures, he sank more and more deeply into depression.

It had to stop.

In 1979, coming full circle, Gary returned in *Les Cerfs-volants* [The kites] (1980) to the themes he had explored thirty-five years earlier in *Education européenne*: World War II, Polish Resistance fighters, desperate love between two adolescents, the dubious redemptive powers of art . . . He dedicated the book "To Memory." Just as it came out, in September, Jean Seberg committed suicide.

Following this work, Gary stopped inventing. He spent the year 1980 revising several of his earlier books; he legally emancipated his son Diego (at seventeen, technically still a minor), and he penned an explanation of the Ajar hoax, *Vie et mort d'Emile Ajar* (1981), for publication after his death. Then he lowered the curtain.

The curtain down, the mystery remains. Who was Romain Gary? A Franco-Russian writer? Franco-Polish? Jewish? American? A world citizen, or, as he himself liked to claim, a "rue du Baciste"? No other novelist of this century succeeded as he did in getting "out of his skin," traveling to other times and places, becoming *everyone* thanks to the fact that he was no one, embracing the totality of human experience. No other novelist suffered such absolute distress, either, or such a crippling incapacity simply to be alive. Gary rejected all the security blankets that bring happiness to common mortals—and by "security blankets" I mean not only political, religious, or national appurtenances, but also life's most mundane activities. Everyday existence with its reassuring regularities— shopping, cooking, watching a child sleep, listening to music, chatting over tea, walking in the woods—was forbidden to him. He needed to remain constantly on edge, naked, flayed, exposed to the misery of the world.

He needed to take upon himself the sins of mankind.

Some of the similarities between Gary and Jesus Christ have already been mentioned. Jesus was an important figure in Gary's novels virtually from the beginning. In *Tulipe* (1970 [1946]), we find him evoked by a New York journalist named Grinberg in a sort of oral crossword puzzle. " 'The only beautiful spiritual figure in history. . . . It starts with a C. Six letters.' " Grinberg's friend Flaps makes wild guesses ranging from Chiang Kai-shek to Cagliostro. No, insists Grinberg. " 'A great and beautiful and pure human figure. It starts with a C. Six letters. There aren't two of them!' 'There ain't one of 'em,' " replies Flaps [— La seule belle figure spirituelle de l'histoire. . . . Ça commence par un C. Six lettres. . . . — Mais non. Une grande et belle et pure figure humaine. Ça commence par un C. Six lettres. Il n'y en a pas deux! — Il n'y en a pas une] (1970 [1946]: 74).

The Jewish comedian Genghis Cohn was also, explicitly, a reincarnation of Jesus Christ (and one cannot help but notice the phonetic resemblance between their initials). Here is the next-to-last paragraph of Gary's own English translation, *The Dance of Genghis Cohn*: "King of the Jews, in fact, once more. They've already crowned him, indeed, and he looks quite dazed under his thorns, but at least he is still there, Cohn the invincible, Cohn the immortal, *mazel tov*. He is bent double under the weight, but he can still perform, as long as there is an audience, and he obstinately follows his beloved [i.e., humanity], dragging his heavy cross on his back" [Il est d'une maigreur effrayante, il est couvert de plaies, il a un œil poché, il vacille, ils ont déjà eu le temps de le couronner et il a l'air completement ahuri, sous ses épines, qu'il n'essaie même plus d'enlever, mais enfin, il est toujours là, *mazltov*! Cohn l'increvable, l'immortel, il est plié en deux, mais il tient debout, et il suit obstinément Lily, en trainant sur l'épaule Son enorme Croix] (1968a: 243–44).

Outside his books, as well, Gary spoke increasingly highly of Jesus with every passing year. When feminism gained prominence in the 1970s, he took every opportunity to extol Christ's "feminine" qualities (tenderness, compassion, love) and to bemoan the fact that his message had not been heard. The world, said Gary, was increasingly ruled by the displays of destructive force which were not true "masculinity," but rather a sign of the fear of impotence, a horrifying *substitute* for virility (he saw atom bombs not as symbolic penises but as overblown dildos).

"I've always had a tremendous weakness for Jesus," Gary told his friend François Bondy in 1974. "If you take any interest at all in the myth of mankind, in that tiny particle of poetry which is the only difference between us and reptiles, it's impossible to avoid Jesus. . . . Do you realize that when Jesus came along, we finally had everything we needed to build a civilization? And even a Church? And what did we make of it?

A big polemical debate about the sacredness of sperm, about the birth-control pill, for heaven's sake!" [J'ai toujours eu un grand faible pour Jésus. Si tu t'intéresses au mythe de l'homme, à cette parcelle de poésie qui, seule, nous différencie du reptile, tu passes par Jésus. . . . Tu te rends compte qu'avec Jésus, enfin, il y avait tout ce qu'il fallait pour bâtir une civilisation et même un Eglise? Et qu'est-ce qu'on en a fait? Une polémique sur le caractère sacré du foutre, sur la pilule, c'est là qu'on va chercher] (1974a: 227).

Mathieu, the hero of *The Gasp* (1968b), comes as close as any of Gary's characters to professing the author's personal philosophy when he says, "Okay, . . . we are all shit eaters. . . . The point is you can't end the shit without putting an end to the *other* gasp [i.e., soul] qualities. . . . You put an end to the shit and there's no more *beauty*, Professor. No more icons. No more golden halos. No more love." To which the professor retorts, "You came all the way here to quote Jesus Christ to me?" [—C'est entendu, . . . nous sommes tous des bouffe-merde. . . . Mais il se trouve qu'on ne peut pas mettre fin à la merde en nous sans mettre fin au reste. . . . Vous mettez fin à la merde et c'en est fait aussi de la beauté, professeur. Plus d'icônes. Plus d'auréoles dorées. Plus d'amour. . . .— Vous avez fait tout ce chemin jusqu'ici pour me citer les paroles de l'Evangile?] (ibid.: 230).

In reality, of course, Jesus Christ said nothing whatsoever about eating shit. This might indeed have been why he didn't manage to save humanity: though he washed the feet of prostitutes and kissed lepers, he himself was too perfect. People cannot use perfection as their model; they know they can never live up to it. When one takes Gary's life and work as a whole, it is difficult to escape the impression that he did everything in his power to become a second Jesus, but an imperfect one this time, a Jesus with flagrant shortcomings—ambitious, fast-talking, skirt-chasing, hungry for success and material reward—so that we would no longer feel humiliated by the comparison. A Jesus who was *human*, not only because he suffered and bled, but because he ate and made love voraciously, befriended and betrayed, laughed and cried and tore his hair out, hurt himself and others, didn't give a damn, died of it. A fatherless, heavenless Jesus who had recognized as part of himself (and thus part of humanity) *both* God and the devil, both purity and filth, *both* Genghis Cohn the Jew (whose name evokes hordes of murderers) and Schatz the Nazi (whose name means darling). And to become this savior, Gary was willing—even anxious—to sacrifice himself. This is why, throughout his life, he frenetically went on broadening his horizons, gulping down other people's existences and integrating new dimensions, melting down and remolding the most wildly diverse experiences — until at last, a chameleon gone mad, succumbing to the temptation of playing God himself, he began to treat the real world like a novel and the people who loved him most like fictional characters. At last, aged sixty-six (twice Christ's age at his death), having orchestrated and attended his resurrection in advance, it only remained for him to die. His suicide can be construed as a self-crucifixion.

There are no simple lessons to be drawn from the life and work of Romain Gary, both of which were imperfect and magnificent. They definitely do not point toward an improvement of the human species — "I doubt we'll ever invent a new mankind," Gary once said (1973a); and yet, whatever the absurdity of hope, the crucial thing, in his eyes, was to preserve it. He lived obstinately at the heart of this contradiction and laid claim to it just *in order* to emphasize the irreducible complexity of human beings.

Yes, like you, Romain, all of us are hybrid bastards tossed onto this earth for no reason whatever, condemned to deal as best we can with the noble and the ignoble, the grace and disgrace that inhabit us.

A few months before he slipped the barrel of a .38-caliber Smith and Wesson into his mouth, Romain Gary said in a radio interview devoted to his final novel, *Les Cerfs-volants*: "I don't always manage to apply to my life the precepts of my books, but this whole book is the story of people who don't know how to despair" [Je n'arrive pas toujours à appliquer à ma vie les préceptes de mes livres, mais tout ce livre est l'histoire de gens qui ne savent pas désespérer] (1979).

REFERENCES

Blanch, Lesley
  1993 "Romain Gary: Une Vie, une oeuvre" (radio interview with Nancy Huston), France-Culture, December.
Gary, Romain
  1944 *Forest of Anger*, translated by Viola Gerard Garvin (London: Cresset).
  1956 [1944] *Education européenne* (Paris: Gallimard).

1960a *Promesse de l'aube* (Paris: Gallimard).

1960b *Nothing Important Ever Dies* (Paris: Gallimard).

1961 *The Talent Scout*, translated by John Markham Beach (New York: Harper).

1965 *Pour Sganarelle* (Paris: Gallimard).

1966 *La Danse de Gengis Cohn* (Paris: Gallimard).

1968a *The Dance of Genghis Cohn*, translated by Romain Gary with the assistance of Camilla Sykes (New York: World).

1968b *The Gasp* (New York: Putnam).

1970 [1946] *Tulipe* (Paris: Gallimard).

1971 *White Dog* (London: Cape).

1972 *Europa* (Paris: Gallimard).

1973a Radio interview with Patrice Dalbo, *La Vie entre les lignes*, France-Culture.

1973b *Les Enchanteurs* (Paris: Gallimard).

1974a *La Nuit sera calme* (Paris: Gallimard).

1974b *Les Têtes de Stéphanie* (Paris: Gallimard).

1975 *La Vie devant soi* (Paris: Gallimard).

1976 *Pseudo* (Paris: Mercure de France).

1979 Radio interview with Jacques Chancelle, *Radioscopie*, France-Culture.

1980 *Les Cerfs-volants* (Paris: Gallimard).

1981 *Vie et mort d'Emile Ajar* (Paris: Gallimard).

HENRY LOUIS GATES JR.

THE WELCOME TABLE: JAMES BALDWIN

IN EXILE

TAKE ONE YOUNG, EAGER, BLACK American journalist—that was me. One aging actress-singer/star—that was Josephine Baker. And one luminary of black letters—James Baldwin. I was twenty-two, a London-based correspondent for *Time* magazine, and I felt like a mortal invited to dine at his personal Mount Olympus.

My story, for which the magazine had sent me to France, was on "The Black Expatriate." One of my principal subjects was Baldwin. Another was Josephine Baker who, being a scenarist to her very heart, put a condition on her meeting with me. I was to arrange her reunion with Baldwin, whom she hadn't seen since leaving France many years before to live in Monte Carlo.

Well into her sixties in 1973, Josephine Baker still had a lean dancer's body. One expected that. She was planning a return to the stage, after all. What was most surprising was her skin, smooth and soft as a child's. The French had called her "cafe-au-lait," but that says nothing of the trans-lucency or the delicate shading of her face. Her makeup was limited to those kohl-rimmed eyes, elaborately lined and lashed, as if for the stage. She flirted continually with those eyes, telling her stories with almost as many facial expressions as words.

I do not know what she made of me, with my gold-rimmed cool-blue shades and my bodacious Afro, but I was received like a dignitary of a foreign land who might just be a long-lost son. And so we set off, in my rented Ford, bearing precious cargo from Monte Carlo to Saint Paul de Vence, Provence, chez Baldwin. In case I was in any danger of forgetting that a living legend was my passenger, her fans mobbed our car at regular intervals. Invariably, she responded with elaborate grace, playing partly the star who expects to be adored, partly the aging performer who is simply grateful to be recognized.

Baldwin made his home just outside the tiny ancient walled town of St. Paul de Vence, nestled in the alpine foothills that rise from the Mediterranean Sea. The air carries the smells of wild thyme, pine, and centuries-old olive trees. The light of the region, prized by painters and vacationers, at once intensifies and subdues colors, so that the terra cotta tile roofs of the buildings are by turns rosy pink, rust brown, or deep red.

His house—situated among shoulder-high rosemary hedges, grape arbors, acres of peach and almond orchards, and fields of wild asparagus and strawberries—was built in the eighteenth century and retained its original frescoed walls and rough-hewn beams. And yet he had made of it, somehow, his own Greenwich Village café. Always there were guests, a changing entourage of friends and hangers-on. Always there was drinking and conviviality. "I am *not* in paradise," he assured readers of the *Black Scholar* that year, 1973. "It rains down here too" (Baldwin 1973: 36). Maybe it did. But it seemed like paradise to me. And if the august company of Jo Baker and James Baldwin wasn't enough, Cecil Brown was a guest at St. Paul, as well: Cecil Brown, author of the campus cult classic, *The Life and Loves of Mister Jiveass Nigger,* and widely esteemed as one of the great black hopes of contemporary fiction.

The grape arbors sheltered tables, and it was under one such grape arbor, at one of the long harvest tables, that we dined. Perhaps there was no ambrosia, but several bottles of Cantenac Braun provided quite an adequate substitute. The line from the old gospel song, a line Baldwin had quoted toward the end of his then latest novel, inevitably suggested itself: *"I'm going to feast at the welcome table."* And we did.

I wondered why these famous expatriates had not communicated for so long, since St. Paul was not far from Monte Carlo. I wondered what the evening would reveal about them, and I wondered what my role in this drama would be. It was the first time Jo and Jimmy had seen each other in years; it would prove the last.

At that long welcome table under the arbor, the wine flowed, food was served and taken away, and James Baldwin and Josephine Baker traded stories, gossiped about everyone they knew and many people they didn't, and remembered their lives. Both had been hurt and disillusioned by the United States and had chosen to live in France. They never forgot, or forgave. At the table that long, warm night, they recollected the events that led to their decisions to leave their country of birth and the consequences of those decisions: the difficulty of living away from home and family, of always feeling apart in their chosen homes, the pleasure of choosing a new life, the possibilities of the untried. A sense of nostalgia pervaded the evening. For all their misgivings, they shared a sense, curiously, of being on the winning side of history.

And with nostalgia, anticipation. Both were preparing for a comeback. Baker would return to the stage in a month or so, and it was on stage that she would die. Baldwin, whose career had begun so brilliantly, was now struggling to regain his voice. The best was yet to come, we were given to understand.

People said Baldwin was ugly; he himself said so. But he was not ugly to me. There are, of course, faces that we cannot see simply as faces because they are so familiar that they have become icons to us, and Jimmy's visage was one of these. As I sat there, in a growing haze of awe and alcohol, studying his lined face, I realized that neither the Jimmy I had met — mischievous, alert, and impishly funny — nor even the Jimmy I might come to know could ever mean as much to me as James Baldwin, my own personal oracle, that gimlet-eyed figure who had stared at me out of a fuzzy dust jacket photograph when I was fourteen. For that was when I met Baldwin first and discovered that black people, too, wrote books. You see, that was *my* Baldwin. And it was strictly Private Property. No trespassing allowed.

I was attending an Episcopal church camp in eastern West Virginia, high in the Allegheny Mountains overlooking the South Branch of the Potomac River. It was August 1965, a month shy of my fifteenth birthday. This, I should say at the outset, was no ordinary church camp. Our themes that year were "Is God Dead?" and "Can you love two people at once?" (*Dr. Zhivago* was big that summer, and Episcopalians were never ones to let grass grow under their feet.) After a solid week of complete isolation, a delivery man, bringing milk and bread to the camp, told the head counselor that "all hell had broken loose in Los Angeles" and that the "colored people had gone crazy." Then he handed him a Sunday paper, which screamed the news that Negroes were rioting in some place called Watts.

I, for one, was bewildered. I didn't understand what a riot was. Were colored people being killed by white people, or were they killing white people? Watching myself being watched by the white campers — there were only three black kids among hundreds of campers — I experienced that strange combination of power and powerlessness that you feel when the actions of another black person affect your own life, simply because you both are black. For I knew that the actions of people I did not know had become my responsibility as surely as if the black folk in Watts had been my relatives in the village of Piedmont, just twenty or so miles away.

Sensing my mixture of pride and discomfiture, an Episcopal priest from New England handed me a book later that day. From the cover, the wide-spaced eyes of a black man transfixed me. *Notes of a Native Son,* the book was called, by one James Baldwin. Was this man the *author,* I wondered to myself, this man with a closely cropped "natural," brown skin, splayed nostrils, and wide lips, so very Negro, so comfortable to be so?

It was the first time I had heard a voice capture the terrible exhilaration and anxiety of being a person of African descent in this country. From the book's first few sentences, I was caught up thoroughly in the sensibility of another person—a black person. The book performed for me the Adamic function of naming the complex racial dynamic of the American cultural imagination. Coming from a tiny, segregated black community in a white village, I knew both that "black culture" had a texture, a logic of its own *and* that it was inextricable from "white culture." That was the paradox that Baldwin identified and negotiated, and that is why I say his prose shaped my identity as an Afro-American, as much by the questions he raised as by the answers he provided. If blackness was a labyrinth, Baldwin would be my cicerone, my Virgil, my guide. I could not put the book down.

I raced through this book, then others, filling my commonplace book with his marvelously long sentences, bristling with commas and qualifications. Of course, Baldwin's biblical cadences spoke to me with a special immediacy, for I, too, was to be a minister, having been "saved" in a small black evangelical church at the age of twelve. (From this fate as well, the Episcopalians—and, yes, James Baldwin—diverted me.) I devoured his books: first *Notes,* then *Nobody Knows My Name, The Fire Next Time,* and then *Another Country.* I began to imitate his style of writing, using dependent clauses whenever and wherever I could—much to my English teacher's chagrin. Consider: "And a really cohesive society, one of the attributes, perhaps, of what is taken to be a 'healthy' culture, has, generally, and I suspect, necessarily, a much lower level of tolerance for the maverick, the dissenter, the man who steals the fire, than have societies in which, the common ground of belief having all but vanished, each man, in awful and brutal isolation, is for himself, to flower or to perish." There are sixteen commas in that sentence; in my essays at school I was busy trying to cram as many commas into my sentences as I could—until Mrs. Iverson, my high school English teacher, forbade me to use them "unless absolutely necessary!"

Poring over his essays, I found that the oddest passages stirred my imagination. There were, for example, those moments of the most un-

Negro knowingness, a cosmopolitanism that moved me to awe, such as his observation that, unlike Americans, "Europeans have lived with the idea of status for a long time. A man can be as proud of being a good waiter as of being a good actor, and in neither case feel threatened. And this means that the actor and the waiter can have a freer and more genuinely friendly relationship in Europe than they are likely to have here. The waiter does not feel, with obscure resentment, that the actor has 'made it,' and the actor is not tormented by the fear that he may find himself, tomorrow, once again a waiter" (Baldwin 1961: 20). I remember the confident authority with which I explained this insight (uncredited, I suspect) about French and American waiters to a schoolmate. It hardly mattered that there were no waiters in Piedmont, W.V., unless you counted the Westvaco Club, which catered to the management of our one industry, a paper mill. It mattered less that there were no actors. How far was Paris, really? Baldwin wrote about an epiphany experienced before the cathedral in Chartres. In Piedmont, true enough, we had no such imposing monuments, but I struggled to collect his noble sentiments as I stood before our small, wooden church, in need though it was of a fresh coat of white paint.

Of course, I was not alone in my enthrallment and, much as it vexed me, Baldwin was *not* my private property. When he wrote *The Fire Next Time* in 1963, he was exalted as *the* voice of black America. The success of *Fire* led directly to a cover story in *Time* in May of 1963; soon he was spoken of as a contender for the Nobel Prize. ("Opportunity and duty are sometimes born together," Baldwin wrote later.) Perhaps not since Frederick Douglass a century earlier had one man been taken to embody the voice of "the Negro." By the early sixties, his authority seemed nearly unchallengeable. What did the Negro want? Ask James Baldwin.

The puzzle—as anyone who read him should have recognized—was that his arguments, richly nuanced and self-consciously ambivalent, were far too complex to serve straightforwardly political ends. Thus he would argue in *Nobody Knows My Name* that

the question of color, especially in this country, operates to hide the graver question of the self. That is precisely why what we like to call "the Negro problem" is so tenacious in American life, and so dangerous. But my own experience proves to me that the connection between American whites and blacks is far deeper and more passionate than any of us like to think. . . . The questions which one asks oneself begin, at last, to illuminate the world, and become one's key to the experience of others. One can only face in others what one can face in oneself. On this confrontation depends the measure of our wisdom and compassion. This energy is all that one finds in the rubble of vanished civilizations, and the only hope for ours.   (Ibid.: 12–13)

One reads a passage like this one with a certain double-take. By proclaiming that the color question conceals the graver questions of the self, Baldwin leads us to expect a transcendence of the contingencies of race, in the name of a deeper artistic or psychological truth. Instead, with an abrupt swerve, Baldwin returns us to them.

In America, the color of my skin had stood between myself and me; in Europe, that barrier was down. Nothing is more desirable than to be released from an affliction, but nothing is more frightening than to be divested of a crutch. It turned out that the question of who I was was not solved because I had removed myself from the social forces which menaced me — anyway, these forces had become interior, and I had dragged them across the ocean with me. The question of who I was had at last become a personal question, and the answer was to be found in me.

I think that there is always something frightening about this realization. I know it frightened me.   (Ibid.: 11)

Again, these words are easily misread. The day had passed when a serious novelist could, as had Thomas Mann at thirty-seven, compose his *Betrachtungen eines Unpolitischen.* Baldwin proposes not that politics is merely a projection of private neuroses, but that our private neuroses are shaped by quite public ones. The retreat to subjectivity, the "graver questions of the self," would lead not to an escape from the racial drama, but — and this was the alarming prospect Baldwin wanted to announce — a rediscovery of it. That traditional liberal dream of a nonracial self, unconstrained by epidermal contingencies, was hopefully entertained and, for him at least, reluctantly dismissed. "There are," he observed, "few things on earth more attractive than the idea of the unspeakable liberty which is allowed the unredeemed. When, beneath the black mask, a human being begins to make himself felt one cannot escape a certain awful wonder as to what kind of human being it is. What one's imagination makes of other people is dictated, of course, by the laws of one's own personality and it is one of the ironies of black-white relations that, by means of what the white man imagines the black man to be, the black man is enabled to know who the white man is" (Baldwin 1985b: 452).

This is not a call for "racial understanding"; on the contrary, we understand each other all too well, for we have invented one another, derived our identities from the ghostly projections of our alter egos. If Baldwin had a central political argument it was that the destinies of black America and white were profoundly and irreversibly intertwined. Each created the other, each defined itself in relation to the other, and each could destroy the other.

For Baldwin, then, America's interracial drama "not only created a new black man, it has created a new white man, too." In that sense, he could argue, "the history of the American Negro problem is not merely shameful, it is also something of an achievement. For even when the worst has been said, it must also be added that the perpetual challenge posed by this problem was always, somehow, perpetually met" (ibid.: 532).

These were not words to speed along a cause. They did not mesh with the rhetoric of self-affirmation that liberation movements require. Yet couldn't his sense of the vagaries of identity serve the ends of a still broader, braver politics? As an intellectual, Baldwin was at his best when exploring his own equivocal sympathies and clashing allegiances. He was here to "bear witness," he insisted, not to be spokesman. And he was right to insist on the distinction. But who had time for such niceties? The spokesman role was assigned him willy-nilly.

The result was to complicate further his curious position as an Afro-American intellectual. On the populist Left, the then favored model of the oppositional spokesman was what Gramsci called the "organic intellectual," someone who participated in and was part of the community he would uplift. And yet Baldwin's basic conception of himself was formed by the familiar (and still well-entrenched) idea of the alienated artist or intellectual, whose advanced sensibility entailed his estrangement from the very people he would represent. Baldwin could dramatize the tension between these two models—he would do so in his fiction—but he was never to resolve it.

A spokesman must have a firm grasp on his role and an unambiguous message to articulate. Baldwin had neither, and when this was discovered a few years later, he was relieved of his duties, shunted into the position of elder, retired statesman. The irony is that he may never fully have recovered from this demotion from a status he had always disavowed.

And if I had any doubts about that demotion, I was set straight by my editor at *Time* once I returned to London. They were not pleased by my choice of principal subjects. Josephine Baker, I was told, was a period-piece, a quaint memory of the twenties and thirties. And as for Baldwin, well, wasn't he passé now? Hadn't he been for several years?

Baldwin, *passé*? In fact, the editor, holding a wet finger to the wind, was absolutely correct, and on some level I knew it. If Baldwin had once served as a shadow delegate for black America in the congress of culture, his term had expired. Besides, soldiers, not delegates, were what was wanted these days. "Pulling rank," Eldridge Cleaver wrote in his essay on Baldwin, "is a very dangerous business, especially when the troops have mutinied and the basis of one's authority, or rank, is devoid of that inter-dictive power and has become suspect" (Cleaver 1968: 104).

Baldwin, who once defined the cutting edge, was now a favorite tar-get for the *new* cutting edge. Anyone who was aware of the ferment in black America was familiar with the attacks. And nothing ages a young Turk faster than still younger Turks. Baldwin was "Joan of Arc of the cocktail party," according to the new star of the black arts movement, Amiri Baraka. His "spavined whine and plea" was "sickening beyond be-lief" (Jones 1966: 117). He was, according to a youthful Ishmael Reed, "a hustler who comes on like Job" (Leeming 1994: 304). Eldridge Cleaver, the Black Panther's Minister of Information, found in Baldwin's work "the most gruelling, agonizing, total hatred of the blacks, particularly of himself, and the most shameful, fanatical, fawning, sycophantic love of the whites that one can find in any black American writer of note in our time" (Cleaver 1968: 99). Above all, Baldwin's sexuality represented trea-son: "Many Negro homosexuals, acquiescing in this racial death-wish, are outraged because in their sickness they are unable to have a baby by a white man." Baldwin was thus engaged in "a despicable underground guerilla war, waged on paper, against black masculinity" (ibid.: 102). Young militants referred to him, unsmilingly, as Martin Luther Queen.

Baldwin was, of course, hardly a stranger to the sexual battlefield. "On every street corner," Baldwin would later recall of his early days in Greenwich Village, "I was called a faggot" (Baldwin 1985d: 684). What was different this time was a newly sexualized black nationalism that could stigmatize homosexuality as a capitulation to alien white norms and correspondingly accredit homophobia — a powerful means of polic-ing the sexual arena — as a progressive political act.

This new generation, so it seemed, was determined to define itself by everything Baldwin was *not*. By the late sixties, Baldwin-bashing was almost a rite of initiation. And yet Baldwin would not return fire, at least not in public. He responded with a pose of wounded passivity. If a new and newly militant generation sought to abandon him, Baldwin would not abandon them.

In the end, the shift of political climate forced Baldwin to simplify his rhetoric or else risk internal exile. As his old admirers saw it, Baldwin was now chasing, with unseemly alacrity, a new vanguard, one that esteemed rage, not compassion, as our noblest emotion. "It is not necessary for a black man to hate a white man, or to have particular feelings about him at all, in order to realize that he must kill him," he wrote in *No Name in the Street,* a book he started writing in 1967 but did not publish until 1972. "Yes, we have come, or are coming, to this, and there is no point in flinching before the prospect of this exceedingly cool species of fratricide" (Baldwin 1985b: 508). That year he told the *New York Times* of his belated realization that "our destinies are in our hands, black hands, and no one else's." A stirring if commonplace sentiment, this, which an earlier Baldwin would have been the first to see through.

How far we had come from the author of *The Fire Next Time,* who had forecast the rise of black power and yet was certain that "we, the black and the white, deeply need each other here if we are really to become a nation — if we are really, that is, to achieve our identity, our maturity, as men and women. To create one nation has proved to be a hideously difficult task; there is certainly no need now to create two, one black, and one white" (Baldwin 1962: 131). All such qualms were irrelevant now. In an offhand but calculated manner, Baldwin affected to dismiss his earlier positions: "I was, in some way, in those years, without entirely realizing it, the Great Black Hope of the Great White Father" (Baldwin 1985b: 498). Now he knew better.

In an impossible gambit, the author of *No Name in the Street* sought to reclaim his lost authority by signaling his willingness to be instructed by those who had inherited it: this was Baldwin and the new power generation. He borrowed the populist slogans of the day and returned them with a Baldwinian polish. "The powerless, by definition, can never be 'racists,'" he writes, "for they can never make the world pay for what they feel or fear except by the suicidal endeavor that makes them fanatics or revolutionaries, or both; whereas those in power can be urbane and charming and invite you to those homes which they know you will never own" (ibid.: 499). This sentiment in its unadorned rendering — that blacks cannot be racist — is now a familiar one, and often dismissed as an absurdity. But the key phrase here is "by definition," for this is not a new factual claim but a rhetorical move. The term "racism" is redefined to refer to systemic power relations, a social order in which one race is subordinated to another. (A parallel move is common in much feminist theory, where "patriarchy"—naming a social order to which Man and Woman have a fixed and opposed relation—contrasts with "sexism," which characterizes the particular acts of particular people.) It cannot, therefore, be dismissed as a factual error. And it does formulate a widely accepted truth: the asymmetries of power mean that not all racial insult is equal. (Not even a Florida jury is much concerned when a black captive calls his arresting officer a "cracker.")

Nonetheless, it is a grave political error, for black America needs allies more than it needs absolution. And the slogan—a definition masquerading as an insight—would all too quickly serve as blanket amnesty for our dankest suspicions and bigotries. It is a slogan Baldwin once would have repudiated, not for the sake of white America—for them, he would have argued, the display of black prejudice could only provide a reassuring confirmation of their own—but for the sake of black America. The Baldwin who knew that the fates of black and white America were inextricable also knew that if racism was to be deplored, it was to be deplored *tout court* and without exemption clauses for the oppressed. Wasn't it this conviction, above all, that explained his repudiation of Malcolm X?

I should be clear. Baldwin's reverence for Malcolm was real, but posthumous. In a conversation with the psychologist Kenneth Clarke, recorded a year and a half before the assassination, Baldwin ventured that by preaching black supremacy, "what [Malcolm] does is destroy a truth and invent a myth." Compared to King's appeal, Malcolm's was "much more sinister because it is much more effective. It is much more effective, because it is, after all, comparatively easy to invest a population with false morale by giving them a false sense of superiority, and it will always break down in a crisis. That is the history of Europe simply—it's one of the reasons that we are in this terrible place." But, he cautioned, the country "shouldn't be worried about the Muslim movement, that's not the problem. The problem is to eliminate the conditions which breed the Muslim movement." (Five years later, under contract with Columbia Pictures, Baldwin began the task of adapting Malcolm to the silver screen.)

That ethnic scapegoating was an unaffordable luxury had been another of Baldwin's lessons to us. "Georgia has the Negro," he once pithily wrote, slicing through thickets of rationalization, "and Harlem has the

Jew" (Baldwin 1985a: 72). We have seen where the failure of this vision has led: the well-nigh surreal spectacle of urban activists who would rather picket Korean grocery stores than crack houses, presumably on the assumption that sullen shopkeepers with their pricey tomatoes — not smily drug dealers and their discount glass vials — are the true threat to black dignity.

The sad truth is that as the sixties wore on, Baldwin, for all his efforts, would never be allowed to reclaim the cultural authority he once enjoyed. To give credit where credit is due, the media can usually tell the difference between a trend-maker and a trend-follower. What did the Negro *really* want? Ask Eldridge Cleaver.

I did. Several months after my visit to St. Paul de Vence, I returned to France to interview the exiled revolutionary. We had moved with the times from cosmopolitan expatriates to international fugitives. ("How do I know you're not a CIA agent?" he had demanded when we first talked.) This was not a soirée on the Riviera. It was an apartment on the Left Bank, where Eldridge and Kathleen lived, and where he put me up in his study for a couple of weeks; here, ostensibly, was the radical edge that Baldwin now affected to covet.

Between Cleaver and Baldwin, naturally, no love was lost. Eldridge complained to me that Baldwin was circulating a story about him impugning his manhood. He wanted me to know it was untrue. He also wanted me to know that he would soon be returning and would take up where he had left off. The talk was heady, navigating the dialectical turns of Fanon and Marx and Mao and Ché. (Jesus would be added a few months later.) His shelves were lined with all the revolutionary classics but also with W.E.B. Du Bois, Richard Wright, and, yes, James Baldwin. Young Baldwin may have warned of "the fire next time," but Cleaver, determined to learn from the failures of his revolutionary forebears, was busily designing the incendiary devices.

What came as a gradual revelation to me was that Cleaver really wanted to be a writer and that Baldwin was, perforce, his blueprint of what a black writer could be. He was at work, he told me, on a memoir, to be entitled *Over My Shoulder;* on a novel, to be called *Ahmad's Jacket.* But commitment, to be genuine, had to spill over the page. And in case I forgot our parlous position in the nether-zone of the law, there was that hijacker — armed, dangerous, and definitely deranged — who had insisted on staying with them, too. Eldridge, who had adopted me as a younger brother for the nonce, handed me a butcher's knife to keep under my pillow and made sure I propped a filing cabinet in front of the door before I went to sleep at night.

Times had changed all right. That, I suppose, was our problem. But Jimmy wanted to change with them, and that was his.

We lost his skepticism, his critical independence. Baldwin's belated public response to Cleaver's charges was all too symptomatic. Now, with slightly disingenuous forbearance, he would turn the other cheek and insist, in *No Name in the Street,* that he actually admired Cleaver's book. Cleaver's attack on him was explained away as a regrettable if naïve misunderstanding: the revolutionary had simply been misled by Baldwin's public reputation. Beyond that, he wrote,

> I also felt that I was confused in his mind with the unutterable debasement of the male—with all those faggots, punks, and sissies, the sight and sound of whom, in prison, must have made him vomit more than once. Well, I certainly hope I know more about myself, and the intention of my work than that, but I *am* an odd quantity. So is Eldridge, so are we all. It is a pity that we won't, probably, ever have the time to attempt to define once more the relationship of the odd and disreputable artist to the odd and disreputable revolutionary. . . . And I think we need each other, and have much to learn from each other, and, more than ever, now. (Baldwin 1985b: 539)

It was an exercise in perversely *willed* magnanimity, meant, no doubt, to assure us that he was with the program and to suggest, by its serenity, unruffled strength. Instead, it read as weakness, an ill-disguised appeasement by a creature whose day had come and gone.

Did he know what was happening to him? His essays give no clue, but then they wouldn't. Increasingly, they came to represent his official voice, the carefully crafted expression of the public intellectual, James Baldwin. His fiction became the refuge of his growing self-doubts. In 1968, he published *Tell Me How Long the Train's Been Gone.* Formally speaking, it was his least successful work. But in its protagonist, Leo Proudhammer, Baldwin created a perfectly Baldwinian alter-ego, a celebrated black artist who, in diction that matched that of Baldwin's essays, could express the quandaries that came increasingly to trouble his creator. "The day came," he reflects at one point, "when I wished to break my silence and found that I could not speak: the actor could no longer be distinguished from his role" (Baldwin 1968: 57). Thus did Baldwin, our elder statesman, who knew better than anyone how a mask could deform the face beneath, chafe beneath his own.

Called to speak before a civil rights rally, Proudhammer ruminates upon the contradictions of his position. "I did not want others to endure my estrangement, that was why I was on the platform; yet was it not, at the least, paradoxical that it was only my estrangement which had placed me there? . . . [I]t was our privilege, to say nothing of our hope, to attempt to make the world a human dwellingplace for us all; and yet—yet—was it not possible that the mighty gentlemen, my honorable and invaluable confreres, by being unable to imagine such a journey as my own, were leaving something of the utmost importance out of their aspirations?" (ibid.: 43).

These are not unpolitical reflections, but they are not the reflections of a politician. Contrast Leroi Jones's unflappable conviction, in an essay published in 1963: "A writer must have a point of view, or he cannot be a good writer. He must be standing somewhere in the world, or else he is not one of *us*, and his commentary then is of little value" (Jones 1966: 118). It was a carefully aimed arrow and it would pierce Baldwin's heart.

The threat of being deemed "not one of *us*" is a fearful thing. *Tell Me How Long* depicts a black artist's growing sense that (in a recurrent phrase) he no longer belongs to himself, that his public role may have depleted the rest of him. There is a constituency he must honor, a cause he must respect; when others protect him, it is not for who he is but what he stands for. To be sure, what Baldwin once termed "the burden of representation" is a common malady in Afro-American literature, but few have measured its costs—the price of that ticket to ride—as trenchantly as he. Baldwin risked the fate that Leo Proudhammer most feared: to be "a Jeremiah without convictions." Desperate to be "one of us," to be loved by us, Baldwin allowed himself to mouth a script that was not his own. The connoisseur of complexity tried to become an ideologue. And with the roaring void left by the murders of Malcolm X and Martin Luther King, he must have felt the obligation ever more strongly.

However erratic some of his later writing might have been, I believe he could still do anything he wanted with the English essay. The problem was that he no longer knew what he wanted . . . or even what we wanted from him. Meanwhile, a generation had arrived that didn't want anything from him—except, perhaps, that he lie down and die. And this, too, has been a consistent dynamic of race and representation in Afro-

America. If someone has anointed a black intellectual, rest assured that others are busily constructing his tumbrel.

In an essay he published in 1980, he reflected on his role as an elder statesman: "It is of the utmost importance, for example, that I, the elder, do not allow myself to be put on the defensive. The young, no matter how loud they get, have no real desire to humiliate their elders and, if and when they succeed in doing so, are lonely, crushed, and miserable, as only the young can be" (Baldwin 1985c: 674). The passage is eloquent, admirable . . . and utterly, utterly unpersuasive.

Baldwin and I stayed in touch, on and off, through the intervening years, often dining at the Ginger Man when he was in New York. Sometimes he would introduce me to his current lover or speak of his upcoming projects. But I did not return to St. Paul de Vence until shortly after his death in 1987, when my wife and I went to meet his brother, David.

St. Paul had changed remarkably in the twenty or so years since Baldwin settled there. The demand for vacation homes and rental property had claimed much of the farmland that once supported the city and supplied its needs. Luxury homes dotted the landscape on quarter-acre plots, and in the midst of this congestion stood Baldwin's ten acre oasis, the only undivided farm acreage left in St. Paul. Only, now the grape arbors were strung with electric lights.

There we had a reunion with Bernard Hassell, Jimmy's loving friend of so many decades, and met Lucien Happersberger, the friend to whom *Giovanni's Room* is dedicated. After a week of drinking and reminiscing, David Baldwin asked me just when I had met Jimmy for the first time. As I recounted the events of our visit in 1973, David's wide eyes grew wider. He rose from the table, went downstairs into Jimmy's study—where a wall of works by and about Henry James faces you as you enter—and emerged with a manuscript in hand. "This is for you," he said.

He handed me a play entitled "The Welcome Table," the last work Jimmy completed as he suffered through his final illness. The play was set in the Riviera, at a house much like his own, and among the principal characters were "Edith, an actress-singer/star: Creole, from New Orleans," "Daniel, ex-black Panther, fledgling playwright" with more than a passing resemblance to Cecil Brown, and "Peter Davis, Black American journalist." Peter Davis—who has come to interview a famous star and whose prodding questions lead to the play's revelations—was, I should say, a far better and more aggressive interviewer than I was, but of course Baldwin, being Baldwin, had transmuted the occasion into a searching drama of revelation and crisis. Reading it made me think of all the questions I had left unasked. It was and is a vain regret. Jimmy loved to talk and he loved language, but his answers only left me with more questions.

Narratives of decline have the appeal of simplicity, but Baldwin's career will not fit that mold. "Unless a writer is extremely old when he dies, in which case he has probably become a neglected institution, his death must always seem untimely," Baldwin wrote in 1961, giving us fair warning. "This is because a real writer is always shifting and changing and searching" (Baldwin 1961: 187). Reading his late essays, I see him embarking on a period of intellectual resurgence. I think he was finding his course, exploring the instability of all the categories that divide us. As he wrote in "Here Be Dragons," an essay published two years before his death and with which he chose to conclude *The Price of the Ticket*, his collected nonfiction: "[E]ach of us, helplessly and forever, contains the other—male in female, female in male, white in black, and black in white. We are a part of each other. Many of my countrymen appear to find this fact exceedingly inconvenient and even unfair, and so, very often, do I. But none of us can do anything about it" (Baldwin 1985d: 690). We needed to hear these words two decades ago. We need to hear them now.

Times change. An influential intellectual avant-garde in black Britain has resurrected Baldwin as a patron saint, and a new generation of readers has come to value just those qualities of ambivalence and equivocality, just that sense of the contingency of identity, that made him useless to the ideologues of liberation and anathema to so many black nationalists. Even his fiercest antagonists seem now to have welcomed him back to the fold. Like everyone else, I guess, we like our heroes dead.

REFERENCES

Baldwin, James
  1961 *Nobody Knows My Name* (New York: Dell).
  1962 *The Fire Next Time* (New York: Dell).
  1968 *Tell Me How Long the Train's Been Gone* (New York: Dial Press).
  1973 "Black Scholar Interviews James Baldwin," *Black Scholar* 5: 33–42.
  1985a [1955] *Notes of a Native Son,* in *The Price of the Ticket,* 127–46 (New York: St. Martin's Press).

1985b [1972] *No Name in the Street,* in *The Price of the Ticket,* 448–552 (New York: St. Martin's Press).

1985c [1980] "Notes on the House of Bondage," in *The Price of the Ticket,* 667–75 (New York: St. Martin's Press).

1985d "Freaks and the American Ideal of Manhood," reprinted as "Here Be Dragons," in *The Price of the Ticket,* 677–90 (New York: St. Martin's Press).

Cleaver, Eldridge

1968 *Soul on Ice* (New York: McGraw-Hill).

Jones, Leroi

1966 [1963] "Brief Reflections on Two Hot Shots," in *Home: Social Essays* (New York: William Morrow).

Leeming, David

1994 *James Baldwin* (New York: Knopf).

ZYGMUNT BAUMAN

ASSIMILATION INTO EXILE:

THE JEW AS A POLISH WRITER

TO BE IN EXILE means to be out of place; also, needing to be rather
elsewhere; also, not having that "elsewhere" where one would rather be.
Thus, exile is a place of compulsory confinement, but also an unreal
place, a place that is itself out of place in the order of things. Anything
may happen here, but nothing can be done here. In exile, uncertainty
meets freedom. Creation is the issue of that wedlock.

What makes the exile an unreal place is the daily effort to make it
real—that is, to cleanse it of all things that are out of place. In exile,
one is pressed to stop being in exile; either by moving elsewhere, or by
dissolving into the place, not being anymore out of it. The latter is the
pressure of assimilation. To be like anyone else. Not to be odd—anymore
to renounce one's nonidentity, that is, to renounce one's identity in the
name of a new identity, which would be nonidentity.

Not all assimilation is tragic, nor is all culturally creative. As a matter
of fact, the opposite seems to be the case—and ever more so, as throughout the Western world the crusading spirit of nationalism dissipates into
vague historical memory and do-it-yourself, and shop-supplied and personally assembled identities replace the etiological myths of common
fate, blood, soil, and collective missions. The daily life of assimilation is
dull and uninspiring. It is hardly a source of agony and certainly not a
stimulus to iconoclasm and intellectual adventurism. With the exit of the
tragedy and cruelty of politically inspired homogenization, the cultural
explosiveness of the assimilatory context is all but gone.

For the great majority of diasporic Jews, comfortably settled now in
the middle classes of their respective countries—local, yet not militantly
parochial—assimilation means no more than keeping up with the
Joneses. *Thou shalt not step out of line with thy neighbor* is assimilation's
sole commandment—one easy to observe, as Cynthia Ozick caustically
commented, by "rushing out to buy a flag to even up the street" (1984:
159). Assimilation has dissipated in a general conformity of public appearances peacefully cohabiting with a variety of privatized contents.
Overt conformity is all the easier to maintain, since diversity (particu-

larly as long as it remains unobtrusive) has been recognized as the foremost of personal virtues, a duty and a pride. Amid the cornucopia of class, generational, occupational, or just socially unattached, freely wandering lifestyles, it is difficult to set apart, as a special challenge, such forms of life as may be ethnically rooted and thus subject to other, more worrisome rules than the rest of the manifold dimensions of diversity. The memory of past uniqueness survives, if at all, in the older and fast-aging generation's occasional hiccups of shame and embarrassment. On the whole, it seems, attention is focused, undramatically, on the efforts of affluent Jewish residents of suburbia to "be like" the rest of the affluent residents of suburbia, the efforts of Jewish youth to absorb and replicate the up-to-date lifestyle of the young, of Jewish professionals to live and dress and decorate their offices in the way right and proper for professionals of their standing, of Jewish academics to act in accordance with the latest campus fashion.

The sting has been taken out of assimilation not because the Jews have performed what assimilation ostensibly pressed them to perform, but because the pressure is not there anymore—in this late modern, or postmodern, world of universal particularity; a world integrated through its diversity, a world little worried by difference and resigned to ambiguity.

The agony and the splendor of assimilation was a relatively brief, and relatively localized, episode in the history of the modern world. It encompassed a few generations spanning the stormy, short period needed for modern states to entrench themselves in their historically indispensable, yet transitory, nationalist forms. It also encompassed just a few generations thrown into the cauldron of seething nationalist passions; generations already cut off from their roots but yet unabsorbed by the new compound; generations forced to stretch themselves to the utmost, to build from scratch a domicile that others around them thought of as something one normally inherits. It is of such generations that Kafka spoke as four-legged animals (truly, they would not pass muster as humans by the standards then in force), whose hind legs had already lost touch with the ground while the forelegs sought a foothold in vain. The empty, extraterritorial space in which these "men without qualities" were suspended felt like an uncanny mixture of paradise and hell: the paradise of infinite chances, the hell of infinite inconclusiveness. For a few generations, the travelers—forced to take off, prohibited from landing—had no other abode. The agony and splendor of assimilation was confined to that brief flight through the world of nonidentity. Enticed,

blandished, or coerced to take to the air, the flyers—whether keen or reluctant—made easy prey for gamekeepers and poachers alike. But they
also enjoyed the brief privilege of that vast and sharp vision called, with
a touch of awe and jealousy, the "bird's eye view."

THE AFTERLIFE OF ASSIMILATION

Two events, both closely related to the outbreak, fifty years ago, of World
War II, are universally admitted to weigh heavily on contemporary Jewish identity.

The Holocaust has never moved far from the center of contemporary
Jewish consciousness. It is as if the collective memory of the wounded
nation followed Elie Wiesel's injunction: "Anyone who does not actively engage in remembering is an accomplice of the enemy" (1977:
16). There is wide (if incomplete) agreement that the Holocaust could
not but leave its imprint on the meaning of Judaism. For some contemporary theologians, like Richard Rubenstein (1966), the Holocaust
marked the failure of God, of the Jewish exilic tradition, of the centuries-
long customary strategies of Jewish survival, and thus opened up an
altogether new era in which Jews must learn to exist in the absence of
God and without the habitual and trusted grounds of secure identity. For
others, like Emil Fackenheim, the Holocaust has proved once and for all
that the flight from Jewish destiny is impossible. To embrace that destiny
has also become a Jewish *moral* duty. The Jews "are forbidden to despair
of the God of Israel, lest Judaism perish. . . . They are commanded to
survive as Jews, lest the Jewish people perish" (1970: 84). However strong
their dissent on this and other points, most writers agree that the Holocaust was a watershed not only in *Jewish* history. If anything, it brought
the Jews closer still to the ethical center of the world at large, as living
witnesses to the dark underside of modern civilization. Because of the
Holocaust, Jews are people with a new mission: they are the carriers of
the truth that humanity would otherwise be liable to forget at its moral
and physical peril.

Whether praised or censured, revered or berated, the State of Israel
and all its works provide the reference point for present-day Jewish
identity. Zionism "has become the underlying ideology of the diaspora Jews—an ironic success, since classical Zionism argues for *shlilat
hagolah*." For most Jews, "a sovereign Jewish state is a necessity for the

Jewish people as a whole" — even if not for them personally (Biale 1986: 190, 188). The State of Israel is now that fate to which Jewish identity has given itself (or was given away) as a hostage. Like all fate, it cares little about the feelings of its hostages. The best and most ethically sensitive among the latter, like Gershom Scholem, have been acutely aware of the severe test to which the creation of the state had put Jewish history. Having asked "whether or not Jewish history will be able to endure this entry into a concrete realm," they soon found that the state's "presumptive demand that its mundane interests should be identified with moral precepts" were "manifestly impossible" (Scholem 1971: 36; 1982 [1976]: 297). And yet like all fates, the State of Israel is unlikely to loosen its grip over the hostages. The hostages would not permit it to be broken, nor would they *be allowed* to break it if they tried.

By comparison with these two events, the consequences of the third — the disappearance of Central European Jewry — are somehow off-center. More often than not confined to commemorative rituals, memory of Central European Jewish history is seldom contemplated in terms of its cultural significance. And yet it is difficult to overestimate the profundity of change in the meaning of Jewishness, and in the role of Jews in contemporary culture, brought about by the tragic death and dissipation of Central European Jews. It is still to become fully evident and fully fathomed. It is perhaps too early yet for a complete assessment. The best one can do at the moment is to sketch some of the most salient areas in which the disappearance of Central European Jewry changed the context of Jewish existence and the Jewish political and cultural role.

Elsewhere (Baumann 1991), I have discussed the role played by, or assigned to, Central European Jewry (under the stereotypical name of the *Ostjude*) in the assimilatory processes in Western Europe. "Though both groups called themselves Jews, they none the less encountered each other within a framework of cultural stereotypes and ideological preconceptions," wrote Ritchie Robertson, summing up a century of uneasy coexistence (1988: 87). Even such an encounter was, however, limited. During the era of assimilation, Western European Jews — whether calling themselves "German," "French," or "English" — were preoccupied more with acceptance by their own respective national hosts than with other branches of the diaspora. Loyalties and cultural orientations followed the general European tendency of the nationalist age in enclosing themselves within the boundaries of nation-states. And yet the encounter with Eastern Jews could not be avoided altogether, however much their assimilated cousins in the West found it inconvenient and embarrassing. Successive waves of anti-Jewish persecution by the late-arriving and thus particularly virulent East European nationalisms, combined with deepening poverty in the undeveloped region of a rapidly modernizing Europe, lay behind a steady stream of Jewish immigration to more secure and prosperous parts of Europe. In Jack Wertheimer's apt assessment, "The newcomers threatened to revive an image of the Jew that natives had worked so hard to obliterate" (1987: 160).

The reaction of the affluent elites of the West to this threat was swift and often verging on hysterical. In France, for instance, the various strands of the Jewish establishment joined ranks with native anti-immigrationists in an effort to stem the influx (according to an official statement published by the Alliance Israélite Universelle) of "these contemptible people" who, like Bedouins, moved their tents about with complete indifference; while the Paris Comité de Bienfaisance spared no effort to repatriate the orientals back to where they belonged, or pass them over to less inhospitable places, but at any rate out of France (Marrus 1971: 160–70). In England, in March 1871, the *Jewish Chronicle* noted with satisfaction "a very material increase" in the number of poor Jewish immigrants "who have left this country to seek subsistence elsewhere" (Fishman 1975: 64–65). One of the first steps taken by the newly formed Jewish Board of Guardians was to allocate £50 (a huge sum at the time, and a deep hole in the Board's meager budget) to post notices all around the Russian pale discouraging immigration to England. As Eugene C. Black commented in his recent study, "After half a century of almost unbroken, if slow, success, Jewish leaders perceived their work endangered" by these distant cousins of "bizarre appearance and bad habits" (1988: 285). In November 1904, British Jewish leaders convened a European conference dedicated to moving the Jews escaping Russian persecution away from Western Europe. To the great relief of the gathering, a shipping company had been found which not only offered cheap fares and kosher food, but promised to sail directly to America without touching England on the way (ibid.: 292).

To Western Jews, it seemed that the final success of their own assimilation, just around the corner, was systematically thwarted if not prevented altogether by the influx of backward and uncivilized Jewish masses virtually untouched by the "process of enlightenment" and still sunk in the "superstitions" whose memory the "more advanced" sections of Jewry tried hard to wash out. Indeed, as David Feldman has recently rediscovered, "some of the greatest efforts of Anglo-Jewish institutions were spent in preventing migrants from settling in Britain" (1989: 209). What was true of Britain was equally applicable to France or Germany (though in the last case all efforts were bound to remain inconclusive because of the *Drang nach Osten* tendency of the expansionist German state).

When finally breaking through the barricades erected by state powers with the eager help of their loyal Jewish subjects, the immigrants were subjected to a zealous "civilizing" drill. In practice, that meant a concentrated effort to instruct the newcomers in the ways of their new countries and in how to shed both the spiritual traditions and the visible behavioral symptoms of their past identities—to make them, in other words, English, French, or German, just like the elites of the established Jewish communities. It is in the context of that effort that the stereotype of the *Ostjude*, that virtual inner demon of Jewish assimilation, was born and derived its vitality. The stereotype served as a genuine storehouse for all those "shameful and disgracing" aspects of Jewish identity, all those best-forgotten attributes of the recent past, which the native nationalist elites had stamped as alien and alienating. The assimilation-induced *shame* of one's own unreformed identity was displaced as the *embarrassment* felt at the sight of the close kin's otherness. Ever-renewed embarrassment did not allow the shame to die out, but it deflected the most painful assimilatory pressures and indefinitely postponed the moment of truth. Despite the facts of the matter, one could go on believing that assimilatory diligence would have been rewarded in full if not for the influx of the "aliens" who put off the moment of completion. One could, in other words, go on trusting the sincerity of assimilatory promise and believing in its ultimate success.

The civilizing mission aimed at the East and Central European immigrants, and the phantom of the *Ostjude* that haunted Western Jewry's still insecure sense of achievement, were the twin sources of the continuous vigor of assimilatory efforts. The very existence of Central European Jewry added to the inherent inconclusiveness of assimilation, keeping assimilation on the agenda and stimulating the never-ending search for the "right strategy." It had decisively contributed to the emergence of "assimilation by other means"—among which socialism and Zionism enjoyed pride of place. For many an educated and assimilated Jew barred from prestigious positions and rejected by the native elites, joining the socialist movement was the shortest and most realistic way to the status of "man as such"; what the ultimate revolutionary goal of socialism promised in the distant future, the spirit and daily practice of the ostensibly nonnationalist and nondenominational movement delivered right away. As for Zionism, it was the improbability of an early fulfillment of the assimilatory project, in view of the sheer size of backward East European Jewry, which inspired the idea of a "Jewish national home" where the unassimilated sections of European Jewry could be shuffled away. According to David Biale, for Theodor Herzl the "problem" was the population of poor, mostly East European Jews; in Herzl's pre-Zionist phase, it was the poor who were expected to emigrate (Biale 1986: 132). With the poor and uneducated Jews out of reach and out of sight, the established West European Jewry (so it was hoped) would be able to enjoy the fruits of its assimilation, while at the same time performing its own civilizing mission among the residents of the distant "Jewish national home."

It seems that with the disappearance of a massive, "substandard" East European Jewry, many sources of the past assimilatory zeal, as well as of the urgency with which "alternative ways of assimilation" were sought, have now dried up. There is no reminder of the "shameful past" around, no cause for embarrassment. The fullness of assimilation is not subjected to a permanent and never-conclusive test. There is no reason now to look desperately for solutions to a problem that local, established, and orderly national societies cannot accommodate. Weaker than before is the stimulus for the Jewish intelligentsia to seek a revolutionary transformation of society, or to escape from the inhospitable "great society" into the alternatives offered by movements of dissent. And whatever the habitual rhetoric, the Jewish state must claim the attention and interest of diaspora Jewry on other grounds than that of a substitute solution to otherwise insoluble domestic problems. All in all, much of the inner fire of the assimilatory dream and practice has been, for the time being at least, extinguished.

Another profound effect of the extinction of East and Central European Jewry is a drastic change in the social structure of diaspora. The East European ghettos were the main—and seemingly inexhaustible—suppliers of the Jewish working class and the Jewish poor in general. Whatever the official versions, the influx of East European paupers confronted affluent West European communities with a class as much as a cultural problem. The established elites had to gain class domination as much as cultural hegemony over the immigrants. And the immigrants were resisted both as conveyors of alien, incomprehensible habits and customs and as class adversaries and exploiters. If, in the view of the elites, class conflict seemed to dissolve in the struggle for cultural domination, from the vantage point of the immigrant poor, cultural resistance was a weapon in the continuing and all-absorbing class resistance. For all practical purposes, the defense of indigenous Jewish tradition and the pursuit of class interests looked like two sides of the same coin. Hence the phenomenon of *Jewish socialism*, not to be confused with the sociologically distinct phenomenon of participation by Jews (mostly Jewish intelligentsia) in the socialist movements of the host nations. In the historical episode of Jewish socialism, loyalty to traditional Jewish culture was a breeding and battleground of class struggle, and class resistance against Jewish capitalists involved a defense of Jewish language, beliefs, and customs.

There was, we may say, a continuity between the growing rebellion of the poor against the rising class division and exploitation inside the Jewish community of arrival, and the interest of the Jewish poor in socialism, which offered a class-oriented interpretation of their misery, complete with a clear prescription for its relief. In a sense, the socialism of the Jewish poor was a struggle to redefine (not to abandon) the Jewish tradition in terms better attuned to the position of the Jewish masses amid an increasingly capitalist environment. This is how Aaron Lieberman, the first Jewish socialist who began his lifelong romance with socialism in Lithuania and later brought the good tidings to the Jewish poor of London and New York, defined his credo in 1875:

Socialism is not alien to us. The Community is our existence; the revolution— our tradition, the commune—the basis of our legislation as quite clearly indicated by the ordinances forbidding the sale of land, by those on the Jubilee and sabbatical years, on equal rights, fraternity, etc. Our ancient Jewish social structure—anarchy; the real link between us across the surface of the globe— internationalism. In the spirit of our people, the great prophets of our time, such as Marx and Lassalle, were educated and developed.   (Quoted in Frankel 1981: 33)

Similarly, Abraham Rosenberg, the president of the ILGWU, could not find a better way to express his feeling at the sight of the great walkout of the New York cloak makers in 1910 than to recall the scene which "must have taken place when the Jews were led out of Egypt" (quoted in Sorin 1985: 82). Gerald Sorin has recently estimated that over half of

American Jewish socialists "were consistently, unambiguously, and often assertively identifying as Jews. An additional 16% were imbued with a 'dual orientation'—with some degree of Jewish consciousness peacefully coexisting with the belief that Jews will gradually acculturate" (ibid.: 119).

Even when the logic of the socialist project to which they dedicated their lives led them to renounce all particularism and parochialism, including their national varieties, and assert instead the universality of human values and the homogeneity of the human species, they tended to construct their new "general human" identities by using thoroughly Jewish symbols, such as displaying the nonobservance of divisive rules as prescribed by Jewish religious authorities. Even in this negative way, their socialism was given shape and expression by the community in which they grew up and with which—if only by opposition—they identified.

Thus, paradoxically, Jewish socialism constituted another challenge to the dominant—bourgeois and educated—version of Jewish assimilation; it either rejected assimilation altogether, or promoted an alternative understanding of assimilatory strategy and purpose that was hardly acceptable to the Jewish elite. By the very fact of its opposition, Jewish socialism obliquely kept the assimilation drama on stage. It was another badge of Jewish distinctiveness. It drew even further away the fulfillment of the assimilatory dream and therefore, inadvertently, even further stimulated the assimilatory effort. With the traditional tributaries of Jewish socialism all but dried up, another powerful stimulus of the assimilatory drama ground to a halt.

The third and perhaps decisive blow to assimilatory zeal has been delivered by the dissipation of that unique social/political/cultural Central European setting which originally gave Jewish assimilation its romantic appeal and bore responsibility for its tragic course. East-Central Europe was a cauldron of conflicting nationalist pressures and demands. Facing the tasks typical of the "primitive accumulation of legitimacy," and unsure of their grounding and chance of survival, the old and new nationalisms of the area were particularly vicious and ruthless—all the more so because hardly any of their claims went uncontested. As the mutually contradictory national ambitions could not be placated simultaneously, and surrender to one of the many nationalist calls meant necessarily antagonizing all the others, groups located at the receiving end of conflicting claims (*all* conflicting claims at once), that is, the groups without prospective homelands of their own, found themselves in an unenviable position: they were doomed no matter what they did. If they tried, obligingly, to uproot themselves, they ended up in the void, as no other soil was willing to accept them. If they stayed rooted in their own tradition, they were classified as weeds overdue for extermination. Since no progress in acculturation was assessed as satisfactory, each generation felt as if it were starting its work from scratch, as if the road covered by its predecessors did not count and no lasting rights were ever to be earned. Above all, since even a tiny step toward an *approchement* with one of the competing national cultures meant antagonizing the rest, assimilation threatened to earn the Jews more enemies than friends.

This situation generated a great deal of human misery, yet simultaneously made the assimilatory episode into a period of unprecedented cultural creativity and spiritual discovery. East-Central European Jewry, which bore the brunt of that misery and offered most of that creativity, is no more (though this statement can at any moment be belied; one cannot forget the continuing copresence of great numbers of Jews, and of unsated, yet mutually incompatible nationalisms, frozen in their "pre-historic" stage on the vast expanses of the European part of the former Soviet Union). With the departure of East-Central European Jewry, Jewish assimilation lost much of its animus and drama.

In the West, where today most of the Jews live, the era of militant nationalisms, of modern states cultivating and deploying nationalist sentiments as instruments of sociopolitical control and integration, or cultural crusades and state-managed homogenizing pressures, is in all probability over. We are witnessing a double erosion of the powers and ambitions of the national state. There is, first, a pronounced tendency toward the transfer of state sovereignty to poorly coordinated supranational or international agencies, which by no stretch of the imagination can claim national sources of legitimation, and which do not need national loyalty as a guarantor of effective action. There is, second, a tendency to limit and undermine the power of the national state from below, through a growing scope of regional self-management, of ethnic and religious self-determination, and of cultural autonomy. What we are witnessing, in other words, is the progressive separation between nationhood and societal powers; a sort of *denationalization* of the state. Nationhood is fast shedding much of its past political significance, and is shifting from the area of political rule and control to a predominantly cultural function.

As the assimilatory pressures recede, so peters out the urge to assimilate. There are few rewards for the dissolution of communal identity, and too high a price to pay for the loss of an important and generally valued resource of self-construction. Homogeneity and cultural facelessness, as it were, are today decidedly out of fashion. Once particularity (and preferably, uniqueness) has become the only universally praised universal attribute of humans, all serious concern with assimilation acquires a curiously archaic flavor. It seems that in the postmodern atmosphere of the West the only place where assimilation can live is in historical memory. As Milton Himmelfarb has observed, Jewish distinctiveness, once disdained as "parochial," may now "go from pejorative to honorific. If that happens, it will be helped along by the spectacle of Jews who understood all the particularisms—black, Chicano, Welsh, Basque, Breton, Palestinian—except the Jewish" (1973: 62). The perpetual wanderers can now settle down—in a universal otherhood.

THE HAUNTED LANDS

Where once the Central European Jews lived, Jewish gravestones slowly disintegrate for lack of grieving descendants to tend them. The corpses beneath the gravestones have not truly been put to rest, however, in the haunted memories of the then-witnesses, now survivors.

From time to time, in a desperate yet vain attempt to exorcise the ghosts of murdered neighbors, great hearts repent for the sins of the silent and indifferent ones. Polish poet Jerzy Ficowski confesses that repentance will never be final in the haunted land:

> I'd wish to be silent
> But keeping silence, I lie
>
> I'd wish to walk
> But while walking, I trample

Czeslaw Milosz bemoans the guilt that, even if not earned, cannot be washed out:

> What will I tell him, I, a Jew of the New Testament,
> Waiting two thousand years for the second coming of Jesus?
> My broken body will deliver me to his sight,
> And will count me among the helpers of death:
> The Uncircumcised.
> (Milosz 1988: 65)

The crimes could be individual and private, but the guilt is collective and shared. The survivors are guilty, and their guilt is their survival. This is not a guilt that will be recognized in any human court of justice. But then moral conscience cannot be exonerated by human courts. In the words of another Pole, Wladyslaw Bartoszewski, only those who lost their lives can say that they have done everything they could.

No evidence of innocence will ever argue a guilty conscience away. The Polish-Jewish scholar Emanuel Ringelblum, writing in hiding shortly before his deportation to a death camp in April 1943, left a balanced picture of Polish reactions to the rounding up and mass murder of their Jewish neighbors:

The attitudes of the Poles to Jews were not uniform. . . . Polish fascism, embodied in an excrescent, bestial anti-Semitism, created conditions unfavorable to saving the Jews massively murdered by German, Ukrainian, Lithuanian and Latvian SS men. . . . Taking into account special conditions in Poland, we must admit that the acts of Polish intelligentsia, workers or peasants who do hide the Jews are exceptionally noble, loyal to the spirit of tolerance which permeated Polish history. (1988: 176–77)[1]

Each Jew who survived can recite a long list of Poles who helped him, often putting their own lives at risk. And each Jew who survived will never forget those countless unknown enemies whose hatred or greed made an act of heroism out of the helpers' human impulse. Those who died will never, of course, give us the count of weeping, joyful, or cold eyes that watched their last journey. On the other hand, all such counting, even if possible, would not help much. The stubborn fact cannot be wished away: a great nation, which for eight hundred years shared the glory and the misery of Polish history, was rounded up and murdered, and its death was not prevented. This means guilt. One may try to argue the guilt away; rational arguments can be advanced that the potential rescuers stood little chance of success, and stood a huge chance of add-

---

1. In a thorough, insightful, and carefully balanced analysis of the survival and transformation of "Jewish memory" in contemporary Poland, Iwona Irwin-Zarecka (1989: 166) admits the crucial role of the suppressed memory of Holocaust horrors: "The problem here might be that Poles were such close witnesses that they automatically interpret any general questions about the Holocaust as a challenge."

All translations from the Polish are mine.

ing their own lives to the millions that perished. But *rational* arguments cannot absolve a *moral* guilt.

"It is too late; this linen will never be washed clean," wrote Polish writer Andrzej Kusniewicz. And because it will never be washed clean, it is unlikely ever to be pulled out from the remote corner of the family wardrobe and aired in public. The suppressed memory of mass murder poisons the consciousness of the nation that witnessed it; the fact that this nation of silent witnesses did not contribute actively to its perpetration does not make the matter much easier. And because the subconscious knows that the guilt is there and will hardly ever go away, the consciousness rebels and vehemently seeks excuses. If only the victim could be blamed . . .

This seems to be the secret of the most spectacular of Holocaust survivals: anti-Semitism. It now lives, so to speak, without its traditional environment: it is truly out of its element. It has no new nourishment, no living experience to forage and fatten on. It is not alive, as a matter of fact. The hatred that outlived its objects is more like a rock. A solid rock, immovable and resistant to the sharpest of cutters. And suppressed guilt is its foundation. Gravestones remain of the Polish Jews; stony, *fossilized* anti-Semitism remains after eight hundred years of joint Polish-Jewish history.

How this joint history is retrospectively read depends on what one wants to find in it. From the perspective of the fossilized hatred, most visible in that history is a long record of Jewish treachery. In filmed interviews with witnesses of the Kielce pogrom, two persons remember the hostel run by the Jewish Committee in which the homeless remnants of the once lively Jewish community were housed. According to one, "These people were sad and frightened, somehow out of place, not intending to stay; they did not fit the landscape at all." The other saw more: "They were well off, well fed, well provided for. They got food parcels and money from America." The interviewees were asked to speak of the militiamen and the thousands of ordinary residents of the town who pursued dozens of Jews through the streets and beat them to death; instead, some spoke of the injustices they believed the Jews were guilty of committing: "They, the Jews, boasted: the streets belong to you, but the houses are ours. . . . No wonder people did not like them."

The memory of the millions of men, women, and children herded to their deaths under German occupation was not the only guilt that needed to be suppressed. Isaac Deutscher has pointed out more sinister reasons for renewed postwar anti-Semitism:

The grave of the Jewish middle class became the cradle of a new gentile middle class in eastern Europe . . . a *lumpenproletariat* which turned overnight into a *lumpenbourgeoisie*. The death certificates of the murdered Jews were their only valid trade licenses. . . . The only way in which the new "middle class" can save not so much its newly acquired wealth but its nerves and a pretense of respectability is by smoking out the surviving Jews.   (Deutscher 1968: 88–89)

Empty houses, shops, and workshops did not stay empty for long. When the few survivors among their past owners emerged from hiding or boarded westward trains from their Russian exile or refuge, they were met with eyes filled with fear and fear-fed hatred, lest they should claim their property and in doing so remind the new owners of moments they would prefer to forget.

Twisting history to blame the victim was not a particularly difficult task. Long Polish-Jewish cohabitation was pliable stuff, fit to be molded to suit many interpretations and to supply telling, cogent, convincing arguments for almost any thesis. The theses themselves changed over time. One that gradually became dominant among Poles in the twentieth century was that the Jews were an alien, hostile, and poisonous body in the emerging Polish national organism, threatening the health and the very existence of a precarious Polish national identity.

This sentiment, however, could hardly appear before "Polish national identity" acquired its modern shape, that is, took on a purpose calling for conscious political administration of social development, cultural crusades, and the forceful transformation of chaotic leftovers of past history into a designed order. As Alina Cala, a most perceptive student of Polish-Jewish shared history, points out:

The idea of a single nation state, and the programmes associated with it of assimilating national and ethnic minorities, was foreign to premodern Polish thought. If a nineteenth-century peasant were ever asked if Jews should assimilate or emigrate, he would have been surprised and unable to respond. For him they were part of the unchangeable landscape as God had first created it. A demand to change the existing order would have seemed revolutionary to him that is, contrary to God's will, a prelude of apocalypse. The Jews with their side-curls and kaftans were part of life as created by God, testimony to the Passion of Christ, something threatening and strange, but necessary and unalterable. (1986: 148)

It was modern Polish nationalism, with its program of cultural homogeneity and its struggle for a *Polish state* which was to become a *state of the Poles*, that delivered a decisive blow to the habitual and natural, God-ordained order of things and set the world in turmoil. The ambiguity of the new situation and the sudden disappearance of divine sanction was deeply upsetting and frustrating. "The frustrations caused by participation in these stormy changes were channelled in the direction of totalitarian utopias. One of them was anti-Semitism. . . . It is one of the paradoxes of history that anti-Semitism strengthened the role of the Jew (or rather his myth) as a determinant of Polish national consciousness. Whole social groups discovered their national allegiance as an offshoot of the feeling of separateness from the Jews" (ibid.: 149).

National identity offered an escape and a shelter against that threatening ambivalence of which the Jews had now become the prime example. Note that Russians or Germans, by far the more threatening enemy by any standard, came second to the Jews as a negative support of the budding Polish national identity. They were enemies all right but too *unambiguously* hostile for the purpose. Only the Jews were truly fit to exemplify in a clearly visible form "the other" of the national identity, that chaos against which national unity promised to defend. In no way were the Jews ambivalent before modernization took off. Jewish ambivalence, destined to serve as a focal point of nation forming processes, was itself a product of these processes. A crucial part of the *Kulturkampf* of the rising nation was the achievement of Polish cultural hegemony over the territory of the future nation-state, and thus the cultural conversion of ethnic minorities: this, first and foremost, meant the assimilation of Jews. Yet the assimilatory program was (and had to be) as ambiguous as the cultural map it aimed to homogenize; in its operation more ambivalence was generated than eliminated. Jews who stuck to their traditional ways were singled out as proof of the essential estrangement of Jews from the Poles and their national ambitions. The real ogres were, however, the Jews attracted by the indubitable splendors of Polish culture, those responding with goodwill and enthusiasm to the invitation to join. It was they who become Kafka's *odradeks*—mongrel creatures of unclassifiable identity, neither strangers nor "our own," eluding all straightforward assignment and by the same token discrediting in advance the order yet to be installed. The more successful their Polonization was, the more threatening was the resulting ambivalence. They dressed like Poles, behaved like Poles, spoke like Poles, lived like Poles; for all one knew, they could easily be mistaken for Poles. Hence their ambivalence was of the worst possible kind because it could escape discovery. Such ambivalence calls for constant vigilance. Vigilance against Jewish duplicity and slyness became the major weapon of the border defense of the Polish nation.

Though the pool of assimilating Jews keen to embrace Polish culture never dried up, it had become clear well before the Polish nation-state was created that, for the ever more conspicuously resented Jewish masses, assimilation was not a realistic prospect. Already toward the end of the nineteenth century alternative ways out of the ghetto began to be sought, debated, and tried. The distinctly modern forms of Jewish national identity grew out of the most popular of these alternatives: Jewish nationalism in the shape of several varieties of Zionism, and Jewish socialism in the shape of the Bund (with its program of guarding and developing Jewish cultural uniqueness in the context of a humane, socialist Polish state, tolerant of human differentiation). This political map survived through the twenty-one year period (1918–39) of Polish independence. During that period, relations between the Polish state and its large Jewish minority were tense and fraught with mutual acrimony. Jewish political elites attracted the suspicions of Polish nationalists by siding with other national minorities of the multiethnic state in their shared resistance to the monopolistic aspirations of the ethnically Polish political elite. (Jewish political leaders, in fact, initiated a sort of "united front" with the Ukrainians, Belorussians, and other non-Poles, hoping to force the government to observe the rights of minorities.) On the other hand, the rising Polish nationalism and anti-Semitic sentiments, aided and abetted by the authoritative explanations of the persisting economic depression, made it increasingly clear to the Jews that they were unwanted; their right of residence in the land where their ancestors had lived for centuries was now questioned.

In the last years of Polish independence, Poles constantly discussed but never introduced anti-Jewish legislation of the Nuremberg type, and the Polish foreign minister urged European governments to "solve the Jewish problem" by providing outlets and resources for a massive Jewish emigration from Poland. The Jew most feted by the Polish government was Zhabotynski, the leader of the revisionist branch of Zionism, who promised cooperation in organizing the exodus of the Polish Jews.

No wonder that by the time the war broke out many a Pole was sufficiently primed to think, or at least not to object to his neighbor saying, that "after the war we would have to erect Hitler a monument." Jan Tomasz Gross (1986) has suggested that if the Germans punished all assistance to the Jews in Poland much more severely than in any other occupied country, and if their threat proved effective in preventing massive resistance to the Holocaust, a large part of the explanation resides in the resentment that a majority of Poles felt toward the Jews and the resulting isolation of that resented population. The "righteous among the Poles" often felt as isolated and abandoned by their own society as the hunted Jews they saved.

The Germans were not the only invaders of Polish soil. The eastern lands of Poland, where most of the national minorities lived, were occupied in 1939 by Soviet forces. To the Poles, there was little difference between the two enemies. For the Jews, the difference was one between life and death. Horrified, the Poles watched the enthusiasm with which most Jews greeted the Red Army. In his well-balanced account of Polish-Jewish antagonisms, Aleksander Smolar writes:

Very many Jews greeted the Red Army with enthusiasm, because they did not treat Poland as their Fatherland; they were pushed out of it, as the way to get rid of the Jews became the main topic of public debate. . . . The Jews, communists and non-communists, educated and half-educated, as trustworthy people, entered the local administration and helped to organize Soviet power. Worse still, they assisted Soviet authorities in their chase of Polish army officers and members of the prewar Polish administration. (1986: 97)

This treachery was neither forgotten nor forgiven by the Poles. As if a textbook example of the self-fulfilling prophecy, the Jews behaved exactly as the Polish anti-Semites kept saying they would, and by saying it the anti-Semites prompted them to do so. After the war, the same situation repeated itself. Smolar notes:

[The Jews], grateful to the USSR for saving their lives, socially isolated, culturally uprooted, aware of the resentment or hostility of their environment but dreaming of equality, fraternity, and of giving a good lesson to the 'forces of reaction,' made an excellent material for the new power. Not to mention the committed communists of the old guard, among whom the percentage of Jews was very high. (Ibid.: 119)

Transformed by assimilatory pressures into the frightening and hateful symbol of ambivalence and threat to national existence, the Jews (and *particularly* the assimilating Jews, Jews eager to embrace Polish culture and Polish nationhood) were forcefully excluded from membership in the Polish national community and faced with choices that could only deepen their estrangement and erect new obstacles to mutual understanding. Acceptance predicated on assimilation proved contradictory. On both sides, the drama left a pungent aftertaste which made the "washing of dirty linen" all the more difficult. Suppressed and never faced in all their unpleasant truth, the memories fester and poison. There is more than enough food for the unhealed Jewish aggravation against this erstwhile homeland, and for the bizarre phenomenon of Polish anti-Semitism in the absence of Jews.

LANGUAGE AS SHELTER

Of Julian Tuwim, one of the most influential and innovative Polish poets of the twentieth century, another Polish Jew and formidable literary theorist and critic, Artur Sandauer, wrote: "Essentially, assimilation did not succeed; what succeeded was the poetry, born of that failed assimilation and of unhappy love for Poland. . . . As the other Poland refused to accept him, Polish language remained his true homeland" (1985a: 467–68).[2] The true homeland and the *only* homeland (as all true homelands are). Also, in no small measure, an unshared homeland, its landscape little known and still less understood by those who happened to be born into the "other Poland," closed to Tuwim, or by those who, put off by

2. Of himself, Sandauer writes (1985a): "Sandauer's life is a history of a Jew persecuted for his origin. As a writer, however, he is someone very (perhaps excessively?) Polish on account of his language. His purism betrays a neophyte." One can discern a self-portrait in Sandauer's fictional hero *Mieczyslaw* (an ultra-Polish Christian name) *Rosenzweig*—"a hero built of two halves hating each other." Caught between the equally unprepossessing alternatives (an inauthentic and bleached identity, or a self-hating and demonizing personality), Sandauer admits to being suspended in a state of "unstable balance," in which he "sees any choice as naiveté" (1985b: 526–29). At no stage of the checkered political history of postwar Poland did Sandauer quite fit the prevailing mood. Always an outsider, a debunker by nature, a pedantic, pungent, sullen, and quarrelsome critic, he succeeded in antagonizing all the otherwise warring camps of the Polish literary world in more or less equal measure.

the locks, never knocked on the door and thus did not need to seek sub-stitute shelters. In an unshared land, Tuwim's creative force could be let loose. The result was great poetry and a landscape which, though famil-iar, made many ill at ease. The landscape of Tuwim's homeland had been carved by assimilation: "Their look shapes us from inside, grafts itself upon us as a mistletoe, so that we can only see ourselves through their eyes." Together with the culture of the society he enters, an assimilating Jew also absorbs its myths, "including such myths as are hostile to him." So did Tuwim; in his poetic homeland, the war was waged against priggishness, yet the knight-errant was "seen through the prigs' eyes" (ibid.: 103, 107).

Original and unique as a poet and a stylist, Tuwim was nevertheless a specimen of a type. He was an artist called upon to join a nation fighting for its place in a world filled with nations, and to help develop a culture which could make such a place secure and honorable. He was also a Jew whose place *in the nation* was put in doubt at the moment when the place of *the nation* had been made secure by statehood.

In the age when modern nations were born, the Poles were not only deprived of the political instruments of national self-constitution but were divided between the realms of three foreign dynasties. However hard the core, the peripheries of such a nation must have been diluted and the boundaries unclear. Polish nationalists had to fight off not only the political pretenses of hostile and powerful states but also the cultural claims of rival, strong or weak, militant and ambitious nationalisms. Without a state of its own, Polish nationalism could rely only on the power of cultural proselytism. It needed as many allies as it could muster among the creators and distributors of culture. No one asked too many questions about the birth certificates of the writers and artists who treated the magnificence of Polish culture as their sacred cause. The cul-tural door of the nation-in-search-of-statehood remained ajar and the newcomers were welcome. (The door would be slammed later, but not before real border guards manned real political entries and exits.) The nation needed cultural strength to compensate for its political weakness. Whatever the cause, the invitation seemed—and was—unconditional.

It did attract an uncounted number of Jews seeking escape from the ghetto. Polishness meant to them, as to all others within the orbit of Polish cultural influence, the chance to share in a highly attractive cul-ture—but it also meant the liberation from a caste-like (or, rather, outcast) condition. Since, however, membership in Polish culture in the case of refugees from the ghetto was *acquired* and hence precarious, the Polishness of the Jews was easily distinguished by the exaltation: "An exaggerated care for the excellence of language, pedantic observance of all customs considered distinctly Polish, a cult of Polish literature and art, often a truly fanatical nationalism and chauvinism." This exaggeration followed (almost logically) from a situation in which the examiners' attentions never relaxed, testing never ceased, and there was no way of guessing whether one's performance, however spectacular, would be accepted as satisfactory (Hertz 1988: 164–66).[3] However understandable, Jewish zeal was nevertheless destined to be sooner or later interpreted as a sign of inborn tactlessness, arrogance, and pushiness.

Thus, paradoxically, the Polish excellence of the Jews carried the seeds of Polish *allo*-Semitism: though split into anti- and philo-Semite camps, the Poles in their majority agreed on the *otherness* of Jews. Whether because of their exceptional slyness or exceptional gifts, the Jews *were not quite like the Poles* and neither could nor should be treated as Poles.[4] The less that remained of the once highly visible peculiarity of the Jews, which locked them in their caste-like existence without any need of ideological or scientific formula, the more the repellency had to be theorized and made into the topic of public discourse and political initiative.

In the independent Polish state that came into existence after World War I, Polish nationalism lost (or, rather, discarded and disowned) its proselytizing zeal. The project of cultural conversion of non-Polish ethnic groups inhabiting the territory of the Polish state went on unabated, now assisted by administrative manipulation and political coercion—but only in relation to the larger national groupings whose main habitat remained outside the borders of the new Polish state;

3. Aleksander Hertz remembers a letter he received from a friend, decorated with the highest Polish distinction awarded for supreme military gallantry. The friend wrote: "I had to be courageous. Did I falter, it would be said that the Jew was a coward" (Hertz 1988: 166).

4. A striking example of the allo-Semitic view can be found in the *Diaries* of Witold Gombrowicz, hardly an anti-Semite: "When I hear from those people that the Jewish nation is like other nations, I feel like listening to Michelangelo insisting that he does not differ from the others." "Those who received the right to superiority have no right to equality." "History of that nation is a secret provocation, similar to the biography of all great men—a provocation of fate, inviting disasters that can help fulfill the mission of the chosen nation" (1957: 121).

groupings, in other words, that could raise their own reunification claims against Polish territorial possessions. Since the Jews could not possibly come forward with such a demand, their declarations of Polishness offered little political profit. For the Polish nationalists, and particularly for the rising Polish national intelligentsia, the three million Jews residing inside the Polish state constituted a tangible threat to Polish domination of cultural life: it was in the area of culture, through which the Jews were once called to enter the Polish nation, that a sizable part of the Jewish minority most spectacularly excelled. The emergent modern culture of Poland was full of converted and unconverted Jews. Coming from urban centers and boasting the best education Poland could offer, they easily assumed the role of cultural umpires to whom the native poets and writers, more often than not of rural if not of peasant extraction, looked for guidance and accolades. Expectedly, the growth of their importance in Polish cultural life went hand in hand with the increase in the intensity and spread of Polish anti-Semitism. Hence the "unique phenomenon: the most beloved writers became, as persons, the most hated" (Sandauer 1985a: 460). This incongruity profoundly affected both the Jews and their hosts. Because much of Polish culture was now the product of persons "tainted" with an alien, resented origin, culture and intellectualism as such became suspect; the nation did not trust its own artistic and literary culture, and such suspicion offered fertile soil for all sorts of anti-intellectual, obscurantist, and retrograde movements for which interwar Poland became notorious. For the Polish cultural creators of Jewish origin, on the other hand, this duality turned out to be something of an asset, on top of the usual artistic and philosophical stimuli inherent in the contradictions of the assimilatory process.

To quote Sandauer again, "to assimilate" means to "stay, defenseless, under the gaze of the others" and to accept without murmur the judgmental canons and the aesthetic criteria of others. In so doing, the "assimilating individual" must also "consent to his own ugliness" (ibid.: 468).[5] Jewishness was declared ugly, and so were all the so-called Jewish

---

5. Of the interwar life of the Jews assimilated into Polish culture, Efraim Kaganowski, a Jewish writer from Warsaw, left a few shuddering, perceptive sketches: "Cafe Ziemianska, where the avant-garde of the Polish-Jewish congregate. Writers, poets, artists come here—a curious family, which on every opportunity complains of the 'Jewish gathering.' They are not yet sure of their Polishness and suddenly notice that they are surrounded only by other Jews. This is why they feel so well

traits. One could do something (at least in theory) to escape the ugliness of Jewish religion by conversion, or of Jewish habits or manners of speaking by self-drill. There was nothing one could do about one's looks — and this heinous gift of the genes tended to emerge unscathed from no matter how many bucketsful of baptismal water. The Polish poet Antoni Slonimski, born to an already Christian father, inherited from his ancestors a distinctly Jewish face together with their passionate adoration of Polish culture; the second did not help him against the first. Like the others — the unconverted, those who openly flaunted their Jewish roots and those who tried to hide or deny them — Slonimski was disqualified because he was a Jew. The more racist Polish anti-Semitism became, the more unambiguously it operated.

All this left little ground for self-deceit. Anti-Semitism, and particularly the staunch refusal of cultural membership on noncultural grounds, became in effect a powerful antidote to the parochialism that always lurks at the end of the nationalist itinerary. As cultural creators, Jews of all shades of assimilation stood out for their power to see through and beyond parochial constraints. This quality antagonized the nationalists but it also made the cultural creators among Polish Jews the carriers of modern experience and the articulators of modern culture.

Treated as aliens by the Polish public, Polish-Jewish writers found their retreat and shelter in the Polish language. Here, they felt at home. As the home stood in the midst of a social desert, they lavished on it all their otherwise unspent emotions. The language benefited, though its benefactors did not. Most of the latter perished as Jews, and were only posthumously upgraded to the rank of Poles — in recognition of their martyrdom rather than of their creative lives. The few who survived easily recognized in postwar Poland the all-too-familiar atmosphere of surveillance and vigilant censorship. Now, to be sure, they were not charged with the crime of Jewishness. The accusation was rephrased and reworded to suit the changing circumstances. Sometimes they were re-

---

here. . . . It is hopeless in the narrow Jewish streets. But it is also gloomy in the affluent Jewish flats. And only late at night in a large Jewish bourgeois restaurant. . . . can you meet creatures from another world, whom you have never seen so far in any Jewish place. . . . But this Jewish nightlife does not intoxicate. On their way back home the night guests do not feel drunk. The Jewish eyes are fearful and vigilant. These men want to be crushed in the crowd so that they can stop feeling how lonely they are" (1958: 174–75).

sented simply as the carriers of an unspecified "alien spirit." At other times as "cosmopolitans." Or "Zionists." Or "Communists." Or "Russian helpers" (when it came to the account-settling with the Stalinist episode, the Jewish collaborators, as always, bore the brunt of responsibility shared with countless others, and were expected to engage in much louder breast-beating than anyone else; with much less effect, however, than anyone else).

After the last survivors of the Holocaust ran away from the survivals of anti-Semitism, no Jewish community, Jewish culture, or Jewish institutions of any importance remained on Polish soil. All the more remarkable is the towering presence of two blatantly and demonstratively Jewish, yet superbly Polish, writers: Adolf Rudnicki and Julian Stryjowski. Their language, originally a shelter, has become the temple of a nationwide cult. Their books are sold out the day they are published. Readers love them, and critics lavish praise on them. For whom do they write? Who reads them? What for?

ADOLF RUDNICKI, OR, POLES LIKE JEWS

Like so many other survivors, Rudnicki greeted the new socialist Poland with hope. In the mouth of the hero of one of his stories written shortly after the war, he put a bitter reproach addressed to a Jewish mother who complained about her son's refusal to leave the "land of the graveyards": "National, radical differences will find nothing to feed on—and for this reason, young people will not find them in themselves" (1957). He deleted these words from a later version; wiser by a few years of dashed hopes and frustrated expectations, he wrote instead:

This new breed was to be made of gold—and yet it is not made of gold. In those "first things" in spiritual matters, nature has the upper hand, and nature derides beautiful words. Nature did not allow itself to be evicted and made fools of those who imagined that she would surrender easily. The new breed was to be antichauvinistic, antiracist, rational, internationalist. It is not.

In view of such an experience, the question of self-identity becomes crucial. At the beginning, the answer is ambivalent, as are the situations of Rudnicki's literary characters whose conversations only thinly disguise the author's own agonized soul-searching. (Often several characters are needed to convey the author's torments in full, as no single character burdened with them all — illogical, perhaps inane, in their coexistence — would seem credible as a sane subject.) One, speaking in the first person, declares bluntly: "I always think of myself as a Pole; the rest is my complicated business. If Poland thinks otherwise, it is Her complicated business" (Rudnicki 1957: 68).

When the Warsaw ghetto burned, people in the street told each other: "This fire is in the ghetto," which sounded like "somewhere far away." They said, "It is in the ghetto," and recovered their calm. Detonations shook the earth and the streets, but not the people. These were the years of contempt. Smart and adroit German troops made the residents of Warsaw into hunchbacks — first some of them, the selected ones, the Jews, then a bit later the others. They made sure that turns were properly taken, that the others had had their share of laughs before they were told of their own humps.[6]

This was a contempt felt by a lackey proud of using a WC, for an "Eastern" creature who uses only a wooden shack, and by a lackey proud of shaving every day, for a creature who did not shave daily. . . . Since the war, I am in deadly fear of people too well dressed, too well washed, as this very fact cuts them off from the rest, prompts them to look down at the slightly less well dressed. I always see them as they enter their huge offices early in the morning, sit in front of their big diagrams, the products of their cold, dry, orderly nights, containing designs for destruction of millions of lesser humans, like you and me. . . . I am in deadly fear of excessive order, even of the sportsmen, whose exaggerated smartness — it always seems to me — cannot lead to any good.

The experience of being at the receiving end of contempt was staged, but it was shared. We all know now, or at least we could know if we wished, that for everyone there is an order, a standard of smartness, a measure of dressing that could make him into a hunchback. Is not culture about making the humps grow? Is not contempt, that license to snub and despise and kill, what culture is about? "Culture is a narrow, rotten plank thrown over a pool teeming with crocodiles, who will get in the end what they want. True, one always needs a task, one time it could

6. The hump is a well-established trope in Polish-Jewish literature. Perhaps the most famous example of its use is Julian Tuwim's poem of a hunchback imagining his suicide; he would buy a most beautiful necktie and hang himself with it. To no avail, though: "No one will say 'what a wondrous necktie' / Everybody'll comment 'what an awful hump.'"

be culture, some other time an anti-culture, but whether it is culture or anti-culture the pride is always the same — the pride, arrogance, conceit."

What Rudnicki has in mind is a culture arrogant, self-assertive, militant, aggressive, and intolerant. A culture sufficiently sure of itself to subordinate or kill; one that uses its splendors as a mask of oppression. Sooner or later, it may become a bait set to attract the crocodiles. Promise of safe passage is loud yet unreliable. The threat of disaster grows in strength alongside trust in the promise.

This is the wisdom the Jews learned earlier and more profoundly than their neighbors. They derived it first from the unhealed wound of rejected acculturation. Then, as if to remove the last trace of doubt, the truth of their wisdom was confirmed by the tragedy of the Holocaust — a tragedy that revealed the loneliness that centuries of shared life and suffering had not removed. This is the lesson hammered home by the work of Rudnicki — a legatee, warden, and messenger of that wisdom. It is perhaps because they feel that they need this wisdom or may well yet need it in the future, that young and not-so-young Poles avidly grasp each successive Rudnicki story. Or perhaps they do it, at least for the time being, only because they wish to learn more about these strange, incomprehensible people whom they agree to promote only posthumously to the rank of their compatriots.

JULIAN STRYJKOWSKI, OR THE DUTY TO REMEMBER

At the age of eighty-five, Julian Stryjkowski has no time to waste. He writes avidly, greedily, obsessively. In a span of four years, he recorded the stories of Moses, King David, Judah Maccabbee–in his own words, "the greatest prophet, the greatest king, and the greatest hero" in the tormented history of the Jews, these "people with a hump on their backs — not the wings of freedom, as in fairy tales, but rags of slavery" (1957: 194).

By his own admission, this Jewish writer, as a child, took refuge in the Polish language. With that language he fell in love. The depth of feelings did not help the suitor, though. In the new Polish secondary school in the new independent Poland, the headmaster asked children to name their nationality. Little Aaron Stark called himself a Jew. He explained his nationality, we imagine, in a pure, precise, and pleasing Polish. Yet he was expelled on the spot. "The boy was thrown out from his Paradise." The headmaster did not quite succeed, however: "The child found his refuge. The Word accepted him. The Word and the child remained faithful to each other forever after" (Stryjkowski 1987: 188). The Word offered shelter to the homeless. It has also proved his exile.

Replying to the inquiry on the "Meaning of Polishness," conducted by the Catholic literary journal *Znak*, Stryjkowski wrote: "When, as a Jewish child who spoke Yiddish only, I heard a Polish word, I was dazzled" (ibid.). The hero of *Voices from Darkness*, woven out of the author's childhood memories, explains what being dazzled meant. His sister Miriam, a teacher in a Polish school, speaks Yiddish with her parents and older brother, but she addresses her kid brother in Polish: "Little Aaron smiled and nodded. Did he, or did he not understand? The words sounded beautiful. Those he heard most often the child linked with glittering objects: with mirror, glasses, hanging candlestick" (1957: 266). When Aaron finally enters — not without a struggle — a Polish primary school, his teacher of Polish is Berta Apfelgrün. "One Jew teaches another Jew how to be a Pole," Aaron's uncle comments caustically, sadly — and truthfully (ibid.: 269).

The shtetl had its own dreams. Like all dreams, they were cut to the dreamer's measure. On a Saturday evening, in a rapidly darkening synagogue ("they lit the candles in the synagogue as late as they could; let Saturday last as long as possible amidst the Jews"), little Aaron listens to the quiet, low voice of the Rabbi. He does not understand the complexities, but he knows the Rabbi is telling the story of the Messiah. The Messiah rides into town on a white horse. And after that glorious moment, no one needs to study in the *kheder* anymore, nor does his mother need to freeze in her market stall. Bread grows on trees. The *Sabbath*, that most Jewish measure of happiness and beauty, is on the other side of the invisible walls of the ghetto. It moves massively to that side once the walls, poorly guarded on the outside, are repaired and kept solid by those who stay inside them. The Messiah pitches his tents in the priest's orchard. Melodic sounds of Polish words, those holes in the black fence, allow little Aaron to catch a glimpse of the eternal Sabbath.

Julian Stryjkowski did not just look through the hole. Enchanted by what he saw and propelled by the Jewish messianic impatience, he flew over the black fence into the astounding beauty of the Polish language. He has become a venerated master of Polish prose. His novels capture the shine, the clarity, the unique emotional tension, and the human warmth of the language in which he writes. The critics report the pleasure which grows and overwhelms them with every page of Stryjkowski's prose. His language, they say, is "pure like spring water" (1988: 67).

Stryjkowski came into the Polish language to celebrate the Jewish Sabbath. The same force brought him into the ranks of the clandestine Polish Communist Party. The messianic urge pointed clearly and unambiguously to the world of tolerance and forgiveness, of light and beauty, of holiness on earth, of the Sabbath seven days a week, which the Communists promised. Disenchantment came fast. At the same time, the news came that the nation that had dreamed of perpetual Sabbath faced the greatest threat of its history.

Cast by war into remote places in Soviet Central Asia, Stryjkowski began to write his first great Jewish epic, *Voices from Darkness* (published twelve years later) — and he has not stopped writing since. Stryjkowski writes of the dead for the sake of the living. The memory of the nation that disappeared must live in the memory of the nation that survived. Let the selfsame Polish language, which lured the dead with its splendor and yet proved a cage for many, become their permanent and secure shelter now that they are no more. Let them enter through this language the enchanted land they once lived in without being a part of.

In the shtetl of *Voices from Darkness* and *The Echo* (1988), life went in circles with melancholic monotony. It was as cyclical as that of the peasant. Peasant time is kept in motion by the annual rhythm of field work attuned to the succession of the natural seasons. Jewish time was calibrated by the alternation of the holy and the profane, by the repeated order of the Holy Calendar. As if to underline the cyclical nature and completeness of the holy order, each of the two novels confines its action to one year. In *Voices from Darkness*, it is a year between Aaron's two successive birthdays. In *The Echo*, the year runs between the endings of two successive school years. The holy and the secular merge, as the rhythm of human life mirrors the timeless replay of the holy cycle. This applies to the old and aging as much as to the young and growing. The second year differs from the first by being seen through eyes that have grown one year older. Like the preceding year, it is measured by the passage from New Year to the Day of Atonement, to Sukkoth, to Chanukkah, to Purim, to Passover. And, of course, both years are punctuated by the weekly spots of beauty, tranquility, and serenity: the Sabbaths. The quotidian draws meaning from waiting for the holy days.

In the course of both years, the community whose life rests on that timeless repetition fights for its survival. In the first year, the threat comes from Scharie. In the second, from Manes. Scharie is a rich property owner who has robbed two impoverished sisters-in-law of their inheritance. Manes is a twelve-year-old boy who, on the Day of Atonement, eats a ham sandwich in public. The community loses its fight against Scharie and rejoices in the defeat. It gains a gruesome victory over Manes (the boy hangs himself to escape the curse) and bewails it.

Modche Stark, little Aaron's older brother, who is with Manes's brother in Hungary when the disaster happens, leaves the community for good. For Palestine. Aaron will go instead to a Polish school, where at the celebration of his first promotion he will recite the poem: "Who are you? A little Pole. What is your sign? The White Eagle."

The hump made of the rags of serfdom: How to shake it off? As a Jew sharing the land of Poles? As a Jew leaving behind the land of Poles? As a Jew who pretends to be a Pole? Can one do it with the community? Outside the community? Against the community?

Visitor from Narbonne (1978) is a novel Stryjkowski dedicated to the fighters of the Warsaw ghetto. In that ghetto, the choices that the resident of Stryj spent two full years pondering without getting wiser were forced upon people in a flash. Instantly, it had become clear who was the enemy and who was the brother. Yet the choices were not clearer than before. Their condensation and urgency made their complexity all the more evident, and conclusions all the more difficult to reach.

In the novel, Eli Ibn Gaist arrives from his native Narbonne at a small Spanish town that is writhing in the clutches of the Inquisition. Young, confident, and proud of his wealth, ancestry, and the public respect in which he has bathed since childhood, Eli is ill-prepared for what he finds. Furtive glances, whispers, half-finished sentences, stealthy gaits, faces frozen into masks—all this is difficult enough to comprehend. Something else, however, is yet more bewildering. "In Narbonne, everything was clear and simple. Evil was evil, good was good. When touched by suffering, however, evil and goodness mix up, swirl." When told that sometimes evil ought to be covered up for the sake of good, Eli feels baffled and confused. "So the world is like this? This gives me no peace. . . . The worst is the first crack in the thought. It is like a blemish on the surface of a fruit which inside is already rotten" (1978: 279).

The cracks are, indeed, many. In the span of the few days which divide Eli's arrival from his heroic and grotesque, redeeming yet purposeless death, goodness is soiled by evil, evil dressed as mercy, so that in the end one can no longer tell where the boundary between them runs. Before he dies, Eli is confused. With his last breath, the meaning of his death escapes.

Another visitor, this time to the town of Stryj, the hometown of Aaron Stark, is Martin Heiber: a highly educated, big-town lawyer, spreading the Zionist gospel among the baffled and incredulous residents of the shtetl. Like Eli, he feels humiliated by the confusion and indecision of the ghetto, not very different from that of the barrio. Few listen to his appeals to courage and dignity; fewer still comprehend; no one agrees.

We live in fast flowing, but shallow times. In such water only small fish can live. Our Jewish life is like a stagnant puddle. If a carp happens to be there, it must die. It will suffocate. . . . I searched, tussled like fish on a sandy beach. I found nobody, nobody. Only minnows. On whom could I lean? On whom could I rest my faith? I wandered from town to town, looked people in the eyes. Emptiness everywhere. And I spoke of the Great Renewal!   (1957: 399)

What makes the shtetl routine repulsive and unbearable to Heiber is the stench of serfdom and its spiritual sediment: complacency. It is a slavery that has been sucked in, digested, woven into the bodies and souls of people who feel at home only in the ghetto. Consent to such a life is indignity. Nonconformity is the only way to spiritual regeneration. A powerful idea is needed. Yet more than an idea, powerful men are needed, men who can stand up and say no. What they say "no" to is less important.

To Heiber, one such man was Herzl. Since Herzl's death, Heiber has looked for another one capable, as Herzl had been, of waking the sleeping giant of the nation. What the cost of such determination might be, Heiber does not yet know. The century is still young and innocent, and so is Heiber's Zionism.

Old Tag, the hero of another Stryjkowski novel, *The Inn*, tells the following story which his grandfather allegedly heard from no lesser authority than the Holy Besht.

There is a huge mountain, and a big stone on the top of that mountain, and pure water flows from beneath. There is a soul on the other end of the world. That thirsty soul longs all its life for this source with its clean water. But the soul will never reach this source and will never quench its thirst. That will happen only when Messiah comes. The soul must wait till he comes. Then, it will be all the same for everybody. In the meantime, the heart may burst.   (1966: 89)

The source has not been reached yet. For all the suffering and its tragic end, the source seems not to be nearer now than it was all along. But the effort to reach it can and should be recorded, if only to know where it cannot be found. This, at least, is how Julian Stryjkowski remembers Aaron Stark's reasons for hiding in the shelter of the Polish Word.

Given such reasons, this was not just a hiding, and not merely a shelter. The refugees burdened the Word with all their unfulfilled hopes, promises received but not kept, and first and foremost with their dreams of a world of moral purity. They made the Word grow, expand, and rise to seldom-visited moral heights. If it is true that assimilation arrived from outside as a painful pressure, it is true as well that it was filled from inside by the ethical urge. It will thus forever be remembered as a folly, perhaps, but not a sin.

The refugees brought a gift to the hosts, and the gift will stay with them even if they are slow to acknowledge its reception. It is Polish science, literature, poetry, and art that gained most from the episode of assimilation.

REFERENCES

Bauman, Zygmunt
  1991 *Modernity and Ambivalence* (Ithaca, NY: Cornell University Press).
Biale, David
  1986 *Power and Powerlessness in Jewish History* (New York: Schocken).
Black, Eugene C.
  1988 *The Social Politics of Anglo-Jewry, 1880–1920* (Oxford: Blackwell).
Cala, Alina
  1986 "The Question of the Assimilation of Jews in the Polish Kingdom (1864–1897): An Interpretive Essay," in *Studies in Polish Jewry*, Polin, general editor Antony Polonsky (Oxford: Blackwell).
Deutscher, Isaac
  1968 *The Non-Jewish Jew and Other Essays* (London: Oxford University Press).
Fackenheim, Emil
  1970 *God's Presence in History: Jewish Affirmations and Philosophical Reflections* (New York: New York University Press).
Feldman, David
  1989 "Jews in London, 1880–1914," in *Patriotism: The Making and Unmaking of British National Identity*, edited by Raphael Samuel, 2: (New York: Routledge).

Fishman, William J.
  1975 *East End Jewish Radicals, 1875–1914* (London: Duckworth).
Frankel, Jonathan
  1981 *Prophecy and Politics: Socialism, Nationalism, and the Russian Jews, 1862–1917* (Cambridge: Cambridge University Press).
Gombrowicz, Witold
  1957 *Oziennik, 1953–1956* (Paris: Instytut Literacki).
Gross, Jan Tomasz
  1986 "Ten jest z ojczyzny mojej . . . ale go nie lubie" [He is of my country . . . but I don't like him], *Aneks* 41–42: 13–35.
Hertz, Aleksander
  1988 *Zydzi w kulturze polskiej* [Jews in Polish culture] (Warszawa: Wiez).
Himmelfarb, Milton
  1973 *The Jews of Modernity* (New York: Basic).
Irwin-Zarecka, Iwona
  1989 *Neutralizing Memory: The Jew in Contemporary Poland* (New Brunswick, NJ: Transaction).
Kaganowski, Efraim
  1958 *Warszawskie Opowiadania* [Warsaw stories] (Warszawa: Iskry).
Marrus, Michael R.
  1971 *The Politics of Assimilation: A Study of the French Jewish Community at the Time of the Dreyfus Affair* (Oxford: Clarendon).
Milosz, Czeslaw
  1988 "A Poor Christian Looks at the Ghetto" [Biedny chrzéscijanin patrzy na getto], in *The Collected Poems: 1931–1987*, translated by Czeslaw Milosz, 64–65 (New York: Viking).
Ozick, Cynthia
  1984 *Art and Ardor* (New York: Dutton).
Ringelblum, Emanuel
  1988 *Stosunki Polsko-Zydowskie w czasie drugiej wojny swiatowej* [Polish-Jewish relations during the Second World War] (Warszawa: Czytelnik).
Robertson, Ritchie
  1988 "Western Observers and Eastern Jews: Kafka, Buber, Franzos," *Modern Language Review* 83: 87–105.
Rubenstein, Richard
  1966 *After Auschwitz: Radical Theology and Contemporary Judaism* (New York: Bobbs-Merrill).
Rudnicki, Adolf
  1957 *Zywe i martwe morze* [Live sea, dead sea] (Warszawa: Czytelnik).
  1963 *Kupiec Lodzki* [Tradesman from Lodz] (Warszawa: Czytelnik).
  1967 "Regina, Regina Borkowska," in *Wspolne Zdjecie* [Joint picture], 156–207 (Warszawa: Wydawniczy).
  1988 *Sto Jeden* [One hundred and one], vol. 3 (Krakov: Wydawnic Literackie).

Sandauer, Artur

    1985a "O sytuacji pisarza polskiego pochodzenia zydowskiego w XX wieku" [On the situation of the Polish writer of Jewish origin in the twentieth century], in *Pisma Zebrane*, 3: (Warszawa: Czytelnik).

    1985b "O czlowieku ktory byl diablem" [On the man who was a devil], in *Pisma Zebrane*, 1: (Warszawa: Czytelnik).

Scholem, Gershom

    1971 *The Messianic Idea in Judaism* (London: Allen & Unwin).

    1982 [1976] *On Jews and Judaism in Crisis* (New York: Schocken).

Smolar, Aleksander

    1986 "Tabu i niewinnosc" [Taboo and innocence], *Aneks* 41–42:

Sorin, Gerald

    1985 *The Prophetic Minority: American Jewish Immigrant Radicals, 1880–1920* (Bloomington: Indiana University Press).

Stryjkowski, Julian

    1957 *Glosy w ciemnosci* [Voices from darkness] (Warszawa: Czytelnik).

    1966 *Austeria* [The inn] (Warszawa: Czytelnik).

    1971 Interview with J. Niecikowski, *Wspolczesnosc* 22: 3.

    1972 Interview with Zbigniev Taranienko, *Literatura* 35: 3.

    1978 *Przybysz z Narbony* [Visitor from Narbonne] (Warszawa: Czytelnik).

    1987 "Azyl," *Znak* 390–91.

    1988 *The Echo* (Warszawa: Czytelnik).

Wertheimer, Jack

    1987 *Unwelcome Strangers: East European Jews in Imperial Germany* (New York: Oxford University Press).

Wiesel, Elie

    1977 *Dimensions of the Holocaust* (Evanston, IL: Northwestern University Press).

TIBOR DESSEWFFY

STRANGERHOOD WITHOUT BOUNDARIES:

AN ESSAY IN THE SOCIOLOGY OF KNOWLEDGE

STRANGERHOOD MOVES ALL OF US, making us spit in anger or swallow in desire, but in any case urging us to act. This effect is not as obvious as it may seem. Why do the people of Balassagyarmat, a small town in Hungary, get excited if Muslims buy the run-down hostel next door? Why are the black players of visiting basketball teams welcomed in similar Hungarian towns? Let us first try to understand what makes the stranger so exciting for us moderns.

The first possible explanation would be the essential sameness of the stranger and the modern man, who rediscovers — or wishes to rediscover — himself in this metaphor. The result of a thousand years' reflection on the stranger is the recognition that in the "homelessness" of *Geworfenheit* we all become strangers. Instead of annihilating strangerhood we have turned it into general experience, making domesticated homelessness our home. The curiosity we feel toward the exoticism of the alien has turned into an astonishment over our own personalities split into irreconcilable roles. Even if these two sentiments merge deep in our souls, it is important to separate them theoretically, to distinguish the outer, wandering, physical, social stranger from the inner, introverted, psychological, anxious, alienated self. The distinction between these two types of strangerhood helps to clarify the border between them. Besides, the particular characteristics of one type also illuminate the hidden features of the other.

COMMUNITY AND STRANGERHOOD

Emigration, exile, migration, refugees, persecution, immigrants, personae non gratae: pictures on the covers of magazines, the modern representations of the ancient archetype of the stranger. The stranger, as Georg Simmel (1964) points out in his brilliant essay written at the turn of the century, is the other who arrived today and stays tomorrow.[1]

1. The history of the unidentified creature offers a storehouse of encounters with the stranger where the definition suggested above tends to lose its significance.

His presence is not dimmed by distance, we bump into him, we cannot help seeing him and cannot ignore his existence. He is neither the exotic native of faraway lands nor a bizarre nomad; for a Central European city dweller, an Eskimo or an Indian is not a stranger but a mythical figure. Likewise with the tourist, the traveler, and the wanderer, who give us a reassuring feeling of peace: because we are not forced to live with them, we are only temporarily disturbed by their presence. The stranger, by contrast, "stays on for tomorrow."

Simmel's definition of the stranger is basically geared to spatial movement, but I wish to extend it to other dimensions as well. Besides the forms of spatial foreignness, my examples cover a whole range of types of strangerhood in social, sexual, and cultural behavior patterns that carry the stigma of otherness. The stranger in any form embodies otherness, making the confrontation with ourselves inevitable and upsetting our previously unproblematic existence. The wanderer, though temporarily among us, may move on at any time, stepping out from our collectively built everyday life and thereby questioning it. This otherness, by definition, is maintained until the moment of integration into the group. As long as the newcomer is regarded as a stranger, he cannot be a natural and fully incorporated part of the community or a member of a historical nation or state. Metaphorically speaking, he is not entitled to own the motherland, and indeed he is often literally cut off from this opportunity. The mere possibility of the stranger's stepping out can severely upset the individual who is bound to the soil. The stranger is a strange mixture of nearness and distance, for although he lives close to us, we are always haunted by the nightmare of infinity embodied in his personality. He is a menacing hurricane that can turn our everyday life, peacefully babbling in its gently sloping bed, into an overflowing cataract.

To find an outlet for this psychological tension, the rejecting community can resort to a whole range of traditional and horrifying measures that lead to the stranger's isolation and annihilation. When, after the

---

Consider, for example, virulent anti-Semitism against a virtually nonexistent Jewry, no longer to be encountered in the flesh. It is true, however, that in this case we are dealing not with the problem of strangerhood, but with one sociopathological type of encounter with it, based on the distorted interpretation of a former historical situation. In that interpretation, the other stayed here and would not go. It is sad enough that the notion of the collective unconscious, so dear to psychologists, can be verified precisely by this pathological form of objectless hatred.

declared End of History, you look at the colored map of wars raging on the earth, the smaller fires that stand for ethnic disturbances (the bigger ones mark wars) will remind you of the firelit nights of your childhood scout camps: there are tiny fires all around, the dream of the pyromaniac scoutmaster seeming to have come true. The conservative sages of the Western world consider these to be the ephemeral, localized, and repressed flames that repel the danger of the all-devastating Great Conflagration.

Although the negative definition of the stranger is not universal, it nevertheless seems to be used more often than should be acceptable, for in this case there are no morally acceptable proportions. Even though peaceful encounters with the stranger outnumber the flames dotting the map, we cannot be proud of the position the stranger occupies in the civilization of the turn of the millennium. Apart from the field of gastronomy, where the foreign flavors of Thai, Chinese, French, or Ethiopian cuisines are irresistibly tempting, the general tendency is still to reject otherness. Whether we take up arms and set out for insane expeditions of "ethnic cleansing," or merely curse the primitive inhabitants of neighboring countries over our beer, the logic of rejection is at work. Even if the Korean stores are not permanently on fire in Los Angeles, racial tension persists; and the absence of street fights in Hungary does not mean that public opinion regarding Gypsies is devoid of prejudice. As the Hungarian writer Péter Esterházy remarked: "A slightly anti-Semitic person" is a nonsensical expression.

Simmel, a Jew living in Berlin, the restless, scintillating metropolis of the beginning of the century, was himself an expert on strangerhood, though his main concern was with the host community and its possible reactions. Despite his admired intellect, Simmel was refused a professorship in Berlin, experiencing firsthand the disadvantages of rootlessness and the vicissitudes of the outcast, but also calling attention to another, surprising feature that arises from the "lack of a past." In times when battles between rival clans are pushed to extremes, the stranger, so despised and stigmatized up to this point, is the one to get hold of positions of trust, since he does not have his hands tied by the past and is not enmeshed in local history.

Lewis A. Coser (1974) cites several historical examples of the trust put in such a stranger. Although it is not geographical foreignness he deals with, his examples are still relevant: the careers of the numerous lovers of Louis XIV and of his two successors to the throne prove that those who came from far below could bathe longer in glamor and could count on a more abundant allowance. As social strangers, they belonged only to the king, so that the king, caught in webs of courtly intrigue, could place absolute trust in them.

The best-known example is no doubt that of the Jews in the German courts in the seventeenth and eighteenth centuries. Excluded from political action (since they were not allowed to carry weapons) and restrained in economic life (since they were not entitled to own land), the Jews could give aid to the monarch that he could not accept from anyone else. After being deprived of one-half of the notion of "man" as defined by the age, the Jew became an almost human homunculus and, even more important, could live under the monarch's protection.

In certain historical situations and social systems, the functional importance of strangers grows and they become the pillars of a given society. For example, in the dynamic, conquering period of the Ottoman empire in the fifteenth and sixteenth centuries, when the sultans enlarged not only the territory of the empire but also their own internal sphere of power, they defeated their potential internal rivals by relying almost solely on renegade Christians. The military elite, the Janissaries, kidnapped or bought as children, belonged only to the sultan and, through lack of families or other forms of integration, remained ever strangers and fighters. The administrative managers of the empire were recruited from the most talented children who, after being educated in the schools of the palace, became the leaders of the court and provinces and the main supporters of the sultan in defeating the oligarchies. Of the forty-eight military leaders central to Ottoman history between 1453 and 1623, only five had Turkish origins.

Annihilation and elevation to a distinguished position are the two poles of possible relation to the stranger. To illuminate the diversity of possibilities between these poles and to see to what extent these solutions characterize a given society, let us refer to a peculiar case of sexual strangerhood. If there is one cultural phenomenon that surely cannot be limited to the Western world, it is the division of all human beings into two biological sexes. Although this division defines a fundamental and rarely questioned segment of our identity, it takes no account of such extreme cases as hermaphrodites.

This particular case of strangerhood, though rare, is more than just a curiosity; it is a real cultural challenge responded to variously by different cultures. Precisely because it involves categories of identity and worldview that are of the greatest significance, it provides us with important information on the social responses to strangerhood and otherness. As Clifford Geertz (1983) points out in his essay on the cultural aspects of common sense, we find a fascinating contrast in the views of hermaphroditism taken by different societies. Based on the research of Robert Edgerton, Geertz's essay deals with three different cultures: the American, the Navaho, and the Pokot.

In the case of the Americans — and European thought is no different — the first commonsense reaction is horrified paralysis. How is the sex to be indicated on a birth certificate? Is military service relevant? Can such a person marry? How can "it" choose the right public bathroom? Such questions arise, and in our rational Western culture this is the point where the mind boggles and dread numbs all responses. But our reaction often involves undisguised forms of pressure as well, mostly through parental influence. The "illegitimate" individual who does not fit into our schemes of comprehension is pressured to choose, to adopt either a male or a female role, to become at last a normal "he" or "she" like the rest of us. In late modernity, where social control is achieved by the tabulation of bodies, the organizing rules of the table and the demands of conceptual clarity are much more important than the flesh that completes the Order; the unwanted, unfitting parts have to be removed — literally.

The Navaho's attitude toward hermaphroditism — or in Geertz's terminology, intersexuality — is quite different. For the Navaho, too, of course, intersexuality is strange and abnormal, but rather than evoking horror and distrust, it inspires respect and even reverence. In Navaho society, intersexuality is the divine symbol of fertility, well-being, and wealth. Thus, the hermaphrodite is divinely blessed, chosen to be both a man and a woman in one person. The Navaho often choose their leaders from among the hermaphrodites to ensure the reproduction and wealth of the society. "If there were no more left, the horses, sheep, and Navaho would all go. They are leaders, just like President Roosevelt" (ibid.: 82).

The third group, the Pokot tribe of Kenya, takes a middle position. Their attitude toward intersexuality is neutral: they are not horrified by hermaphrodites, but do not regard them highly either. The Pokot think that even God could make a mistake when creating the world, and regard intersexuals as useless, like a botched pot. As one discards a broken pot, so intersexed children are sometimes killed, not with hatred but in an offhanded way. In this culture, the place of the intersexual is defined by "its" functional uselessness, being unable to give birth to a child; nor can "it" enjoy what the Pokot say is the most pleasant thing in the world—sex. They are often allowed to live, but are simply regarded as not Pokot. Interestingly enough, the Pokot hermaphrodites are relatively well-to-do since they have neither the obligation to support a family nor the ordinary drains of kinship on their wealth.

What concerns us in the cross-cultural study of intersexuality is not to illustrate afresh the irrationality of Western rationality. More significantly, through such an approach to the alien we can develop an important argument against the ideas of vulgar materialism, which overestimate social and economic factors. The example above urges us to devote particular attention to cultural-conceptual elements as organizers of social behavior. "[Common sense] is what the mind has filled with presuppositions—that sex is a disorganizing force, that sex is a regenerative gift, that sex is a practical pleasure," Geertz concludes. "God may have made the intersexuals, but man has made the rest" (ibid.: 84).

It would be economic reductionism to explain the various forms of racism and nationalism simply as the result of poverty, of a competition for limited resources, without considering the worldview, the "order of things," involving space and time and the system of cultural presuppositions in its complexity. In the rational culture of Western Europe, this system of presuppositions does not promote the tolerant acceptance of the stranger. The modern nation-state has spectacularly failed in this sphere; it is enough to remember the French or the German *Völkish* model, the former laying stress upon equal rights at the expense of otherness, and the latter upon blood, giving priority to the German people and ignoring state borders. The East European intelligentsia, stunned by the horrors of the post-Yugoslavian crisis, is inclined to self-chastisement, with good reason. It is important to see that this is a nationalist war, and as such it arises from the essence of modernity. While I disagree with those who claim that the Habermas-Lyotard debate was settled in Sarajevo, surely this war does not speak in praise of modernity.

We can see that the system of presuppositions that unite to form a whole culture largely determines the relation to the alien. Let us now reconstruct this encounter the other way around, from the stranger's point of view.

At first sight, the stranger simply does not exist. If we enter an unknown group or another country, *they* are the strangers, while we are ourselves as we have always been. A large number of interactions are necessary for us to give up after a while our own former knowledge and self: not to regard *them* as strangers but to see ourselves and our own world as unusual in the new environment. Yet, no matter how we define or name the new situation, it will differ fundamentally from our former everyday lives in one respect: the lack of custom. We can no longer rely on the routines that help us through the labyrinth of everyday communication; the automatisms that smoothly control our behavior are no longer operative. The newcomer, from the moment he realizes that he has fallen into a foreign environment, becomes tense and alert: he must begin to learn, and this learning is accompanied by a serious personal crisis.

I mentioned earlier how irritating the otherness of the stranger can be for the host community, since it questions the community's conceptual apparatus. On his part, the stranger — unless he is a conqueror, which is another story — cannot expel the hosts but instead must go through a purgatory of uncertainties. For when, during the process of learning, he realizes the constructed nature of the system of rules in the given culture, the clarity and uniqueness of his own former culture collapse as well. The sociologists' favorite example in the case of kinship relations bears mentioning: the stranger who learns that in a given community the incest prohibition is extended even to the third cousin may come to doubt the eternal truth of his own incest prohibition. Similarly, seeing that others eat heartily the flesh of hare and camel, pig and swarming things, the Jew is liable to doubt the teachings of Mosaic law (in Leviticus), which pronounce these impure and repellent. After becoming acquainted with a culture built on rational efficiency and profit making, we can still follow other patterns with the traditional family as a basis, but we may no longer believe that they represent the "order of things," the only possible way.

The stranger's reactions to this dissonance of consciousness can vary between the extremes of intransigent opposition and overcompensating assimilation. Yet in most cases, the process of learning continues, though in a sense it is bound to fail. As Alfred Schütz says in "The Stranger: An Essay in Social Psychology":

To be sure, from the stranger's point of view, too, the culture of the approached group has its peculiar history, and this history is even accessible to him. But it has never become an integral part of his biography, as did the history of his home group. Only the ways in which his fathers and grandfathers lived become for everyone elements of his own way of life. Graves and reminiscences can neither be transferred nor conquered. The stranger ... may be willing and able to share the present and future with the approached group in vivid and immediate experience; under all circumstances, however, he remains excluded from such experiences of its past. Seen from the point of view of the approached group, he is a man without history. (1976: 96–97)

The learning of the unlearnable means much more than the inaccessibility of the past: it is the general existential experience of the stranger. The fabric of culture keeps fraying instead of wrapping protectively around us; the possibility of making mistakes exists in even the most perfect action. Remember the foreigner who speaks a language with absolute precision and subtlety, and yet betrays himself by his own perfect pronunciation, for it is the clumsiness and negligence in the use of the native tongue that are impossible for a foreigner to learn. He is caught in an unavoidable trap. If his behavior deviates from cultural norms, he will be stigmatized as a stranger; if, however, he wants to acquire them, he will lose naturalness and ease through the act of learning.

CREATIVITY AND STRANGERHOOD

It would be very difficult to speak in general terms about the reaction of the personality to the experience of being a stranger. From the viewpoint of social productivity, the experience of strangerhood can lead to either exceptional creativity or apathetic passivity. Most actual cases of strangerhood range between these extremes.

Let us take one example from the field of the social sciences, involving a member of an extraordinarily successful generation that arrived in the United States in the late 1920s and 1930s. Alfred Schütz (1899–1959) represents the type of personality that responds to foreignness with an explosion of creativity. This choice may be surprising, for Schütz is known to have published only one book during his lifetime and, what is more, not even in the United States but in Austria before his emigration. However, considering the fact that, except for his last few years, Schütz worked as a banker and a part-time teacher, spending an hour each day playing the piano and writing essays in his spare time, the three-volume *Collected Works* published in the late 1960s and the massive collection of manuscripts edited by Thomas Luckman are evidence of an exceptional productivity. His creativity is not merely or primarily quantitative, but original and deep. The unique place Schütz's writings occupy in sociology is perhaps due to the fact that their author remained a stranger — not only in America but within the discipline as well.

Schütz, born in Vienna, became Husserl's student and the prospective inheritor of his university chair. Under the threat of the Anschluss, however, he emigrated first to Paris, then the following year to the United States, where he taught at the New School for Social Research until the end of his life. His intellectual career illustrates the pathbreaking bravery of the stranger.

It was Schütz who mixed Husserl's phenomenology with Weber's cognitive sociology, or simply turned the phenomenology of science of ideas into sociology, the study of the transcendent, floating ego into the analysis of the individual social consciousness, thus discovering and developing a new field: the phenomenologist sociology of knowledge. This approach, radically different from the classical European one, was also rather shocking to the emerging canonical American sociology.

On his arrival in America, Schütz wrote a study of mainstream American sociology, titled "Parsons' Theory of Social Action." Following an intellectually fascinating, but in its tone very dry correspondence with Parsons, he decided against publication, because of the antagonism revealed in the controversy. Given Parsons's authority in contemporary American social science, this affair did not help to integrate him into his new home. Most importantly, neither was the structuralist, functionalist trend in American sociology favorable to the new interpretative sociology of Schütz.

In a certain sense, Schütz cannot be regarded as a lonely hero since this peculiar intermingling of originality, intellectual achievement, tolerance, and nonparticipation characterizes other thinkers of his generation as well. The postwar history of the American social sciences could hardly have been written without the contributions of Hannah Arendt, Eric Vogelin, Leo Strauss, and Franz Neumann in political theory, Karl Wittfogel, Paul Lazarsfeld, and Pitrim Sorokin (a refugee from Lenin's Russia) in sociology, or Wilhelm Reich, Bruno Bettelheim, and Eric Fromm in psychology. Members of the same generation, they all produced significant oeuvres and, because of their originality, became "odd man (or woman) out" in their own professions.

To present the other extreme, that of apathetic passivity, let us consider a case studied by Erik Erikson, a classic figure — and reformer — of historical psychology, and himself a German émigré of the generation mentioned above. Observing the adaptation strategies of the Sioux Indians, Erikson divided the inhabitants of the reservations into two groups, the offended resisters and the opportunistic resisters (in Riesman 1950: 151). Sioux of the first group were seen by whites as incorrigible and problematic, while the diligent "opportunists" tried to impress the whites by "overachievement." Erikson primarily studied the children of the reservation for whom, along with the obligation of attending a "white school," assimilation into white culture was a must. Cultural adaptation clashed with Sioux tradition and knowledge.

As David Riesman has pointed out, this conflict "drains out the emotional energies of the child, thus he seems to be lazy. Therefore both the resisters and the seeming opportunists show indifference towards white culture and white politics" (1950: 95). What seems to be the Indian's laziness and idleness is in fact a painful and self-destructive mitigation of the trauma of strangerhood.

We have to make it clear that this approach, stressing the aspect of intellectual achievement, does not deal with cultural values as such, but with the chances of assimilation and cooperation with the dominant culture. Who could say that Native American textiles and carvings inspired by the horrors of ostracism and genocide are inferior to Thomas Mann's "Mario the Magician," or Picasso's *Guernica*? From the standpoint of Western cultural values, however, it is fair to say that not all forms of strangerhood lead to creative work. The intellect's longing for categorical assertion would be more easily met if this statement were reversed: all creative work is a form of strangerhood. So we must return to the theme that we put aside in the beginning, that of the genuine anxiety and internalized experience of estrangement.

The universal experience of strangerhood in late modernity can be reconstructed in the metaphors that attempt to describe the isolation, solitude, and alienation of the individual toward the end of the millennium. The common characteristic of these metaphors is the reinterpretation of strangerhood by way of reversal. Viewing the stranger as a character within ordinary existence and thus as a metaphor for society as a whole, we step out of the conceptual framework in which the stranger is seen as a newcomer or a minority confronting the majority.

Zygmunt Bauman (1993) describes the internally controlled character of classic modernity by using the image of the pilgrim, who knows where he comes from but, having a sacred cause in view, is even more certain about his destination. The meaning of his life is not simply found in the enjoyment of moving, sightseeing, and discovering foreign lands. Although he might not refuse these worldly pleasures, the real meaning of his journey is to reach the Holy Place. In the late modernity of the present day, a new metaphor of the wanderer is needed to grasp the character of society: that of the tourist. The tourist has nothing sacred in view, only places listed in a guidebook. The web of these places forms an imaginary world dazzling him with the illusion of experience. For the tourist, the world is a source of sensual pleasures, mouthwatering flavors, spectacular events, and camera-ready monuments: pure enjoyment without the slightest intention of participation or the burden of responsibility. It is freedom, in Simmel's famous words, the freedom of the "physically near, spiritually distant" alien from the obligation of turning physical proximity into spiritual identification. "Freedom from moral duty is paid for in advance; the package tour kit contains the preventive medicine against pangs of conscience next to the pills preventing air sickness. . . . Nowhere as much and as radically as in the tourist mode is the uniqueness of the actor disavowed, erased, blotted out" (Bauman 1993: 242). The tourist drowns the natives in numbers, making them all alike. The pleasures of the fantasy world, staked out by the business professionals of tourism and the dream factories of the media, can in no way be disturbed; in an ideal state one's entire life would be a delirious holiday. It would be an overstatement to say that in sociological terms the entire world has turned into Nescafé-travelers, but as the ever rising star of the tourism industry and the publicity of commercialized desires show, the tourist has become a legitimate metaphor for our age.

In this touristic world there is not much possibility for creative work. Of course, judging this statement true or false depends upon what we mean by creative work. It is enough to consider the world of science, that undoubtedly limited sphere of the intellect, to find striking counterarguments. To horrify his readers, the mathematician and social historian Fokasz Nikosz (1993) loves to point out that in the last three hundred years, the number of scientific journals has doubled every fifteen years with monotonous regularity. This process, leading up to the present, obviously contradicts the statement above—provided, of course, we agree with the quantitative view that identifies intellectual achievement with the length of the list of publications. As I have pointed out in connection with Schütz's lifework, it would be more correct to counterbalance quantity with the depth and originality of thought, although this proposal is more a dream than a possibility. But here, with fearsome power over the text in my hands, by creative work I mean only a contribution to the imaginary construction of the intellect and "adding a piece to the puzzle of the world." I do not think that this definition requires further elaboration: first, because it might be impossible and second, because it is not of decisive importance. Our concern is not with the nature of intellectual value but with the creation of those values, in other words, not with the evaluation of results but with the process itself. It is not important whether someone values Mozart's music more or less than Salieri's; in the case of genuine creation, the creative process is identical.

This sameness leads us back to strangerhood in the touristic world, for the morality of a creative person is fundamentally different from that of a tourist. Creative work, in the sense in which I use the word, can only be accomplished after taking responsibility for other people, for the world. The much-emphasized solitude of creation stands opposed to tourism, even if the created work is the tourist's apotheosis. Since the creator wishes to speak about and to other people, she must first step on the walkway of responsibility to which the tourist consciously gives a wide berth. However, the strangerhood of the creative person cannot be grasped only in relation to the tourist. The process of creation is nothing less than casting off the roles and conventions that help us get along in our everyday lives. The creator is a lonely ropedancer, never seeing the end of the rope but feeling it, knowing the direction and the right steps. Anyone who dares to tackle the ropedance of creation becomes a stranger, even to himself.

It is not iterativity or reproducibility but the urge to step out of roles and give up identities that makes Fernando Pessoa, the Lusitanian miracle, the archetype of creation at the close of the millennium. As the Hungarian poet György Somlyó writes: "In Portuguese *pessoa* means person, man, someone, anyone. . . . It is the most general and most abstract word for human being, in which individual, genus, and species are integrated. The original meaning of the Latin *persona* mask also vibrates deep down in it. If a nomen, which is really an omen, were ever to exist, then the name of the most peculiar poet of the century surely is one" (1969: 173; my translation). Pessoa was born in 1888 in Lisbon but spent his youth in South Africa; he spoke perfect English, and wrote his first poems in it. Since he did not want to give up literary independence, he worked as a clerk, just like Kafka. After returning home he wrote poems in Portuguese until, on March 8, 1914, something happened that is called a "Cartesian moment" in modern poetry. Wanting to play a joke on a friend, he tried to write a poem in another persona. His attempt was nearly unsuccessful until, one day, "he stepped to a tall table . . . , put a piece of paper in front of him, and started to write standing, as he usually did whenever he had the time. And he wrote in some kind of a trance more than thirty poems in a row, in the name of another poet who appeared fully armed within him" (ibid.: 176). The author of the poems, the resigned philosopher Alberto Careiro, was soon followed by the epicurean Ricardo Reis, fond of antique forms, and Alvaro Campos, the poet of free verse recalling Whitman's style and devotion to civilization. These are not poems written under pseudonyms. As Pessoa said, he only gave form to the heteronyms that had long existed in himself. "The personality broke into four parts and behold, these did not become four quarters but four different, entire personalities with their own biographies, aesthetics, worldviews, styles, syntaxes, and moreover with their own methods of writing" (ibid.: 177). The poet of modernist free verse, Alvaro Campos, exchanged the tall table for the devil's piano, the typewriter. Not only the ecstatic moments of creation, but also the continuous cohabitation with the otherness emerging from the depths of personality, define the essence of Pessoa's existence, as opposed to the tourist society which molds the stranger into a nameless, impersonal mass. "This does not mean that 'nothing human can be alien' to a human being, but that the human being is identical to anything human. The notion of 'not alien' can soften the forming of judgments, can encourage forgiveness and *wriggling out of responsibility; while the notion of 'identity' emphasizes the universal responsibility of each and every man*" (ibid.: 178; my emphasis).

Heroically guarding the integrity of personality by entirely giving it up through this "explosion of the self," Fernando Pessoa becomes a cult figure for the next thousand years, in which the primary question of the increasingly important politics of identity is: How can the unity of identity be maintained in the flood of roles that has become our destiny?

MORALITY AND STRANGERHOOD

Looking back from our not very promising situation on all the horrors of the century, the greatest achievement of humanity may appear to be the mere fact of survival, which earlier remained unnoticed, natural. The most archaic technique for enduring the horrors is supposedly the division into Us and Them, in which We, the good and innocent, not only regard helplessly the incomprehensible, horrible deeds committed by the evil Them, but also free ourselves from any responsibility for the psychological burdens of crime and the ghosts of punishment. This mechanism can work in two directions. On the one hand, we tend to attach a positive ontological status to the notion of our own group, often definable only in contrast to the stranger. Among the building blocks that make up the national identities of the small Central European countries, charming examples can be found of this phenomenon. Lacking social welfare and effectiveness, national identity can be based on such elements as the "plainness" of the Great Hungarian Plain or the "patriotic spirit" of homemade spirits, the idea of being a world power in sports or of having blood ties with nonexistent empires. The stranger can only come into this picture as a retarded, primitive boor.

On the other hand, if "our" group has committed undeniable crimes, we try to project them onto another group; in addition to the victim Them, we create the evil Them, so that we can stay clean. A sad example is the lack of shame and responsibility among Hungarians for the 1944 deportation of Hungarian Jews and Gypsies. György Csepeli's research describes it as one of the weak points of Hungarian national identity:

Hungarian gendarmes rounded up, before the Hungarian people's eyes, hundreds of thousands of their fellow citizens into ghettos, and then crammed them into wagons carrying them toward certain death. The question has been asked in several polls who is to blame for this unpardonable crime, in the opinion of Hungarian people today. The majority consistently insists on disclaiming responsibility, saying that Nazi Germany and the German army occupying the country were to blame. They reject the opinion that the Hungarian churches and Hungarian public opinion could have done much more to prevent this enormous national shame from happening. Admiral Horthy, the Regent of the country, who had kept his position during the Occupation, simply blamed Fate in his memoirs. (Forthcoming; my translation)

There are numerous anthropological data — consider, for example, the structuralist research of Mary Douglas (1966) — that are evidently applicable to our century's culture of global modernity. Sociology, the science par excellence of modernity, used the metaphor of glorious development as a set of blinders. "The history of class struggle," "the process of rationalization," "the process of civilization," "the conversion from

Gemeinschaft to *Gesellschaft,*" and "the development of organic solidarity" were all infamous emblems manufactured by sociology, dependent on victorious modernity, and proudly worn by those in the field.
(From this point of view, the pessimism of individual classic authors—
especially Weber—and their personal attitudes toward modernization
were irrelevant. What was important was what modernity adopted from
their works to serve its own myth.) Modernization's perception is morally that of a rise out of barbarism, and it sees the process of civilization as a step-by-step movement from bad to good. In this schema,
reincarnations of evil appear as the intrusions of barbarity, as wounds
left untreated by the process of modernization, which can be salved by
the imposition of a more modern, more civilized system. Perhaps this
explains the hysterical attempts to deny the modernizing features of the
Stalinist regime.

The first event of earthshaking importance that interfered with this
sociological and historical-philosophical vision of modernity was the
Holocaust and its modern organizational, technological, administrative, and industrial nature (Bauman 1988). The period following World
War II, with its environmental pollution, and above all the irrationality
of the arms race and the nuclear arsenal left behind by the Cold War, have
led to a strengthening of the environmental movement and a rethinking
of values that Inglehart (1977) has called the "silent revolution." Perhaps
a better term would be *counterrevolution*, for this revolution has led to
a repression of modernity's revolutionary mutations and values, a refusal of the rationalization of growth and conquest. But even if, with
the exception of a few irredentist conservatives and lost utopians, very
few people still see modernity as a radiant angel, we are far from being
free of its moral effects. The simple reversal of belief systems is no help:
the claim that evil is embodied by modernism and "progress" is just
as wrong as belief in the "goodness" of modernism. Under the circumstances of our fin de millennium, those who sail through the straits into
the next millennium will not be those who continually search for evil in
all its guises outside, among "others," among "them." It is historical philosophy, not history itself, that has come to an end. We can no longer
look to the simple working of logic for the creating force of events. And
certainly we can no longer—for the sake of history or to change the
spirit of the world—simply attempt to adjust human values.

All this, naturally, does not mean that "good" and "evil" will cease
to exist; it simply means that we cannot use the Us and Them schema

any longer, and must instead begin to think in terms of the dichotomy between what is possible and what exists. This duality is less comforting than its predecessor, for it bears little promise of psychic relief. It does not allow us to step out of history by simply saying that the grand inquisitors, SS campguards, or communist commandos were fanatically insane or rotten with cynicism. On the contrary, this duality forces us to accept that those capable of monstrous evil are not Them and do not belong to a separate species, but are people like Us. To put it more precisely, they are what we might have become under different circumstances. The sickening, raving evil we see around us in time and space lies dormant within each of us.

Although the chances for the expansion of this worldview are rather low, there is one factor that supports it: the identity politics closely linked to the problem of strangerhood. The way of living characteristic of late modernity imposes more and more roles upon us. We have to learn various roles we never wanted to: we drive cars and, clumsy penmen that we are, we use computers. These are not mere activities but compulsory roles: the computer user must buy software, the car owner must talk to the mechanic. We have to live up to different role expectations at political meetings, in our families, at work, or playing football in a park.

Because of the increase of cultural consumption and the globalization of its structure, we have become members of various symbolic communities. This plurality of roles makes metamorphosis an everyday personal experience. Even if spared the change into a monstrous insect, we wake up to find ourselves in new roles. This role explosion, in a sense undoubtedly frightening, is also promising in two respects. First, it is hard to imagine a man playing all his roles with the same skill—being a wonderful father, a brilliant artist, an excellent athlete, and a witty politician, yet at the same time knowing how to fix a leaky faucet. For this reason we all have to learn the role of the loser as well. This recognition can lead to frustration and hatred, but also to empathy for the weak. Second, realizing the mosaic-like complexity of our own identities, the potential stranger in ourselves, may enable us to pass over the dimension of difference that constitutes strangerhood; recognizing the potential stranger in ourselves, we will then be able to attach importance to similarities, the aspects of our identities through which we can cooperate (Suleiman 1994). One might ask whether it is necessary for a Serbian who meets a

Croatian schoolmate to define himself by his national identity, his first reaction being the impulse to kill. What makes him choose this role from among the bulging bag of identity components, rather than the part of the father playing with his daughters, the tipsy jazz fan, the Volkswagen owner hunting for needed parts, the enthusiast recording on videotape the episodes of *Miami Vice* each Wednesday, or the Madonna fan? All of these roles can be his as well as the other's. Are we predestined to kill or is there a possibility for us to break away from modernity's violence-breeding division between Us and Them? For us, guests in the carnival of roles of late modernity, the latter possibility might not be completely illusory. We cannot be certain whether the chances of a positive attitude toward the stranger are greater today than in the last fin de siècle, but the consequences surely are. This time we cannot afford to miss the opportunity.

REFERENCES

Bauman, Zygmunt
  1988 "Sociology after the Holocaust" *British Journal of Sociology* 39: 496–97.
  1993 *Postmodern Ethics* (Oxford: Blackwell).
Coser, Lewis A.
  1974 *Greedy Institutions: Patterns of Undivided Commitment* (New York: Free Press).
Csepeli, Gyorgy
  forthcoming *Regionális átok magyar zsakutca.*
Douglas, Mary
  1966 *Purity and Danger* (London: Routledge and Kegan Paul).
Geertz, Clifford
  1983 "Common Sense as a Cultural System," in *Local Knowledge*, 73–93 (New York: Basic Books).
Ingelhart, Ronald
  1977 *The Silent Revolution* (Princeton, NJ: Princeton University Press).
Nikosz, Fokasz
  1993 "Lattuk-e hogy jon," *Replika* (November 11–12): 2–21.
Riesman, David
  1950 *The Lonely Crowd* (New Haven, CT: Yale University Press).
Schütz, Alfred
  1976 "The Stranger: An Essay in Social Psychology," in *Collected Works*, 3: 91–106 (The Hague: Martinus).

Simmel, Georg

    1964 "The Stranger," in *The Sociology of Georg Simmel*, translated and edited by Kurt H. Wolff, 402–7 (New York: Free Press).

Somlyó, Gyorgy

    1979 "Fernando Pessoa: The Four-Faced Poet," afterword to *That Ancient Angst* [Hungarian] (Europa: Budapest).

Suleiman, Susan R.

    1994 "The Politics of Postmodernism after the Wall; or, What Do We Do When the Ethnic Cleansing Starts," in *Risking Who One Is: Encounters with Contemporary Art and Literature*, 225–42 (Cambridge, MA: Harvard University Press).

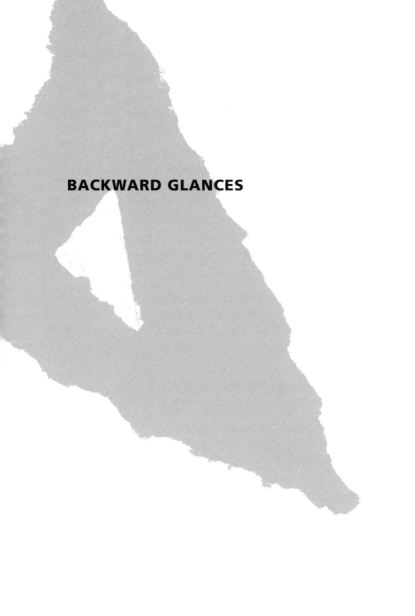

BACKWARD GLANCES

LEO SPITZER

PERSISTENT MEMORY: CENTRAL EUROPEAN

REFUGEES IN AN ANDEAN LAND

The Masai when they were moved from their old country . . . took with them the names of their hills, plains and rivers; and gave them to the hills, plains and rivers in the new country . . . carrying their cut roots with them as a medicine.
ISAK DINESEN, Out of Africa

Nostalgia is memory with the pain removed.
HERB CAEN, quoted in Fred Davis, Yearning for Yesterday

When the brass band on the shore strikes up the jaunty mazurka rhythms of the Polish anthem, I am pierced by a youthful sorrow so powerful that I suddenly stop crying and try to hold still against the pain. I desperately want time to stop, to hold the ship still with the force of my will. I am suffering my first, severe attack of nostalgia, or *tesknota* — a word that adds to nostalgia the tonalities of sadness and longing. It is a feeling whose shades and degrees I'm destined to know intimately, but at this hovering moment, it comes upon me like a visitation from a whole new geography of emotion, an annunciation of how much an absence can hurt.
EVA HOFFMAN, Lost in Translation

Photos taken at the Austrian Club in La Paz, Bolivia, in 1947, two years after the end of the war, show my mother, father, and friends at a Dirndl *ball.*[1] *My parents and the others in the group are dressed in Austrian folk*

A modified version of this essay appears in my book *Hotel Bolivia: The Culture of Memory in a Refuge from Nazism* (1998). I am grateful to the National Humanities Center for a residence fellowship in 1992 enabling me to begin work on this project, and to the Lucius N. Littauer and John Simon Guggenheim Memorial Foundations for additional fellowship support.

1. In the late 1930s, and until the end of the first year of World War II, thousands of refugees from Nazi-dominated Central Europe, the majority of them Jews, fled to Bolivia to escape increasingly vehement persecution. Initially, soon after the Nazis came to power, wealthier, "better-connected," or perhaps more prescient, emigrants acquired visas or fled to the so-called countries of choice — Great Britain, the United States, Australia, Palestine, Argentina, and Brazil. The tightening of immi-

costumes—my mother and the women in full-skirted peasant dresses and tight bodices, and my father and the men in lederhosen, white and tasseled Alpine kneesocks, and Tyrolean hats. They all seem happy, perhaps a little tipsy, and they are obviously having a good time.

Pictures of the same vintage are from an Austrian Club banquet. Scores of people in semiformal dress, including my parents, are seated at long, set dinner tables, apparently enjoying the occasion with wine, plentiful food, and smiling conversation. In the background one can clearly see the club's wall hangings: two Austrian flags, a lithograph of Old Vienna, and lampshades emblazoned with the Austrian republican coat of arms. No precise date is marked on the photos; the occasion being celebrated is not indicated. The attendant music can only be imagined.

I see these photos first as visual examples—accessible, direct, even amusing—of the reproduction of "Austrianness" in Bolivia by refugees who had fled or been expelled from their country in the aftermath of the Anschluss and Nazi persecution. I view them as photographic manifestations of cultural memory and national identity—of nostalgic remembrance acted out in national costume, cultural practice, and symbolic representation. They seem to record performances engendered by Heimweh *and* Sehnsucht, *homesickness and longing, feelings commonly expressed in refugee discourse. Yet the photos also seem discordant to me: so removed from the Andean physical and cultural setting in which they were located as to appear almost quaint and ingenuous in their incongruity and difference. And they come laden with irony. Taken not very long after the conclusion of the war—after Auschwitz, the death camps, and confirmation of extensive Austrian involvement and collaboration in the Final Solution—their depictions of enthusiastic celebrations of Austrian nationality strike me as disturbing and distressing examples of denial, if not amnesia.*

---

gration to these countries, however, virtually closed off entry for the large number of persons desperate to leave in the late 1930s. By the end of the decade Bolivia was one of the very few places that accepted Jewish immigrants. Some twenty thousand refugees from Germany and Austria arrived between 1938 and 1940—a number which, when calculated as a percentage of Bolivia's small "non-Indian" population at the time, gives some sense of how substantial the demographic impact of this Central European immigrant influx must have been. The new arrivals settled primarily in La Paz, 12,500 feet above sea level, as well as in Cochabamba, Oruro, Sucre, and in small mining and tropical agricultural communities throughout the land.

Over time, my initial responses to these pictures are not eradicated. But, in my efforts to contextualize the photos more precisely and to reread them historically, I realize that they also manifest a political dimension that is not immediately apparent. For the refugees within them to proclaim "Austrianness"—to reclaim an identification with an Austrian republic after the Anschluss, Nazi rule, and the defeat of the German Reich—was also to reassert rightful belonging within a body politic and cultural tradition from which the Nazis had attempted to sever them. "You have failed," they seem to assert. "We survive. We have a claim on the best of the past, and we welcome the future!" And beneath the surface comicality of the lederhosen, dirndl, and Tyrolean outfits, lurks the reality that Jews had been legally forbidden to dress in "national costume" when the Nazis came to power. Nostalgic memory, cultural reconnection, ethnic mimicry—their surface readings—take on an additional dimension. Defiance, resistance, victory—these too are being proclaimed . . .

1. NOSTALGIC MEMORY

Literally translated, the German word *Heimweh* means "home hurt" or "home ache," and its sense is closest to the English term *homesickness*. Few persons nowadays would think of the feelings associated with home-sickness — "missing home," or "the desire to return to one's native land" — as a medical problem. But that is exactly how they were considered for almost two centuries after Johannes Hofer, an Alsatian, first coined the word "nostalgia" in a 1688 Swiss medical thesis. His intent was to translate Heimweh, the familiar emotional phenomenon primarily associated at the time with exiles and displaced soldiers languishing for home, into a medical condition (1934 [1688]: 376–91). Through its formal identification as a disease, "nostalgia" (from the Greek *nostos*, to return home, and *algia*, a painful feeling) could thus be opened to rational inquiry and possible cure. As such, learned physicians would soon observe that the "melancholic," "debilitating," "sometimes fatal" symptoms of nostalgia could be triggered in its victims through the associations of memory — by sounds, tastes, smells, and sights that might remind individuals of the homes and environments they had left behind. A "homecoming" and return to the familiar and local, however, could also be restorative, ending the problem and curing the affliction (Starobinski 1966: 81–103; Lowenthal 1975; Davis 1979; Vromen 1993: 69–86).

But in the years after its coinage as a medical term, the meaning of nostalgia, as well as that of its equivalent in German popular usage, Heimweh, expanded and shifted. By the nineteenth century nostalgia was transformed, in David Lowenthal's words, "from a geographical disease into a sociological complaint" (1975: 2). Although its association with absence or removal from home and homeland persisted, nostalgia now also defined "loss" in a more generalized and abstracted way, including the yearning for a "lost childhood," for "irretrievable youth," for a "world of yesterday" from whose ideals and values one had become distanced and detached. In this usage, nostalgia became an incurable state of mind—a signifier of "absence" and "loss" that could never be made into "presence" and "gain" except through memory and the creativity of reconstruction.

For the Central European refugees fleeing Nazi persecution who arrived in Bolivia in the late 1930s and early 1940s, Heimweh and the nostalgic look back was certainly a common affliction—but one that often combined yearnings for a lost homeland, cultural milieu, and past existence with the bitterness of rejection and expulsion. "Dunk'le Naechte dehnen sich voll Grauen / und mein Sehnen sucht den fernen Strand" [The dark dread-filled nights lengthen / yet my longing seeks the distant shore], a poem published in the refugee newspaper *Rundschau vom Illimani* in December 1939 declared,

nur im Traum kann ich Dein Bild noch schauen,
Deine Stroeme, deine Waelder, Auen,
VATERLAND!

. . . . . .

Qual des Heimweh's, das ich nie gekannt,
lern ich jetzt erst schmerzhaft tief verstehen,
seit ich Dich so lang nicht mehr gesehen . . .
VATERLAND!

[only in dreams can I still see your image,
your streams, your woods, your meadows
FATHERLAND!

. . . . . .

Torments of homesickness that I never knew before,
only now do I understand the painful affliction deeply,

having not laid eyes on you for such a long a time,
FATHERLAND!]
(Nielsen 1939)[2]

"Despite the pain, and my anger for what we had been made to endure there," wrote my grandmother Bertha Wolfinger in a letter from La Paz in the early 1940s, "I still have strong feelings for the Vienna in which I spent so many years, and I miss small pleasures that I was forced to give up" (B. Wolfinger 1941?). "In an unassuming Bolivian store my eyes suddenly caught sight of a poster on the wall," Bruno Stroheim, brother of the actor Erich von Stroheim, narrated in the *Rundschau* in February 1940:

How amazing that in Bolivia, practically at the end of this side of the globe, one could glance at a poster depicting a woman dressed in Tyrolean costume. . . . A poster that also displays mountains, a snow-covered field in bluest sunlit sky, skiers, and a one-word inscription: Austria! And in a flash, like an electric shock, I am transported back. . . . Within seconds a film whirs before my eyes — a film whose title should be *Verlorene Heimat!* [Lost homeland!].   (Stroheim 1940)

Commenting with some irony on the character and pervasiveness of the refugees' nostalgic memory in Bolivia, Egon Schwarz noted how often his fellow immigrants began their sentences with the phrase "Back home in Germany . . ." or "Back home in our country . . . ," and how one man had actually exclaimed to him: "Back home in our concentration camp . . ." (1979: 73). The negativity reflected in this darkly humorous recollection was, of course, specifically connected to the circumstances of the refugees' expulsion by their fellow Germans and Austrians, and was not intended as a critique of nostalgic memory as a general phenomenon. But the overall practice of nostalgia itself, and the societal functions and effects of nostalgic memory in general, have been the subject of sharp reproach by many social critics. Detractors — especially those in the Marxist vein — have denounced it as "reactionary," "escapist," "inauthentic," "unreflexive," and as a "simplification" if not "falsification of the past" (Vromen 1993: 71). Christopher Lasch termed nostalgia "a betrayal of history," and saw "nostalgists," as "worse than . . . reactionary," "incurable sentimentalist[s]" who are both "afraid of the

2. All translations in this essay are my own.

future" and "afraid to face the truth about the past" (1984: 65–70). Robert Hewison viewed nostalgic memory in Britain as a tool of the "heritage industry" and as a "spurious . . . uncreative . . . miasma" that counterfeited "authentic memory" (1987: 132–34). For Raymond Williams, it was an opiate with dysfunctional consequences, enticing people to take refuge in an idealized past while avoiding a critical examination and engagement with their present. As such, nostalgia induced acceptance of the status quo and impeded social change (1973: 20–21).[3]

But examined from different perspectives, nostalgic memory has also been seen in a much more positive light. The notion of nostalgic memory as an "escape from the present," for example, was interpreted by the French sociologist Maurice Halbwachs as one of its great virtues. Nostalgia, he argued, frees individuals from the constraints of time; in effect, it enables a transcendence of the irreversibility of time, permitting persons to stress positive experiences and aspects of the past selectively (1925: 103–13; Vromen 1986: 55–66). It recalls, in Suzanne Vromen's words, "a world from which the pain has been removed." In so doing, however, it is neither dysfunctional nor reactionary because it presents a benign past as a contrast to the present, and enables a "pleasantly sad dialogue" between the two (ibid. 1993: 77). As a "retrospective mirage" constructed through hindsight, nostalgic memory thus serves an important comparative and, by implication, animating purpose. It sets up the *positive* from within the "world of yesterday" as a model for creative inspiration, and possible emulation, within the "world of the here and now." And, by establishing a link between a "self-in-present" and an image of a "self-in-past," nostalgic memory also plays a significant role in the reconstruction and continuity of individual and collective identity (Davis 1979: 31–50).

Nostalgic memory—employed to connect the present to a particular version of the past—certainly did serve the thousands of Central European refugees in Bolivia as a creative tool of adjustment, helping to ease their cultural uprootedness and sense of alienation. No sooner had they arrived in the country when a process began by which the immigrants recalled, negotiated, and reshaped their memories of Europe in light of their new circumstances. Concretely, in their everyday practices and in the economic, social, and cultural institutions they established, or

---

3. My discussion in this section is informed by the work of Vromen (1993: 71–74) and Lowenthal (1989: 20–21).

symbolically, in the names they bestowed on these institutions, they re-created a version of a way of life and of a cultural reality that they had previously known. Nostalgic memory, creatively reconfigured, became one source through which they built a new communal culture and constructed a new collective identity to serve their changed needs.

They did not, of course, physically recreate "Hamburgs and Viennas in the Andes," as one of the refugees jokingly referred to the German and Austrian communities that were established in La Paz, Cochabamba, Oruro, and Sucre (E. Taus 1992). But a glance through the pages of the refugee-established German-language newspaper *Rundschau vom Illimani* in 1939–40, or of the *Jüdische Wochenschau* (the Buenos Aires German-Jewish paper that covered Bolivian immigrant news on a monthly basis during the same period) illustrates the range of the immigrants' economic and institutional adjustment in Bolivia, and confirms the character of their symbolic reconnection with Central Europe. Advertisements for the Café Viena, Café-Restaurant Weiner, Pension Neumann, *Lebensmittelgeschaeft* (Foodstore) Brückner & Krill, and for other eateries and groceries like them, promise foods at moderate prices: coffees, Bolivian-produced "European" sausages, pastries, delicatessen items, and lunch and dinner menus identified with culinary pleasures from "back home." "Saûfst, stirbst / saûfst net, stirbst a. Also saûfl!! aber, 'Imperial!'" [If you booze, you die / if you don't booze, you also die. So booze!! But [at the] "Imperial!"] reads an advertisement in Viennese dialect for a newly established café-restaurant—which also promises a pleasant dining experience and daily musical entertainment. Made-to-order clothing, cut in the "latest European styles," is featured in the advertisements of the Haberdashery Berlin, the Casa Paris-Viena, and the Peletería Viena, but secondhand European men's and women's apparel, brought from overseas and sold by the refugees through the Lipczenko brothers' Casa Wera, is offered as an affordable alternative as well. The *Buchhandlung* (Bookstore) La América listing German editions of authors such as Franz Werfel, Paul Zech, and Bruno Weil, is regularly publicized in the weekly papers, as is the German-language rental library Osmaru, which lends out a wide range of previously owned fiction and nonfiction books at very low fees. The *Kleinkunstbühne* (Cabaret theater)—presenting scenes from Schnitzler, von Hoffmansthal, and Beer-Hoffmann, as well as readings of German classics and Viennese dialect skits—advertises its cultural offerings often, as does the refugee-organized Collegium Musicum, with its chamber music concerts and recitals featuring Mozart, Beethoven, and Schubert played by musicians trained at conservatories in Vienna, Prague, and Berlin. In each issue, starting in late August 1939, the *Rundschau* also carries a weekly schedule for the daily, hour-long German-language program on Radio Nacional, a Bolivian radio station. The broadcasts, produced and staffed by refugee actors and performers, consist of brief news summaries, lectures and recitals, dramatizations of German plays, mystery stories, and live and recorded performances of European classical and Viennese dance music.

In my own memories of childhood in Bolivia, I often recall the many occasions when my parents took me along to the Austrian Club—to the "Hogar Austriaco" (Austrian Home) as it was generally known in Spanish, or the "Federación de Austriacos Libres en Bolivia" (Federation of Free Austrians in Bolivia), as it was officially called. With special fondness, I remember family meals taken in the club's dining room, a large multipurpose room convertible into a theater or cabaret hall, with a small stage (curtained in the red and white colors of the Austrian flag) located at one end. My favorite dishes there, as well as at home, were the icons of Hapsburg cuisine: Viennese Schnitzel with potatoes and cucumber salad (Wiena Schnitzel mit Erdäpfel und Gurkensalat) or Hungarian goulash with 'Nockerl (dumplings), made complete with *Apfelstrudel* for dessert. I also recall a number of "entertainments" at the club to which I was taken by my parents—piano and violin recitals, theatrical skits, and one magic show in particular in which Heini Lipczenko, blowing on a flute and wearing a turban in imitation of a Hindu swami, "charmed" a snake out of a basket to perform a rhythmic dance.

Sifting through memorabilia of which I became the keeper when my mother died, I discover an "Hogar Austriaco" cabaret program, undated but clearly from the early 1940s. It introduces a show, *Radio Wien Sendet: Ein Wunschkabarett* [Radio Vienna broadcasts: A cabaret on demand] and lists, among its entertainment numbers, "In einem Wiener Vorstadtvarieté" [In a Viennese suburban music hall], "Ein Maederl aus Moedling" [A lass from Moedling], "Frauen sind zum Kuessen da" [Women are made to be kissed], and various other skits in Viennese dialect. "Der Wandrer, irrend in der Ferne" [The wanderer, astray in a distant land], declares a poem in an Austrian Club publication,

Wo fremd das Tier, der Baum, das Kraut,
Wo fremd die Nacht und ihre Sterne,
Wo fremd und tot der Menschenlaut,

Wie fuelt er sich allein, verstossen,
Wie Jauchzt sein Herz im fremden Land,
Wenn ploetzlicht er den Sprachgenossen,
Den heimatlichen Bruder fand!

[Site of strange animal, tree, and plant,
Site of a strange night and alien stars,
Site of unfamiliar and lifeless human sound,
How lonely and displaced he feels.
But how, in that strange land, his heart rejoices
When suddenly he comes upon,
A brother native from his home,
A speaker of his language.]
(Federación de Austriacos Libres 1944: 54)

Feelings of nostalgia, I realize, lie at the core of my own memories of the Austrian Club, and my recollections are layered and quite complex. They are not merely about the club's importance in my parents' communal life, or about the happy childhood hours I spent there with them. They also involve the cultural universe to which I connected *through* the club: to food, music, and theater certainly, but also to lively adult group conversation in the German spoken by Austrians, and to a mode of cultural communication—to jokes, conventions, etiquette, and an outlook on the world that derived from the common language and the common cultural background that the club's refugee members shared with one another. It connected me, in that sense, to a reconstructed version of Viennese bourgeois culture in particular, and to Austro-Germanic *kultur* more generally—to a cultural environment and discourse that I had never really known in its actual setting, but had only encountered as an already nostalgic reconstruction within a situation of displacement. Indeed, I now recognize that the nostalgic memory engendered in me—nostalgia about nostalgia, so to speak—was precisely one of the aims of the persons who founded the Austrian Club in 1941. In a "Festschrift" published in 1944, to display the club's activities after its first three years and to reaffirm the collective mission of its members, this goal is explicitly indicated: "To provide to the older generation some type of substitute (*Ersatz*) for that which they had lost [through emigration], and to the young, some rendering of a native cultural education they had been forced to give up or miss altogether in their displacement from [their Austrian] 'home'" (Federación de Austriacos Libres 1944: 14).

In employing nostalgic memory to perform this creative function—the recollection and recreation of aspects of the past within an institutional ambience able to reinforce the refugees' sense of cultural and historical continuity—the Austrian Club was effective but not at all unique. Other organizations, involving many of the same individuals as participants, played similar roles. It was no doubt from their recollections of the various Israelitische Kultusgemeinden in the larger cities of Central Europe, that one of the first centers of collective immigrant activity, the Comunidad Israelita, was founded in La Paz in 1939 by a group of Jewish refugees from Germany and Austria (Círculo Israelita 1987; Schwarz 1979: 81).[4] This communal organization established a Jewish synagogue, an old people's home, and two institutions that I attended: a *Kinderheim* serving as kindergarten, boarding school, and day care center, and a school, La Escuela Boliviana-Israelita. But, from its inception, the Comunidad also fulfilled a less utilitarian social function. Its quarters in the city, and its Sunday "garden retreat" in rural Obrajes, became meeting places where Jewish refugees could gather, eat meals, read newspapers, play cards, chess, or table tennis—where they could gossip, socialize, exchange information, and reminisce.[5] The Comunidad's quarters, in other words, like those of the "Hogar Austriaco" (but less identified with a single country of origin), were turned into a version of an institution that many of the immigrants would certainly have looked upon with a fond nostalgia: the *Klublokal* or coffeehouse of Central Europe.

Children of the refugees, like me, especially during the early years of

4. The Círculo Israelita, founded in 1935 by Polish and Rumanian Jews, was the first Jewish community organization in Bolivia. Although it would continue to exist as a separate entity throughout the war years and in the 1950s would absorb the by then much-diminished Comunidad, it was the Comunidad, with its larger Central European membership (in the 1940s) and its affiliated institutions, that dominated the community life of Jewish immigrants. For a history of the Círculo Israelita, see Círculo Israelita 1987.

5. In August 1939 the Asociación Judía was established in Cochabamba. In July 1940, the name of the organization was changed to Comunidad Israelita. It served Bolivia's second largest Jewish community, which officially was recorded as having five hundred registered members—but which, in all likelihood, was significantly larger. See "Historia de Nuestra Comunidad" 1989.

the immigration, received both formal and informal instruction strongly influenced by cultural memories of Europe. The purpose behind the establishment of the Escuela Boliviana-Israelita, for example, was two-fold: the school offered courses in Spanish so that recently arrived and Bolivia-born children of the immigrants might learn the local language, and it taught them to read, write, and do mathematics. It also provided optional supplemental instruction in basic elements of Jewish religion and history. But although Bolivian officials required the school to hire at least one Bolivian teacher to instruct its pupils in local and national history—in what the Bolivians called *educación cívica*—the pedagogical philosophy and curricular content of the Escuela Boliviana-Israelita differed little from those of elementary schools in Germany and Austria before the rise of Nazism (Círculo Israelita 1987: 171–75). The examples the immigrant teachers used in their subjects of instruction derived, as one might expect, from their Central European cultural background and experience.

Looking back through my report cards for grades one through four from the Escuela Boliviana-Israelita, and focusing on my grades in geography, I recall that I was in my second year of school when Dr. Ascher first taught us to locate the "Blue Danube," the "Rhine with its many castles," and the "beautiful Austrian Alps" on a map of Europe. And finding a *"Satisfecho"* (Satisfactory) mark as my final grade in music at the end of my third year reminds me that it was our teacher, Mr. Aaron, playing on a portable piano or an accordion, who taught us to sing German folk songs.

2. CRITICAL MEMORIES / LAYERED IDENTITIES

I am unable to remember with any certainty whether some type of nostalgic affect—in tone of voice, gesture, or sigh—was ever apparent to me in the course of the instruction we received from our immigrant teachers. I find it difficult to imagine, however, that such expressions of longing and bittersweet remembrance would have been altogether *absent* from the faces and bodies of teachers instructing the children of fellow refugees about a European world they had been forced to abandon. And yet, as I think back on Mr. Aaron, Dr. Ascher, the Escuela Boliviana-Israelita, the Austrian Club, and the refugee environment in which I was raised, I am also wary of privileging nostalgia too much, and mindful of simplification and distortion. The culture and community created by the refugee immigrants in Bolivia should certainly not be misrepresented as merely a curious and somewhat ironic reconstruction in the Andes of a nostalgically remembered and sanitized Central European culture and past — one from which Hitler, and the persecutions and policies that had engendered refugeehood, had been obliterated. The immigrants were, after all, *refugees* and not voluntary émigres. Before their departure from Europe, each of them had been identified as undesirable and stripped of citizenship and possessions. Their "present" in Bolivia — the "here and now" from which they looked back upon the past and confronted the future — had come about as a consequence of oppression and expulsion, and it was indelibly marked by painful loss, separation, and the ongoing war in Europe. Within that present, nostalgic memory certainly did *help* the refugees to transcend the negativity of their recent history by reconnecting them to broadly shared values and social practices that had characterized the Austro-German bourgeois culture to which they had belonged, or aspired to belong. In this respect, the creative communal reconstruction engendered by nostalgic memory was also a manifestation of cultural resistance and cultural survival — a denial of success to Nazi efforts to disconnect and expel Jews and other "undesirables" from the Austro-German *kulturkreis* in which they had played such an integral part. But nostalgic memory, and the selective emphasis on the positive from the past, was only one layer of recollection affecting the construction, as well as the content and character, of refugee culture in Bolivia. *Critical memory* — memory incorporating the negative and the bitter from the immediate past — was always present as well. As nostalgia's complicating "other side," it too became a prominent creative force and influence within Bolivian refugee society.

At one level, of course, critical memory of persecution "experienced" and "remembered" was the overarching framework of refugee collective identity in Boliva. Within a present clouded by displacement, insecurity, and war, the critical memory of their recent past was the connective tissue of their "refugeehood" — the ubiquitous bond that bridged many distinctions among them. The refugees, after all, had never been a homogeneous group. Despite their cultural affinities and the common language background that the largest group among them, from Germany and Austria, had in common, their origins and social status had been diverse in Central Europe, ranging across generational, educational, political, and class lines. Although the majority of those who came to Bolivia were Jews, or married to Jews, perhaps some 6 to 8 percent of them were non-Jewish *political* refugees: communists, socialists, and others persecuted by the Nazi regime (Guttentag 1991; Wolfinger 1990; E. Taus 1992; U. Taus 1992; Pinschower 1991; von zur Mühlen 1987). The Jews themselves differed greatly in the degree of their identification with their religion and its traditions. There were Zionists among them, atheists, orthodox believers, "High Holiday" Jews, and nonpracticers. They shared a common identity as Jews only in the sense, perhaps, that they had all been "othered" as "Jews" from the outside—by the Nazis in particular and Christian Europe generally.

But no matter what the background differences had been, or how the particularities of their individual life experiences varied among the refugees, their common history of persecution had placed them all in "the same boat." They were collectively conscious of the ongoing war in Europe, and were bonded by the fact that so many had relatives and friends from whom they had been separated. And the consciousness of that reality, in combination with the recent critical memories of their own persecutions and displacements, added a distinctly *political* dimension to many of the institutions they created, and to the culture and community they developed. If nothing else, this political dimension affirmed that, even though they had all been victimized, they had neither been crushed nor extinguished. "Everyday, we came together at a park bench in the Plaza 14 de Septiembre," commented Eva Markus about a refugee practice that became a routine in Cochabamba during the war years, "and we talked about the war from accounts in the press and radio. We weren't a consistent bunch. The same people weren't always there, and no one stayed very long. But we felt tied together, and our chats sometimes inspired activities—personal or in small groups—connected to the general effort to defeat the Nazis" (Markus 1995).

And yet, even though many of the refugees' differences were submerged within a collectivity broadly based on a common history of persecution and its critical remembrance, no single political grouping or organization ever emerged among them that would incorporate and reflect their common concerns and interests. "Refugeehood" always remained an amalgam of multiple and occasionally overlapping histories and identities. In this regard, critical memory also acted as an instrument of much more specific recollection and reaction—functioning as an overall "connector" among the refugees to be sure, but also stimulating a variety of responses to the past, and challenges to the present, that were based on very particularistic "national," "political," and "ethnic" identifications.

Again, the Austrian Club provides a clear illustration. While nostalgic memory had animated and shaped its function as a social and cultural institution that reproduced elements of a "lost homeland" in the Bolivian refuge, critical memory engendered and influenced the club's role as an activist political organization. The formal name of the club, after all, was "Federación de Austriacos Libres en Bolivia" (Federation of Free Austrians in Bolivia). In its charter document, and in the course of a number of "general assemblies" called during the war years, its members proclaimed the club as "nondenominational" and "above party affiliation," a democratic organization open to all Austrians—Gentiles as well as Jews, persons who were left, center, even monarchist in political identification. But members considered two fundamental tenets to be at the very heart of the club's existence and function: its reassertion of an Austrian national identity distinct from that of Germany, and its political work to reestablish a "free," "independent," "democratic" Austria that would negate Austria's Anschluss to the German Reich and battle Nazi domination (Federación de Austriacos Libres 1944: 9–10). "We were politically active on a number of levels," recalls Heinz Kalmar, who returned from Bolivia to Vienna after the war:

We stayed out of Bolivian national politics, but we did convince Bolivian officials to modify the forms for the "census of foreigners" of 1942 to include a separate "Austrian" category of identification—thus precluding the necessity of our having to identify ourselves as "German," or "Stateless." From admission receipts and collections taken at some of our functions, we donated funds and materials for the Allied war effort.   (Kalmar 1992)[6]

Writing on behalf of the "Free Austria Youth Group" of the La Paz Austrian Club to the international headquarters of the Austrian World Youth Movement in London in 1943, Heinz Markstein confirmed this activism and patriotic zeal. "We have had the opportunity," he declared,

to address Bolivians on radio to explain Austria's plight and to affirm our readiness to fight against Nazi fascism. Some of our men have even volunteered

6. The publication *Federación de Austriacos Libres* 1944 confirms Kalmar's recollections.

to join the Allied forces on the battlefield but have been refused. . . . We thus work to unify all Austrian youth in this country, and to inculcate within ourselves an even greater love for our homeland and for democracy.   (Markstein 1943?, 1945 [1943]: 21)

In formal gatherings and speeches, members of the club marked the March 11 anniversary of the Anschluss—which they viewed as the commemoration of "Austria's subjugation"—as well as the November 9 memorialization of *Kristallnacht*. In November 1942, on the fourth anniversary of that infamous event, Dr. Georg Terramare, a Catholic Austrian refugee who, as a novelist, playwright, actor, and director, was one of the club's most creative and engaged members, composed the words for an anthem, "Hymn der Freien Oesterreicher" [The hymn of the free Austrians]. Sung to the melody of the last movement of Beethoven's Eroica symphony, this alternative *Exilshymne* enabled Austrians in Bolivia to avoid the tune of their old anthem—the Haydn theme which the Germans also employed in *Deutschland, Deutschland, Über Alles*.[7] "Es wird ein Tag im Osten stehn" [In the East a day will come], the Terramare lyrics declared,

Und ueber's Land
Wird sich ein Sturm erheben,
·   ·   ·   ·   ·   ·   ·   ·   ·

New erstehn wirst du, Oesterreich!
·   ·   ·   ·   ·   ·   ·   ·   ·

Wir wollen einig stehen
·   ·   ·   ·   ·   ·   ·   ·

Mit neuer Kraft
·   ·   ·   ·   ·

Wollen dich, du heil'ges Land der Freiheit, wiederbaun.
Neu erstehn wirst du, Oesterreich!

[And o'er the land
A storm will lift,
·   ·   ·   ·   ·   ·

7. The old Austrian national anthem, "Gott erhalte Franz den Kaiser" [God save our Emperor Franz], was used by Joseph Haydn as a basis for the theme and variations in the second movement of his Quartet no. 3 in C Major (The "Emperor" Quartet), and then appropriated by the Germans as a tune for their anthem.

Newly risen will you be, Austria!

. . . .

United we wish to stand

. . . .

[And] With new strength

. . . .

We wish to rebuild you, you sacred land of freedom.
Newly risen will you be, Austria!]
(Federación de Austriacos Libres 1944: 22–23)

German refugees in Bolivia, unlike the Austrians, found it much more difficult to join together on the basis of national origin, under a single organizational umbrella. Many German Jewish and non-Jewish refugees, among them people like Ernst Schumacher, Willi Karbaum, Ernst Altmann, Hugo Efferoth, Erhart Löhnberg, and Wolfgang Hirsch-Weber, had been politically active in Germany, and had been persecuted for their activities in the banned Social Democratic Party (SPD) or in other anti-Nazi political organizations. Scores of members of the SPD had been helped to emigrate to Bolivia from Germany, or from their interim places of European refuge, by the Social Democratic Refugee-Aid organization, headquartered in Prague before the war (von zur Mühlen 1988: 217). Many of these Social Democrats, as well as other German "political" refugees, viewed their stay in Bolivia as an exile that would terminate as soon as the Nazi dictatorship was defeated and a return home to Germany became possible once again. In this respect they differed little from their Austrian counterparts. But members or supporters of competing German refugee political organizations like Freundschaft (Club Amistad), Das Andere Deutschland, Vereinigung Freier Deutschen, and Freies Deutschland, refused to coalesce into a larger anti-Fascist "popular front" association. An important effort in this regard—initiated in La Paz in 1942 by Ernst Schumacher, editor and owner of the widely circulated *Rundschau von Illimani*—to establish an "above party" "Free German" counterpart to the Austrian Club, with branches in Sucre, Cochabamba, and Oruro, fell apart within a relatively short period (von zur Mühlen 1988: 217–39).

The failure of German refugees to unify institutionally and to combine and act politically "as Germans" can certainly be attributed in part to ideological differences and long-standing antagonisms among supporters of competing political factions. The Vereinigung Freier Deutschen, like its sister affiliates in Argentina, Brazil, Chile, Uruguay, and Ecuador, attracted refugees who had been communist sympathizers or members of the Communist Party (KPD) in Germany. Das Andere Deutschland tended to be left-leaning but noncommunist in orientation—attractive to the considerable number of German refugees in Bolivia sympathetic to the SPD. Freies Deutschland, a third alternative, had a right-of-center appeal, and relatively few supporters. Political arguments among German refugees about the Hitler-Stalin pact, the politics of the USSR, and about their divergent expectations for the character and ideological direction of a post-Hitler Germany abounded. Such a range of political opinion, of course, and similar divisions, existed among Austrian refugees as well. But the intensity and uncompromising nature of political disagreement among German refugees appears to have been exacerbated by the clash of individual personalities and by what has been termed a "legendary" acrimony among German refugee "leaders"—characteristics reflected in many *Rundschau von Illimani* newspaper columns from the period, and noted in several refugee memoirs and accounts (von zur Mühlen 1988: 221–31). Among German refugees, it would seem, neither nostalgic remembrance of an absent German homeland, nor shared memories of persecution and expulsion, nor the universal desire for Nazi defeat, were sufficient to submerge the political divisions and animosities that they had imported to Bolivia—and which, within a period of months (after their arrival in 1938–39), surfaced once again.

Focusing only on the failure of German refugees to unite "as Germans" beneath a single umbrella organization, however, distorts the multilayered character of refugee identity in Bolivia, as well as the complexity of refugee responses and adjustments over time. Read more "thickly," taking into account the broader context of the Bolivian immigration, German refugee responses—like those of other national groups—clearly transcended the boundaries of national origin. *Individual* refugees from Germany, after all, like all refugees in Bolivia, were identified, and identified themselves, according to a number of other criteria. Their politics, their religion, their age, gender, class background, and, if Jewish, the nature and strength of their identification with Judaism all influenced and affected responses and adjustments to the world in which the refugees found themselves. At different moments, depending on circumstances, any one or combination of these identifications might emerge as primary and influential.

Thus among Jewish refugees in Bolivia, whether originally from Germany or not, the political dimension of critical memory was displayed in the very assertion of an ongoing Jewish existence and vitality in the public sphere — in the openness of the refugees' collective presentation of themselves "as Jews" both institutionally and symbolically. This was, on the one hand, reflected in the range of Jewish public organizations that were established not long after the large-scale influx of refugees from Central Europe began in the late 1930s: synagogues in La Paz and Cochabamba, a Jewish kindergarten, primary and secondary schools, a home for the aged, cemeteries, Jewish cultural and refugee-aid associations, and the largely German-Jewish dominated central community organization, the Comunidad Israelita. (The older Círculo Israelita had been created by Jews from Eastern Europe in 1935.) Each of these institutions, generally identified by a sign or placard in Spanish as well as in Hebrew lettering, occupied physical space within the urban surroundings — acreage, a building, a portion of an edifice — and was a tangible manifestation of Jewish presence and endurance.

But Jewish vitality was also reflected through the refugees' participation, "as Jews," in parades and public events celebrating Bolivian national holidays, and through their activities in public athletic and gaming competitions. Carrying the blue-white-blue banner and the Star of David insignia associated with a promised Jewish national homeland, young immigrant women and men in Bolivia's largest cities represented local branches of Maccabi, the international Jewish-Zionist sports association that had flourished throughout Europe before the outbreak of World War II (Savidor 1972).[8] They engaged in wide-ranging athletic and gaming contests open to spectators table tennis, tennis, soccer, swimming, track and field, chess — competing against one another within the association, but also against Bolivian and other Latin American teams (Círculo Israelita 1987: 263–310).

Clearly, the public presentation of continuing Jewish communal existence and spirit functioned politically as a concrete negation of images of Jewish degeneration and dissolution projected in anti-Semitic propaganda. During the war years, especially when news of German military victories and Nazi brutalities and killings brought fearful shudders to so many, they not only proclaimed survival but promised reconstruction and renewal. They displayed Judaism as an enduring religion and living

8. The Maccabi World Union was known as Maccabi in Bolivia. Its preadolescents' branch was Maccabi Hazair.

culture, and Jewish communal identity as a basis for the Zionist dream of nationhood.

At the same time, however, the positive political functions of Jewish communal self-representation should not obscure the fact that indisputable differences — social, political, and economic, as well as in the degree of connection to Jewish religion and practice — continued to exist among individual Jewish refugees and between Jewish groups. For many Jewish refugees in Bolivia, the tie to Judaism in its broadest communal sense remained secondary to other connections and identifications. Was one a Jew *first*, and *then* a German or an Austrian? Or was political identification and ideology the primary allegiance — to social democracy, to communism, to some version of internationalism? And what about differences within Judaism? Between the religious and the secular? Among Labor Zionists, other Zionists, and assimilationists? Among Jews from different cultural backgrounds, with distinctly different cultural memories? Cultural distinctions and prejudices imported to Bolivia from Europe, for example, helped to maintain an old rift between the German-speaking Jewish refugee majority from the Austro-German *Kulturkreis*, and the smaller, predominantly Yiddish-speaking group from Poland, Russia, and other parts of Eastern Europe (Archivo de La Paz 1942).[9] The German speakers, who were considered "highly assimilated" and referred to as *Yekkes* by the East Europeans, tended to fraternize with one another, keeping their social distance from the *Polacos* (as the East Europeans were called) whom they often viewed as "more primitive," and "less cultured" (Wolfinger 1990; Weinheber 1995). While Yekkes and Polacos, Austrian Jews and German Jews, Zionists and assimilationists, the orthodox and the secular, were all at times able to elide distinctions among themselves — in the course of their economic and athletic interactions, as well as on those occasions when they rallied together to present themselves to others *as Jews* — the multilayered character of refugee identity, and the complexity and dynamic nature of refugee adjustment, remained a central characteristic of the Bolivian immigration.

9. Though a minority in Bolivia's refugee population overall, East European Jews were at the core of the smaller-scale Jewish immigration to Bolivia that preceded the 1938–1941 influx from Central Europe. In addition, a second wave of Jewish immigration to Bolivia, consisting largely of persons of Eastern European origin, many of whom were camp survivors, occurred after the end of the war. Ironically, ex-Nazis like the notorious Klaus Barbie also found refuge in Bolivia in the late 1940s.

3. LOOKING BACK: THREE VIGNETTES

July 1991. Julius Wolfinger, in the living room of his apartment in Queens, New York:

For many of us from Austria and Germany, Bolivia was like a hotel. We arrived there, found a safe place to stay a while, and then many of us packed up again and left. Some didn't go far—maybe to Argentina, or Chile, or Brazil—places in South America that were a little more European. Others, like me and my parents, were able to come to the US after the war. Ferry Kohn, and other younger people emigrated to Palestine—Israel—in '48 or '49. And then some, who couldn't be happy anywhere else, actually went back—to Vienna, to where they had come from in Austria and Germany.

I've been in this country for forty-five years. But you know, if I didn't have a bad heart, I would really like to visit Bolivia. I would like to see it again—to eat salteñas,[10] see the mountains. I was a young man when I was there. We had some good times. Bolivia took us in. I feel a deep attachment to the place. I miss it. (Wolfinger 1990)

April 1995. Liesl Lipczenko is speaking to me on the telephone. Originally from Vienna, she and her husband and two sons emigrated from Bolivia to New York in 1951, but they have lived in Cleveland for over thirty years.

LS: *Even though I left La Paz when I was ten, I feel a strong connection—everything seems familiar.*

Liesl: *I have such good memories of those years. I wish I was younger and could go there again. I have real longing* [Sehnsucht] *for the place. Not for Vienna, not at all. But for Bolivia, I have* Sehnsucht. (Lipczenko 1995)

A Nostalgic Recollection:

My mother's apartment in Kew Gardens, New York. The framed, artist-signed lithograph of St. Stephen's Cathedral and the Stefansplatz—originally acquired in La Paz—hangs in the living room. As it had been in our apartment on Calle México, it is again centrally placed. But here, on a shelf beneath the picture, my mother has also displayed an old, one-armed, plaster of paris ekeko—a Bolivian Aymara folk god of good fortune and plenty. Standing on short legs, fat-bellied,

---

10. *Salteñas*, eaten at midmorning, consist of a stew of beef or chicken, peas, potatoes, hard-boiled eggs, and a spicy sauce, wrapped in sweet dough and baked.

wearing sandals made from recycled auto tires, a knit Indian cap, and a manta, he is laden with miniaturized versions of wished-for goods and possessions: currency, sacks of grain and sweets, noodles, beans, baskets, utensils, tools, suitcases, and other foodstuffs and essentials. The belief is that ekeko *must be "fed" annually by its owner—rewarded with a gift—so that he, in turn, will bring luck and prosperity. Every year, my mother put a fresh cigarette in* ekeko's *mouth.*

POSTSCRIPT: NOTES FROM A RECENT VISIT TO BOLIVIA

La Paz's main boulevard, Avenida 16 de Julio, better known as El Prado, has changed considerably over the years since my family left Bolivia for the United States. The most visible changes occurred after the mid-1970s, when many of the street's stately private homes and public buildings, with their massive, carved wooden doors, ornate stained-glass windows, and elaborate iron latticework and balustrades, were razed and replaced by large hotels, tall office buildings, and numerous shops and eateries with electric signposts and flashing placards. The Prado's impressive central promenade still remains much as I remember it, with its trimmed flower beds, its elaborately designed burnt orange and white tiled walkway lined by trees and white bubble lampposts, its French-designed fountain displaying a statue of Neptune in the center, and its monuments honoring Cristóbal Colón and Bolivia's heroic founder, José Antonio de Sucre. But the once-genteel promenade and avenue is now thickly crowded until the late hours of the evening with pedestrians and street hawkers—a reflection of La Paz's immense population growth during the last two decades and its roadway is often packed bumper to bumper with cars and loud minibuses. Gone is the slow-moving electric tram that ran on tracks on the Hotel Sucre side of the Avenida 16 de Julio—the *tranvía* that I often took to school, and the steel rails on which we children placed bottletops to be flattened into objects of play. And the whitewashed turn-of-the-century building that housed the synagogue and my first-grade classroom now stands boarded up, seemingly ready for demolition, having failed in its most recent function: as a hamburger and fast food restaurant.

The "Confitería Elis," however, owned by an Austrian Jew who had emigrated to Bolivia in 1939 on the same ship with my parents, continues to thrive on this street. On signs in its showcase and on its printed menu, it advertises its longevity and quality as an establishment specializing in excellent European meals and baked goods for over forty-five years. And although it is now connected by name and ownership to a trendier New York–style pizzeria on the same block that caters to a younger crowd, it has remained a popular restaurant with local *Paceños* (residents of La Paz) and with tourists who appreciate its well-prepared food, elaborate pastries, and reasonable prices. It offers daily specials and a wide-ranging blend of cuisines: Bolivian *chairo*, matzoball soup, *Wienerschnitzl*, goulash, arroz con pollo. "Elis" is also the place that continues to attract a regular crowd of "old customers"—mostly Jewish men in their sixties and seventies who came to Bolivia as refugees in the late 1930s, or as Holocaust survivors after the war. The number of Jewish refugees still remaining in Bolivia has dwindled to under a thousand. Every weekday around five in the evening, a group of them comes together at "Elis," frequently at the same table—the *Stammtisch*, as one of them calls it—and they order tea, coffee, or juice and try to resist the temptation of indulging in a slice of *Mohnstrudel, Apfelstrudel, Streuselkuchen*, or whichever cake or pastry looks most appealing in the display case near the kitchen. Their conversation is wide ranging, their opinions strong, and their arguments animated and (sometimes) loud. They speak to one another in many languages—Yiddish, Spanish, English, Polish, German—but usually in what sounds like a multilingual blend. They discuss business, the decline of the dollar, the world situation, the outlook of the future, and they compare recollections of the past. None of them, they tell me, would ever think of returning to Europe. Many have sent their children to the United States to college or for professional training, and some have relatives in North America or in other South American countries whom they visit occasionally. Still, they feel themselves established in Bolivia, permanent residents, fixtures in the landscape. Like the "Confitería Elis" that they frequent, they have maintained much of the old world within them: its memories, its tastes, aspects of its culture. Yet in a very real sense, they are *no longer of that old world*. Nostalgia for their homeland, for Europe, if it still arises within them on occasion, is recognized as nostalgia for an irreplaceable loss. But they describe the feeling in more accepting terms—as more akin to leave-taking and final separation than to a yearning for return.

REFERENCES

Archivo de La Paz
  1942 "Censo de Extranjeros (Judíos)," Boxes 1–13.
Asociación Israelita de Cochabamba
  1989 *Historia de Nuestra Comunidad*. Mitteilungsblatt der Asociación Israelita de Cochabamba (Bolivia): Publicación de Gala en Conmemoración de las "Bodas de Oro" de la Colectividad Israelita de Cochabamba, Noticiario no. 29, Noviembre.
Círculo Israelita
  1987 *Medio Siglo de Vida Judía en La Paz* (La Paz: Círculo Israelita).
Davis, Fred
  1979 *Yearning for Yesterday: A Sociology of Nostalgia* (New York: Free Press).
Federación de Austriacos Libres en Bolivia
  1944 *Zum Dreijaehrigen Bestehen der Federación de Austriacos Libres en Bolivia* (La Paz: Federación de Austriacos Libres en Bolivia).
Guttentag, Werner
  1991 Video interview with author, July 31.
Halbwachs, Maurice
  1925 *Les Cadres sociaux de la mémoire* (Paris: Alcan).
Hewison, Robert
  1987 *The Heritage Industry: Britain in a Climate of Decline* (London: Methuen).
Hofer, Johannes
  1934 [1688] "Medical Dissertation on Nostalgia," translated by Carolyn K. Anspach, *Bulletin of the History of Medicine* 2: 376–91.
Jüdische Wochenschau
  1939–42 Monthly "Bolivia" section of the Buenos Aires newspaper.
Kalmar, Heinz
  1992 Video interview with author, June 3.
Lasch, Christopher
  1984 "The Politics of Nostalgia," *Harper's*, November, 65–70.
Lipczenko, Liesl
  1995 Telephone interview with author, April 6.
Lowenthal, David
  1975 "Past Time, Present Place: Landscape and Memory," *Geographical Review* 65(1): 1–36.
  1989 "Nostalgia Tells It Like It Wasn't," in *The Imagined Past: History and Nostalgia*, edited by Christopher Shaw and Malcolm Chase, 18–32 (Manchester: Manchester University Press).
Markstein, Heinz
  1943? "La Juventud Austriaca hable [*sic*] a la Juventud Boliviana." Typed radio script.

1945 [1943] Letter published in *Jugend Voran: Anti-Nazi Periodical of the Austrian World Youth Movement* (London): 21.

Markus, Eva
1995 Video interview with author, March 22.

Nielsen, F. W.
1939 "Vaterland," *Rundschau vom Illimani*, December 29.

Pinschower, Heinz
1991 Video interview with author, April 10.

Rundschau vom Illimani
1939–46 Weekly newspaper (La Paz).

Savidor, Menachem
1972 "Maccabi World Union," in *Encyclopaedia Judaica*, 11: 664–65 (New York: Macmillan).

Schwarz, Egon
1979 *Keine Zeit für Eichendorff: Chronik unfreiwilliger Wanderjahre* (Königstein: Athenäum).

Starobinski, Jean
1966 "The Idea of Nostalgia," *Diogenes* 54: 81–103.

Stroheim, Bruno
1940 "Kleiner Emigrationsfilm," *Rundschau vom Illimani*, February 2.

Taus, Egon
1992 Video interview with author, April 21.

Taus, Ursula
1992 Video interview with author, April 21.

von zur Mühlen, Patrik
1987 "Jüdische und deutsche Identität von Lateinamerika-Emigranten," *Exilforschung. Ein Internationales Jahrbuch* 5: 55–67.
1988 *Fluchtziel Lateinamerika: Die deutsche Emigration 1933–1945: Politische Aktivitäten und soziokulturelle Integration* (Bonn: Neue Gesellschaft).

Vromen, Suzanne
1986 "Maurice Halbwachs and the Concept of Nostalgia," in *Knowledge and Society: Studies in the Sociology of Culture Past and Present: A Research Annual*, edited by H. Kuklick and E. Lond, 6: 55–66 (Greenwich, CT: JAI).
1993 "The Ambiguity of Nostalgia," in *YIVO Annual*. Vol. 21, *Going Home*, edited by Jack Kugelmass, 69–86 (Evanston, IL: Northwestern University Press).

Weinheber, Alfredo
1995 Video interview, March 29.

Williams, Raymond
1973 *The Country and the City* (New York: Oxford University Press).

Wolfinger, Bertha
1941? Undated letter to Eugen (Jevö) Spitzer, in my possession.

Wolfinger, Julius
1990 Video interview, July 2.

SUSAN RUBIN SULEIMAN

MONUMENTS IN A FOREIGN TONGUE: ON

READING HOLOCAUST MEMOIRS BY EMIGRANTS

What would happen if all the members of my family disappeared? I would
maintain for some time the habit of attributing a meaning to their first names.
MAURICE HALBWACHS, On Collective Memory

TRAUMA, PSYCHOANALYSTS tell us, has a timeless quality: age does
not wither it. The literature of testimony about the trauma of the Holocaust bears out this fact. Thirty, forty, fifty years after the events, survivors of Nazi persecution in Europe continue to feel the necessity "to
speak out, to tell it all" (T. Levi 1995:3). Or "to tell at last" (Rosenberg
1993), for many affirm that the memory of the events has never left them;
only their telling has been delayed. As the century approaches its close,
the body of autobiographical writings by survivors, already immense,
keeps growing.[1]

My thanks to Marianne Hirsch for her important suggestion about the structure
of this essay; to Froma Zeitlin for her wisdom and erudition about the Holocaust,
which she has generously shared with me, along with her impressive library; and to
Brian McHale, Orly Lubin, Alan Rosen, Meir Sternberg, and Hana Wirth-Nesher
for their careful reading of an earlier version of this essay and their very helpful
comments.

1. As far as I know, there exists no exhaustive bibliography of survivors' memoirs; Young (1988) and Dwork (1991) list hundreds of titles between them, but these
are already outdated. The recent spate of publications is partly due, no doubt, to
the systematic efforts (stepped up as the number of survivors dwindles) by museums and centers for Holocaust studies to collect survivors' testimonies. While
these efforts have focused mainly on collecting videotaped oral testimonies by the
largest number of witnesses possible, the publication of written memoirs has been
encouraged by series like the Holocaust Library in the United States and the recently created Library of Holocaust Testimonies in England. Besides Jewish presses
such as Ktav or the Jewish Publication Society, some American university presses
have published survivors' memoirs in the past few years. The hierarchy of publishing houses for such work, ranging from major New York publishers to tiny operations in New Jersey or California, is fascinating. However, every publication implies
the belief (both by the writer and the publisher) that a responsive public exists for

I want to focus here on a small segment of that body: recent memoirs by survivors who are not writing in their native tongue, nor in a second language learned in early childhood, but in a language to which they came as teenagers or adults and which, for that reason, they must experience as foreign. Even more specifically, and to add an extra twist to the discussion, I will consider books written in English and French by Hungarian survivors — the twist being that I, too, am Hungarian by birth, though English does not feel to me like a foreign tongue. This, then, will be an exercise in shuttling between two shores of foreignness — or perhaps it's a single shore seen from opposite sides.

While students of Holocaust literature are keenly aware of problems of language and representation, they have paid surprisingly little attention to a problem one might call representing — or remembering, or memorializing — the Holocaust in translation.[2] Yet the first thing that strikes any viewer of videotaped oral testimonies by survivors living in the United States (and this must be true of other countries as well) is that almost all of them speak English with a heavy Eastern European, or occasionally French or German, accent. In written texts, of course, one cannot actually hear an accent; but there exist written equivalents, and some writers have exploited them to great artistic effect (see Sternberg 1981). Novelists have rendered "foreign accents" by means of fractured syntax (where the syntax of the native language interferes with that of the acquired language), misspelled words (where the misspelling reflects a mispronunciation), or the selective use of foreign words and phrases inserted into the narrative.[3] In the domain of Holocaust literature, Alan

---

the work. This is one difference between published memoirs and archives of testimonies, whether written or taped.

2. Sidra Ezrahi notes in the introduction to her classic study of Holocaust fiction that "Holocaust novels written in English by survivors from Europe . . . bear the salient marks of a translated idiom" (1980: 12). She does not foreground this perception in her readings of individual works, however, and her study does not deal with memoirs. For discussions of general problems of language and representation in relation to the Holocaust, see Ezrahi 1980, Langer 1991, and Young 1988; some recent collections indicate the range of these commentaries: see Friedländer 1992, Hartman 1994, Kritzman 1995, and Lang 1988.

3. Paradoxically, the more the mixing of languages is foregrounded, the greater the degree of "literariness" of the work. As we shall see, the written memoirs of Holocaust survivors who are not professional writers tend to erase the signs of

Rosen has analyzed Art Spiegelman's use of the father's foreign accent in *Maus* (which can actually be heard in the CD-ROM version): Vladek's fractured English when he recounts his concentration camp experiences is meant to emphasize the "foreignness" of the Holocaust itself to human experience, as well as to indicate Vladek's own foreignness in America (Rosen 1995). Spiegelman, however, is a native speaker and writer of English—his use, and indeed exaggeration, of his father's accented speech is an artistic choice, similar to Henry Roth's use of Yiddish and Hebrew to indicate the family's "foreignness" in his modernist masterwork *Call It Sleep* (Wirth-Nesher 1991). It is a quite different matter when the witness in oral testimony or the author of a written memoir is herself or himself a foreign speaker.

Not that the published memoirs of those for whom English is a foreign language lack correct grammar—nothing as obviously "accented" as that, either because the authors have perfect command of English grammar (the way only foreigners do, we're often told) or because they've had the benefit of good editing.[4] I have in mind more subtle marks of foreignness, that is, of separation from one's audience.

The commentators' lack of focus on this phenomenon may be due to its very ubiquity. With few notable exceptions (Primo Levi's being the best known), the large majority of memoirs by Jewish survivors of Nazi persecution have been written by emigrants—people in a permanent state of exile from their countries of origin. There are historical reasons for this: most of the Jewish survivors from Eastern Europe either did not return home after the war (Elie Wiesel is a case in point), or else returned but soon left again in order to avoid further pogroms (e.g., in Poland) or to escape from communist regimes behind the Iron Curtain (e.g., in Poland, Hungary, Czechoslovakia, and Romania). The exceptions are the French or Italian Jews, like Levi, who returned home after deportation and stayed there, writing books in their native language, addressed to a native audience.[5] Some Eastern Europeans also returned and stayed,

---

foreign languages, opting instead for what Sternberg calls the "homogenizing convention" (1981: 224), where everything is rendered in "standard English."

4. Some recent Holocaust memoirs were cowritten, presumably with a native speaker and professional writer (see Lerner 1980 and Wieder 1984).

5. Obviously, Jews were not the only survivor-victims of the camps who published memoirs. Many of the famous testimonies are by non-Jews (Borowski, Delbo,

but in the communist countries they were for a long time discouraged from writing about their experiences as Jewish victims of the Holocaust. What Ivan Sanders has noted about Hungary is also true of other communist countries: "The persecution and annihilation of Jews came under the heading of Fascist atrocities; it was considered unnecessary, inappropriate even, to focus specifically on the Jewish tragedy. There were no Jews, only victims of persecution" (1985: 191).

Among the emigrants, some wrote their memoirs in their native language (Wiesel wrote *La Nuit* [1960] in Yiddish before rewriting it in French), but their relation to the audience "back home" remained problematic. Wiesel's Central European Yiddish-speaking audience no longer existed, except as individuals and small groups dispersed all over the globe. It was only after rewriting his book in French and publishing it in Paris that he found a large audience. Olga Lengyel, a doctor and survivor of Auschwitz, wrote her devastating memoir *Five Chimneys* in her native Hungarian immediately after the war, in Paris; it was first published in a French translation in 1946. She added to it, again in Hungarian, for the American edition that appeared the following year; as far as I know, *Five Chimneys* has never been published in Hungary, or in Hungarian.[6] Jean Améry, an Austrian by birth (his real name was Hans Mayer), wrote *At the Mind's Limits* (1980 [1966]) in his native German, even though he had been living in Brussels for many years. His book was acclaimed in Germany, among other places; yet he explained in his preface that he sought a German public because the Germans "in their overwhelming majority do not, or no longer, feel affected by the darkest and at the same time most characteristic deed of the Third Reich" (ibid.: xiv). Even though he

---

Tillion) who were deported for resistance activities. These works are generally written in the native tongue and for a native audience.

6. The writing and publication history of such works can be difficult to trace. In the case of *Five Chimneys*, I have pieced it together from the acknowledgments to the American and British editions, where the author thanks her French publisher, Editions du Bateau Ivre (Lengyel 1959), and Clifford Coch for translating the work from French to English, as well as Paul P. Weiss "for translating the balance from Hungarian" (Lengyel 1947). Curiously, no other credit is given to the translators, whose names do not appear on the title or copyright pages. According to catalog information, the French version appeared in 1946, translated from the Hungarian by Ladislas Gara. I have not seen this version.

was writing as a "native speaker to native speakers," Améry took pains to remind his first readers that they were radically different from him. He considered himself homeless (ibid.: 41–61).

It might be argued that all Holocaust memoirs are essentially — or as metaphysicians say, transcendentally — homeless. In positive terms, we might call them global. When such works become recognized, their recognition is worldwide; most readers have read Levi, Wiesel, or Améry in translation. But homelessness as a metaphor or a philosophical concept is different from actual homelessness. Améry, after living in Belgium for over twenty years, wrote: "There is no 'new home.' Home is the land of one's childhood and youth. Whoever has lost it remains lost himself, even if he has learned not to stumble about in the foreign country" (ibid.: 48). His view is perhaps extreme in its sense of irreplaceable loss (he committed suicide twelve years after publishing *At the Mind's Limits*), as well as in its idealization of "home" as a place of fulfillment. (Many who possess a "home" rail against it, as we know.) But by its very extremism, it suggests that some people — and some books — are more homeless than others. Nathan Wachtel has pointed out that in the case of Holocaust memoirs, the "lost paradise" of childhood is gone "not simply . . . because time has gone and 'nostalgia isn't what it used to be': [but because] it was brutally destroyed, assassinated" (1986: 324; see also Wieviorka 1994).

One dividing line, I believe, runs between works that were written "at home," in the native language, addressed to an implied native audience, and works that were from the start and in their very composition split off from the writer's first language or public. Among the latter, the most "homeless" are memoirs written not only far from home, but in a foreign tongue (one experienced as foreign); they are "in translation" from the start, with no original.[7]

Anxiety about not being understood runs high among the writers of

7. It's not completely clear where Wiesel's *La Nuit* belongs. First written in exile but in the native tongue, it was rewritten in an adopted tongue that became the author's primary language for writing. French can hardly be thought of as a "foreign tongue" for Wiesel, although technically it is, according to my criteria — he was around sixteen by the time he reached Paris. The significant difference may be between those who only write one memoir and someone like Wiesel, who becomes a professional writer in the adopted language.

Holocaust memoirs, wherever they may be. Primo Levi, writing in Italian in Italy, with huge success,[8] nevertheless felt less and less sure of his public; he doubted, as one commentator writes, "that his voice [would] be heard; and if heard, understood; and if understood, effective" (Horowitz 1994: 52). All the more so for the emigrant survivor writing in a foreign tongue: the abyss that separates his or her experience from the reader's is doubled by the difference in language, which is of course also a difference in worlds. To quote Améry again: "Every language is part of a total reality to which one must have a well-founded right of ownership if one is to enter the area of that language with a good conscience and a confident step" (1980: 53–54). The Eastern European who writes in English or French (or Spanish?[9]) has acquired the reader's language, perhaps even to the point of entering it with a "confident step." But the places and events she/he writes about, including those that preceded the radical break of persecution or deportation, are cut off from the "adopted" reader by multiple separations: of language, geography, traditions, material culture—in short, of collective memory. Such a survivor can affirm literally the metaphor David Lowenthal borrowed from a novel: "The past is a foreign country; they do things differently there" (1985: xvi).

Foreign for whom? At this point we return to the two shores I spoke of earlier; for foreignness is a shifting word, whose referent changes with the speaker and the listener. If I know that my familiar world is foreign to you, I can try to "translate" it for you in various ways; but in that very process, I will also be signaling our mutual foreignness: "Humming a *csárdás*—a Hungarian dance tune" (Isaacson 1990: 3). Presuming the reader's ignorance, the author underlines her difference. This is even more evident when it comes to proper names: "Tolcsva, Hungary. Don't look for it on the map. It exists in relation to other places. More than one hundred kilometers northeast of Budapest. About thirty kilometers from Sátoraljaújhely" (Lerner 1980: 11). No amount of glossing will as-

8. *Survival in Auschwitz* [Se questo è un uomo] (1961 [1947]) sold very few copies when it first appeared in 1947, but became an international best-seller after it was reissued in 1956 (P. Levi 1995: 57, 87).

9. I have not investigated survivors' memoirs written in Spanish, and have not seen any listed in bibliographies; but given the large postwar emigration to South America, I assume some have been published. (If not, that fact is itself worth explaining.) Another body of work I am not competent to deal with is memoirs written in Hebrew by emigrants to Israel.

similate the foreign proper name, nor is it translatable. It is the flag of the foreign a stubborn kernel of otherness.

But this is where my twist occurs, because (as is obvious if I read the sentences aloud) I happen to be a reader to whom these foreign names are familiar, or at least pronounceable; to me and others like me — emigrants, displaced persons from the writer's native land and tongue — the names appear simultaneously as foreign bodies (when seen from the English-speaking shore) and as signals of a home that once was but is no more. My "between" position allows me to see the author's attempts at translation or assimilation, and their failure; it also allows — nay, compels — me to engage in what I have elsewhere called autobiographical reading: reading another's story as if it were, or could have been, one's own (Suleiman 1994: 199–214). Imaginative projection of the self onto another identity probably accompanies all reading of stories, and to that degree all reading can be considered autobiographical; but the strongest kind of autobiographical reading, I have suggested, occurs when the reader's life story actually intersects in some significant way with the story she is reading (ibid.). This may explain my own compelling interest in Holocaust memoirs by Hungarian Jewish emigrants.

Although technically I qualify as a survivor of the Holocaust, I was too young to have lived through that time with a genuine awareness of what was happening to me. When the Nazis marched into Hungary and started rounding up the Jews in the spring of 1944, I was little more than a toddler. Like a handful of other exceptionally lucky children from wartime Europe, I emerged from the war with both my parents, as well as my grandparents and several aunts and uncles, still alive. (A huge extended family was killed, but I never knew them.)[10] Almost all of us left Hungary a few years later. Today, people very rarely notice that I have a slight accent when I speak English. Had I been four or five years older when I arrived here, I would now probably have the unmistakable Hungarian

---

10. Among other Hungarian child survivors of the Holocaust who have published memoirs, the only one I know of who was lucky enough to keep both parents is Andrew Riemer (1992), whose family emigrated to Australia after the war. Susan Varga, who also lives in Australia, lost her father when she was a year old (1995: 3). Riemer and Varga write English as a "stepmother tongue." The same can be said of Saul Friedländer's relation to French, in his beautiful memoir *Quand vient le souvenir* [When memory comes] (1978). Friedländer's first language, abandoned in early childhood, was Czech.

accent, with its rolling *rs* and deep vowels, and difficulties pronouncing *th* or *aw*, that was my mother's way of speaking even after forty years in the United States. I might also have, very possibly, a mastery of the language and a stock of cultural baggage—poetry, proverbs—that would make Hungarian my true mother tongue.

As it is, English is my mother tongue—a kindly stepmother tongue with a twin sister, French. But I have enough investment in Hungarian to make my reading of Holocaust memoirs by Hungarian Jewish emigrants an autobiographical experience. And I would now like to look at that experience more closely. First, names; then, a commonplace.

NAMES; OR, THE POWER OF THE SIGNIFIER

Over the past few months, I have read—devoured would be a more accurate description—close to a dozen books by Hungarian survivors of the Holocaust, all but one published in the last fifteen years (one appeared in 1978). What do they have in common?[11] First, authors who are not professional writers: with one exception (Shlomo Breznitz, a professor

11. Although I may not cite each of these works individually, I perceive them as a corpus which manifests a striking range of shared properties. While I do not consider these works by Hungarians to be a separate subgenre within the genre of Holocaust memoirs, I do think they are part of another subgenre: Holocaust memoirs written by emigrant survivors who are not professional writers, many years after the experience, "in a foreign tongue." Other recent works by Polish, German, and Austrian survivors belong to the same subgenre. My own remarks are based on the following works: Breznitz 1993; Edelstein 1985; Gabor 1981; Isaacson 1990; Leitner 1978; Lerner 1980; T. Levi 1995; Siegal 1981, 1985; Vital-Tihanyi 1981; and Wieder 1984. Even within this group, the degree of artfulness or literary skill varies considerably, but I am less concerned with that here than with what they have in common.

Exactly who should be called a Hungarian Jew is not always clear, because after World War I Hungary lost a large part of its territory and a considerable number of Hungarian speakers, including many Jews, to neighboring countries. Many of these people continued to speak Hungarian and to identify themselves as such; many also spoke Yiddish, and some even spoke Yiddish as their primary language, while considering themselves Hungarian. (Hungary temporarily reoccupied some of these ceded areas during the war.) Among the memoirs I discuss, only the one by Shlomo Breznitz (1993) is in the doubtful category—Breznitz, born in Slovakia, spoke Hungarian at home. He emigrated to Israel after the war with his mother and sister, but wrote his memoir in English.

of psychology who has published scholarly books), they have published no other works besides their memoirs (Aranka Siegal's takes up two volumes). Second (and probably related), these books are "reader-friendly" in their use of language: they generally keep foreign words out (or gloss them if they must use them), try no experiments in polylingualism, and opt for traditional forms of narration, description, and dialogue. Poeticians would say that they emphasize the referential over the poetic function of language, or that they lack literariness. (Leitner's *Fragments of Isabella* [1983 {1978}] is an exception, experimenting with short, emotional fragments.) At the same time, they are all marked as "foreign" to the non-Hungarian reader by the presence of unassimilable linguistic elements, namely, an abundance of Hungarian proper names.

Third, all of these books bear dedications, most of them to those who perished — specific family members, or all those in the camps, or all who died from persecution. The other dedications are divided between supportive family members, some of whom shared the author's trials; and the young, the author's children and grandchildren.

Fourth, they have in common the same story, with variations: a peaceful childhood and adolescence in a provincial city or small village (one in Budapest), a more or less happy, prosperous, educated family, more or less knowledge and observance of Jewish traditions, more or less friendly Christian neighbors, and then the Break: for most, this meant being rounded up into a ghetto, then deported to the netherworld of Auschwitz; for a few, it meant false identities and desperate scrambles from one hiding place to another; for all, it meant the permanent loss of loved ones, of home, of a world — and after the war, sooner or later, alone or with a family member, emigration and a new life elsewhere.

A few accounts end with liberation, but most continue well beyond. Two (Gabor's and Trude Levi's) are full-length autobiographies coming up to the present; these two authors, both of whom were totally alone after the war, appear to have had the most distressing postwar experiences: failed marriages, frustrated hopes, in one case the suicide of an adult child. But like all of these memoirs, theirs at least end on a small note of triumph: despite terrible suffering, the authors have finally found peace, even happiness. All but three of the books (those by Siegal and Breznitz's, which happen to be the only ones published by major "literary" presses) include photographs: of the author and her or his family before the war; of the author, alone or in a group (not family, generally) soon after liberation; of the author today, surrounded by children, spouse, grandchildren. Sometimes the prewar photographs are accompanied by a notation: "Of the people in this picture, I alone survived." But even if it is not explicitly stated, the prewar photographs often function as tombstones, markers of the dead. At the same time, they provide a glimpse into a life untouched, as yet, by catastrophe—the life before the Break, lived by people who had no idea of its approaching end.[12]

Finally, the majority of these books (eight out of eleven in my sample) are by women. This is not the result of a skewed autobiographical choice on my part, but reflects the corpus: more Hungarian women survivors than men have published memoirs in English or French over the past fifteen years. Yael Danieli, a psychologist who works with survivor families, has noted that "compared to the Jewish woman, the Jewish man was at an immense disadvantage in achieving psychological recovery" after the war, for reasons ranging from the physical (circumcised men had been less able to hide, were more easily identified than women) to the psychological (men felt greater pressure to be breadwinners and to assume the role of head of the family, at a time when they had suffered tremendous blows to their self-esteem) (1988: 115). Women survivors were able, on the whole, to make easier adjustments to emigration. Some young women married their American liberators or men in host countries like France or Sweden, thus finding support and protection almost immediately after their ordeals. This may have allowed them more easily to write and bring a project to completion: the truly desperate don't publish books, as a rule. Or if they do, the world hears about it. These memoirs, by contrast, are modest achievements: they are not meditative or philosophical but narrative, needing to tell a story.[13] Améry and Primo Levi also tell stories, but theirs are primarily meditative works.

Terrence des Pres remarked, in his classic study published before any of

12. Such prewar photographs as documentation of a life before catastrophe are an important feature of Holocaust memorializing, as in the Tower of Faces at the United States Holocaust Memorial Museum in Washington. (For a perceptive analysis see Liss 1992.) They are also found in the many "*yizkor* books" commemorating the life of destroyed Jewish communities, published after the war (see Wachtel 1986).

13. The fact that these works were published (and, mostly, written) so many years after the events suggests that even the women survivors were sufficiently traumatized after the war not to want to dwell on—or try to recall—their experiences. Theorists of trauma have noted that there is often a significant delay between traumatic events and their recollection.

these memoirs, that in concentration camp testimonies "from one report to the next the degree of consistency is unusually high" (1976: 29). He attributed this phenomenon to the horrific reality of the camps, which allowed for no "rearranging" or rhetoric: the attention of survivors writing about their experience was directed wholly at "scenes which they can never forget and which, sometimes in hatred, sometimes with amazing tenderness, they feel compelled to record" (ibid.: 44). These recent memoirs do not contradict Des Pres's observation; they are amazingly consistent, not only in their accounts of the camp experience but in other ways as well. Allowing for the variations and vagaries of individual lives and for differing emphases (some spend more time on the world before the war than others), these works are repetitious, like folktales. They seem to bear out Primo Levi's observation about the increasingly stylized nature of survivors' memories with the passage of time, memories that are "often, unbeknownst to them, influenced by information gained from later readings or the stories of others" (1988: 19). David Lowenthal has discussed not only the role of forgetting,[14] but also the role of continuous revision in the way people remember their lives: later events necessarily shape and color the reporting of earlier ones, both to oneself and to others (1985: 204–10).

All this is true, and yet I read these memoirs with an avidity bordering on addiction. Why?

One reason is the names. Beregszász, Szombathely, Kisvárda, Kaposvár, Tolcsva—I've never been to these places, most likely never will be, and have only the vaguest notion of where they fit on a map. But I know exactly how to say them. The *a* of *Szombathely*, deep, way back in the throat, unlike any other *a* I know of; the *á* of *Kisvárda*, light and smiling; the *szs* and *css* which look like tongue twisters but aren't; the heavy first syllables followed by monotony—all this is familiar. I also know how to pronounce the names of people born in those towns and killed before their time: Joli and Manci, the baby sister and niece of Dawidowitz Piri; Dr. Mosonyi Dezső, father of Mosonyi Trudi; Klein Cipi, Izabella's sister; Magyar Judit's best friend Pogány Ilona, her first boyfriend Székely Anti, her father Magyar János, her uncles Józsi, Feri, Dezső, Andor, György,

---

14. Lowenthal reports on a study comparing wartime diaries of people who underwent the London blitz with the same people's retrospective accounts thirty years later: "Most people had forgotten things they could not imagine losing track of" (1985: 206).

and Imre; Glück Lily's parents, Kornel and Zoltán.[15] The very words that to a non-Hungarian reader appear most foreign, to be skipped over unpronounced (the way I skip over some proper names in Polish or Czech) beckon to me as familiars, inviting me to linger.

True, some non-Hungarian readers may dream over the proper names precisely because they are foreign—these may be the most poetic elements in an otherwise prosaic, "homogenized" text. But rare is the reader who can distinguish among a whole series of foreign names: at best, they merge into the single category of the "poetic foreign." I, by contrast, am aware of the unique quality of each name, its particular sound and shape; and in some cases I can also decipher the stories they tell: *Magyar* and *Mosonyi* are "Hungarianized" family names, signs of patriotism and a middle-class desire to assimilate, typical of educated Hungarian Jews to this day. (Assimilated Jews before the war usually didn't renounce their Jewishness, but they considered themselves Hungarians first.) *Dawidovitz*, *Glück*, and *Klein*, by contrast, are names that fit the modest lives of the religious rural Jews who bore them, and who often spoke Yiddish as a first language (generally, they spoke Hungarian as well).

Sometimes, as a gesture of friendship to the English-speaking reader, an author will purposefully delete the accents from all the vowels in a name, or Americanize a consonant (*sh* for *s*, *ch* for *cs*) (Wieder 1984). I note the gesture, then try to restore the correct spelling. Almost always, the author writes full names American-style, first name followed by last name. In Hungarian, it's the other way around: I reverse the names (as I did in the preceding paragraph). Sometimes it's not clear which is which, since usage varies even within a single work: Shafar Joska or Joska Shafar? (Siegal 1981: 73). I feel frustrated at the lack of consistency (besides, *Jóska* should have an accent, as should the name of Piri's brother, *Sándor*). In dialogues, I occasionally find myself trying to reconstitute the original words, as they must have been stated then, before "translation."

Speak of referential reading! It doesn't get more referential than this. Barbie Zelizer (1995), studying photographs of concentration camps published in American newspapers and magazines shortly after liberation, has contrasted referential reading (which asks: which camp? on

15. In order of mention, these names refer to Siegal 1981, T. Levi 1995, Leitner 1983, Isaacson 1990, and Lerner 1980.

what day? who is in the picture?) to universalizing reading, which sees these pictures as icons of human suffering or of "man's inhumanity to man." The two kinds of reading, although different, are not necessarily contradictory. However, if one is reading only for "universal meaning," a single photograph suffices; if one is driven by the referent, one wants as many photographs as possible, for each documents a specific case that resembles the others but is unique.

In my own reading of Hungarian survivors' memoirs, the referential impulse would seem to account for my unflagging interest: each memoir is like the others, but the names are different, and that makes a difference. As I think about it, however, I realize that the real "bait" in these works for me is not the referent but the signifier: *Szombathely* and *Tolcsva* signify Hungary, as *Dezső* and *Imre* (and *Laci, Miklós, Ernő, Pista, Géza, Bandi, Jenő,* and *Béla*) signify Hungarian men, and *Manci, Joli, Rózsi, Magda, Marika, Ibolya, Évi, Zsuzsi, Ági, Ilona, Ica,* and *Jutka* signify Hungarian women. But it is not today's Hungary, or today's Hungarians, that these names evoke most vividly: to go to Szombathely is not my desire. (I have been to Nyíregyháza, my mother's birthplace — once is enough.)

Maurice Halbwachs, the theorist of collective memory, wrote in a posthumously published work:

What would happen if all the members of my family disappeared? I would maintain for some time the habit of attributing a meaning to their first names. . . . To the extent that the dead retreat into the past, this is not because the material measure of time that separates them from us lengthens; it is because nothing remains of the group in which they passed their lives, and which needed to name them, that their names slowly become obliterated. . . . A person who alone remembers what others do not resembles someone who sees what others do not see. He is in certain respects like a person suffering from hallucinations who leaves the disagreeable impression among those around him. As his society becomes impatient he keeps quiet, and because he cannot express himself freely, he forgets the names that are no longer used by those around him. (1992: 73–74)

These comments, although not, as far as I know, written with the Holocaust in mind, apply perfectly to the problematics of Holocaust testimonies by survivors who have lost a world and a language.[16] But unlike

16. Halbwachs, an Alsatian Catholic, was deported from Lyon at age sixty-seven for protesting the murder of his Jewish father-in-law and mother-in-law, Victor and Hélène Basch, by the French *Milice* (on January 10, 1944); he died at Buchenwald in 1945 (see Lewis Coser's introduction to Halbwachs 1992: 6–7.)

the individual described by Halbwachs, who falls into silence, the writers of these memoirs persist in wishing to perpetuate the names of their lost family members. Halbwachs's account does not consider the possibility of written testimonies as an attempt to contravene the societal work of forgetting. A name written down, pronounced, can suddenly revive a forgotten or dead person not only for the writer who remembers the name, but also for the "autobiographical reader" who associates a different person or group of persons with the name: the signifier, being identical, "floats" over to cover the shifting referent (that's why Halbwachs emphasizes first names they can "float" more easily). I had an uncle Laci and an aunt Magda, just like Judith Isaacson. My family had Dezsős and Imres and Pistas, just like the families of all these memoirists. We didn't have Kaposvár or Kisvárda, but we had Nyíregyháza and Ungvár (never mind where they are on a map). The name resurrects the lost objects, but at the same time reinforces the sense of their pastness, their goneness. These people, these places (*as they were*, towns with many Jews in them) no longer exist.[17]

The paradox of naming is precisely this double power, as Mallarmé famously saw: "Je dis une fleur." I say *flower*, and what surfaces is the absence of all bouquets. I say *Uncle Laci* or *Aunt Magda*, I say *Pogány Ilona* or *Mosonyi Dezső*, I say *Szombathely* or *Beregszász*—and what surfaces is their absence. That is the double edge of Holocaust memoirs, as of all *lieux de mémoire*. Pierre Nora writes, with a touch of bitter irony: "There are *lieux de mémoire*, sites of memory, because there are no longer *milieux de mémoire*, real environments of memory" (1989: 15). When you need an archive, the archetypal site of memory, it signals that the life embodied in an ongoing tradition is gone. Holocaust memoirs are archives,

17. Noticeably, I haven't mentioned Budapest or its neighborhoods in any of the above enumerations, even though my own childhood was spent in the capital and several of these memoirs are sited there, wholly or in considerable part (Gabor [1981]; Vital-Tihanyi [1981]; Wieder [1984]). Would I say that Budapest too is irretrievable for Jews? Yes and no. Budapest has a flourishing Jewish community, the largest in Eastern Europe. It's a beautiful city, wonderful to visit briefly or for longer sojourns. But once you have left it as a Holocaust survivor, there is no going back, not for good: you have no family there, the few who may have remained have died or will do so very soon. In this respect, Budapest is like other Hungarian cities or towns, even though most of its Jewish population escaped extermination (see Suleiman 1996).

preserving traces of a living past and at the same marking its destruction. These memoirs are monuments raised to the dead, in a foreign country where their names are unpronounceable save by a few, many years after their death.

TOPOI; OR, THE POWER OF THE COMMONPLACE

My friend Froma tells me I've been "wallowing" in these Hungarian memoirs. Is it only because of the names? "Surely not," she insists. She knows that I've been mulling over a recurring theme as well—a topos, or commonplace. The fact that an event—or rather, its recounting— is a commonplace, a piece of typical or even stereotypical discourse, does not deprive it of power: on the contrary, in some cases it re- inforces the effect. No matter how many times I read about the arrival at Auschwitz—the noise, the stench, the headlights, the dogs, the strange, skeletal creatures in striped pajamas scurrying, unloading the baggage, unloading the dead, the SS officer pointing some to the left, some to the right, the last goodbye—my throat clutches.

That, however, is not the topos I've been haunted by in my autobio- graphical reading of these memoirs. My topos concerns choice—more exactly, choice as opposed to luck; I call it choice versus chance.

Lawrence Langer and others have rightly emphasized that it is im- possible to speak of genuine choices on the part of victims during the Holocaust. Choice implies the freedom to act, and there was very little of that available to Jews in Eastern Europe after war had broken out, not to mention after they were rounded up and deported. Langer coined the phrase "choiceless choice," for example in the case of Jewish leaders who were forced to select the next victims of destruction: "Whatever you choose, somebody loses" (Langer 1995: 46). Other choices became choiceless because victims were lied to or kept in ignorance. A constant theme in survivors' memoirs (but particularly in Hungarian memoirs, because by that late stage of the war many people knew the truth, or a good part of it) is that of being duped. The lies told by the Nazis ("cooperate, and all will go well for you") perverted and parodied the possibility of rational choice. Over and over again, one reads in these survivors' memoirs the pain and outrage of having been tricked: the sick and the old would be taken to the hospital if necessary, or given lighter work assignments, the Nazis assured them on the platform in Auschwitz as they watched their loved ones depart for the gas chamber.

Nor were the Nazis the only perpetrators of deception. Elie Wiesel has spoken angrily about the ignorance in which Hungarian Jews in the provinces were kept by Jewish leaders in Budapest, at a time when they knew about Auschwitz: people would not have gone so quietly into the cattle cars in May and June of 1944, Wiesel writes, if they had known their true destination (1985: xi–xv).

An equally strong theme in these memoirs is that of luck. Deborah Dwork, writing about the 11 percent of Jewish children who survived Nazi persecution in Europe, notes: "There is absolutely no evidence to indicate that survival was due to anything more — or anything less — than luck and fortuitous circumstances" (1991: xxxiii). This can be said of adult survivors as well. Yet I am struck by the strong presence, in these memoirs, of a tension between choice and chance, or choice and blind luck, as if the writers were themselves caught, in trying to account for their own survival, between those two contradictory possibilities. If luck alone accounted for their survival, then none of their specific choices actually mattered. (In fact, they did have occasion to make choices, however constrained they may have been.) If their choices were indeed significant, determining the difference between life and death, then it was not luck or chance alone that led to their survival.

There is obviously no way to resolve this question, except to say that choices often made the crucial difference, but not without luck. Perhaps the most dramatic example is provided by Judith Magyar Isaacson, who survived deportation to Auschwitz with her mother and aunt, and published her memoir more than forty years later. Some time after their arrival in Auschwitz, they were transported to a work camp in Germany but not before a selection took place. The selection, directed by Mengele, involved three possibilities: to the left, straight ahead, or to the right, which Judith interpreted as death, transport for work in Germany, or "the girls' transport" — forced prostitution and mass rape by German troops on the Eastern front. Almost all of the younger women were being sent in that direction. Told by Mengele to go right while her mother went straight ahead, Judith disobeyed and, despite warnings by attendants that Mengele would shoot her, ran after her mother; her aunt Magda, only a few years older than she, did the same. Miraculously, he did not shoot, and all three women were shipped out to Lichtenau in Germany (1990: 85–86).

This is a striking instance of a "free" choice (relatively speaking), based on knowledge of the alternatives: death rather than "the girls' transport." (Was it really a "girls' transport"? It doesn't matter; the factual accuracy of the reporting here is less important than the framing in terms of choice, and its combination with luck.) One could compare this choice to the suicides on the electric fence — terrible, but paradoxically "free."[18] What is different about this choice is that it did not lead to certain death: for once, in that strangely illogical world, Mengele did not shoot. The choice turned out to have been right — that is, lucky, leading to survival.

Later, a "free" choice made by all three women together led to their liberation. During the evacuation from yet another camp, knowing that the mother was too weak to leave, the women decided to risk staying behind in the infirmary (which they knew would be set on fire) rather than march with the others. This too turned out to be the right choice, in retrospect. A few days later, after more adventures, they were freed by American troops (ibid.: 114–18).

Others, under similar circumstances, were not as lucky. Elie Wiesel and his father, faced with a similar choice during the evacuation of Auschwitz in January 1945, decided to join the marchers; the father, exhausted, died in Buchenwald a few weeks later on the eve of liberation (Wiesel 1960). Yet another, slightly different case: Primo Levi, ill with scarlet fever in the infirmary, could not join the marchers (even though he could have chosen to leave like his two Hungarian neighbors, who were shot on the road a few hours later). Levi expected to die in the infirmary, but instead was liberated ten days later by the Russians (1961: 137–57).

Or consider the story told by Isabella Leitner. On the evacuation march from their last camp, her sister Chicha (Csicsa? Cica? I know "Chicha" isn't right) seized the moment to escape from the line, and Isabella and Rachel followed her instinctively; the fourth sister, Cipi, did not and later died. "[Chicha] was the one to notice that the SS men had gone to the rear. She was on the outside of the column. It was a sudden flash of evaluation, of assessing the situation. It was a moment that called for crystal-clear thinking. And she was capable of it. We merely followed" (Leitner 1983: 84). More than thirty years later, Isabella is still

---

18. The choice of suicide is a culminating point in Charlotte Delbo's play about Auschwitz, *Qui rapportera ces paroles?* [Who will carry the word?] (Paris: P. J. Oswald, 1974).

tormented by the question of why Cipi didn't follow. Didn't she see her sisters, or did she choose not to follow them? Should Isabella have pulled her along? "Was I supposed to tug at your ragged sleeve?" (ibid.: 85).

Experiences like this lead to the topos of "What if . . ." If I had done X, or not done X, I'd be dead now. If A had done X, or not done X, she might be alive now. In 1977, on a return visit to Kaposvár, Judith Isaacson reflects: "If I hadn't defied the selection at Auschwitz, hadn't been pulled from the transport at Lichtenau, hadn't escaped the death march at Leipzig, the bombs, the guns, my name would be engraved on this monument, under my father's" (1990: 142–43).

Choice or chance: what fascinates me is not a possible resolution of the contradiction, but the tension between its opposing terms and the impossibility of choosing either one alone. There is no way fully to reason out a right choice—that's life; one can decide whether it was right only retrospectively. But in ordinary life, wrong choices do not, as a rule, lead to death.

Why did my mother take the risk of walking out of our apartment building holding my hand as if none of this concerned her, past soldiers with bayonets, when all the other Jewish tenants were being rounded up? She and my father had planned it, that seems certain. But what if we had been stopped? What if the concierge, standing by the open door, had tapped a soldier's arm: "That woman and her daughter are Jews." Then everything would have been different (Suleiman 1996: 33).

Sometimes, in my safe, middle-class, everyday life here in the United States, I find myself agonizing over small choices—or larger ones, but still within the realm of the ordinary—as if my life depended on them. Lately, I have wondered whether those desperate feelings of possible doom over trifles may not be the legacy of a paradox in the lives of all Holocaust survivors: we are here today because of chance, but also because—miraculously, known only by hindsight—we or those close to us made the right, that is to say the lucky, choices.

REFERENCES

Améry, Jean
  1980 [1966] *At the Mind's Limits: Contemplations by a Survivor on Auschwitz and Its Realities*, translated by Sidney Rosenfeld and Stella P. Rosenfeld (Bloomington: Indiana University Press).

Braham, Randolph, L., ed.

1985 *The Holocaust in Hungary: Forty Years Later* (New York: Social Science Monographs).

Breznitz, Shlomo

1993 *Memory Fields: The Legacy of a Wartime Childhood* (New York: Knopf).

Danieli, Yael

1988 "The Heterogeneity of Postwar Adaptation in Families of Holocaust Survivors," in *The Psychological Perspectives of the Holocaust and of Its Aftermath*, edited by Randolph L. Braham, 109–28 (Boulder, CO: Social Science Monographs).

Des Pres, Terrence

1976 *The Survivor: An Anatomy of Life in the Death Camps* (New York: Oxford University Press).

Dwork, Deborah

1991 *Children with a Star: Jewish Youth in Nazi Europe* (New Haven, CT: Yale University Press).

Edelstein, Dov B.

1985 *Worlds Torn Asunder* (Hoboken, NJ: Ktav).

Ezrahi, Sidra DeKoven

1980 *By Words Alone: The Holocaust in Literature* (Chicago: University of Chicago Press).

Friedländer, Saul, ed.

1992 *Probing the Limits of Representation: Nazism and the "Final Solution"* (Cambridge, MA: Harvard University Press).

Gabor, Georgia M.

1981 *My Destiny, Survivor of the Holocaust* (Arcadia, CA: Amen).

Halbwachs, Maurice

1992 *On Collective Memory*, edited and translated by Lewis Coser (Chicago: University of Chicago Press).

Hartman, Geoffrey, ed.

1994 *Holocaust Remembrance: The Shape of Memory* (Cambridge, MA: Blackwell).

Horowitz, Sara

1994 "Voices from the Killing Ground," in Hartman 1994.

Isaacson, Judith Magyar

1990 *Seed of Sarah: Memoirs of a Survivor* (Urbana: University of Illinois Press).

Kritzman, Lawrence D., ed.

1995 *Auschwitz and After: Race, Culture, and "the Jewish Question" in France* (New York: Routledge).

Lang, Berel, ed.

1988 *Writing and the Holocaust* (New York: Holmes and Meier).

Langer, Lawrence L.

    1991 *Holocaust Testimonies: The Ruins of Memory* (New Haven, CT: Yale University Press).

    1995 *Admitting the Holocaust: Collected Essays* (New York: Oxford University Press).

Leitner, Isabella

    1983 [1978] *Fragments of Isabella: A Memoir of Auschwitz* (New York: Dell).

Lengyel, Olga

    1947 *Five Chimneys: The Story of Auschwitz* (Chicago: Ziff-Davis).

    1959 *Five Chimneys* (London: Granada).

Lerner, Lily Gluck (with Sandra Lee Stuart)

    1980 *The Silence* (Secaucus, NJ: Lyle Stuart).

Levi, Primo

    1961 [1947] *Survival in Auschwitz*, translated by Stuart Woolf (New York: Collier).

    1988 *The Drowned and the Saved*, translated by Raymond Rosenthal (New York: Summit).

    1995 *Le Devoir de mémoire*, translated by Joel Gayraud (Paris: Mille et Une Nuits).

Levi, Trude

    1995 *A Cat Called Adolf* (London: Vallentine Mitchell).

Liss, Andrea

    1992 "Contours of Naming: The Identity Card Project and the Tower of Faces at the United States Holocaust Memorial Museum," *Public* 8:107–35.

Lowenthal, David

    1985 *The Past Is a Foreign Country* (Cambridge: Cambridge University Press).

Nora, Pierre

    1989 "Between Memory and History: *Les Lieux de Mémoire*," *Representations* 26: 7–25.

Riemer, Andrew

    1992 *Inside Outside: Life between Two Worlds* (Pymble, Australia: Angus and Robertson).

Rosen, Alan

    1995 "The Language of Survival: English as Metaphor in Art Spiegelman's *Maus*," *Prooftexts* 15(3): 249–62.

Rosenberg, Blanca

    1993 *To Tell at Last: Survival under False Identity, 1941–45* (Urbana: University of Illinois Press).

Roskies, David

    1984 *Against the Apocalypse: Responses to Catastrophe in Modern Jewish Culture* (Cambridge, MA: Harvard University Press).

Sanders, Ivan
    1985 "The Holocaust in Contemporary Hungarian Literature," in Braham 1985:
        191–202.
Siegal, Aranka
    1981 *Upon the Head of a Goat: A Childhood in Hungary 1939–1944* (New York:
        Farrar, Straus, Giroux).
    1985 *Grace in the Wilderness: After the Liberation, 1945–1948* (New York: Farrar,
        Straus, Giroux).
Sternberg, Meir
    1981 "Polylingualism as Reality and Translation as Mimesis," *Poetics Today*
        2(4): 221–39.
Suleiman, Susan Rubin
    1994 *Risking Who One Is: Encounters with Contemporary Art and Literature*
        (Cambridge, MA: Harvard University Press).
    1996 *Budapest Diary: In Search of the Motherbook* (Lincoln: University of Ne-
        braska Press).
Varga, Susan
    1994 *Heddy and Me* (Victoria: Penguin Books Australia).
Vital-Tihanyi, Isabelle
    1981 *La Vie sauve* (Paris: Minuit).
Wachtel, Nathan
    1986 "Remember and Never Forget," *History and Anthropology* 2: 307–35.
Wieder, Ludvik (with Joel H. Cohen)
    1984 *I Promised My Mother* (New York: Shengold).
Wiesel, Elie
    1960 *La Nuit* (Paris: Minuit).
    1985 "Introduction" in Braham 1985: xi–xv.
Wieviorka, Annette
    1994 "On Testimony," in Hartman 1994: 23–32.
Wirth-Nesher, Hana
    1991 "Afterword: Between Mother Tongue and Native Language in *Call It
        Sleep*," in *Call It Sleep*, by Henry Roth (New York: Farrar, Straus and
        Giroux).
Young, James E.
    1988 *Writing and Rewriting the Holocaust: Narrative and the Consequences of
        Interpretation* (Bloomington: Indiana University Press).
Zelizer, Barbie
    1995 "Memory and the Circulation of Images." Paper presented at the Con-
        ference on Articulations of History: Issues in Holocaust Representation,
        Photographic Resource Center, Boston.

MARIANNE HIRSCH

PAST LIVES: POSTMEMORIES IN EXILE

I neither emigrated nor was deported.
The world that was destroyed was
not mine. I never knew it.
HENRI RACZYMOW, "Memory Shot through with Holes"

IN THE SUMMER of 1991, in the aftermath of the Gulf War, I was very
moved by the Israeli writer Yoram Kaniuk's article in the German newspaper *Die Zeit* (Kaniuk 1991). The article, titled "Three and a Half Hours
and Fifty Years with Günter Grass in Berlin," reported on an open discussion in Berlin a few months earlier between the two writers, and
addressed German intellectuals' opposition to the war in view of Germany's massive sales of arms and poison gas to Iraq during the preceding
years. Kaniuk, up until that moment an active member of Peace Now,
tried to explain how different things looked to him in Tel Aviv from how
they looked to German intellectuals in Munich, Frankfurt, or Berlin.
Kaniuk invited Grass, an outspoken opponent of the war, to contemplate
the enormous distance separating them, who were otherwise friendly
and of very similar yet fatally different backgrounds. For as they were sitting on stage in March 1991, talking about Israel and Germany, Kaniuk
said he could feel the spiritual presence of their two fathers and their four
grandfathers.

   In the article, Kaniuk claimed his right to speak out and to address Grass so aggressively as a birthright. Conceived in Germany, like
Grass, yet born in his parents' exile in Palestine in 1939, Kaniuk grew
up in Tel Aviv. But, he explained, walking down Ben Yehuda Street
as a child, he experienced as more real and more present the streets
of his parents' prewar German world named in the German children's
book *Emil and the Detectives*. His parents' German reality, transmitted
through daily stories and references yet, as a Jewish culture, irrevocably
destroyed, nevertheless had the power to displace and de-realize his own
immediate childhood world in the Middle East. "Ich entscheide hiermit,
dass wir hier in einem kleinen Berlin gewohnt haben, das wir Tel Aviv
nannten und aus dem wir am liebsten wieder zurückkehren oder uns
untermischen würden" [I hereby decide that we lived here in a small Ber-

lin that we called Tel Aviv, and from which we would have wanted to return again or blend in] (ibid.: 18; all translations are mine unless otherwise noted). This "memory" of a Germany in which he had never lived, on whose streets he had never walked, whose air he had never breathed, and whose language he eventually abandoned, remained, until the day of his dispute with Grass fifty years later, the place of identity, however ambivalent. Through words and images, it acquired a materiality in his memory that determined his adult discourse and self-definition as an Israeli writer.

My reading of Kaniuk's article was so overwhelmingly autobiographical that it filters many of my recollections of the Gulf War. Unlike Kaniuk, I was not conceived in my parents' native Czernowitz, but was born in Rumania four years after their exile. (Czernowitz, capital of the formerly Austrian Bukowina, was annexed first by Rumania in 1918 and then by the USSR in 1945.) Still, the streets, buildings, and natural surroundings—the theater, restaurants, parks, rivers, and domestic settings of Czernowitz—none of which had I ever seen, heard, or smelled myself, occupy a monumental place in my childhood memories. All the while, as I was growing up hearing my parents' stories of life in Czernowitz before the war and of the events during the wartime Russian and German occupations that culminated in their exile in 1945, I knew that I would never see that place, and that my parents would never return there. I knew it not only because Czernowitz now belonged to the USSR and travel between there and Rumania was difficult; I knew it also from my parents' voice and demeanor, from the sense they projected that this world, their world, had been destroyed. That left a rift in their lives, and in mine, similar to the rift between Günter Grass and Yoram Kaniuk, one writer living at home, one forever homeless. In our familial discourse, Czernowitz embodied the idea of home, of place, but to me it was, and would remain, out of reach. Kaniuk and I share with many European Jews of our generation this sense of exile from a world we have never seen and never will see, because it was irreparably changed or destroyed by the sudden violence of the Holocaust.

None of us ever knows the world of our parents. We can say that the motor of the fictional imagination is fueled in great part by the desire to know the world as it looked and felt before our birth. How much more ambivalent is this curiosity for children of Holocaust survivors, exiled from a world that has ceased to exist, that has been violently erased. Theirs is a different desire, at once more powerful and more conflicted:

the need not just to feel and to know, but also to re-member, to re-build, to re-incarnate, to replace and to repair. For survivors who have been separated and exiled from a ravaged world, memory is necessarily an act not only of recall, but also of mourning, a mourning often inflected by anger, rage, and despair. As Nadine Fresco (1981: 209) writes: "La destruction avait été telle que pas une image ne subsistait de la vie juive d'avant la guerre qui ne fut désormais grevée, entachée, marquée par la mort" [The destruction was such that not an image was left from the Jewish life before the war that was not in some way encumbered, tainted, marked by death]. Children of survivors live at a further temporal and spatial remove from that decimated world. The distance separating them from the locus of origin is the radical break of unknowable and incomprehensible persecution; for those born after, it is a break impossible to bridge. Still, the power of mourning and memory, and the depth of the rift dividing their parents' lives, impart to them something that is akin to memory. Searching for a term that would convey its temporal and qualitative difference from survivor memory, I have chosen to call this secondary, or second-generation, memory "postmemory."[1]

Postmemory is a powerful form of memory precisely because its connection to its object or source is mediated not through recollection but through an imaginative investment and creation. That is not to say that memory itself is unmediated, but that it is more directly connected to the past. Postmemory characterizes the experience of those who grow up dominated by narratives that preceded their birth, whose own belated stories are displaced by the stories of the previous generation, shaped by traumatic events that can be neither fully understood nor re-created. I have developed this notion in relation to children of Holocaust survivors, but I think it may usefully describe the second-generation memory of other cultural or collective traumatic events and experiences.

Holocaust postmemory, however, attempts to bridge more than just a temporal divide. The children of exiled survivors, although they have not themselves lived through the trauma of banishment and the destruction of home, remain always marginal or exiled, always in the diaspora. "Home" is always elsewhere, even for those who return to Vienna, Berlin, Paris, or Cracow, because the cities to which they can return are no longer those in which their parents had lived as Jews before the genocide, but are instead the cities where the genocide *happened* and from which

1. My discussion of postmemory draws on a previous article (Hirsch 1992–93).

they and their memory have been expelled. As Fresco (ibid.: 211) suggests, "Nés après la guerre, parfois pour remplacer un enfant mort de la guerre, les juifs dont je parle ici ressentent leur existence comme une sorte d'exil, non d'un lieu présent ou à venir, mais d'un temps revolu qui aurait été celui de l'identité même" [Born after the war, sometimes in place of a child killed in the war, the Jews I am describing here experience their lives as a sort of exile, not from a present or future place, but from a completed time which would have been that of identity itself]. This condition of exile from the space of identity, this diasporic experience, is characteristic of postmemory.

Postmemory—even that of a circumscribed population like the children of exiled Holocaust survivors—can take many forms. Based on a series of interviews with others of her generation whose parents never spoke of their abandoned world or their wartime experiences and who thus had virtually no access to the repressed stories that shaped them, Nadine Fresco speaks of an *absent memory*. In her terms, the postwar generation's diasporic life is a *diaspora des cendres*—the place of origin has been reduced to ashes. There is no return.[2] Her contemporary, the French writer Henri Raczymow, insists that this absence, this void, is the condition that must be preserved and should never be bridged. The memory he describes is a *mémoire trouée*, a "memory shot through with holes": "Dans mon travail, un tel vide est rendu possible par cette mémoire absente dont je parlais. Elle est chez moi le moteur de l'écriture. Et mes livres ne cherchent pas à compler cette mémoire absente—je n'écris pas, banalement, pout lutter contre l'oubli—mais à la présenter, justement, comme absente" [In my work, such a void is created by the empty memory I spoke of, which propels my writing forward. My books do not attempt to fill in empty memory. They are not simply part of the struggle against forgetfulness. Rather, I try to present memory *as* empty. I try to restore a non-memory, which by definition cannot be filled in or recovered] (Raczymow 1986: 181; 1994: 104). In his evocation of the absent memory that serves for him as the "motor" for writing, Raczymow adopts Kafka's spatial conception of time, articulated in the 1920s: "Si la terre tourne à droite . . . , je dois tourner à gauche pour rattraper le passé" [If the earth is turning to the right . . . , I must turn left in order to catch up with the past] (1986: 181; 1994: 104). European

2. For a discussion of Jewish identity as inherently diasporic, see Boyarin and Boyarin 1993.

Jews of the postwar generation are forever turning left, but we can never catch up with the past; inasmuch as we remember, we remain in perpetual temporal and spatial exile. Our past is literally a foreign country we can never hope to visit. And our postmemory is shaped, Raczymow suggests, by our sense of belatedness and disconnection: "Et je ne suis ni émigré ni déporté, le monde qui fut détruit n'etait pas le mien puisque je ne l'ai pas connu. Pourtant je suis, nous sommes nombreux à être en position d'orphelins" [I neither emigrated nor was deported. The world that was destroyed was not mine. I never knew it. But I am, so many of us are, the orphans of that world] (1986: 180; 1994: 103).[3]

Nadine Fresco's "absent memory" does not correspond to my own experience as a child of survivors. For me, having grown up with daily accounts of a lost world, the links between past and present, between the prewar world of origin and the postwar space of destination, are more than visible. The Czernowitz of my postmemory is an imaginary city, but that makes it no less present, no less vivid, and perhaps because of the constructed and deeply invested nature of memory itself, no less accurate. The deep sense of displacement suffered by the children of exile, the elegaic aura of the memory of a place to which one cannot return, creates, in my experience, a strange sense of plenitude rather than a feeling of absence: I've sometimes felt that there were too many stories, too much affect, even as at other times I've been unable to fill in the gaps and absences. The fullness of postmemory is no easier a form of connection than the absence it also generates. Full or empty, postmemory seeks connection. It creates where it cannot recover. It imagines where it cannot recall. It mourns a loss that cannot be repaired. And, because even the act of mourning is secondary, the lost object can never be incorporated and mourning can never be overcome. "Nous n'avons même pas *faillis* d'être déportés" [We cannot even say that we were *almost* deported], says Raczymow (1986: 181; 1994: 104). In perpetual exile, this/my genera-

3. Fresco's and Raczymow's reflections echo Alain Finkielkraut's definitions of postwar Jewish identity as a form of absence in *Le Juif imaginaire* (1980: 138): "Ce qui fait de moi un Juif, c'est la conscience aiguë d'un manque, une absence entretenue, l'exil où je vis par rapport à une civilisation dont, 'pour mon bien' et parce qu'il y avait eu Auschwiz, mes parents n'ont pas voulu que je sois dépositaire" [What makes me a Jew is the acute consciousness of a lack, of a continuous absence: my exile from a civilization which, 'for my own good,' my parents didn't wish me to keep in trust] (1980: 138; 1994: 114).

tion's practice of mourning is as determinative as it is interminable and ultimately impossible.

In what follows, I would like to look at this practice of mourning and postmemory among European Jewish children of exiled survivors and at the aesthetic forms it shapes. I would like to suggest that the aesthetics of postmemory is a diasporic aesthetics of temporal and spatial exile that needs simultaneously to rebuild and to mourn. In the terms of Nadine Fresco, it is "comme si ceux qui étaient nés après ne pouvaient pas qu'errer, en proie d'une nostalgie qui n'a pas de droit de cité" [as though those who were born after could do nothing but wander, prey to a longing forever disenfranchised] (1981: 211). What forms does their wandering take? What strategies do they invent to relocate themselves? What are the aesthetic shapes of postmemory?

During the first waves of refugee emigrations from Eastern Europe to the West, following the pogroms in the early part of this century, a Jewish memorial tradition developed among diasporic communities, based on ancient and medieval Jewish practices of commemoration that could serve as a resource and a model to children of survivors. The *yizker bikher*, or memorial books, prepared in exile by survivors of the pogroms, were meant to preserve the memory of their destroyed cultures. The survivors of Nazi genocide built on this memorial tradition and prepared for subsequent generations similar memorial books devoted to the memory of their individual destroyed communities. (Over four hundred memorial books have been written by survivors of Polish communities alone.)[4] They contain historical accounts of community life before the destruction and detailed records of the genocide that annihilated the communities, as well as photographs, individual and group portraits, that evoke life as it was *before*. The books also contain accounts of survivors' efforts to locate the remains of their family members in order to give them a proper burial, and they detail the acts of commemoration devoted to the dead.

The memorial books are acts of witness and sites of memory. Because they evoke and try to re-create the life that existed, and not only its destruction, they are acts of public mourning, forms of a collective

4. See Boyarin and Kugelmass 1983 for an account, excerpts, and a list of these Polish memorial books.

Kaddish. But they are also sites where subsequent generations can find a lost origin, where they can learn about the time and place they will never see. In the words of Jonathan Boyarin and Jack Kugelmass, who collected translated selections from Polish memorial books: "The memorial books are the fruit of the impulse to write a testament for future generations. They constitute an unprecedented, truly popular labor to record in writing as much as possible of a destroyed world" (1983: 6). Yizker books, with their stories and images, are documents to be invested with life: they are spaces of connection between memory and postmemory. Many communal organizations think of them as their memorials or monuments or, as Raczymow says, "tiennent lieu de sepultures pour ceux qui sont morts sans sepulture" [they take the place of graves for those who had no graves] (1986: 179; 1994: 101). As such they can serve as models and inspirations for other acts of remembrance by children of exiled survivors. They provide the paradigms for a diasporic aesthetics of postmemory.

Raczymow's *Tales of Exile and Forgetting* [Contes d'exil et d'oubli] (1979) is a kind of memorial book, but its radically different form illustrates the difference between memory and postmemory. While the yizker books contain testimonies and reminiscences, Raczymow's tales are reconstructions that do not disguise their exploratory and probing relation to the unknown past. "Je ne sais rien de Konsk" [I know nothing about Konsk], insists the protagonist and historian Matthieu Schriftlich (1979: 19) "Qui peut me parler de Konsk, ombre d'ombre et sans tombe?" [Who can speak to me about Konsk, shadow of shadows and without a grave?] (ibid.: 37). Why does he want to know? He is intrigued by a few names and a few stories he heard, particularly by Matl Oksenberg, a grandmother who frequently appears in the tales of his sometimes reluctant informant, Simon Gorbatch: "C'est moi qui suis le vieillard, et c'est vous qui scrutez le passé" [I am the old man and you are the one who questions the past] (ibid.: 51). But can Matthieu ever know Matl Oksenberg and her world? He insists that he can't and that, in fact, a certain distance must be maintained. Even as he writes the stories of Konsk, Schriftlich must inscribe the impossibility of knowing or understanding them. He must preserve the shadows surrounding Konsk and his grandmother, even as he tries to lift the veil of mystery that attracts him in the first place.

His point of access is a network of names; the narrative emerges from the names, slowly becoming coextensive with them. As Simon tells the stories, Matthieu abandons himself to the absence of memory. The names are available and they are richly interrelated. As one name evokes another, we come to find ourselves in an intricately woven social fabric of words that no longer refer to specific people but become separated from their content, generalized and interchangeable, empty vehicles of an absent memory. "Le nom des morts n'est-il pas disponible à nos fantaisies, Simon?" [The names of the dead, aren't they available to our fantasies, Simon?] (ibid.: 103). Matthieu, with the help of the ever more tentative Simon, reinvests them with a narrative, but in the process he loses his individuality: he becomes indistinguishable from his function as scribe and historian, as "Schriftlich."

Just as the authors of the yizker books are agents of memory, so Matthieu Schriftlich is the agent of postmemory, someone who gives narrative shape to the surviving fragments of an irretrievable past. But the stories do not add up; the names continue to resist Matthieu's curiosity, and Konsk never emerges from the fog that surrounds it. This resistance is necessary to the practice of postmemory, as is the elegiac tone of Raczymow's tales. But the mourning Matthieu practices is anything but sentimental: as Raczymow plays on the double meaning of the French word *larme* (both tear and drop), the tear (*larme*) with which the last tale ends is not a tear at all but a *drop* of vodka, "une *larme.*" Nostalgia and sentimentality are always undercut by the knowledge of what occurred in Konsk and by the impossibility, finally, of understanding it. With his *Contes d'exil et d'oubli*, Raczymow has developed an aesthetic that emerges from the absences of his earlier *nouveaux romans* and from his personal need to re-member the forgotten places of his ancestors' exile. His book becomes itself a site of postmemory, a reconstructed village in which, however, no one can live. Too many questions remain. Raczymow's tales evoke not so much Konsk as its absence—the condition of exile from Konsk.

Yizker books contain texts and images, but the book of Matthieu Schriftlich is limited to oral and written stories. There are no pictures of Matl or Noïoch Oksenberg, no photographs of Szlama Davidowicz or the streets of Konsk. Do pictures provide the second- and third-generation questioner with a more concrete, a better, access to the abandoned parental world than stories can? Or, as indexical traces, do they perhaps provide too direct and material a connection to the past?[5] How do photographic images shape the work of postmemory?

When I visited the United States Holocaust Memorial Museum in Washington, DC, I thought a great deal about these questions, for the museum, I realized, is also dedicated to bridging the distance between memory and postmemory. The museum was created not primarily for survivors and the deeply engaged children of survivors like me, but for an American public with little knowledge of the event. At its best, I would argue, the museum would elicit in its visitors the desire to know and to feel, the curiosity and passion that shapes the postmemory of survivor children. At its best, it would include all of its visitors in the generation of postmemory. The museum's architecture and exhibits aim at just that effect: to get us close to the affect of the event, to convey knowledge and information without, however, attempting any facile sense of re-creation or reenactment.

How could the museum give some small sense of the world that was destroyed, beyond concentrating on the destruction alone? Is it possible to show visitors passing through its edifice that Jewish experience was more than only that of victims, to convey the richness and diversity of Jewish cultures before? How could the museum re-create those cultures?

As with most of its exhibits, the museum has chosen to attempt that representation of life "before" through photographic images, allowing us to consider specifically the role of images in the work of postmemory. Thus, there are a number of portraits of famous Jewish artists and intellectuals banned by the Nazis, killed or forced into exile. There are portraits of the writers whose books are being burned in the films of the book burnings. There is a small room devoted to a few of Roman Vishniac's images of the lost world of the Polish shtetl: some faces, some lonely street scenes, a dance. And, in its photographic archive, the museum collects as many photo albums of survivors as it can get, carefully cataloging and dating the prewar birthdays, anniversaries, family outings, and school pictures of random Jewish families. Filling the shelves of the photographic archives, along with notebooks full of images

5. Raczymow speaks of Roman Vishniac's photographs of the world of the shtetl: "Comment peut-on avoir la nostalgie de ce que representent ces photos, c'est-à-dire saleté, tristesse, pauvreté?" [How could they be nostalgic for the filth, the wretchedness, the poverty shown in those pictures?] (Raczymow 1994: 101; 1986: 179).

of horror—ghetto scenes, shootings by *Einsatztruppen*, arrivals at concentration camps, selections, bodies, personal belongings surviving the destruction of their owners—these conventional family pictures testify to the full range of Holocaust photography. They attempt to reverse, as well, the Nazi destruction not only of people and their communities but of the very records—pictures and documents—that might have testified to their former existence. Many survivors, in fact, have no photographs that precede the war years:[6] it is as though the museum collection were trying to repair this irreparable loss.

In my work, I have included in the category of "Holocaust photograph" all of those pictures which are connected to total death and to public mourning—both pictures of horror and ordinary snapshots or portraits, family pictures defined by their context as much as by their content.[7] I recognize, of course, that there are differences between the pictures of a birthday celebration or outing and the documentary images of mass graves, especially in the work of reading that goes into them. Confronted with the latter image, we respond with horror, even before looking at the caption or knowing the context of the image. Knowing that context increases the horror, as we add to the bodies, or the hair or the shoes depicted, all those others we know about but that are not in the picture or are unrecognizable. Confronted with the former image—the portrait or family picture—we need to know its context, but once we do, I would argue, we respond with a similar sense of disbelief. These two kinds of photographs are complementary: it is precisely the displacement of the bodies depicted in the pictures of horror from their domestic settings, and their disfiguration, that brings home (as it were) the enormity of Holocaust destruction. And it is precisely the utter conventionality and generality of the domestic family picture that makes it impossible for us to comprehend how the person in the picture was exterminated. In both cases, the viewer fills in what the picture leaves out: the horror of looking is not necessarily in the image itself but in the story we bring to it. But, the family and community pictures have another function: they provide a part of a record or narrative about the Jewish world lost in the Holocaust and thus place the images of destruction into a needed contextual framework. More than that, they

6. I am grateful to Lori Lefkowitz for continuing to remind me of this sad fact.

7. This discussion of the Holocaust photograph draws on my earlier article (Hirsch 1992–93).

Figure 1   Yaffa Eliach Collection; Photograph by Alan Gilbert, Courtesy of the
United States Holocaust Memorial Museum.

recreate something of what has been destroyed, even as they elicit and facilitate the viewer's mourning of the destruction. The conventionality of the family photo provides a space of identification for any viewer participating in the conventions of familial representation; thus they bridge the gap between viewers who are personally connected to the event and those who are not. They expand the postmemorial circle.

The photos are both icons and indexical traces, or material connections to the people who did not survive. In Roland Barthes's controversial reading, "the photograph is literally an emanation of the referent. From a real body, which was there, proceed radiations which ultimately touch me, who am here" (1981: 80). Photography, then, is precisely the medium connecting memory and postmemory. As traces, photographs record both life (the rays connecting body to eye) and death (the moment they record becomes fixed with the very act of recording). Photographs of the world lost to the Holocaust can thus contain, perhaps more obviously than the names and narrative fragments handed down to Matthieu Schriftlich, the particular mixture of mourning and re-creation that characterizes the work of postmemory.

This is nowhere more visible than in the "Tower of Faces," situated at the very center of the Holocaust Memorial Museum (Figure 1). Chronological in conception, the museum's permanent exhibition begins on the fourth floor with the rise of Nazism, leading to the prewar "terror in Poland" and the Nazi euthanasia program. Next we pass over a glass bridge whose walls are inscribed with hundreds of names, each representing a town or community destroyed in the genocide. In a radical break in chronology, we then enter a room shaped like a tower and constructed entirely of sepia-toned photographic images that hover all around us. An introductory panel explains that what we are seeing are several hundred photographs of the Lithuanian shtetl of Ejszyzski collected by a child survivor of the town, Yaffa Eliach, the granddaughter of the town's Jewish photographers, Yitzak Uri Katz and Alte Katz.

Some of the photos are at eye level, while others are out of reach and difficult to see (Figure 2). We are separated from them by the bridge on which we are standing, which keeps us in the middle of the room, removed from direct contact with the images. The Ejszyzski photographs are ordinary portraits of individuals and groups, of family and group rituals, of candid moments. They are, as the museum's director Michael Berenbaum (1994) insists, the pictures by which we mark life's transitions, the pictures we would send to friends and relatives abroad. In the

Figure 2 Courtesy of the Yaffa Eliach Shtetl Collection.

context of the museum, they are meant to "personalize the story of the Holocaust."

If the Ejszyszki photographs represent the typical Jewish prewar life of the town, they prove the diversity and range of that life. These pictures do not emerge from a narrow historical moment, but span what must be a thirty-year period. We see observant as well as assimilated Jews. We see young and old. We see a great range of class and economic backgrounds—laborers and scholars, farmers and professionals. We see an even greater range of activities: bicycling, eating, boating, mourning, reading, walking, posing with friends or alone. Many types of work and many types of leisure appear.

My first reaction, similar to that of many others, was to marvel at how rich and varied a life was destroyed. The pictures gain by their diversity and their multiplicity: after looking at them for a while, it becomes less important to see individual images than to take in a sense of the whole, and of its relation to one's own family albums. "Look, look, look," I hear people saying all around me, "we have a picture just like this one in our album." Or, "Look, that looks just like grandma!" Interestingly, in the minutes I spend in the room, I find that this identification easily transcends ethnic identity and family history.

The conventional nature of family photography allows for this identification, this erasure of time and space. We might leaf through any of our own family albums and find similar photos. But if the tower is a family album, then we are situated right inside it. Like all family albums, the tower preserves and creates memory: it is a site of commemoration and rememoration. The people depicted diverge from one another in historical moment, occupation, class, and style, and they are separated from us as viewers by at least fifty years and by the radical break the Holocaust introduced into this century. Nevertheless, the conventional and familial nature of the images themselves manages to transcend these distances, figured spatially by the bridge that separates us from the pictures, and to foster an affiliative look that binds the photographs to one another and us to them. Most of the photographs remain anonymous, but some have names and dates inscribed on them; some have arrows leading from a name to a face. Even these names, however, serve less to individualize than to generalize: in the photographs' multiplicity, the names become anonymous and generic, like Raczymow's *Matl*, *Simon*, *Schlomo*, and *Chaim*. When we enter the Tower of Faces, we leave the historical account of the museum and enter the domestic space of a family album that shapes a different form of looking and knowing, a different style of recognition, one that is available to any viewer and that can connect viewers of different backgrounds to one another. This is a collective and not an individual story, yet the process of affiliative familial looking fosters and shapes the individual viewer's relationship to this collective memory. The tower provides for visitors a space in which they can become a community: descendants of those killed in a small shtetl thousands of miles away.

Visitors descending through the museum encounter the Tower of Faces twice, first on the fourth floor, at the end of the exhibits pertaining to the rise of Nazism, and again on the third floor, as a culmination of the exhibits detailing the final solution. After walking through a railroad car used in the Polish deportations, seeing a model of the gas chambers and crematoria in Auschwitz, walking by a pile of shoes brought from Auschwitz, and seeing an actual oven from Mauthausen, we walk across another glass bridge, right below the one that listed the names of lost communities. This bridge is covered with hundreds of first names—I find mine, my mother's and father's, that of each of my grandparents, those of my sons. After a few other memorial exhibits, this bridge leads to the Tower of Faces on a level below the bridge on which we initially stood. Here a panel narrates the town of Ejszyski's destruction by a

Figure 3   Courtesy of the Yaffa Eliach Shtetl Collection.

mobile killing unit in September, 1941. We are told that there were virtually no survivors of that action, though we assume that some people, like
Yaffa Eliach and her parents, had gone into hiding beforehand.

   This is a radically different encounter with the images (Figure 3). The
lower room is much darker since the light comes in from a distant
skylight obscured by the opaque glass bridge above on which other visitors are standing. This lower room is square and we can go right up to
the images—we are no longer separated from them. We see the faces

more closely, we look into the eyes of people who were alive, full of joy, confidence, and hope. The images are at once more accessible, because we are closer to them, and less so because there is so little light. I notice, for the first time, the black borders surrounding the sepia images and I wonder now whether the intent is aesthetic or funereal. And, as I look up toward the next floor and the distant light source way above that, as I see the images rush down toward me, so many much too distant to recognize, I realize, with a shudder, that this tower is in fact a chimney, that this album is also a tomb, that commemoration is also mourning. I am reminded of Paul Celan's famous evocation of the "grave in the air" in his "Todesfuge."

The Tower of Faces brings out most forcefully photography's connection to death, and thus the power of photographs as media of mourning. The "having-been-there" of the object, what Roland Barthes calls the "ça a été," creates the scene of mourning shared by those who are left to look at the picture. This is what Barthes means when he identifies time itself as a sort of *punctum*: "I read at the same time *This will be* and *this has been*; I observe with horror an anterior future of which death is the stake. By giving me the absolute past of the pose (aorist), the photograph tells me death in the future. What *pricks* me is the discovery of this equivalence" (1981: 96). The pictures in the Tower of Faces tell us the immediacy of life at the moment photographed, transformed in the instant of this recognition into the death that we know soon followed. They evoke both the anger and the disbelief accompanying this temporal jolt. With death as the photographs' latent content, commemoration becomes rememoration — a collective act of resistance against forgetting.[8]

By using the most conventional of photographic genres, family pictures, with its characteristically affiliative gaze, the tower preserves power of commemoration into the generations of postmemory. The architecture itself figures the nature of postmemory. As Andrea Liss has said, the double encounter with the tower "functions more in harmony with the layered way in which memories overlap and cross the mental time zones of the past and the present, especially involving circumstances of extreme traumatic dislocation" (1993: 126). Standing in the tower we stand, literally, both inside a photo album and inside a tomb in the shape of a chimney. We reanimate the pictures with our own knowledge of daily life, and we experience, emotionally, the death that took those lives so

---

8. Kristine Stiles (1994) usefully defines this notion of rememoration.

violently. The Tower of Faces has forged a form to contain the contradictory shapes of postmemories of exile and survival.

Yaffa Eliach and her family were able to escape the town's extermination
and to survive in hiding. Yet in 1944, when they returned to Ejszyszki,
they were subjected to a local pogrom in which many of the twenty-nine
surviving Jews, including Yaffa's mother, were killed. Yaffa escaped with
photos hidden in her shoes and strapped to her brother's body. Later,
she assembled the six-thousand picture archive from which the tower
is composed by collecting the pictures that her compatriots had sent to
relatives around the world or had saved in numerous unbelievable ways.[9]
Yaffa Eliach is a child survivor with memories of Ejszyszki; the Tower of
Faces is her memorial book addressed to the subsequent generations that
will visit the museum. With the help of the architect, she has constructed
a site of postmemory and mourning that is at the same time a reconstruction of the town itself.

The tower's memorial form reflects specifically the investment of a
survivor and her effort to create and to reach as inclusive a postmemorial
generation as possible. I would like to compare this form of memorialization to the postmemorial work of the French artist Christian Boltanski.

Unlike Eliach, Boltanski, whose middle name is "Liberté," grew up
after the Holocaust; he was born on the very day that Paris was liberated
from Nazi occupation. Boltanski's father was born a Polish Jew and,
though he had converted to Catholicism, he spent the years of the Occupation hiding under the floorboards of his home in Paris. Although his
mother was Catholic, and although he repeatedly speaks of his "Jewish
culture, non-culture," Boltanski's paternal history has no doubt shaped
his avant-garde photographic career. But the aesthetic of postmemory
that emerges in Boltanski's work differs from that of Eliach's "Tower of
Faces"; it comes closer to the opaque distance claimed by Raczymow,
to Fresco's and Finkielkraut's absence. Also attempting both to re-create
and to mourn a lost world of parental origin, Boltanski signals more
clearly the gap between memory and postmemory, the difficult access
to that world and the complex suspicion that surrounds photography's
documentary claims in a postmodern and post-Holocaust world.

Boltanski's early work, marked by this suspicion, is devoted to

9. Linenthal (1995: 171–86) gives the background to this installation.

uncoupling any uncomplicated connection between photography and truth. Most of his work consists of images that are rephotographed, altered, and replaced with others, thus losing their purported credibility. Boltanski uses this myth of credibility, in fact, to establish as "true" situations he invents, such as an elaborate "record" of a bicycle accident he never had, or the use of images of anonymous children to "document" his own childhood. In Boltanski's work the indexical nature of the photograph is in itself a trace as he succeeds in disguising the arbitrary connection between image and referent. Many of his images are, in fact, icons masquerading as indices or, more radically, symbols masquerading as icons and indices.

The detective function of photography runs through Boltanski's many images of objects through which he traces the lives of individuals and families, images reminiscent both of the cases full of objects in traditional ethnographic museums and of the belongings collected by the Nazis before they gassed their victims — the so-called Canada storehouses. Each of his works aims not toward particularity but toward anonymity, not toward an individual but toward a collective identity. He often speaks of the effort to erase himself, so as to be able to reach a communal memorial layer, an amalgam of unconscious reminiscences and archetypes through which viewers can supply their own stories as they look at his images.

But that deeper layer is not just psychological: it invites historical and political readings as well. The critic Lynn Gumpert, for example, has situated installations such as "The Clothes of François C.," "The Inventory of Objects Belonging to a Woman in Bois-Colombe," and the rearranged photo album of the D. family, 1939–64, within the history of France and Europe during these years (Boltanski 1988: 59). Boltanski uses objects as clues to a communal history: what did the D. family or the woman from Bois-Colombe do during the Occupation? What world did they construct for themselves? Is it a normal everyday world that disguises the presence of the war or do their objects allow us to confront the problematic history of French collaboration and resistance?

Not until the mid-1980s, when he undertook a series of installations grouped under the general title "Lessons of Darkness," did Boltanski confront directly his own postmemory of Holocaust, exile, and survival. "There were all sorts of things about my own childhood that I suppressed in my work because they were too special. For example, in my first works I never mention that I was from a Jewish family, I described it as a normal French family" (quoted in Gumpert 1994: 97). His

Figure 4 Courtesy of the Marian Goodman Gallery.

new series of installations begins with "Monuments: The Children of Dijon" and "Odessa Monument" (1985ff.) — large structures built out of numerous rephotographed faces of his own school picture and a school picture from Dijon, mounted on walls with individual lights or sitting on tin boxes within tin frames, connected by electrical cords that provide the lighting (Figure 4). Boltanski did a number of these installations in Paris, Dijon, Venice, New York, and elsewhere. Although the actual children depicted may well still be alive, their images form altarpieces, reminiscent of Byzantine icons commemorating the dead. Through iconic and symbolic, but not directly indexical, implication, Boltanski connects these images of children to the mass murders of the Holocaust: the pictures themselves evoke and represent the actual victims, but neither we nor the artist have a way of knowing whether the individuals in the photos are Holocaust victims or random schoolchildren. Through their lack of specificity, they represent even more forcefully Boltanski's search for a post-Holocaust aesthetic that would contain his generation's absent memory shaped by loss and mourning. "I have never used images from the camps," Boltanski says in an interview. "My work is not about, it is after" (Marsh 1990: 10).

"Lessons of Darkness" culminates in a series of installations that use photographs of actual Jewish children, in particular a 1931 class picture from a Jewish high school in Vienna, the Chajes Realgymnasium, that Boltanski found in *Die Mazzesinsel* (1984), a book on Vienna's predominantly Jewish second district, and the photograph of a Purim celebration from a French Jewish school in 1939. Again, Boltanski re-photographs and enlarges individual faces, installs them on top of tin biscuit boxes or mounts them on the wall, illuminating each picture with a black desk lamp that creates a large circle of light at the center (Figure 5). The biscuit boxes, empty containers of a life story and of individual memory, are stripped of their contents, just as the faces themselves are stripped of individuality. Even though their indexical, referential function reemerges through the use of the class photo of a group the majority of which certainly ended up in Hitler's death camps, the images, blown up to enormous proportions and thus depersonalized, become icons of untimely death, icons of postmemory and mourning. Stripped of their connection to an actual abandoned and destroyed community, stripped of the narrative the actual class picture tells, the faces from the Chajes school, like the children of Dijon (and the "Monuments" made of Christian's own elementary class picture), echo a collective act of destruction and evoke the post-Holocaust viewer's fears and sorrows, without conveying any specific informational content. The sculptural installations allow Boltanski to rebuild a lost world, but one that looks anonymous, requiring both a certain contextualization (the fact that the high school was Jewish) and a certain investment by the viewer—of his

Figure 5   Courtesy of the Marian Goodman Gallery.

or her own memories and fears—to carry any meaning and power. This is equally true of the subsequent installation, "Canada": here we don't know the identity of the faces depicted or the source of the objects on the floor; we know only the title, "Canada," which evokes, for those who *know*, Hitler's storehouses. The gaze that connects us to these images and installations is affiliative only in the most general sense: we recognize not the people or the world rebuilt, but the forms of memorialization and mourning, the technological shapes of Holocaust persecution and extermination, the names of a destroyed world and of the means of its destruction. "For me it's very important to start with a real image," Boltanski insists. "Then I blow it up to make it universal" (Boltanski 1995). In these new installations, using ghostly sheets and black mesh, the artist impairs visibility severely. This new work highlights, more and more forcefully and brutally, the violence of photographic exposure and revelation. The pictures suggest a truth, but they remain blurry, unforgiving and unyielding (Figure 6).

Like Raczymow's, Boltanski's connection to the world he reconstructs is shaped primarily by his own need to remember and to know, and by a profound ambivalence about that need. "I think," he says in an interview, "that my work is bound to a certain world that is bordered by the White Sea and the Black, a mythic world that doesn't exist, that I never knew, a sort of great plain where armies clashed and where Jews of my culture lived" (Marsh 1990: 5). "Anyway, this is all very fuzzy in my own mind; I have no Jewish culture. I am like the Indians who, in westerns, serve as guides to the soldiers: they forgot everything, but when they drank, the Indian dances came back to them" (quoted in Gumpert 1994: 96).

For Boltanski postmemory is indeed empty, shaped by deep and residual cultural knowledges, overlaid with more present practices. Thus the lessons of darkness bring together Jewish and Christian modes of memorialization (the Jahrzeit or Chanukah candle with the altarpiece and the icon), made more poignant by the transcendently painful figure of the dead child. The objectification inherent in the still photographic image is reinforced by the fact that the faces on the walls are children's faces, looking forward to a life they were never to have, faces reproduced and rephotographed to the point of third- and fourth-generation fuzziness, made hollow and empty by enlargement. Darkness is death, absence of light, the darkroom: photography can recreate this darkness, dependent as it is on light. Family and school photography have lost all sense of comfort and safety, revealing an irreparable darkness and a danger from which our familiar social institutions cannot shield us.

As an aesthetic of postmemory, Boltanski's works reach an extreme. The empty content of the boxes and the generality of the pictures allow us both to believe and to suspect the documentary aspect of the photograph. But to call the truth of pictures into question in view of current Holocaust denial is risky indeed. At the same time, reconstructing a destroyed world in the shape of a memorial and a site of mourning extends the need to remember even as it acknowledges the loss of knowledge and specificity. Boltanski's "Lessons" are not history les-

Figure 6   Courtesy of the Marian Goodman Gallery.

sons: they are lessons about mass destruction and the need to recall an irrecoverable past in the absence of precise, totalizing knowledge. They are lessons about a form of disconnection and loss that is the condition of exile without the hope of return. And, with their unforgiving electric lights, they are lessons about the violence of knowledge, the brutality of exposure, the incapacities of our technologies of revelation.

Boltanski's images are thus particularly compelling at a moment when survivors of the Holocaust are rapidly disappearing from our midst, taking with them the possibility of direct memorial access to the event, however already mediated by the process of recollection. Although they are broadly accessible and disturbingly evocative, I wonder whether the "Lessons of Darkness" nevertheless risk too radical a disconnection from their source and thus the possibility of further manipulation and appropriation, whether they encourage a form of looking too decontextualized and ungrounded. If we look at the original image of the Chajes school graduating class, we recognize a historical moment, with its distinctive clothing, body language, and representational styles. Boltanski's re-creations leave only eerily empty faces and enormous eye sockets waiting to be filled with the viewer's own affective responses. But as a third generation grows to maturity and postmemory becomes dissociated from memory, we are left to speculate how these images can communicate on their own.

A different form of remembrance and perhaps one possible response to Boltanski's dilemma is exemplified in the work of the young American photographer Shimon Attie. By fully exploiting photography's capacity to evoke absence as well as presence, Attie may provide Yoram Kaniuk with a more satisfying way to return to the Berlin into which he might have been born. Visiting Berlin in 1991, Attie began to ask: "Where are all the missing people? What has become of the Jewish culture and community which had once been at home here?" (Attie 1994: 9). A concerted search led him to a number of historical photographs of Berlin's Scheunenviertel, its Jewish quarter during the 1920s and 1930s. Making slides of them and using several powerful projectors, Attie projected these old images onto the precise locations where they were originally taken, thus "rebuilding" the ruined world on the very site of its ruin. Then rephotographing the projections, he created layered images that have become movable memorial sites, which each of us can invest with our own nostalgic and elegiac needs (Figures 7–8). In his work, the site of destruction has been reconnected to the site of commemoration, icon merged with index, context and content restored. But is it? Attie admits that he "made every effort to project the image onto its original site" (ibid.: 11), but it was only possible in about 25 percent of the installations. Sometimes he had to use an adjacent building, sometimes another site altogether. In five of the seventy installations, moreover, he

Figure 7   Courtesy of Shimon Attie.

used images from other Jewish quarters and ghettos in Eastern Europe. "When it was necessary to choose between being a good historian and—hopefully—a good artist, I always chose the latter," he confessed (ibid.).

I can identify with Attie's impulse to rebuild Jewish Berlin through this shadow play. The ghosts in his images and Boltanski's also haunt my imagination. Looking at the children's faces in Boltanski's installations, at the shadow figures haunting Attie's projections, I see the children in my mother's and father's classes who did not survive, I see the buildings of Czernowitz now inhabited by young people who don't remember their parents' neighbors. I see the child I could have been and the child I was in my own early nightmares. As postmodern subjects are we not constructed, collectively, in relation to these ghosts and shadows? Are we not shaped by their loss and by our own ambivalence about mourning them? As we look at them, they look back at us, constituting, as Dominick LaCapra has recently argued, the return of the repressed that identifies the postmodern with the post-Holocaust (1994: 188). Postmodern subjectivity is shaped in this temporal/spatial diaspora, as Fran Bartkowski suggests, "in relation to an elsewhere" (1995: 3). Photographs can suggest what that elsewhere is or was; they can provide a visual content for our

Figure 8   Courtesy of Shimon Attie.

ambivalent longings. And they can also remind us of the distance, the absence, the unbridgeable gap that, in the postmodern, makes us who we are.

For years I thought I would never be able to go to Czernowitz and I shared my parents' sense that their world is simply gone, surviving only in their stories, memories, and friendships. But after 1989, at the same time that East Berlin became available to Attie, Czernowitz, now in the Ukraine, began to admit some visitors from the West. Several German television, radio, and newspaper stories were produced there to capture some of the flavor of the city of Paul Celan, and some tours were organized in Israel so that former residents might return for a few days. I read some of these stories and suggested to my parents that we take a trip to Czernowitz in the summer of 1994. After some research I knew the travel conditions would be harsh whether we chose to go by car or train, and was a bit discouraged by a photo exhibit on the Bukowina which showed a dismal landscape. But I thought that as experienced travelers we could all handle it and that the visit would be well worth the trouble.

My fantasy was that we would spend several days walking around the city, whose prewar buildings are still standing. We would visit my father's cousin Rosa, one of the very few remaining Jews of the prewar population, and we would meet her son Felix who grew up in the Russian Czernowitz. We would have our still camera and our video camera along, and we would record our walks and talks. "Remember, so and so used to live here," I imagined my parents saying to each other; "No, you're wrong, it was over there." Somewhat like Christa Wolf and her family in *Patterns of Childhood* (1976), we would discuss our impressions and share our reminiscences. My parents would show me their old apartments, the schools they attended, the houses of many friends and neighbors. They would retrace their steps, tell me where they met and where they used to spend time together. They would relive the prewar and also the war and they would relive their departure. Together, we would try to make the place come alive, investing it with memories of old, and memories created in the present, memories transmitted across generations.

The trip never happened. Every time I called about making reservations, or to discuss our itinerary, my mother asked was I really so interested in going, and why? It dawned on me that my desire, not theirs, was driving this plan. They were ambivalent and finally dissuaded by the practical difficulties of the trip and, I'm sure, by the fear of seeing, like Attie, only ghosts. The summer passed and we have not mentioned it again. Will I ever go there without them, like many friends who have gone to trace their roots in Poland, Czechoslovakia, and Hungary during the last five years? I doubt it. Instead I will have to search for other, less direct means of access to this lost world, means that inscribe its unbridgeable distance as well as my own curiosity and desire. This search will be inspired by Kaniuk's rage and by the aesthetics of Spiegelman, Raczymow, Boltanski, and Attie. And it will certainly include the numerous old pictures of people and places, the albums and shoe boxes, building blocks of the work of my postmemory.

REFERENCES

Attie, Shimon
  1994 *The Writing on the Wall: Projections in Berlin's Jewish Quarter* (Heidelberg: Edition Braus).
Barthes, Roland
  1981 *Camera Lucida: Reflections on Photography*, translated by Richard Howard (New York: Hill and Wang).

Bartkowski, Frances

1995 *Travelers, Immigrants, Inmates: Essays in Estrangement* (Minneapolis: University of Minnesota Press).

Berenbaum, Michael

1994 Speech to visiting student group, United States Holocaust Memorial Museum, Washington, DC, November.

Boltanski, Christian

1988 *Christian Boltanski: Lessons of Darkness*, exhibition catalog (Chicago: Museum of Contemporary Art; Los Angeles: Museum of Contemporary Art, New York: New Museum of Contemporary Art).

1990 *Reconstitution*, exhibition catalog (London: Whitechapel Art Gallery).

1995 Talk at the Institute of Contemporary Art, Boston, January 25.

Boyarin, Daniel, and Jonathan Boyarin

1993 "Diaspora: Generation and the Ground of Jewish Identity," *Critical Inquiry* 19: 693–725.

Boyarin, Jonathan, and Jack Kugelmass

1983 *From a Ruined Garden: The Memorial Books of Polish Jewry* (New York: Schocken).

Finkielkraut, Alain

1980 *Le Juif imaginaire* (Paris: Seuil).

1994 *The Imaginary Jew*, translated by Kevin O'Neill and David Suchoff (Lincoln: University of Nebraska Press).

Fresco, Nadine

1981 "La Diaspora des cendres," *Nouvelle revue de psychoanalyse*, 205–20.

Gumpert, Lynn

1994 *Christian Boltanski* (Paris: Flammarion).

Hirsch, Marianne

1992–93 "Family Pictures: *Maus*, Mourning and Post-Memory," *Discourse* 15(2): 3–29.

Kaniuk, Yoram

1991 "Dreienhalb Stunden und fünfzig Jahre mit Günter Grass in Berlin," *Die Zeit*, June 26–28.

LaCapra, Dominick

1994 *Representing the Holocaust: History, Theory, Trauma* (Ithaca, NY: Cornell University Press).

Linenthal, Edward T.

1995 *Preserving Memory: The Struggle to Create America's Holocaust Museum* (New York: Viking).

Liss, Andrea

1993 "Contours of Naming: The Identity Card Project and the Tower of Faces at the United States Holocaust Memorial Museum," *Public* 8: 107–35.

Marsh, Georgia

1990 "An Interview with Christian Boltanski," in Boltanski 1990.

Raczymow, Henri

1979 *Contes d'exil et d'oubli* (Paris: Gallimard).

1986 "La Mémoire trouée," *Pardès* 3: 177–82.

1994 "Memory Shot through with Holes," translated by Alan Astro, *Yale French Studies* 85: 98–105.

Stiles, Kristine

forthcoming "Remembering Invisibility: Photography and the Formation of Community in a Nuclear Age."

CONTRIBUTORS

SUSAN RUBIN SULEIMAN is the C. Douglas Dillon Professor of the Civilization of France and Professor of Comparative Literature at Harvard University. Her most recent books are *Risking Who One Is: Encounters with Contemporary Art and Literature* (1994) and a memoir *Budapest Diary: In Search of the Motherbook* (1996).

ERNST VAN ALPHEN teaches comparative literature at the University of Leiden and is a member of the Amsterdam School of Cultural Analysis (ASCA). He is the author of *Francis Bacon and the Loss of Self* (1993) and *Caught by History: Holocaust Effects in Contemporary Art and Theory* (1997).

ZYGMUNT BAUMAN is a retired Professor of Sociology at the University of Leeds. His books include *Legislators and Interpreters: On Modernity, Postmodernity, and Intellectuals* (1987) and *Modernity and the Holocaust* (1991).

JANET BERGSTROM teaches film studies at UCLA. She was a founding coeditor of *Camera Obscura* from 1974 to 1992. She is coeditor with Mary Ann Doane of *The Spectatrix*, a special issue of *Camera Obscura* (1989), and of *Close Encounters: Film, Feminism, and Science Fiction* (1991).

ALICIA BORINSKY is Professor of Latin American and Comparative Literature and Director of the Interdisciplinary Program in Latin American Studies at Boston University. Her most recent books are *Mean Woman* (1993) and *Theoretical Fables: The Pedagogical Dream in Contemporary Latin American Fiction* (1993).

SVETLANA BOYM, Professor of Slavic and Comparative Literature at Harvard University, is the author of *Death in Quotation Marks: Cultural Myths of the Modern Poet* (1991) and *Common Places: Mythologies of Everyday Life in Russia* (1994).

CHRISTINE BROOKE-ROSE was for twenty years Professor of American Literature at the University of Paris VIII. She has written twelve novels and four critical books, *A Grammar of Metaphor* (1958), *A ZBC of Ezra Pound* (1971), *A Rhetoric of the Unreal* (1981), and *Stories, Theories, and Things* (1991). She is now retired and living in Provence.

JACQUELINE CHÉNIEUX-GENDRON is Director of Research at the CNRS, Paris, and Professor at the University of Paris VII. She has published and edited many books, one of which, *Surrealism* (1990), has been translated into English.

HÉLÈNE CIXOUS, born in Oran, Algeria, was instrumental in founding the University of Paris VIII in 1968. She has been Director of the Centre d'Études Féminines since 1974, when she created the first and still the only doctoral program in women's studies in France. She is author of more than thirty works of poetical fiction, as well as numerous plays and collections of critical work. Her publications in English translation include her doctoral thesis, *The Exile of James Joyce or the Art of Replacement* (1972), *The Newly Born Woman* (1986), *"Coming to Writing" and Other Essays* (1991), *Three Steps on the Ladder of Writing* (1993), *Manna* (1994), *The Hélène Cixous Reader* (1994), and *First Days of the Year* (1996).

TIBOR DESSEWFFY is a sociologist at Eotvos Lorand University (ELTE) in Budapest and the editor in chief of the quarterly *Imago*. He has written and lectured on postmodernism, postcommunism, popular culture, and the sociology of knowledge. His recent writings are *Transition in Hungary* (1995), *Blue Hawaii* (1995), and the forthcoming *Seductions of Communism*.

MARIANNE HIRSCH is Professor of French and Comparative Literature and Distinguished Research Professor in the Humanities at Dartmouth College. She is the author of *The Mother/Daughter Plot: Narrative, Psychoanalysis, Feminism* (1989) and coeditor of *Conflicts in Feminism* (1990). The present essay also appears slightly revised in her *Family Frames: Narrative and Photography in the Postmodern* (1997).

DENIS HOLLIER is Professor of French at NYU and general editor of *A New History of French Literature* (1989). He is currently working on narratives of the September 1938 Munich crisis. His most recent publication is *Absent without Leave: French Literature Under the Threat of War* (1997).

NANCY HUSTON is a Canadian-born writer residing in Paris. She is the author of twelve books of fiction and nonfiction in French, including *Cantique des plaines* (1993; published in North America as *Plainsong*), which won the 1993 Canadian Governor General's award for French-language fiction. Her most recent book is *Instruments of Darkness* (1997).

JOHN NEUBAUER is Professor of Comparative Literature at the University of Amsterdam. His publications include *The Emancipation of Music from Language* (1986), *The Fin-de-Siecle Culture of Adolescence* (1992), and annotated editions of Goethe's scientific works.

LINDA NOCHLIN is the Lila Acheson Wallace Professor of Modern Art at the Institute of Fine Arts, New York University. Her publications include *Realism* (1971), *Women, Art, and Power* (1988), *The Politics of Vision* (1989), *The Body in Pieces:*

The Fragment as a Metaphor of Modernity (1994), and *The Jew in the Text* (1995), edited with Tamar Garb.

THOMAS PAVEL teaches French and comparative literature at Princeton University. His publications include *Fictional Worlds* (1986), *The Feud of Language: A History of Structuralist Thought* (1989), and a forthcoming book on French neo-classicism.

DORIS SOMMER, Professor of Latin American Literature at Harvard University, is the author of *One Master for Another: Populism as Patriarchal Rhetoric in Dominican Novels* (1984), *Foundational Fictions: The National Romances of Latin America* (1991), and the forthcoming *Proceed with Caution: A Rhetoric of Particularism.*

LEO SPITZER, the Kathie Tappe Vernon Professor of History at Dartmouth College, is the author of *The Sierra Leone Creoles* (1974), *Lives in Between: Assimilation and Marginality in Austria, Brazil, West Africa, 1780–1945* (1989), and *Hotel Bolivia: The Culture of Memory in a Refuge from Nazism* (1998).

Library of Congress Cataloging-in-Publication Data

Exile and creativity : Signposts, Travelers, Outsiders, Backward Glances / edited
by Susan Rubin Suleiman.

p.   cm.

"All of the essays in this book, with one exception, first appeared in the special
double [issue] of Poetics today . . . vol. 17, nos. 3–4, 1996" — Notes.

ISBN 0-8223-2187-4 (cloth : alk. paper). — ISBN 0-8223-2215-3 (paper : alk.
paper)

1. Exiles in literature.   2. Creativity in literature.   3. Creation (Literary,
artistic, etc.)   4. Literature, Modern — History and criticism.   I. Suleiman,
Susan Rubin, 1939–

PN56.5.E96C74   1998

809'.8920691 — dc21   97-43276